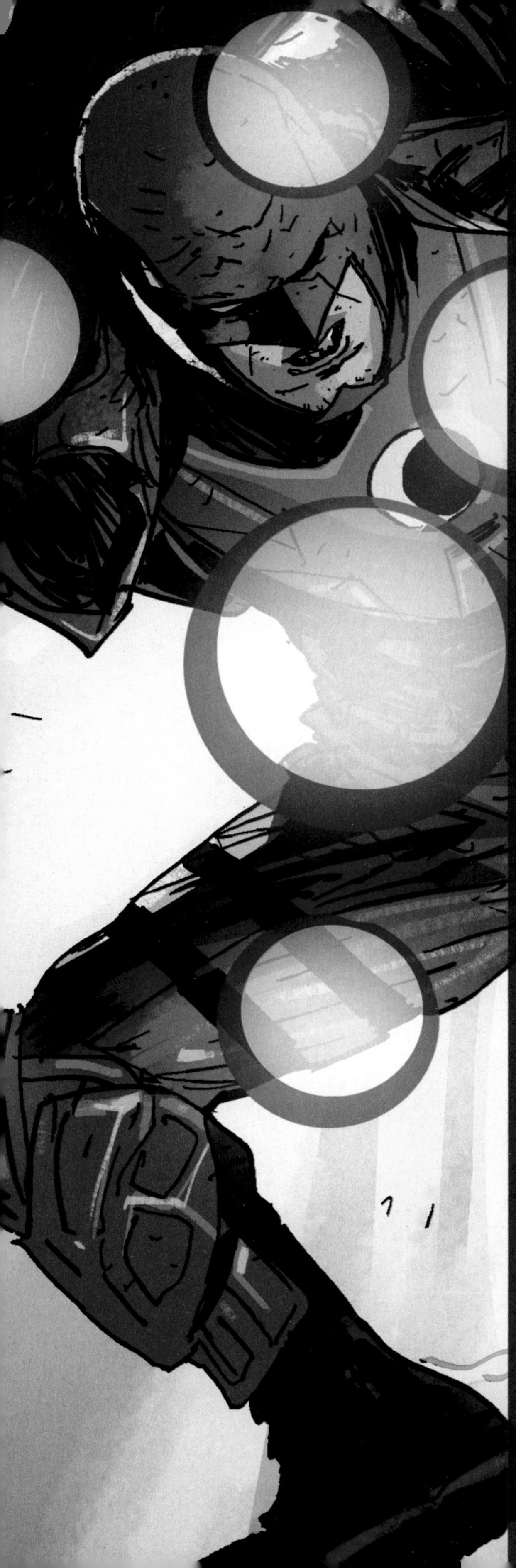

MIDNIGHTER

VOLUME 1
OUT

WRITTEN BY
STEVE ORLANDO

ART BY
ACO
STEPHEN MOONEY
ALEC MORGAN
HUGO PETRUS

COLOR BY
ROMULO FAJARDO, JR.
ALLEN PASSALAQUA
JEROMY COX

LETTERS BY
JARED K. FLETCHER
TOM NAPOLITANO

COVER ART BY
ACO & ROMULO FAJARDO, JR.

ORIGINAL SERIES COVERS BY
ACO & ROMULO FAJARDO, JR.
ARTYOM TRAKHANOV

CHRIS CONROY Editor – Original Series
DAVE WIELGOSZ Associate Editor – Original Series
JEB WOODARD Group Editor – Collected Editions
SCOTT NYBAKKEN Editor – Collected Edition
STEVE COOK Design Director – Books
DAMIAN RYLAND Publication Design

BOB HARRAS Senior VP – Editor-in-Chief, DC Comics

DIANE NELSON President
DAN DIDIO and JIM LEE Co-Publishers
GEOFF JOHNS Chief Creative Officer
AMIT DESAI Senior VP – Marketing & Global Franchise Management
NAIRI GARDINER Senior VP – Finance
SAM ADES VP – Digital Marketing
BOBBIE CHASE VP – Talent Development
MARK CHIARELLO Senior VP – Art, Design & Collected Editions
JOHN CUNNINGHAM VP – Content Strategy
ANNE DEPIES VP – Strategy Planning & Reporting
DON FALLETTI VP – Manufacturing Operations
LAWRENCE GANEM VP – Editorial Administration & Talent Relations
ALISON GILL Senior VP – Manufacturing & Operations
HANK KANALZ Senior VP – Editorial Strategy & Administration
JAY KOGAN VP – Legal Affairs
DEREK MADDALENA Senior VP – Sales & Business Development
JACK MAHAN VP – Business Affairs
DAN MIRON VP – Sales Planning & Trade Development
NICK NAPOLITANO VP – Manufacturing Administration
CAROL ROEDER VP – Marketing
EDDIE SCANNELL VP – Mass Account & Digital Sales
COURTNEY SIMMONS Senior VP – Publicity & Communications
JIM (SKI) SOKOLOWSKI VP – Comic Book Specialty & Newsstand Sales
SANDY YI Senior VP – Global Franchise Management

MIDNIGHTER VOL. 1: OUT

Published by DC Comics. Compilation Copyright © 2016 DC Comics. All Rights Reserved.

Originally published in single magazine form in CONVERGENCE: NIGHTWING/ORACLE 2 and MIDNIGHTER 1-7. Copyright © 2015
DC Comics. All Rights Reserved. All characters, their distinctive likenesses and related elements featured in this publication
are trademarks of DC Comics. The stories, characters and incidents featured in this publication are entirely fictional.
DC Comics does not read or accept unsolicited ideas, stories or artwork.

DC Comics. 2900 West Alameda Ave. Burbank, CA 91505
Printed by RR Donnelley, Salem, VA, USA. 1/15/16. First Printing.
ISBN: 978-1-4012-5978-5

Library of Congress Cataloging-in-Publication data is available.

PEFC Certified

Printed on paper from
sustainably managed
forests and controlled
sources

PEFC™

PEFC/29-31-75   www.pefc.org

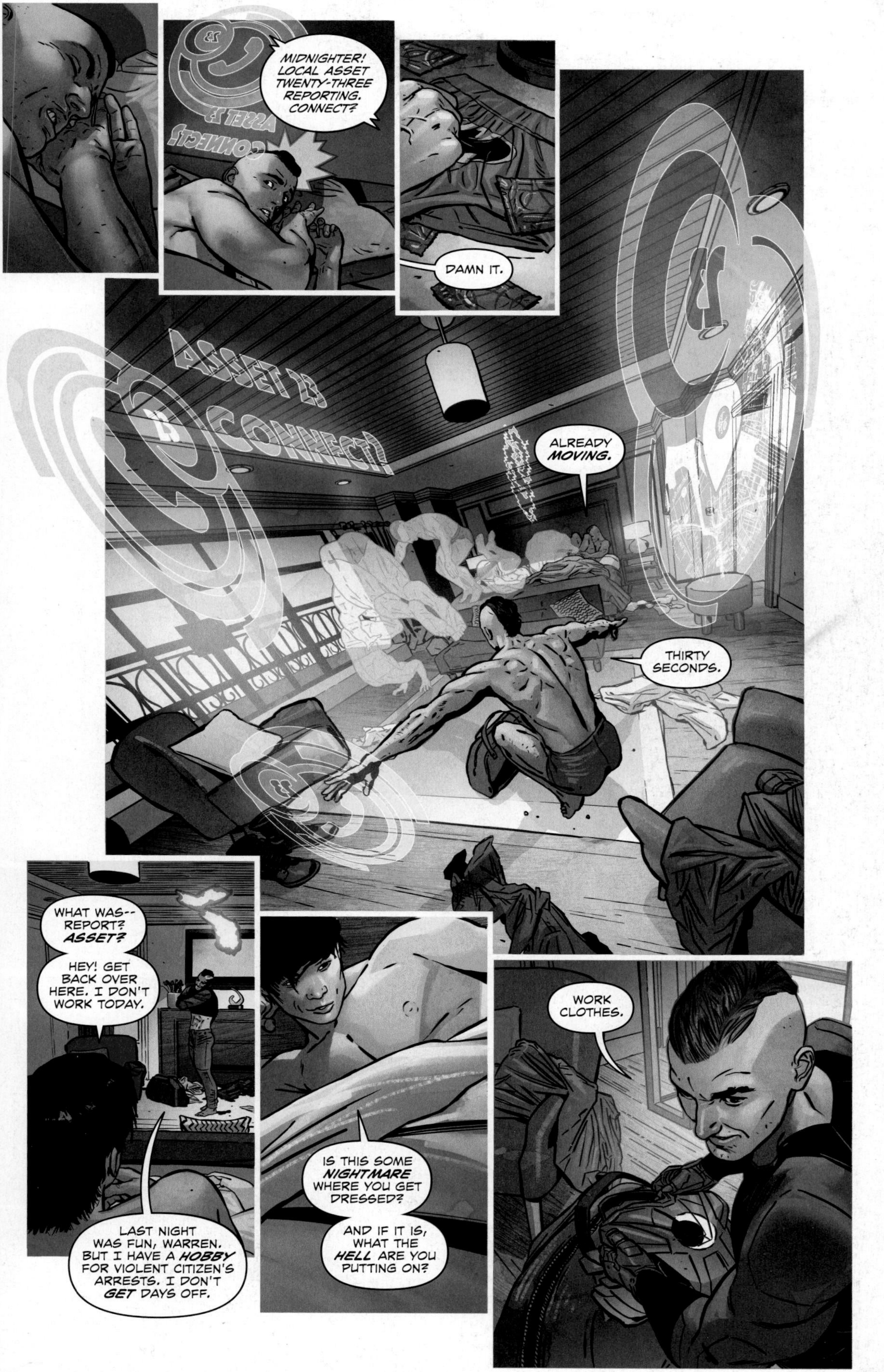
MIDNIGHTER! LOCAL ASSET TWENTY-THREE REPORTING. CONNECT?
ASSET 23
CONNECT?
DAMN IT.
ASSET 23
CONNECT?
ALREADY MOVING.
THIRTY SECONDS.
WHAT WAS-- REPORT? ASSET?
HEY! GET BACK OVER HERE. I DON'T WORK TODAY.
LAST NIGHT WAS FUN, WARREN. BUT I HAVE A HOBBY FOR VIOLENT CITIZEN'S ARRESTS. I DON'T GET DAYS OFF.
IS THIS SOME NIGHTMARE WHERE YOU GET DRESSED?
AND IF IT IS, WHAT THE HELL ARE YOU PUTTING ON?
WORK CLOTHES.

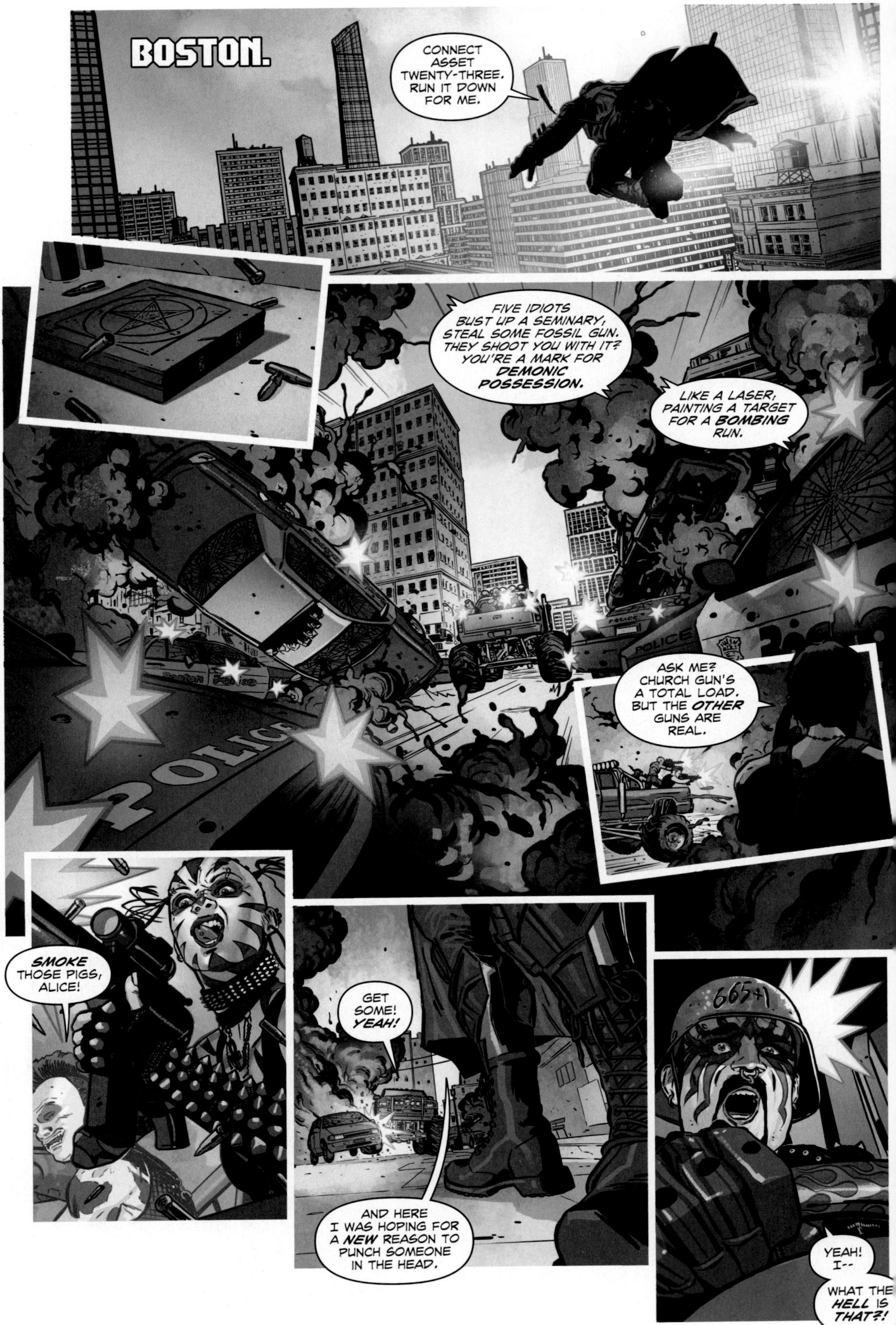
BOSTON.
CONNECT ASSET TWENTY-THREE. RUN IT DOWN FOR ME.
FIVE IDIOTS BUST UP A SEMINARY; STEAL SOME FOSSIL GUN. THEY SHOOT YOU WITH IT? YOU'RE A MARK FOR DEMONIC POSSESSION.
LIKE A LASER, PAINTING A TARGET FOR A BOMBING RUN.
POLICE
ASK ME? CHURCH GUN'S A TOTAL LOAD. BUT THE OTHER GUNS ARE REAL.
SMOKE THOSE PIGS, ALICE!
GET SOME! YEAH!
AND HERE I WAS HOPING FOR A NEW REASON TO PUNCH SOMEONE IN THE HEAD.
665+1
YEAH! I--
WHAT THE HELL IS THAT?!

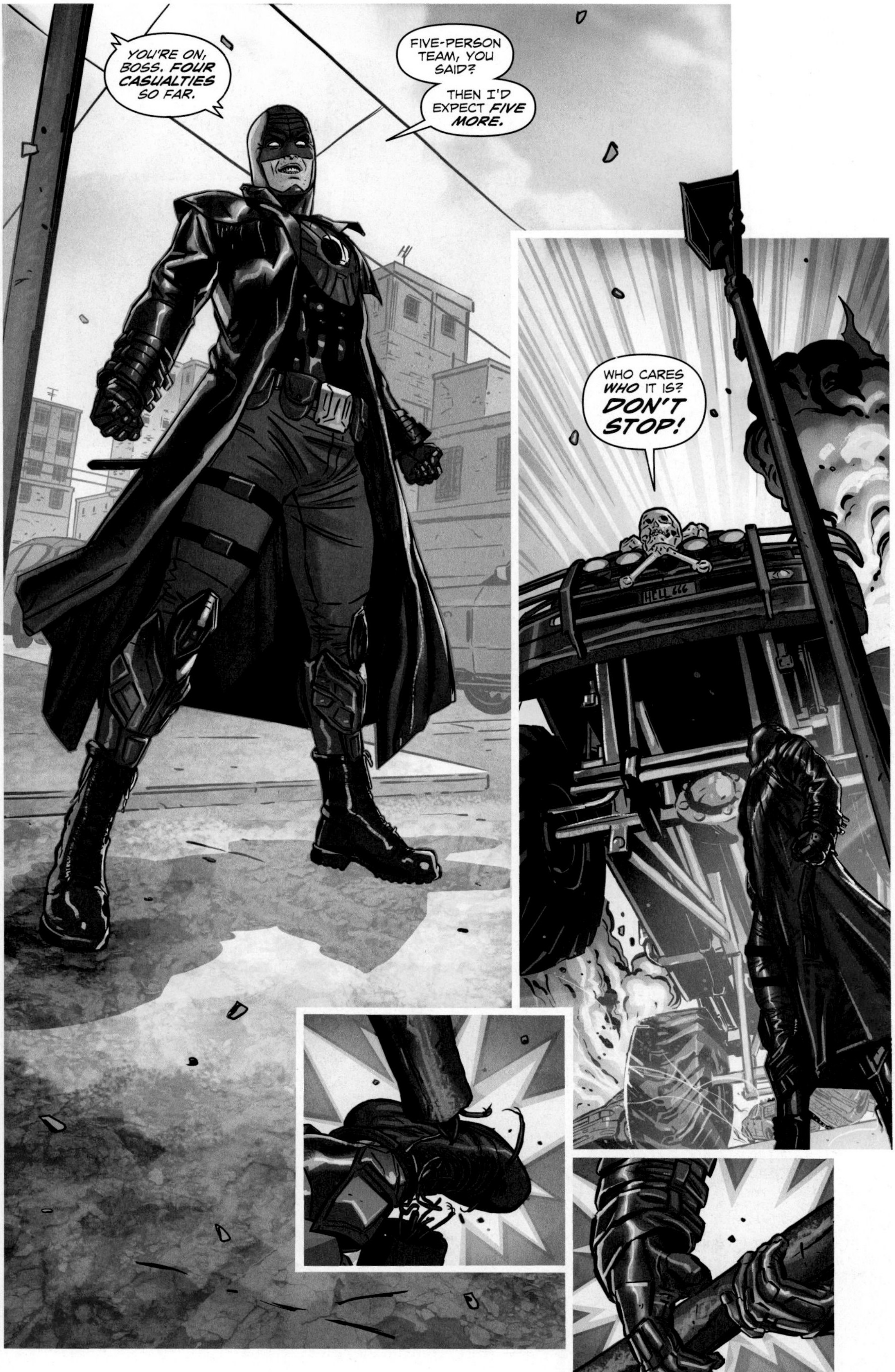
YOU'RE ON, BOSS. FOUR CASUALTIES SO FAR.
FIVE-PERSON TEAM, YOU SAID?
THEN I'D EXPECT FIVE MORE.
WHO CARES WHO IT IS? DON'T STOP!

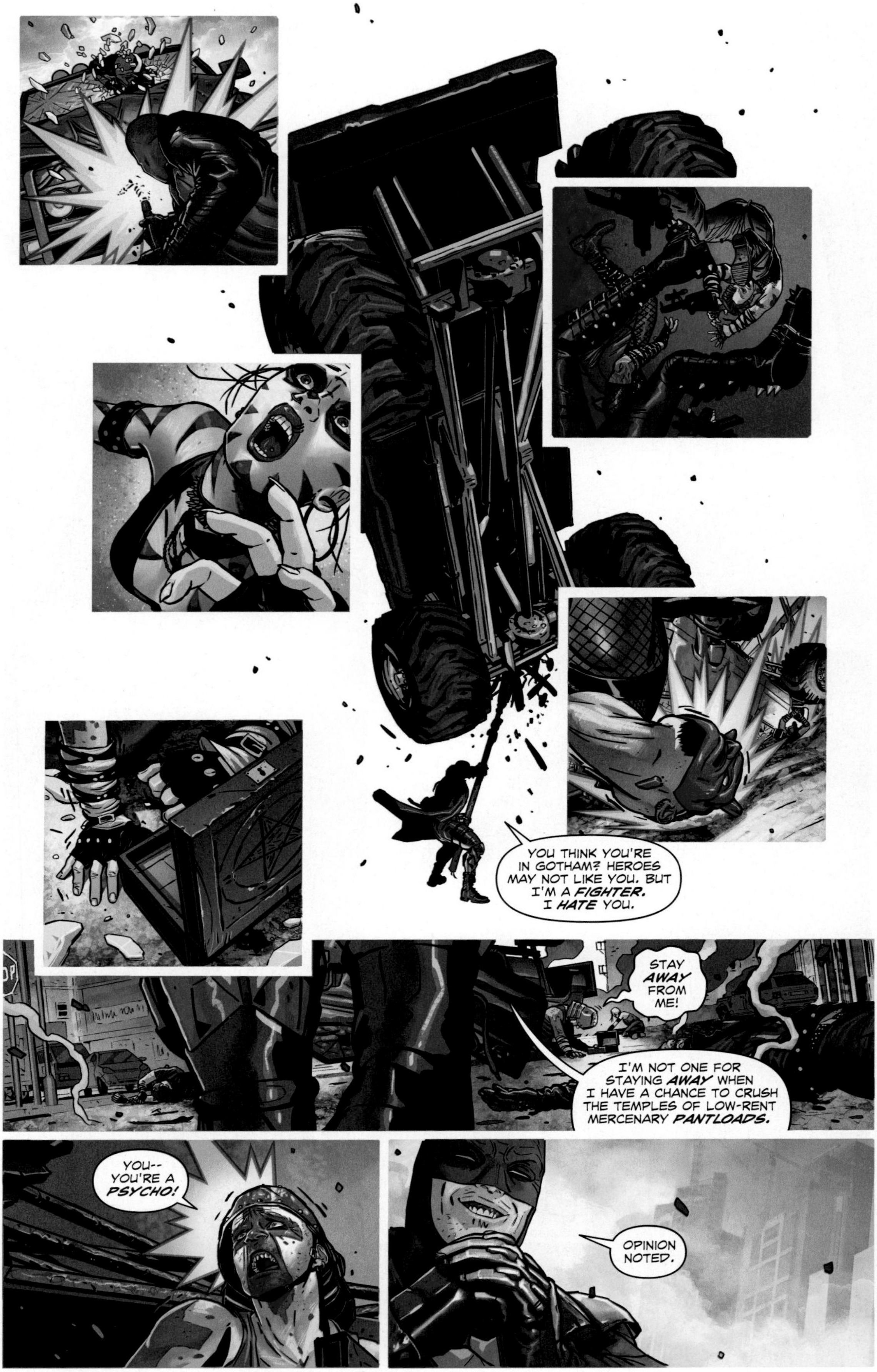
YOU THINK YOU'RE IN GOTHAM? HEROES MAY NOT LIKE YOU. BUT I'M A *FIGHTER.* I *HATE* YOU.
STAY *AWAY* FROM ME!
I'M NOT ONE FOR STAYING *AWAY* WHEN I HAVE A CHANCE TO CRUSH THE TEMPLES OF LOW-RENT MERCENARY *PANTLOADS.*
YOU-- YOU'RE A *PSYCHO!*
OPINION NOTED.

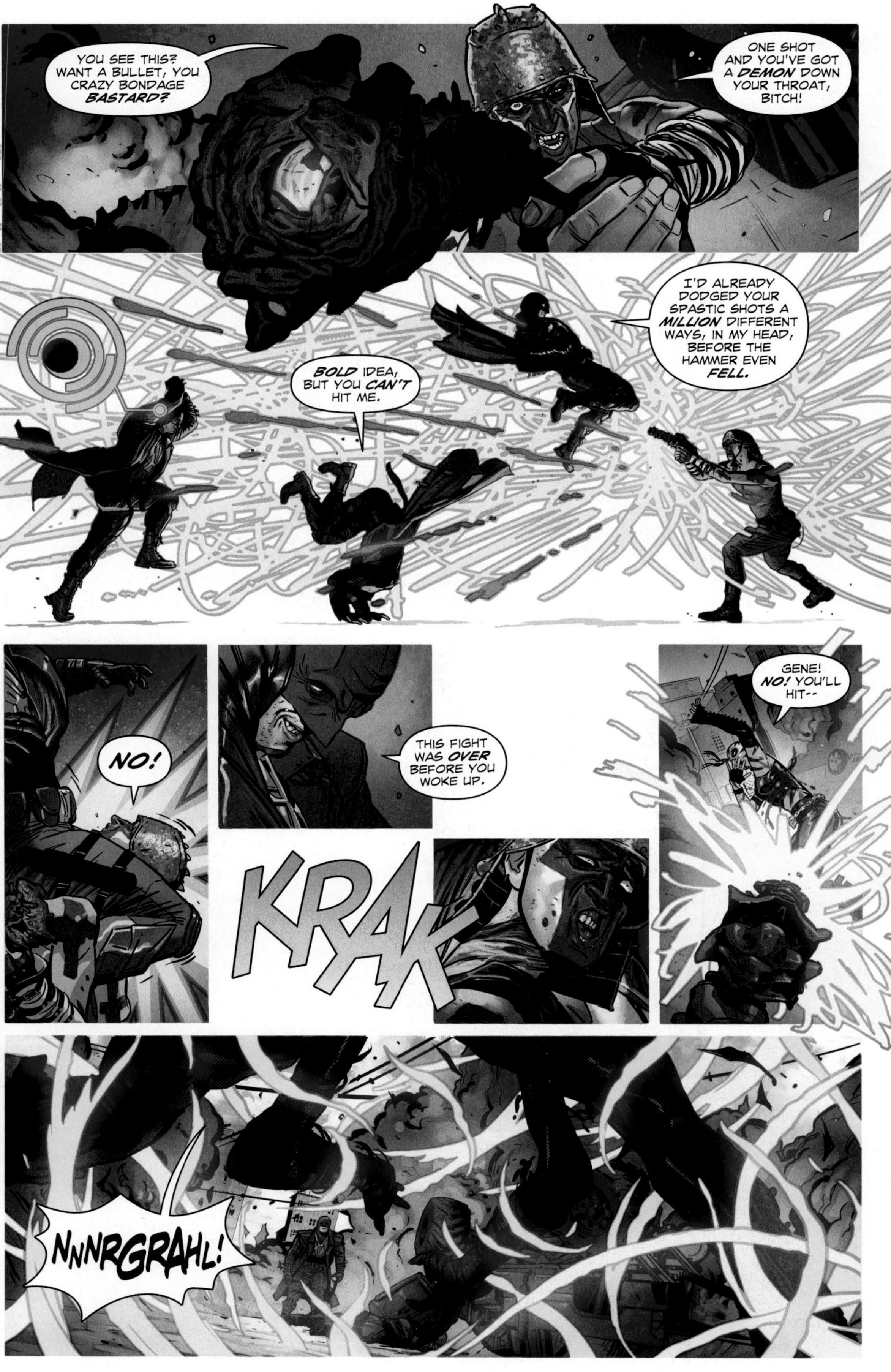
YOU SEE THIS? WANT A BULLET, YOU CRAZY BONDAGE BASTARD?
ONE SHOT AND YOU'VE GOT A DEMON DOWN YOUR THROAT, BITCH!
BOLD IDEA, BUT YOU CAN'T HIT ME.
I'D ALREADY DODGED YOUR SPASTIC SHOTS A MILLION DIFFERENT WAYS, IN MY HEAD, BEFORE THE HAMMER EVEN FELL.
NO!
THIS FIGHT WAS OVER BEFORE YOU WOKE UP.
KRAK
GENE! NO! YOU'LL HIT--
NNNRGRAHL!

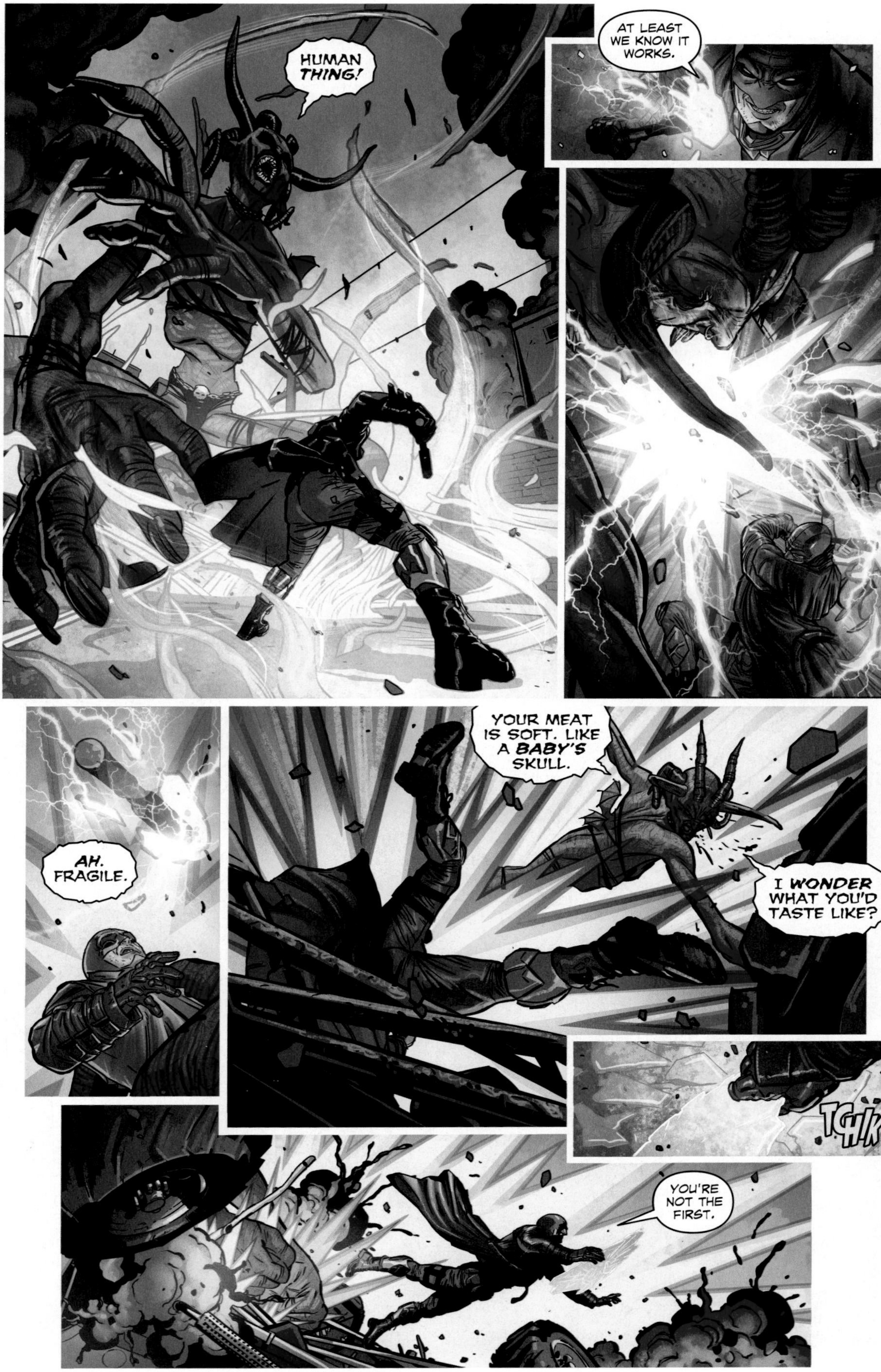
HUMAN THING!
AT LEAST WE KNOW IT WORKS.
AH. FRAGILE.
YOUR MEAT IS SOFT. LIKE A BABY'S SKULL.
I WONDER WHAT YOU'D TASTE LIKE?
TCHIK
YOU'RE NOT THE FIRST.

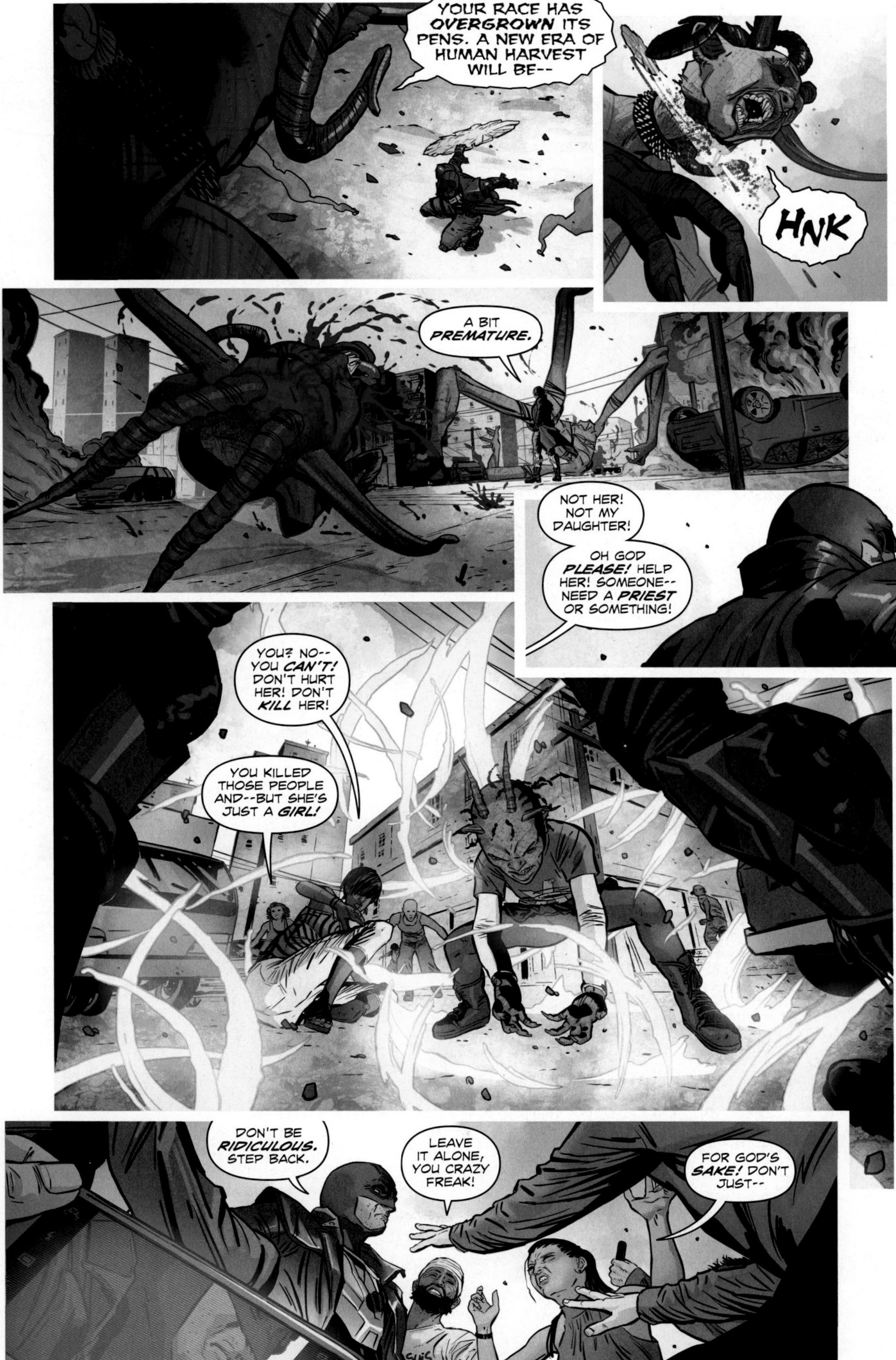

YOUR RACE HAS OVERGROWN ITS PENS. A NEW ERA OF HUMAN HARVEST WILL BE--
HNK
A BIT PREMATURE.
NOT HER! NOT MY DAUGHTER!
OH GOD PLEASE! HELP HER! SOMEONE-- NEED A PRIEST OR SOMETHING!
YOU? NO-- YOU CAN'T! DON'T HURT HER! DON'T KILL HER!
YOU KILLED THOSE PEOPLE AND--BUT SHE'S JUST A GIRL!
DON'T BE RIDICULOUS. STEP BACK.
LEAVE IT ALONE, YOU CRAZY FREAK!
FOR GOD'S SAKE! DON'T JUST--

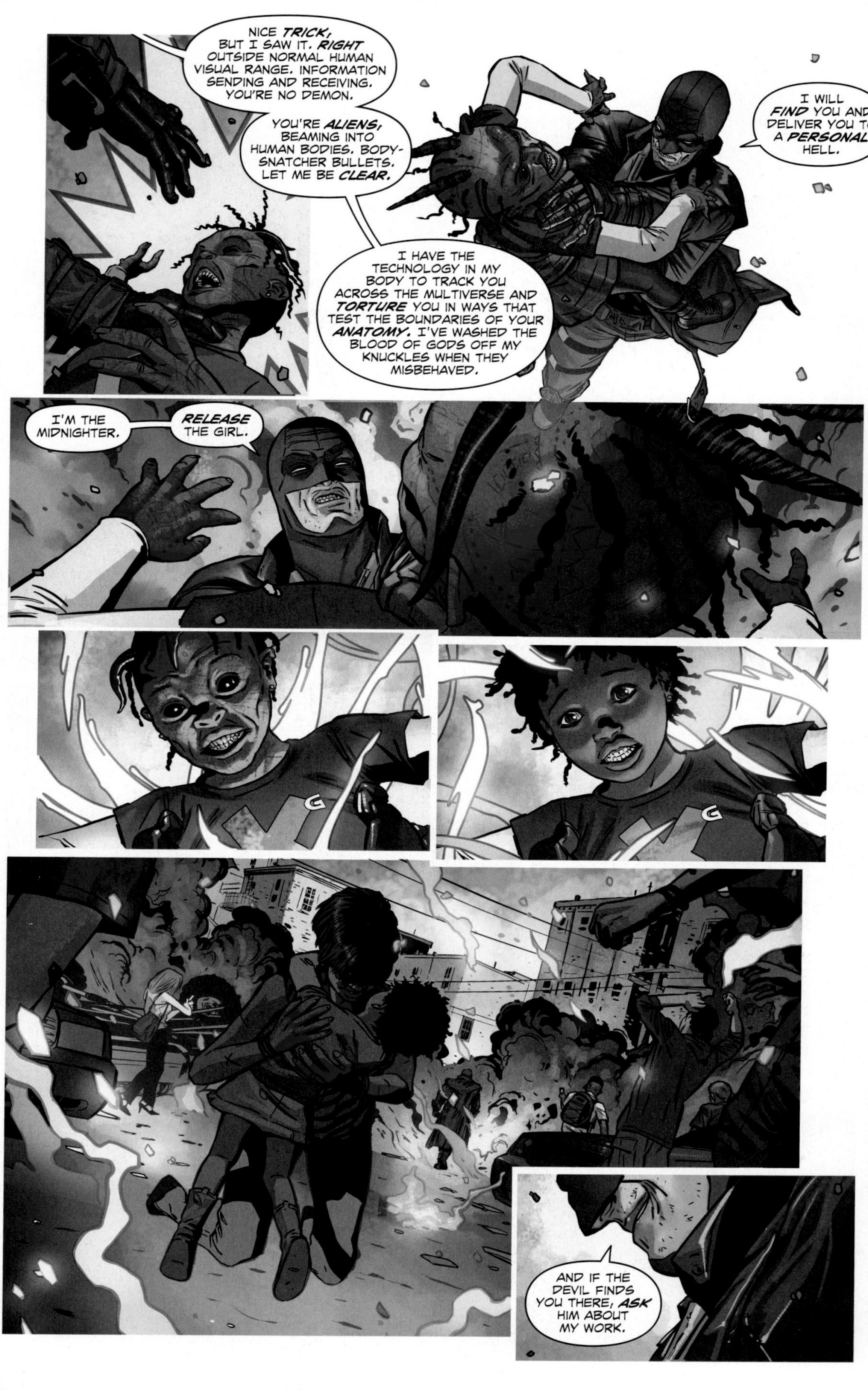
NICE TRICK, BUT I SAW IT. RIGHT OUTSIDE NORMAL HUMAN VISUAL RANGE. INFORMATION SENDING AND RECEIVING. YOU'RE NO DEMON.
YOU'RE ALIENS, BEAMING INTO HUMAN BODIES. BODY-SNATCHER BULLETS. LET ME BE CLEAR.
I HAVE THE TECHNOLOGY IN MY BODY TO TRACK YOU ACROSS THE MULTIVERSE AND TORTURE YOU IN WAYS THAT TEST THE BOUNDARIES OF YOUR ANATOMY. I'VE WASHED THE BLOOD OF GODS OFF MY KNUCKLES WHEN THEY MISBEHAVED.
I WILL FIND YOU AND DELIVER YOU TO A PERSONAL HELL.
I'M THE MIDNIGHTER.
RELEASE THE GIRL.
AND IF THE DEVIL FINDS YOU THERE, ASK HIM ABOUT MY WORK.

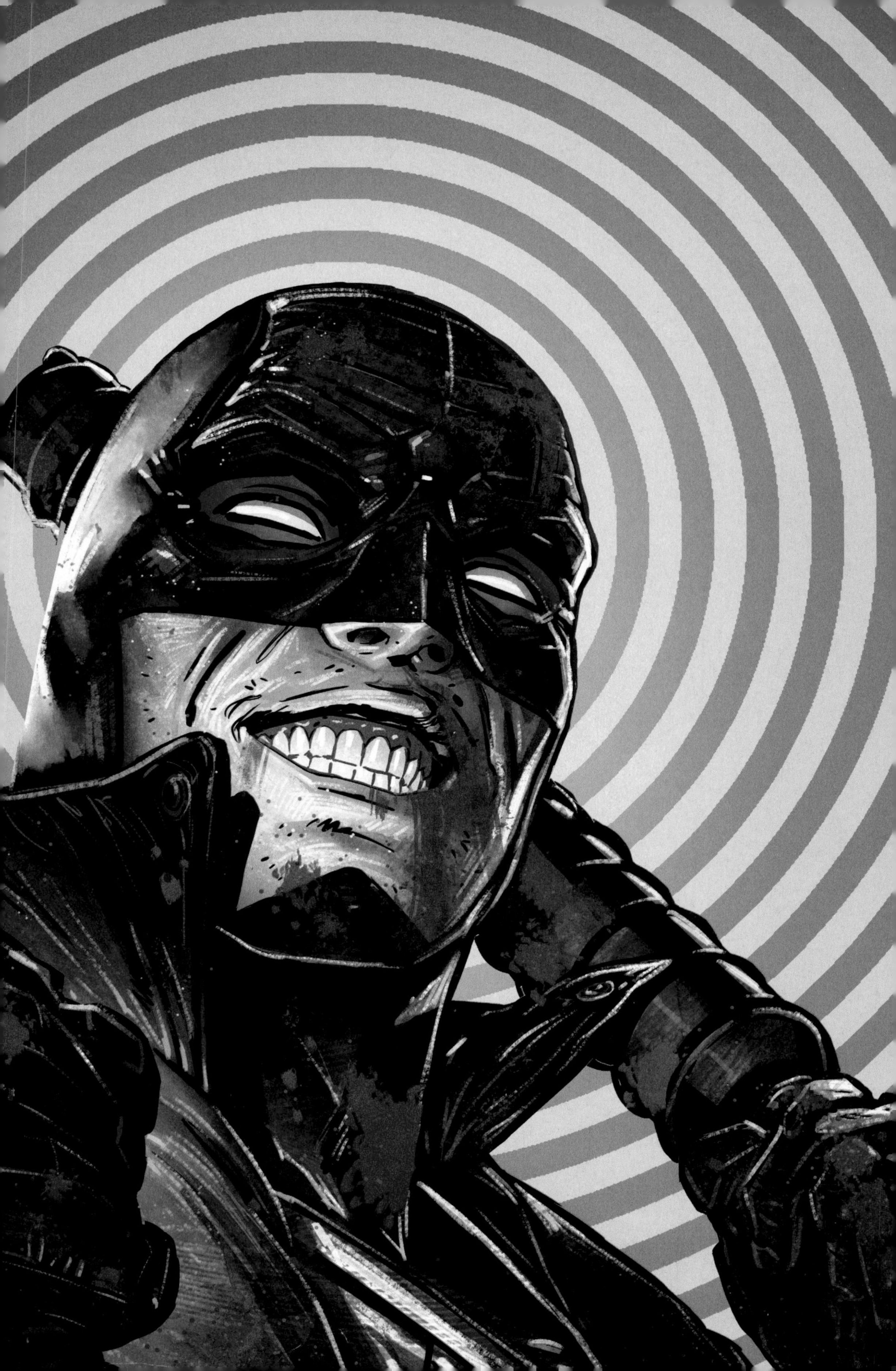

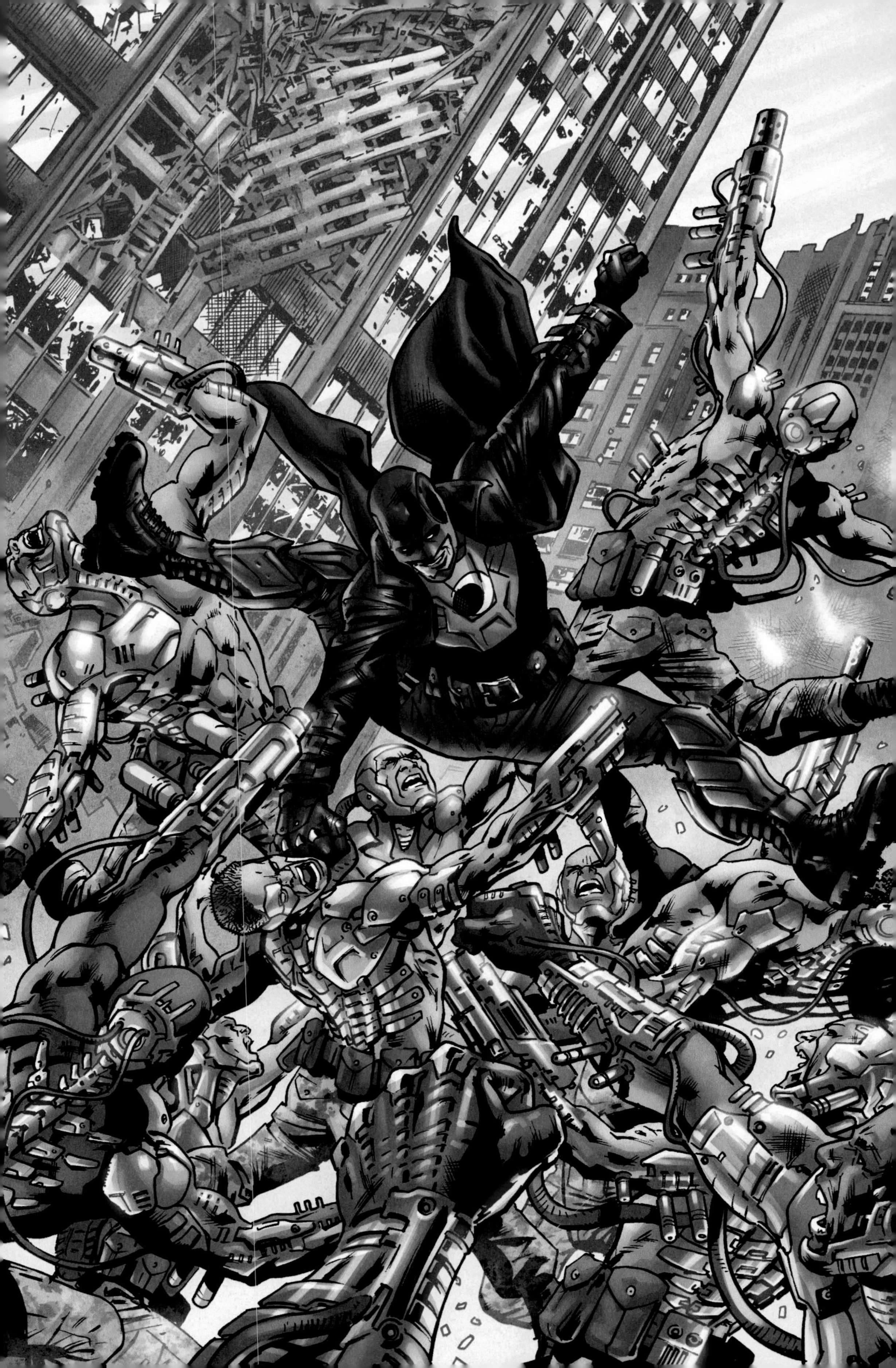

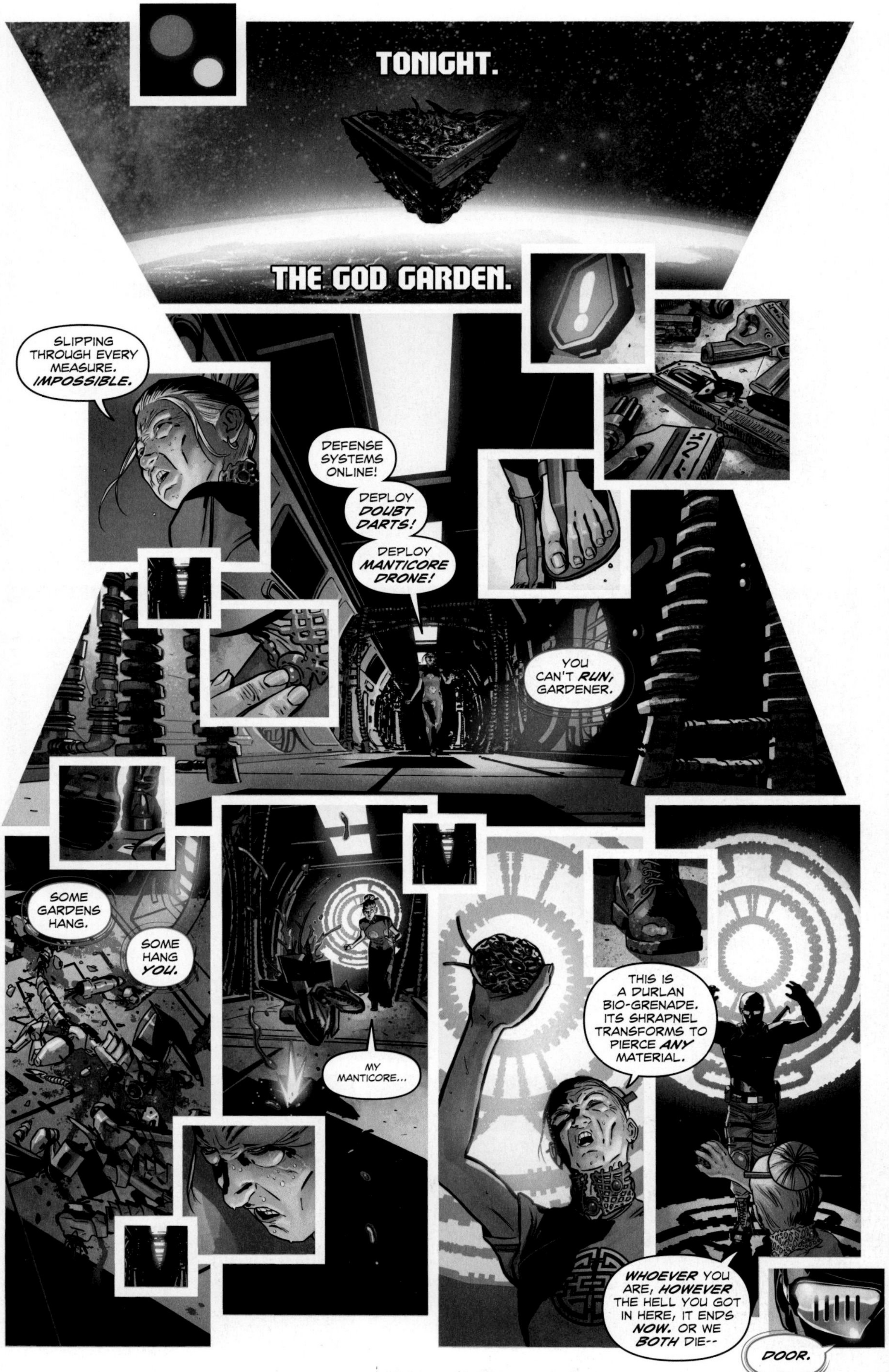
TONIGHT.
THE GOD GARDEN.
SLIPPING THROUGH EVERY MEASURE. IMPOSSIBLE.
DEFENSE SYSTEMS ONLINE!
DEPLOY DOUBT DARTS!
DEPLOY MANTICORE DRONE!
YOU CAN'T RUN, GARDENER.
SOME GARDENS HANG.
SOME HANG YOU.
MY MANTICORE...
THIS IS A DURLAN BIO-GRENADE. ITS SHRAPNEL TRANSFORMS TO PIERCE ANY MATERIAL.
WHOEVER YOU ARE, HOWEVER THE HELL YOU GOT IN HERE, IT ENDS NOW. OR WE BOTH DIE--
DOOR.

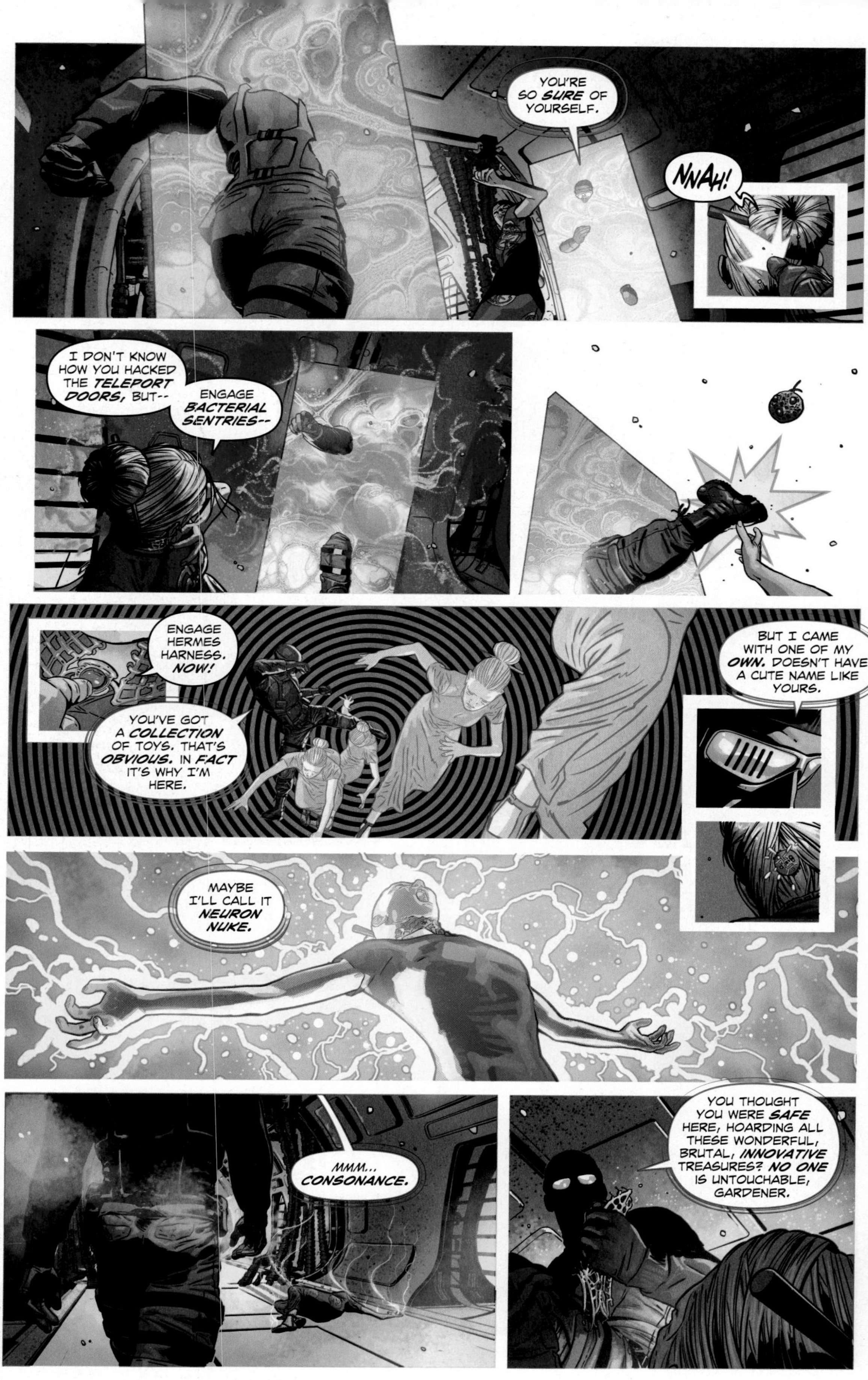
YOU'RE SO SURE OF YOURSELF.
NNAH!
I DON'T KNOW HOW YOU HACKED THE TELEPORT DOORS, BUT--
ENGAGE BACTERIAL SENTRIES--
ENGAGE HERMES HARNESS. NOW!
YOU'VE GOT A COLLECTION OF TOYS. THAT'S OBVIOUS. IN FACT IT'S WHY I'M HERE.
BUT I CAME WITH ONE OF MY OWN. DOESN'T HAVE A CUTE NAME LIKE YOURS.
MAYBE I'LL CALL IT NEURON NUKE.
MMM... CONSONANCE.
YOU THOUGHT YOU WERE SAFE HERE, HOARDING ALL THESE WONDERFUL, BRUTAL, INNOVATIVE TREASURES? NO ONE IS UNTOUCHABLE, GARDENER.

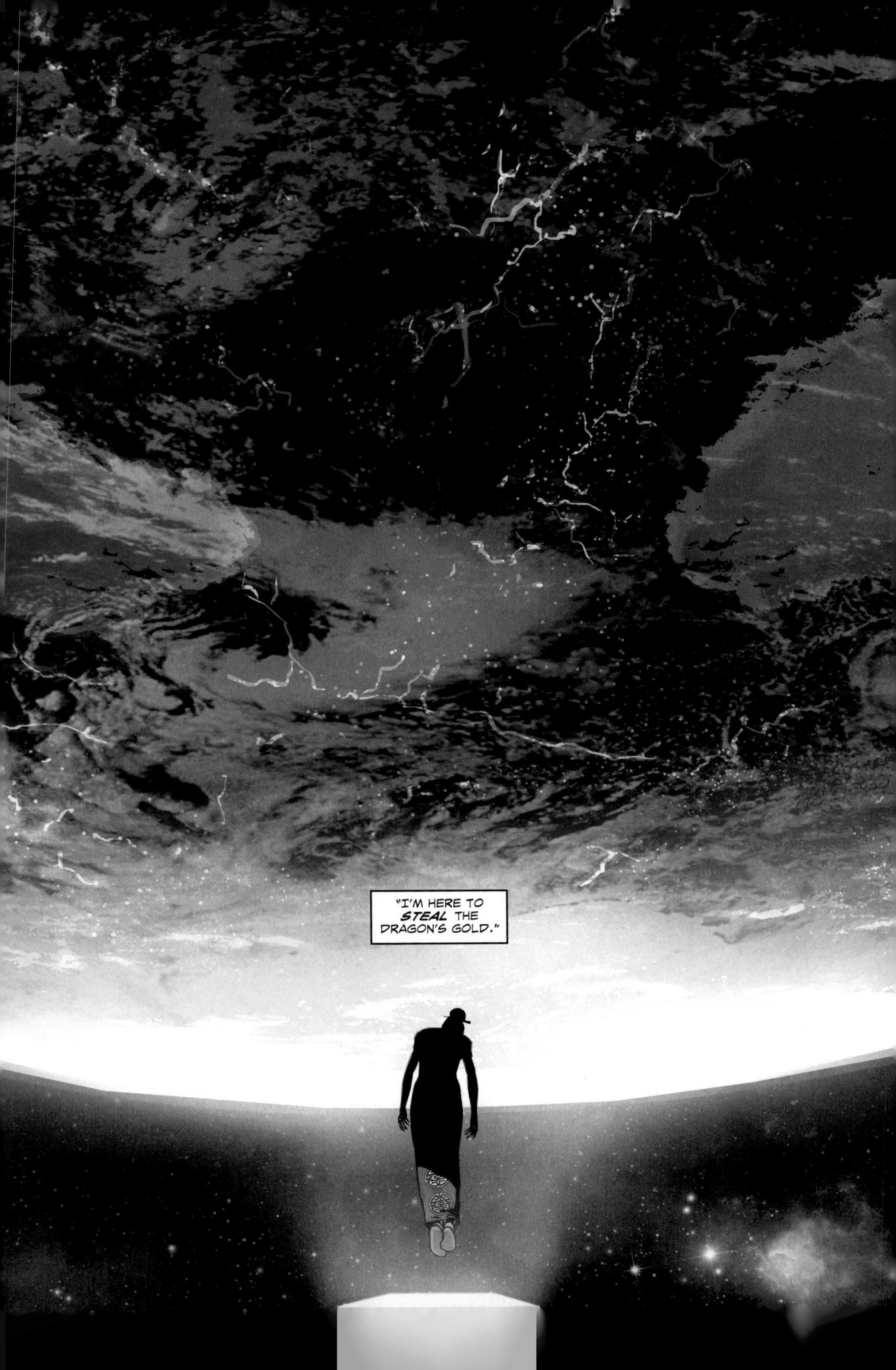
"I'M HERE TO STEAL THE DRAGON'S GOLD."

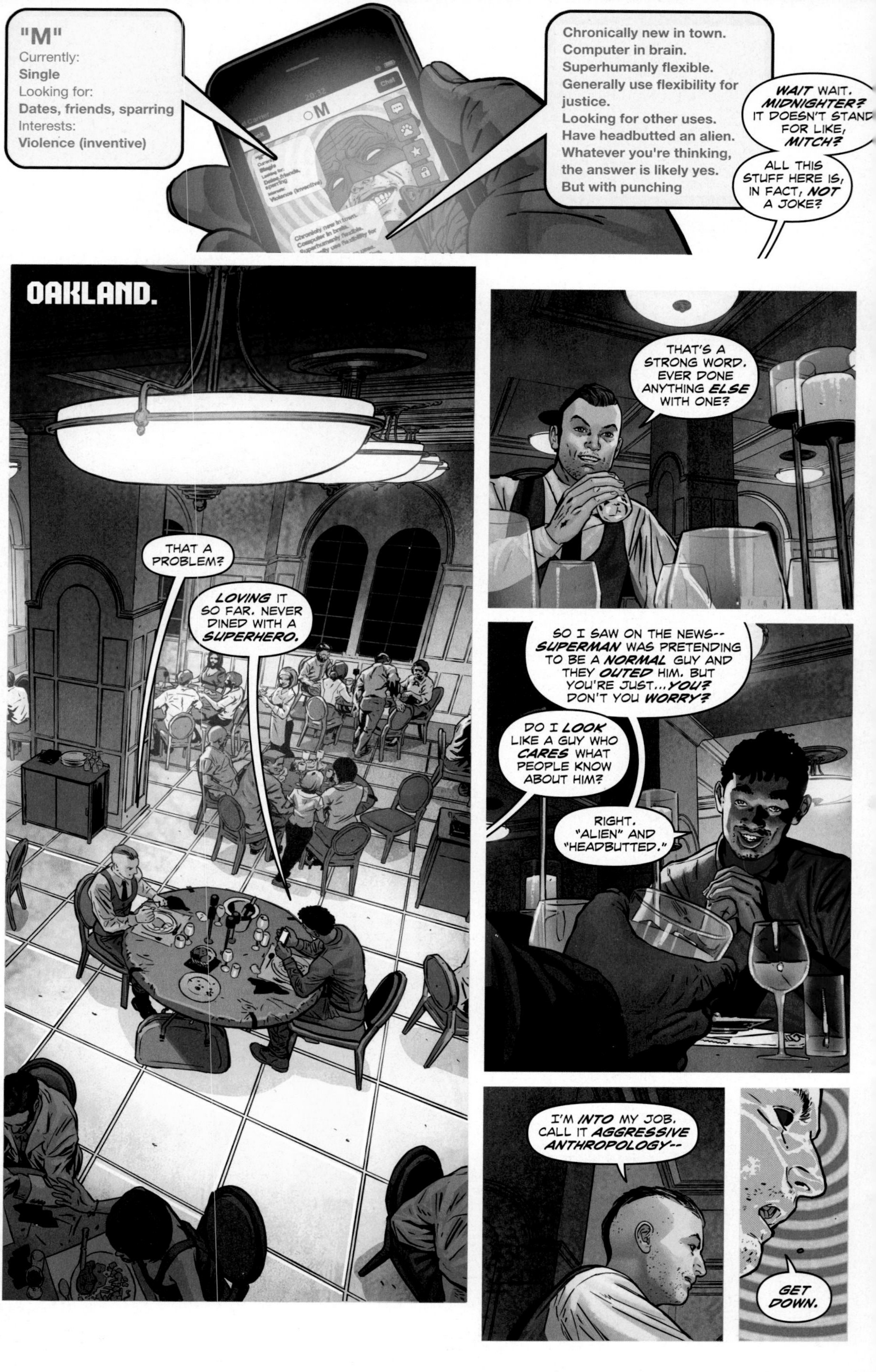
"M"
Currently:
Single
Looking for:
Dates, friends, sparring
Interests:
Violence (inventive)
Chronically new in town.
Computer in brain.
Superhumanly flexible.
Generally use flexibility for justice.
Looking for other uses.
Have headbutted an alien.
Whatever you're thinking, the answer is likely yes.
But with punching
WAIT WAIT. MIDNIGHTER? IT DOESN'T STAND FOR LIKE, MITCH?
ALL THIS STUFF HERE IS, IN FACT, NOT A JOKE?
OAKLAND.
THAT A PROBLEM?
LOVING IT SO FAR. NEVER DINED WITH A SUPERHERO.
THAT'S A STRONG WORD. EVER DONE ANYTHING ELSE WITH ONE?
SO I SAW ON THE NEWS-- SUPERMAN WAS PRETENDING TO BE A NORMAL GUY AND THEY OUTED HIM. BUT YOU'RE JUST...YOU? DON'T YOU WORRY?
DO I LOOK LIKE A GUY WHO CARES WHAT PEOPLE KNOW ABOUT HIM?
RIGHT. "ALIEN" AND "HEADBUTTED."
I'M INTO MY JOB. CALL IT AGGRESSIVE ANTHROPOLOGY--
GET DOWN.

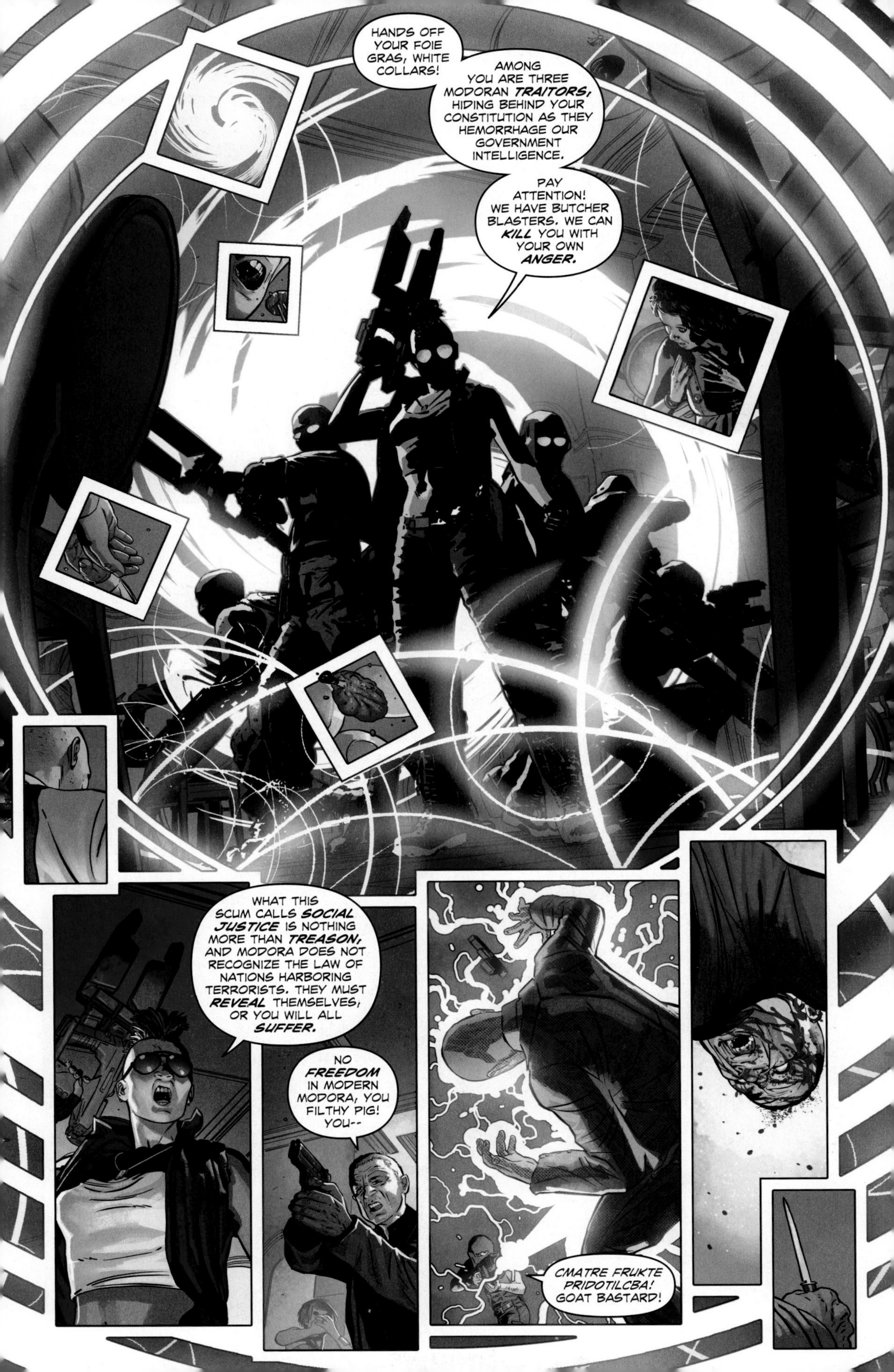
HANDS OFF YOUR FOIE GRAS, WHITE COLLARS!
AMONG YOU ARE THREE MODORAN TRAITORS, HIDING BEHIND YOUR CONSTITUTION AS THEY HEMORRHAGE OUR GOVERNMENT INTELLIGENCE.
PAY ATTENTION! WE HAVE BUTCHER BLASTERS. WE CAN KILL YOU WITH YOUR OWN ANGER.
WHAT THIS SCUM CALLS SOCIAL JUSTICE IS NOTHING MORE THAN TREASON, AND MODORA DOES NOT RECOGNIZE THE LAW OF NATIONS HARBORING TERRORISTS. THEY MUST REVEAL THEMSELVES, OR YOU WILL ALL SUFFER.
NO FREEDOM IN MODERN MODORA, YOU FILTHY PIG! YOU--
CMATRE FRUKTE PRIDOTILCBA! GOAT BASTARD!

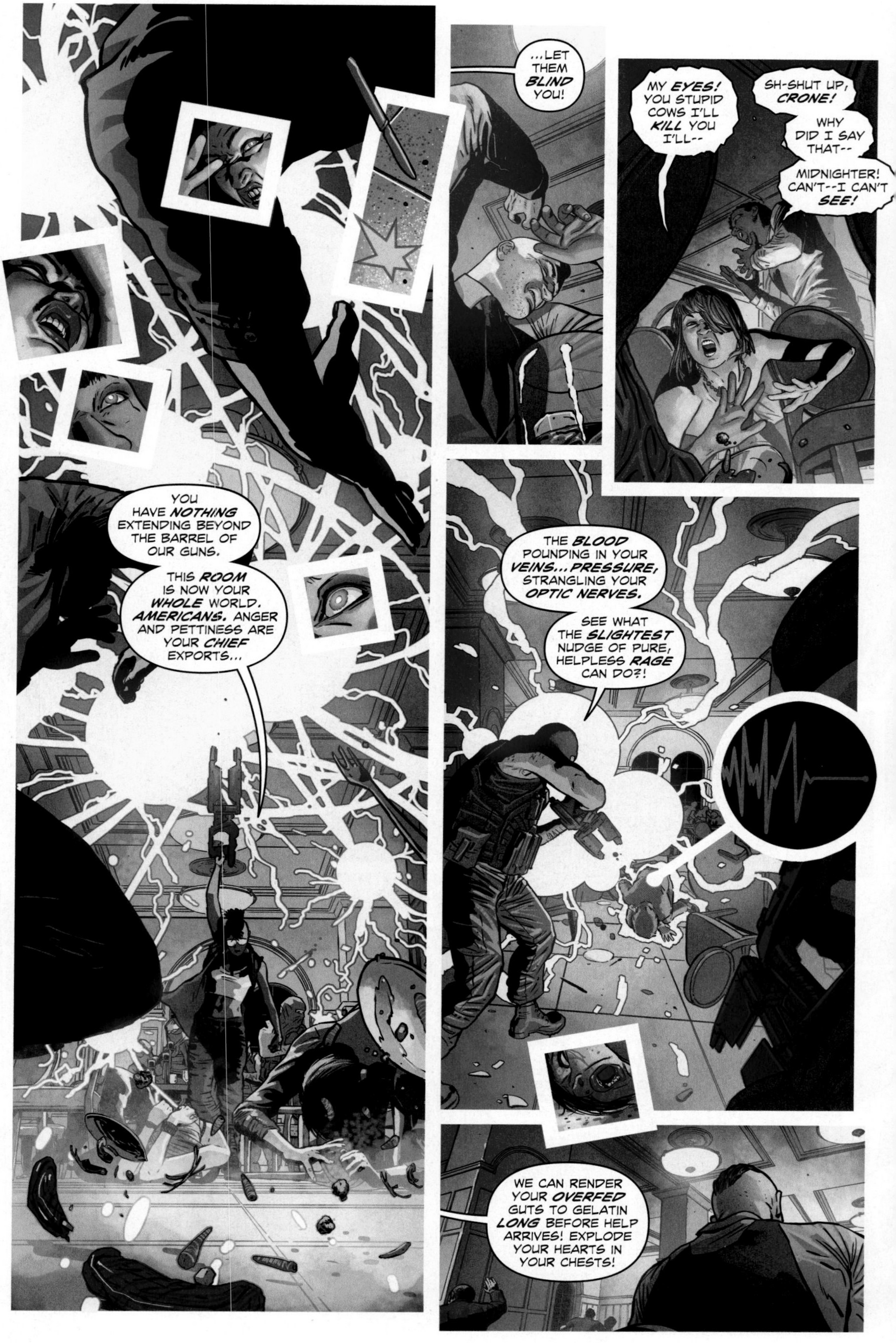
...LET THEM BLIND YOU!
MY EYES! YOU STUPID COWS I'LL KILL YOU I'LL--
SH-SHUT UP, CRONE!
WHY DID I SAY THAT--
MIDNIGHTER! CAN'T--I CAN'T SEE!
YOU HAVE NOTHING EXTENDING BEYOND THE BARREL OF OUR GUNS.
THIS ROOM IS NOW YOUR WHOLE WORLD. AMERICANS. ANGER AND PETTINESS ARE YOUR CHIEF EXPORTS...
THE BLOOD POUNDING IN YOUR VEINS...PRESSURE, STRANGLING YOUR OPTIC NERVES.
SEE WHAT THE SLIGHTEST NUDGE OF PURE, HELPLESS RAGE CAN DO?!
WE CAN RENDER YOUR OVERFED GUTS TO GELATIN LONG BEFORE HELP ARRIVES! EXPLODE YOUR HEARTS IN YOUR CHESTS!

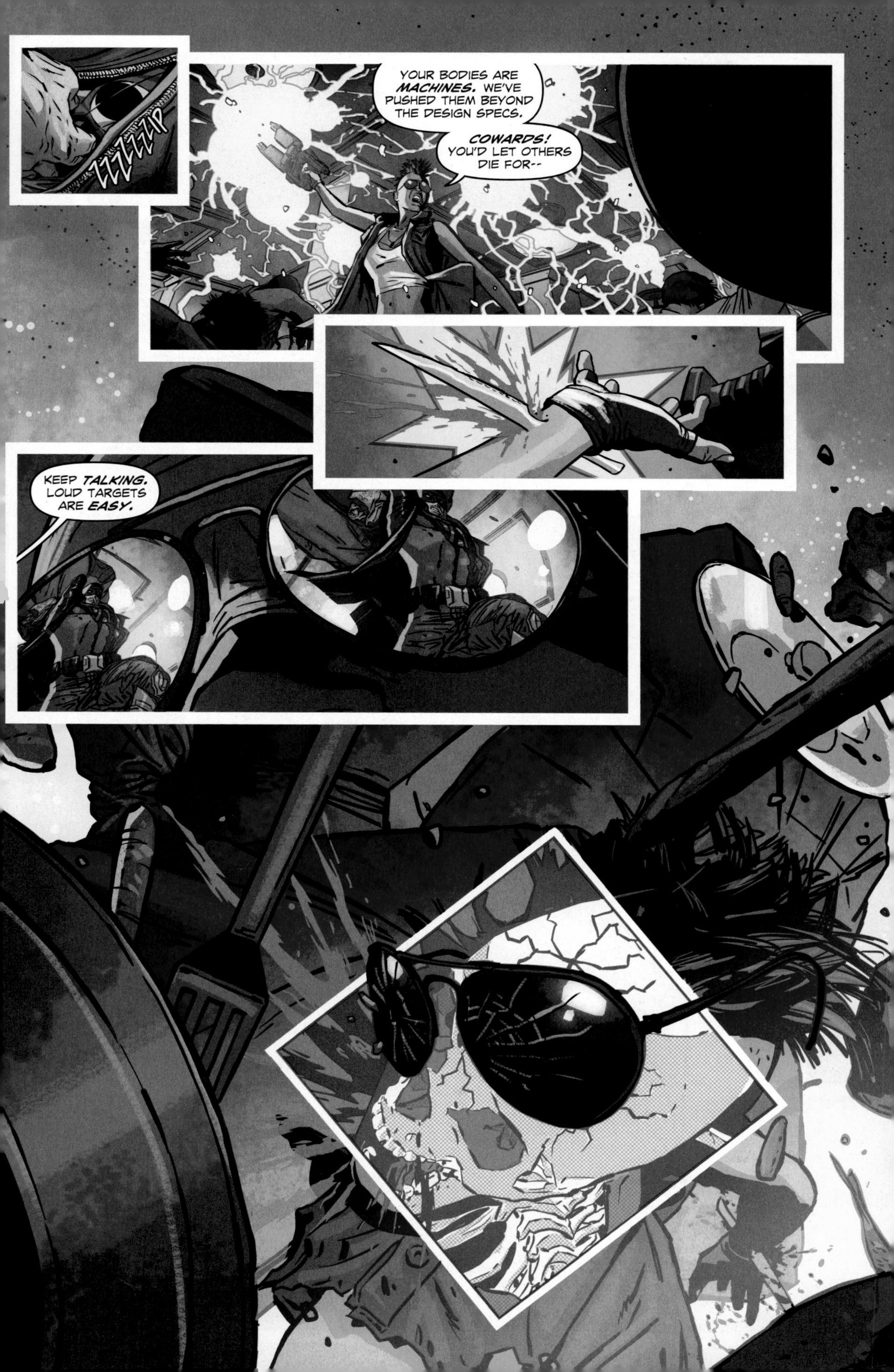
ZZZZZZIP
YOUR BODIES ARE MACHINES. WE'VE PUSHED THEM BEYOND THE DESIGN SPECS.
COWARDS! YOU'D LET OTHERS DIE FOR--
KEEP TALKING. LOUD TARGETS ARE EASY.

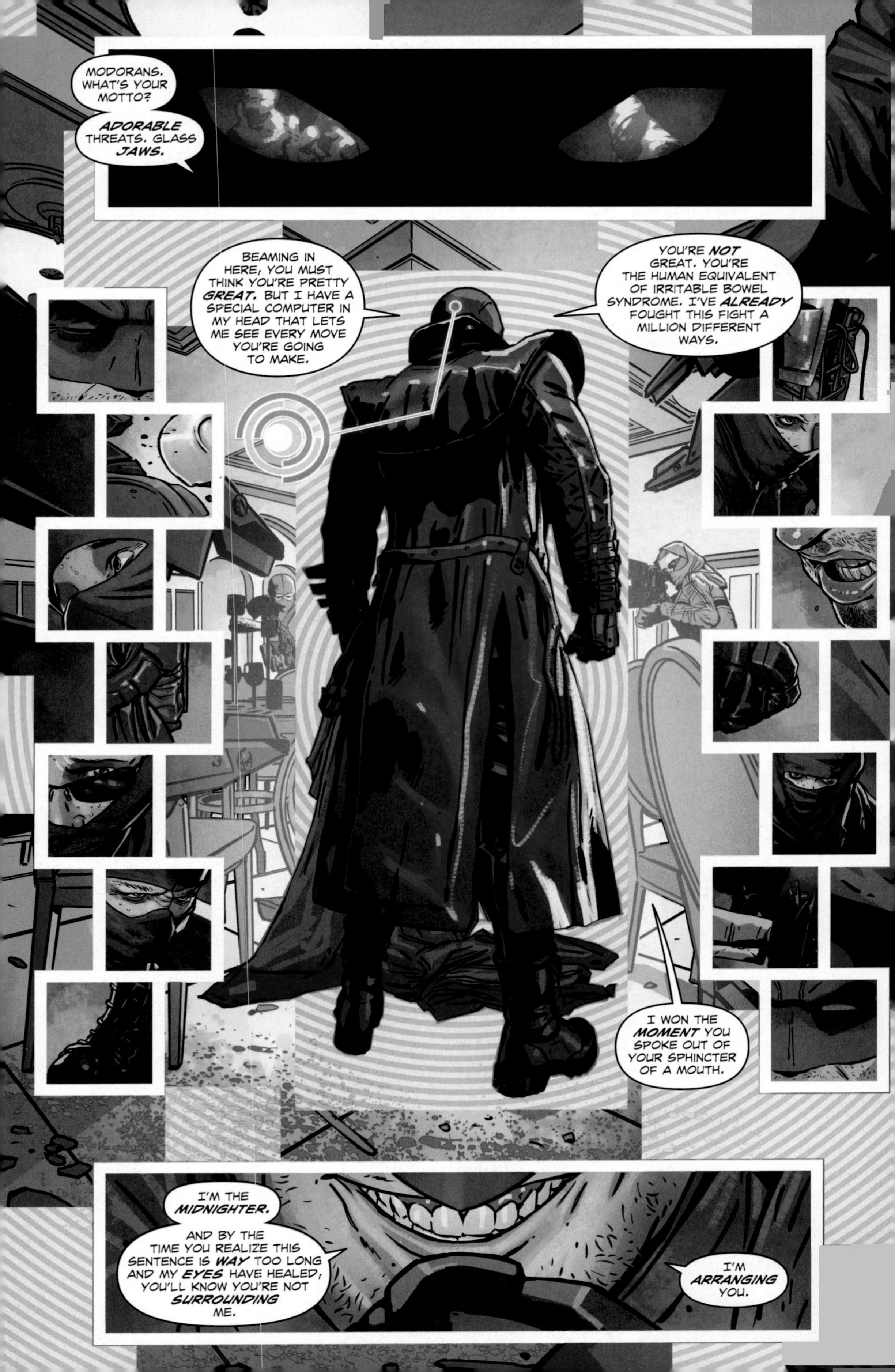
MODORANS. WHAT'S YOUR MOTTO?
ADORABLE THREATS. GLASS JAWS.
BEAMING IN HERE, YOU MUST THINK YOU'RE PRETTY GREAT. BUT I HAVE A SPECIAL COMPUTER IN MY HEAD THAT LETS ME SEE EVERY MOVE YOU'RE GOING TO MAKE.
YOU'RE NOT GREAT. YOU'RE THE HUMAN EQUIVALENT OF IRRITABLE BOWEL SYNDROME. I'VE ALREADY FOUGHT THIS FIGHT A MILLION DIFFERENT WAYS.
I WON THE MOMENT YOU SPOKE OUT OF YOUR SPHINCTER OF A MOUTH.
I'M THE MIDNIGHTER.
AND BY THE TIME YOU REALIZE THIS SENTENCE IS WAY TOO LONG AND MY EYES HAVE HEALED, YOU'LL KNOW YOU'RE NOT SURROUNDING ME.
I'M ARRANGING YOU.

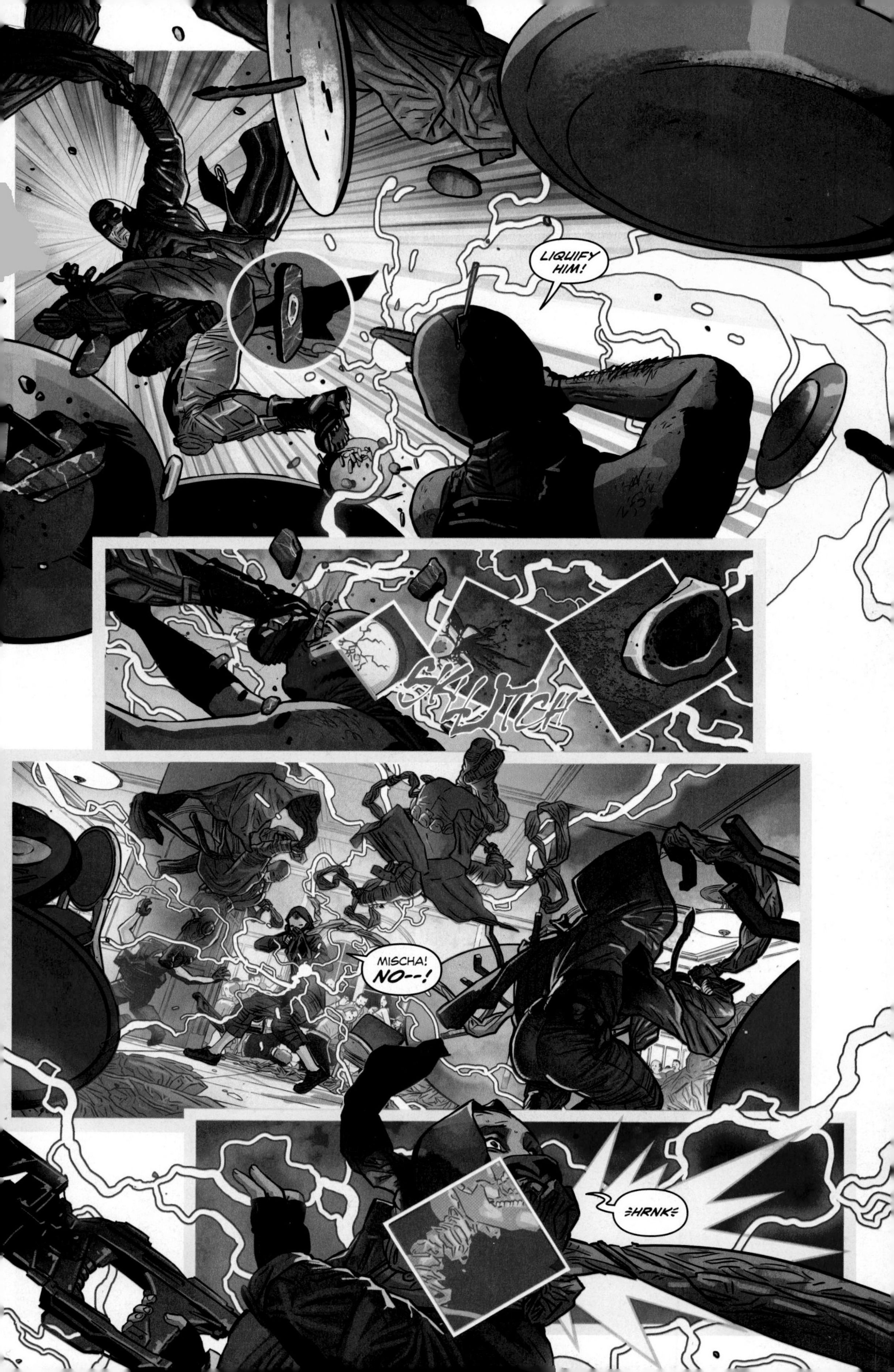
LIQUIFY HIM!
SKLUTCH
MISCHA! NO--!
HRNK

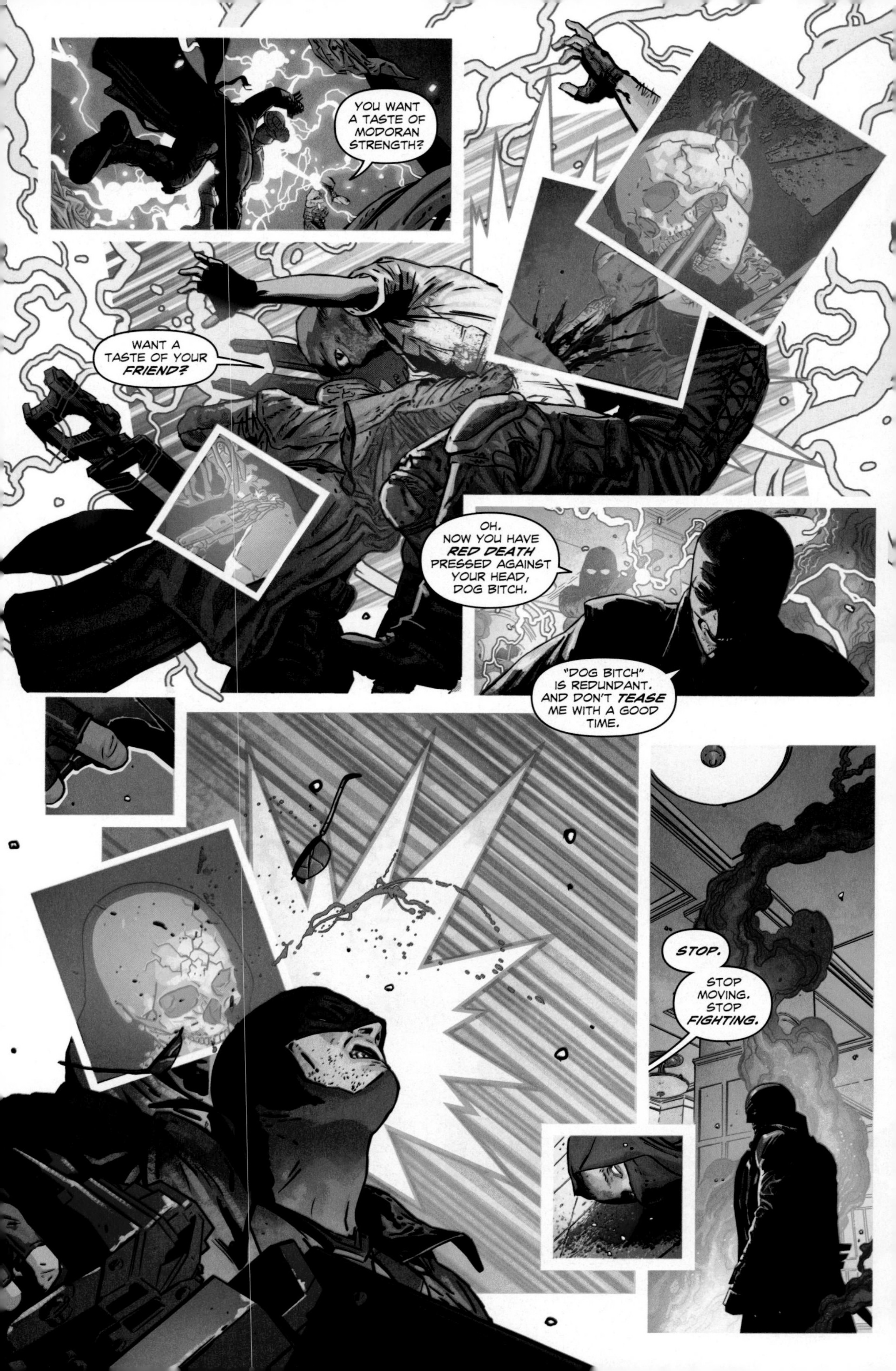
YOU WANT A TASTE OF MODORAN STRENGTH?
WANT A TASTE OF YOUR FRIEND?
OH. NOW YOU HAVE RED DEATH PRESSED AGAINST YOUR HEAD, DOG BITCH.
"DOG BITCH" IS REDUNDANT. AND DON'T TEASE ME WITH A GOOD TIME.
STOP.
STOP MOVING. STOP FIGHTING.

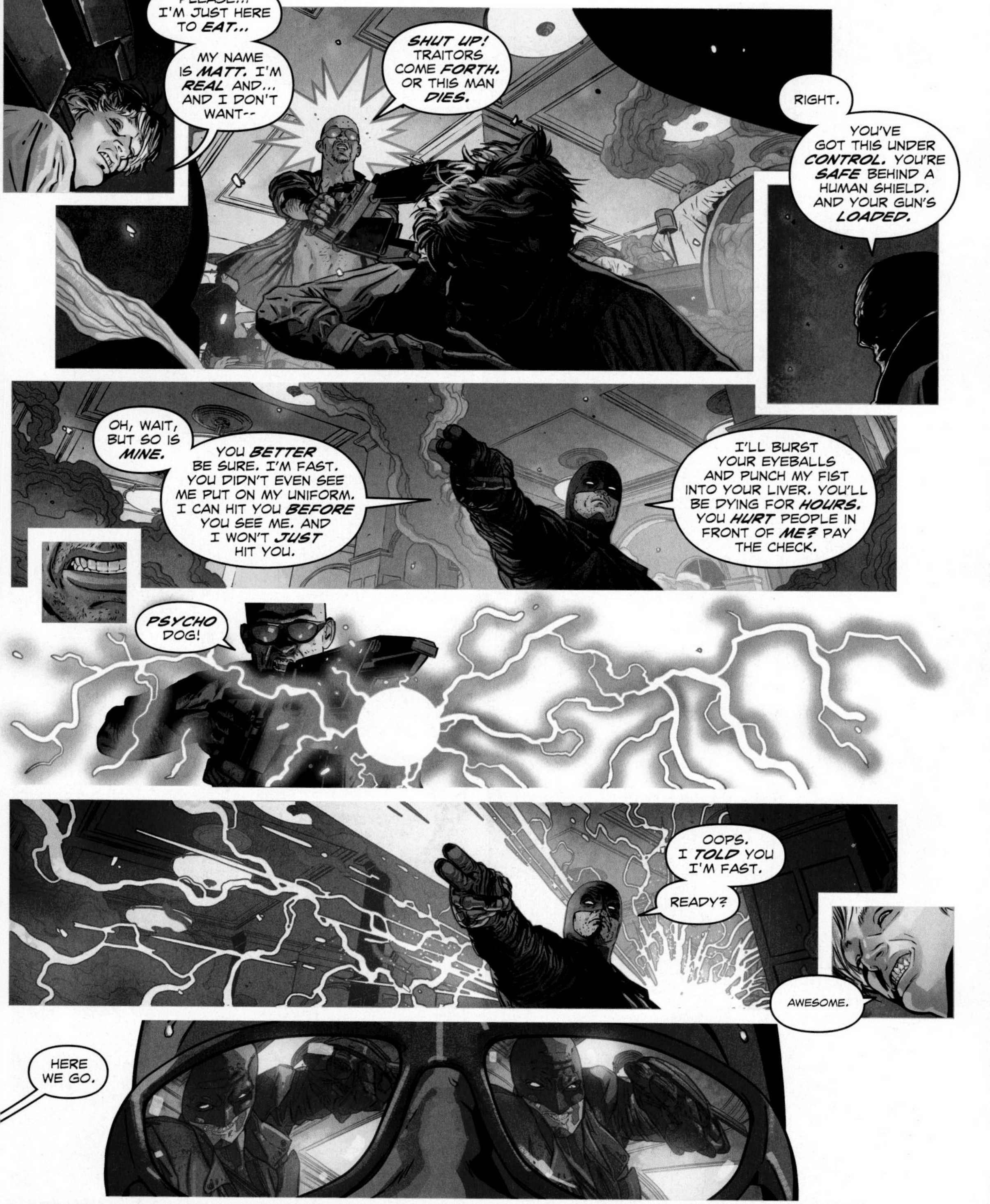
PLEASE... I'M JUST HERE TO EAT...
MY NAME IS MATT. I'M REAL AND... AND I DON'T WANT--
SHUT UP! TRAITORS COME FORTH. OR THIS MAN DIES.
RIGHT.
YOU'VE GOT THIS UNDER CONTROL. YOU'RE SAFE BEHIND A HUMAN SHIELD. AND YOUR GUN'S LOADED.
OH, WAIT, BUT SO IS MINE.
YOU BETTER BE SURE. I'M FAST. YOU DIDN'T EVEN SEE ME PUT ON MY UNIFORM. I CAN HIT YOU BEFORE YOU SEE ME. AND I WON'T JUST HIT YOU.
I'LL BURST YOUR EYEBALLS AND PUNCH MY FIST INTO YOUR LIVER. YOU'LL BE DYING FOR HOURS. YOU HURT PEOPLE IN FRONT OF ME? PAY THE CHECK.
PSYCHO DOG!
OOPS. I TOLD YOU I'M FAST.
READY?
AWESOME.
HERE WE GO.

MIDNIGHTER

STEVE ORLANDO WRITER ACO PENCILLER ACO WITH HUGO PETRUS INKS
ROMULO FAJARDO, JR. COLORS JARED K. FLETCHER LETTERS
ACO & ROMULO FAJARDO, JR. COVER BRYAN HITCH & ALEX SINCLAIR VARIANT COVER
DAVE WIELGOSZ ASST. EDITOR CHRIS CONROY EDITOR MARK DOYLE GROUP EDITOR

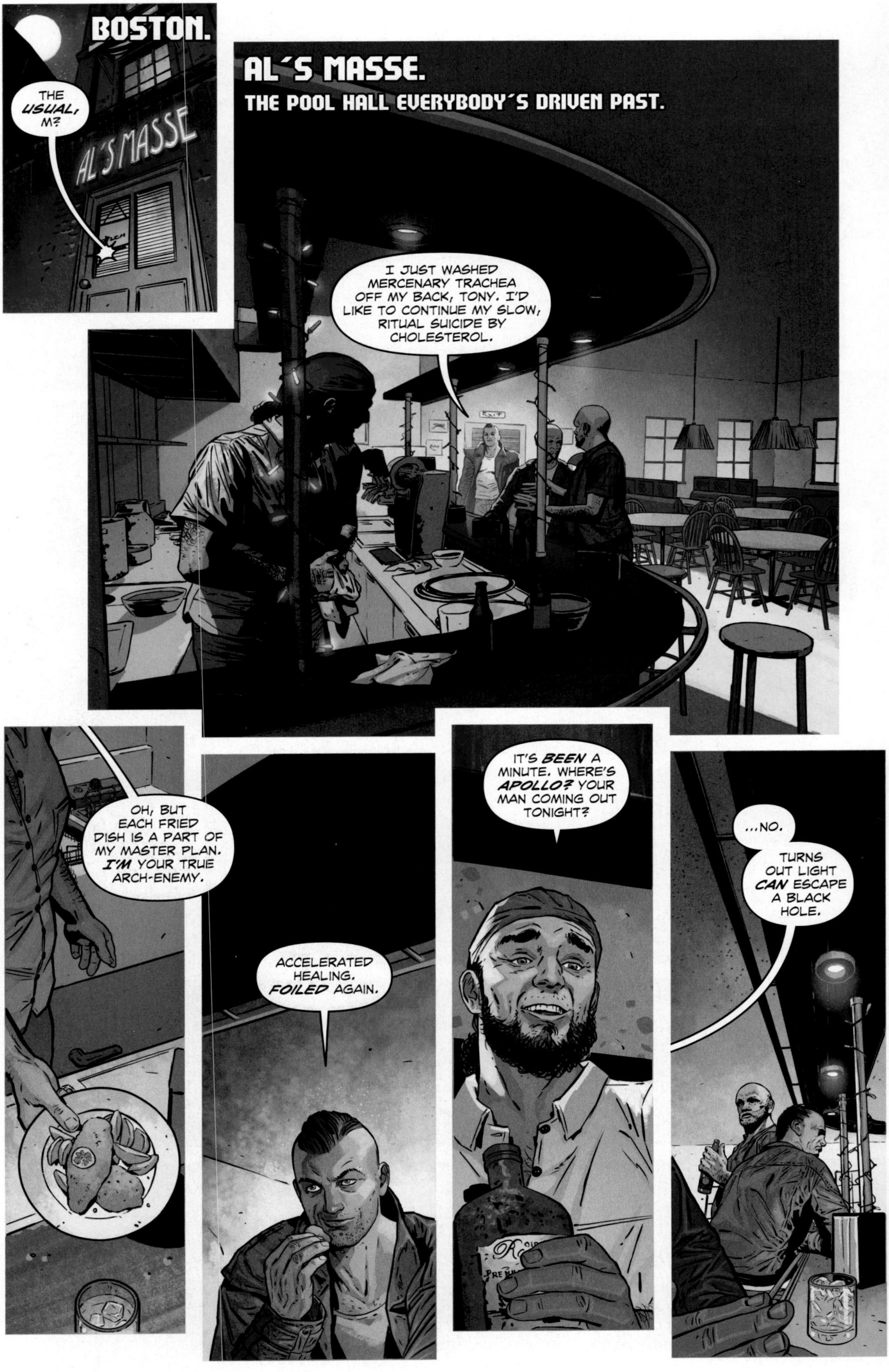
BOSTON.
THE USUAL, M?
AL´S MASSE
AL´S MASSE.
THE POOL HALL EVERYBODY´S DRIVEN PAST.
I JUST WASHED MERCENARY TRACHEA OFF MY BACK, TONY. I'D LIKE TO CONTINUE MY SLOW, RITUAL SUICIDE BY CHOLESTEROL.
OH, BUT EACH FRIED DISH IS A PART OF MY MASTER PLAN. I'M YOUR TRUE ARCH-ENEMY.
ACCELERATED HEALING. FOILED AGAIN.
IT'S BEEN A MINUTE. WHERE'S APOLLO? YOUR MAN COMING OUT TONIGHT?
...NO.
TURNS OUT LIGHT CAN ESCAPE A BLACK HOLE.

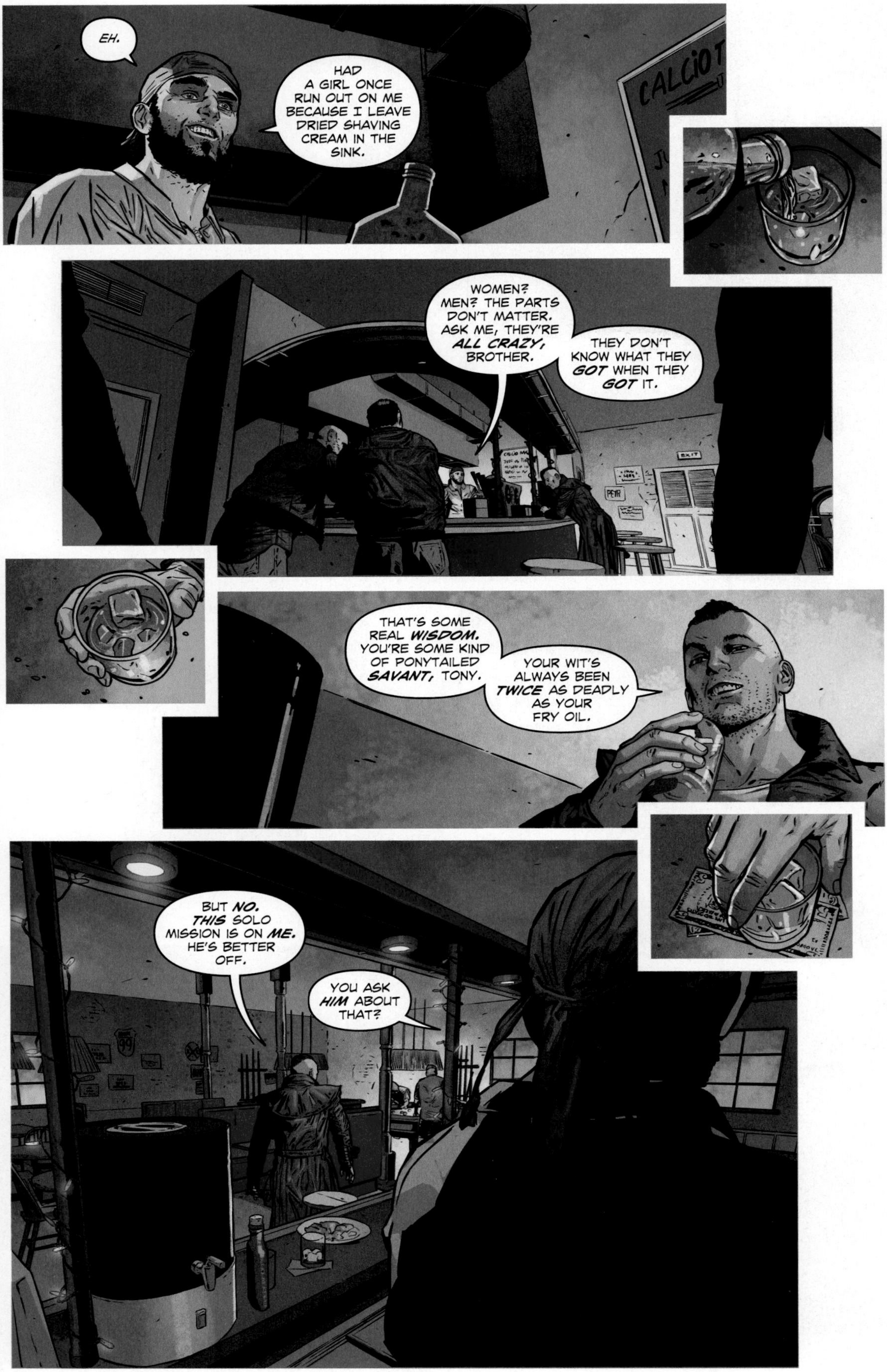
EH.
HAD A GIRL ONCE RUN OUT ON ME BECAUSE I LEAVE DRIED SHAVING CREAM IN THE SINK.
WOMEN? MEN? THE PARTS DON'T MATTER. ASK ME, THEY'RE ALL CRAZY, BROTHER.
THEY DON'T KNOW WHAT THEY GOT WHEN THEY GOT IT.
THAT'S SOME REAL WISDOM. YOU'RE SOME KIND OF PONYTAILED SAVANT, TONY.
YOUR WIT'S ALWAYS BEEN TWICE AS DEADLY AS YOUR FRY OIL.
BUT NO. THIS SOLO MISSION IS ON ME. HE'S BETTER OFF.
YOU ASK HIM ABOUT THAT?

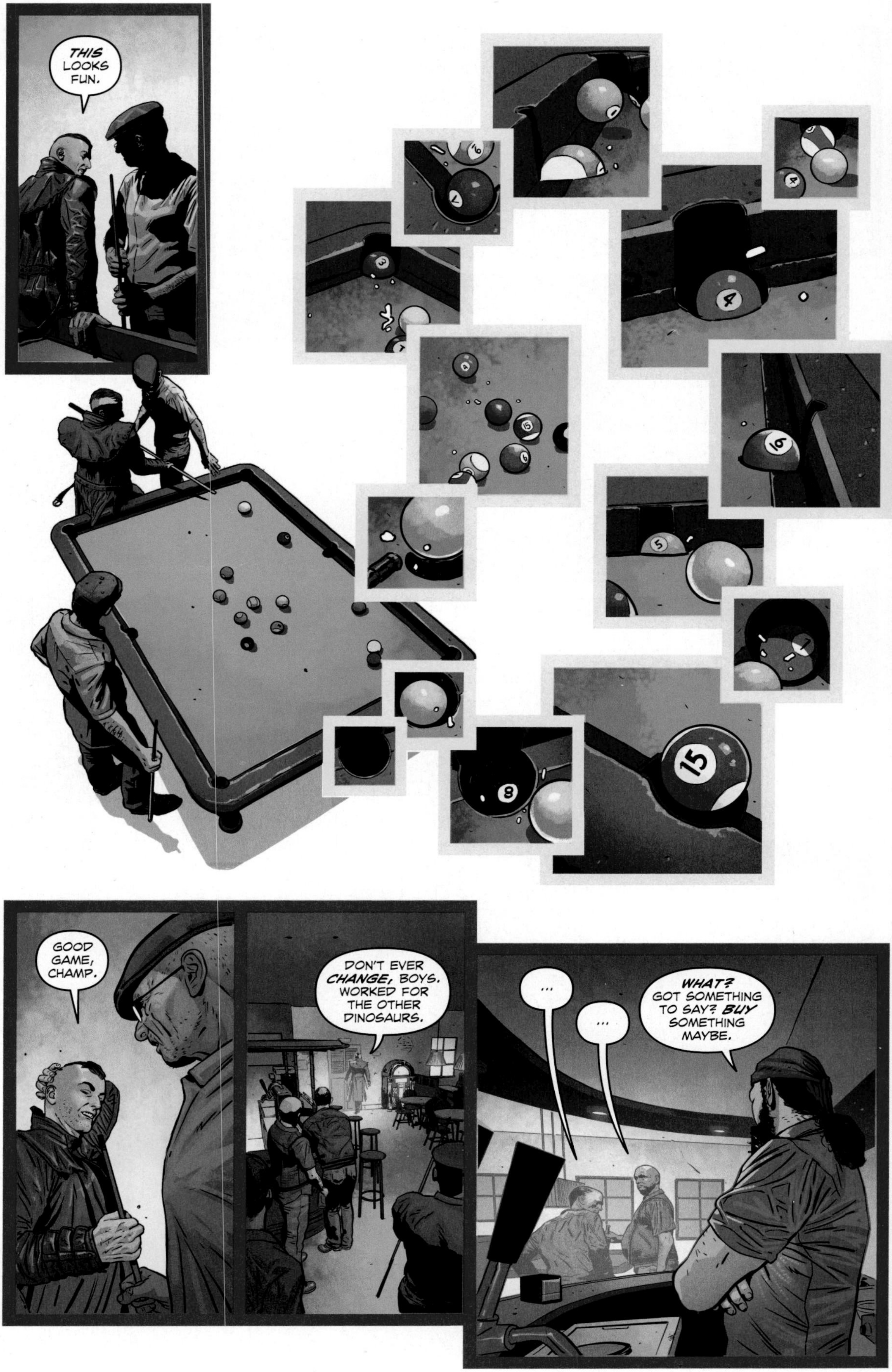
THIS LOOKS FUN.
GOOD GAME, CHAMP.
DON'T EVER CHANGE, BOYS. WORKED FOR THE OTHER DINOSAURS.
...
...
WHAT? GOT SOMETHING TO SAY? BUY SOMETHING MAYBE.

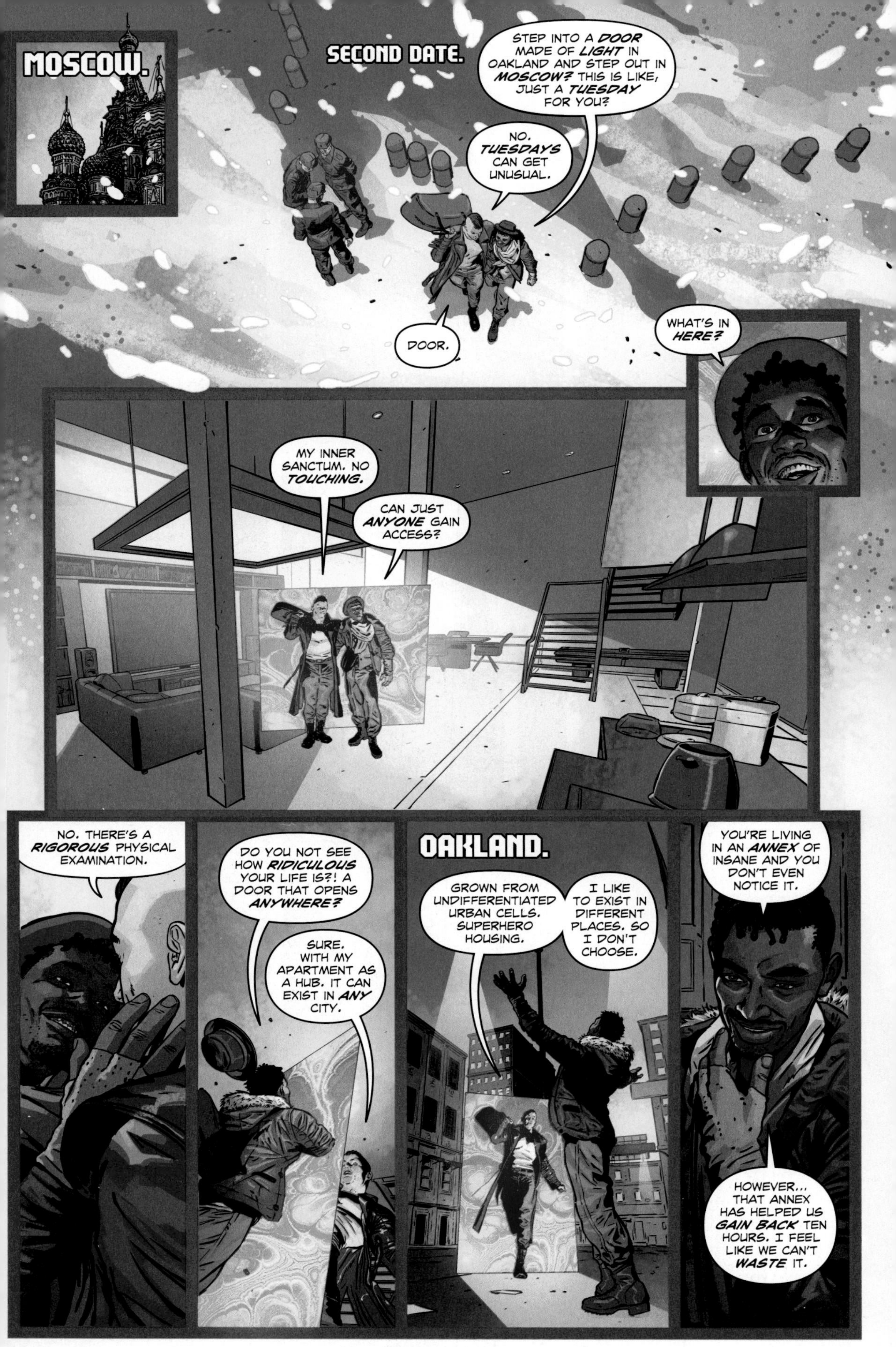
MOSCOW.
SECOND DATE.
STEP INTO A DOOR MADE OF LIGHT IN OAKLAND AND STEP OUT IN MOSCOW? THIS IS LIKE, JUST A TUESDAY FOR YOU?
NO. TUESDAYS CAN GET UNUSUAL.
DOOR.
WHAT'S IN HERE?
MY INNER SANCTUM. NO TOUCHING.
CAN JUST ANYONE GAIN ACCESS?
NO. THERE'S A RIGOROUS PHYSICAL EXAMINATION.
DO YOU NOT SEE HOW RIDICULOUS YOUR LIFE IS?! A DOOR THAT OPENS ANYWHERE?
SURE. WITH MY APARTMENT AS A HUB. IT CAN EXIST IN ANY CITY.
OAKLAND.
GROWN FROM UNDIFFERENTIATED URBAN CELLS. SUPERHERO HOUSING.
I LIKE TO EXIST IN DIFFERENT PLACES. SO I DON'T CHOOSE.
YOU'RE LIVING IN AN ANNEX OF INSANE AND YOU DON'T EVEN NOTICE IT.
HOWEVER... THAT ANNEX HAS HELPED US GAIN BACK TEN HOURS. I FEEL LIKE WE CAN'T WASTE IT.

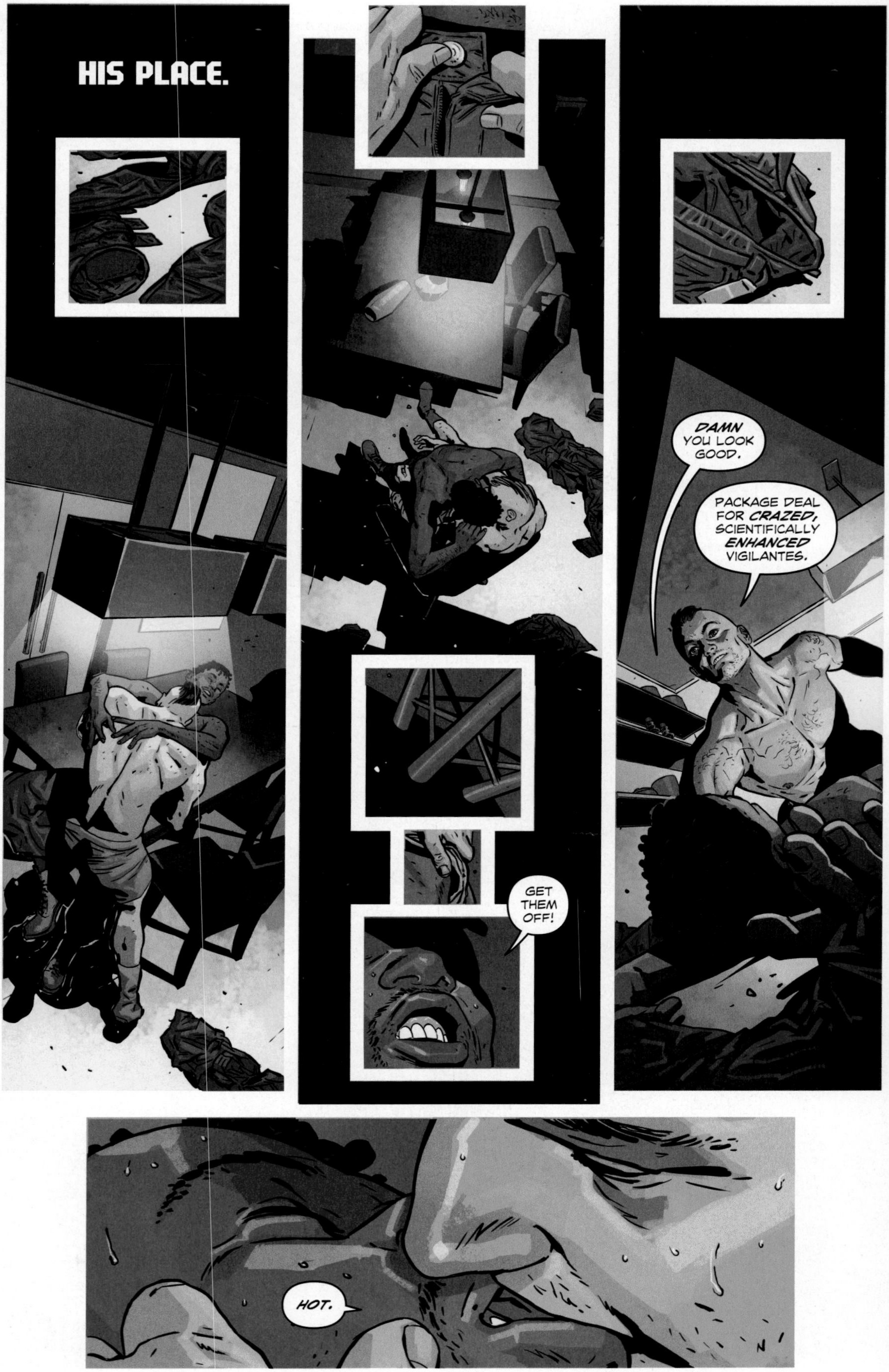
HIS PLACE.
GET THEM OFF!
DAMN YOU LOOK GOOD.
PACKAGE DEAL FOR CRAZED, SCIENTIFICALLY ENHANCED VIGILANTES.
HOT.

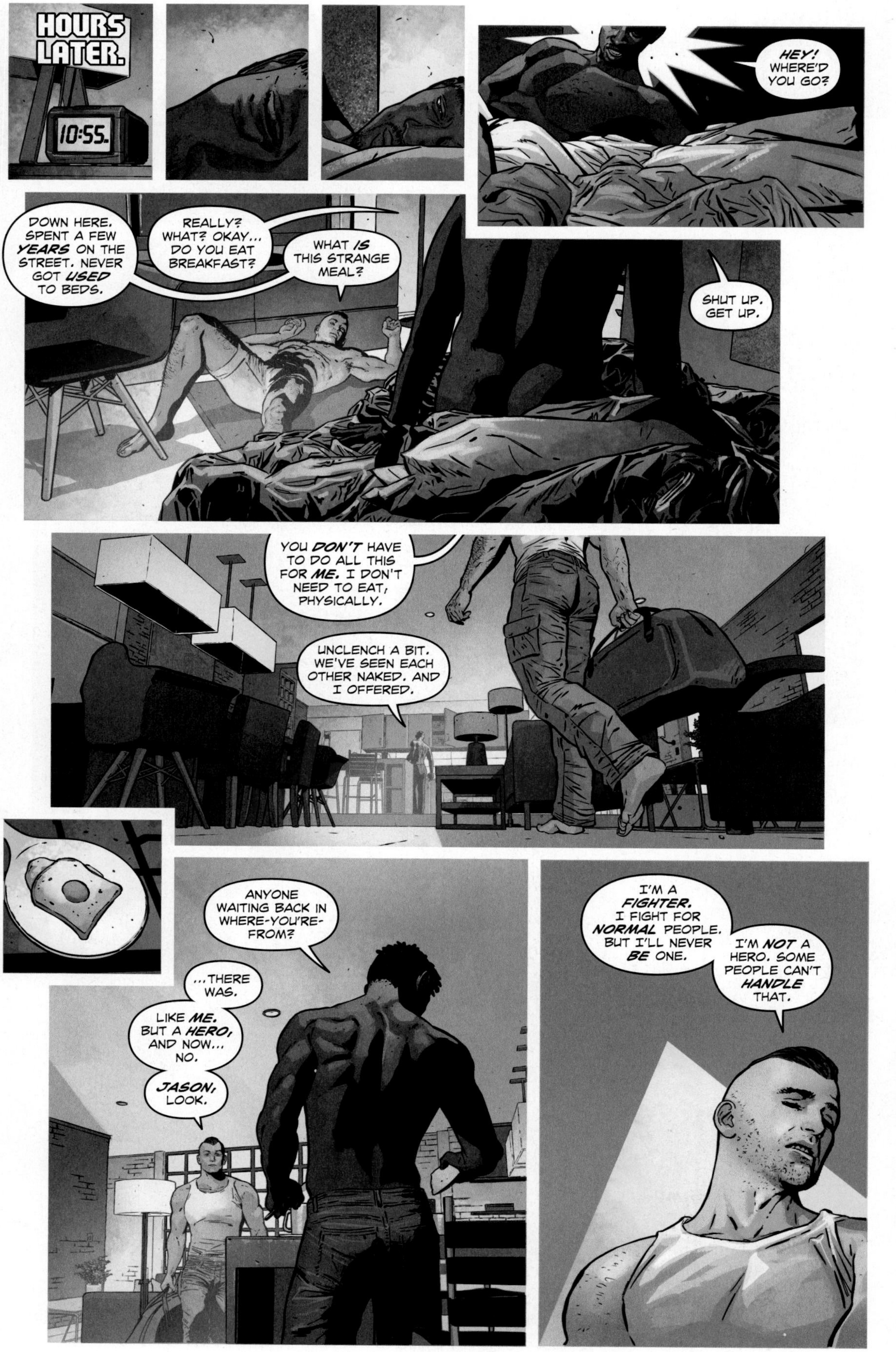
HOURS LATER.
10:55.
HEY! WHERE'D YOU GO?
DOWN HERE. SPENT A FEW YEARS ON THE STREET. NEVER GOT USED TO BEDS.
REALLY? WHAT? OKAY... DO YOU EAT BREAKFAST?
WHAT IS THIS STRANGE MEAL?
SHUT UP. GET UP.
YOU DON'T HAVE TO DO ALL THIS FOR ME. I DON'T NEED TO EAT, PHYSICALLY.
UNCLENCH A BIT. WE'VE SEEN EACH OTHER NAKED. AND I OFFERED.
ANYONE WAITING BACK IN WHERE-YOU'RE-FROM?
...THERE WAS.
LIKE ME. BUT A HERO, AND NOW... NO.
JASON, LOOK.
I'M A FIGHTER. I FIGHT FOR NORMAL PEOPLE. BUT I'LL NEVER BE ONE.
I'M NOT A HERO. SOME PEOPLE CAN'T HANDLE THAT.

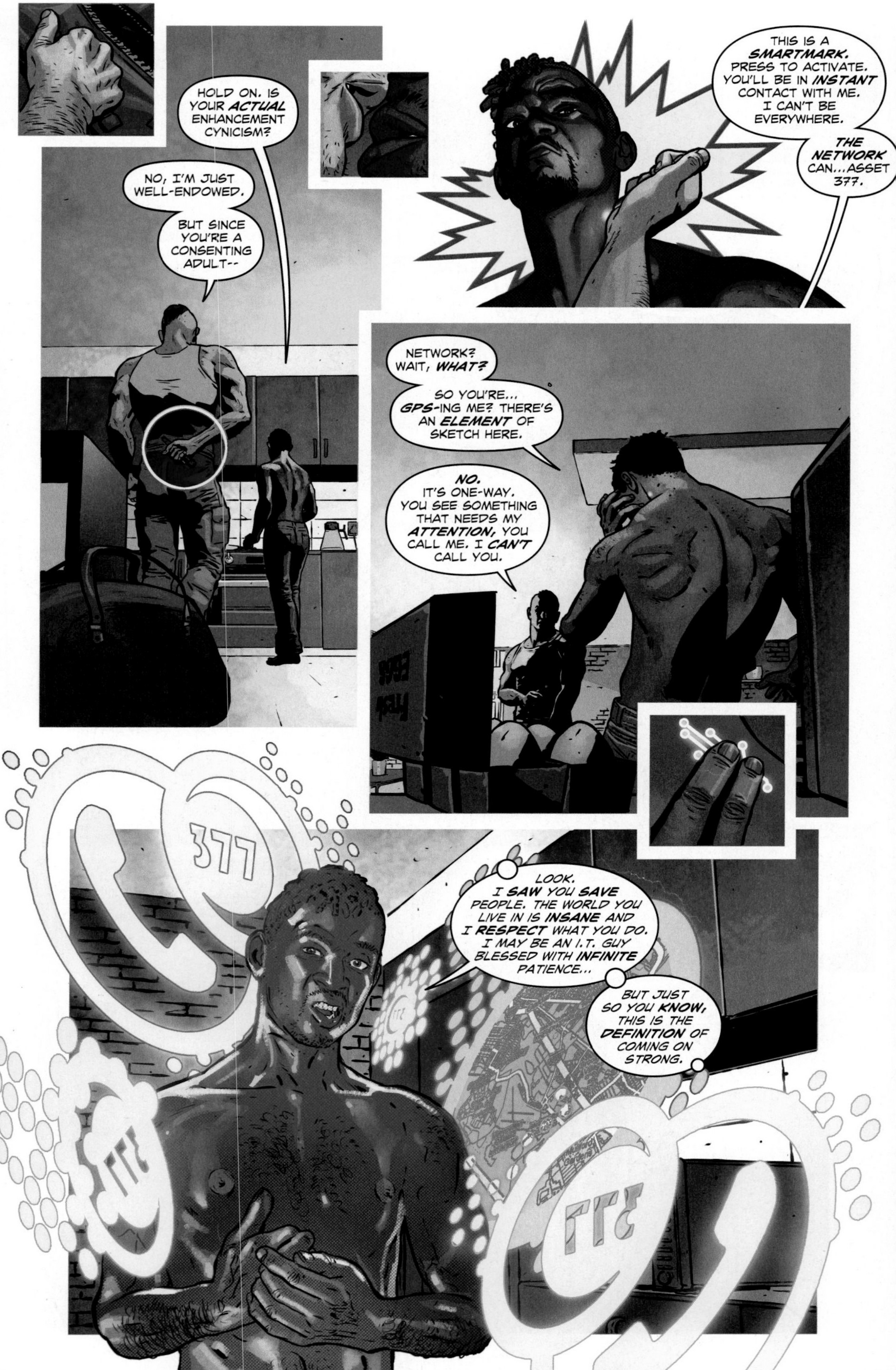
HOLD ON. IS YOUR ACTUAL ENHANCEMENT CYNICISM?
NO, I'M JUST WELL-ENDOWED.
BUT SINCE YOU'RE A CONSENTING ADULT--
THIS IS A SMARTMARK. PRESS TO ACTIVATE. YOU'LL BE IN INSTANT CONTACT WITH ME. I CAN'T BE EVERYWHERE.
THE NETWORK CAN...ASSET 377.
NETWORK? WAIT, WHAT?
SO YOU'RE... GPS-ING ME? THERE'S AN ELEMENT OF SKETCH HERE.
NO. IT'S ONE-WAY. YOU SEE SOMETHING THAT NEEDS MY ATTENTION, YOU CALL ME. I CAN'T CALL YOU.
377
LOOK. I SAW YOU SAVE PEOPLE. THE WORLD YOU LIVE IN IS INSANE AND I RESPECT WHAT YOU DO. I MAY BE AN I.T. GUY BLESSED WITH INFINITE PATIENCE...
BUT JUST SO YOU KNOW, THIS IS THE DEFINITION OF COMING ON STRONG.

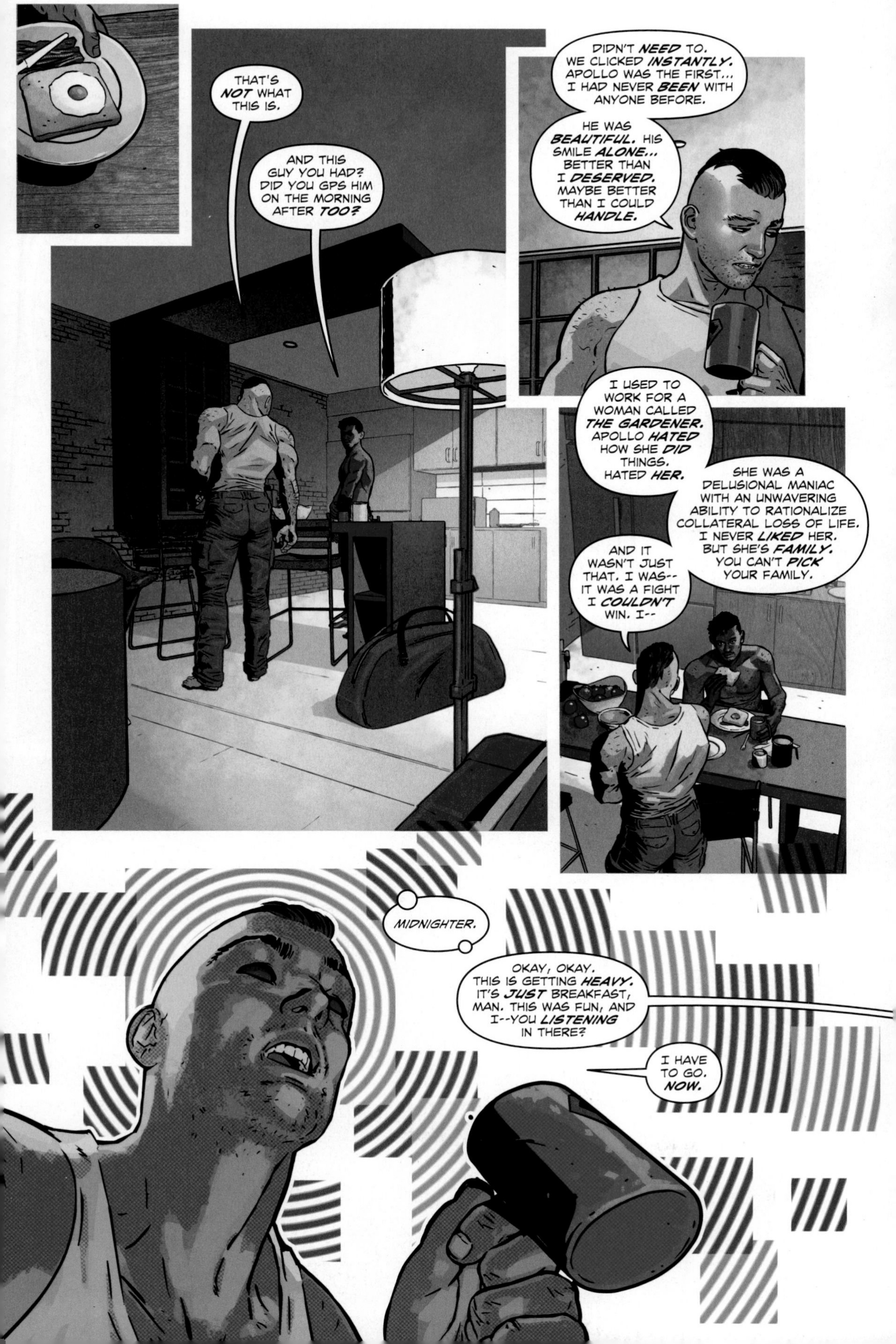
THAT'S NOT WHAT THIS IS.
AND THIS GUY YOU HAD? DID YOU GPS HIM ON THE MORNING AFTER TOO?
DIDN'T NEED TO. WE CLICKED INSTANTLY. APOLLO WAS THE FIRST... I HAD NEVER BEEN WITH ANYONE BEFORE.
HE WAS BEAUTIFUL. HIS SMILE ALONE... BETTER THAN I DESERVED. MAYBE BETTER THAN I COULD HANDLE.
I USED TO WORK FOR A WOMAN CALLED THE GARDENER. APOLLO HATED HOW SHE DID THINGS. HATED HER.
SHE WAS A DELUSIONAL MANIAC WITH AN UNWAVERING ABILITY TO RATIONALIZE COLLATERAL LOSS OF LIFE. I NEVER LIKED HER. BUT SHE'S FAMILY. YOU CAN'T PICK YOUR FAMILY.
AND IT WASN'T JUST THAT. I WAS-- IT WAS A FIGHT I COULDN'T WIN. I--
MIDNIGHTER.
OKAY, OKAY. THIS IS GETTING HEAVY. IT'S JUST BREAKFAST, MAN. THIS WAS FUN, AND I--YOU LISTENING IN THERE?
I HAVE TO GO. NOW.

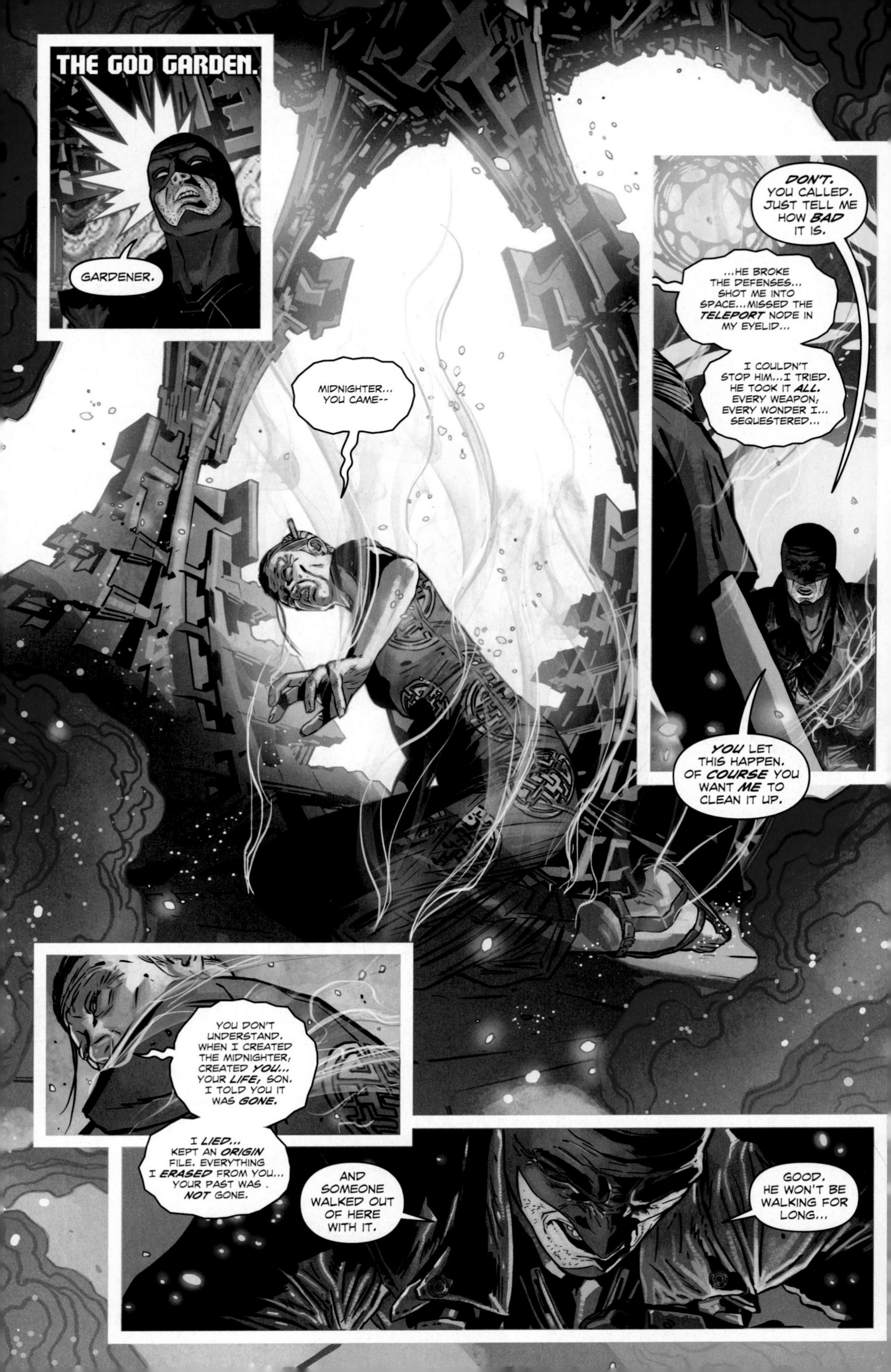
THE GOD GARDEN.
GARDENER.
MIDNIGHTER... YOU CAME--
DON'T. YOU CALLED. JUST TELL ME HOW BAD IT IS.
...HE BROKE THE DEFENSES... SHOT ME INTO SPACE...MISSED THE TELEPORT NODE IN MY EYELID...
I COULDN'T STOP HIM...I TRIED. HE TOOK IT ALL. EVERY WEAPON, EVERY WONDER I... SEQUESTERED...
YOU LET THIS HAPPEN. OF COURSE YOU WANT ME TO CLEAN IT UP.
YOU DON'T UNDERSTAND. WHEN I CREATED THE MIDNIGHTER, CREATED YOU... YOUR LIFE, SON. I TOLD YOU IT WAS GONE.
I LIED... KEPT AN ORIGIN FILE. EVERYTHING I ERASED FROM YOU... YOUR PAST WAS NOT GONE.
AND SOMEONE WALKED OUT OF HERE WITH IT.
GOOD. HE WON'T BE WALKING FOR LONG...

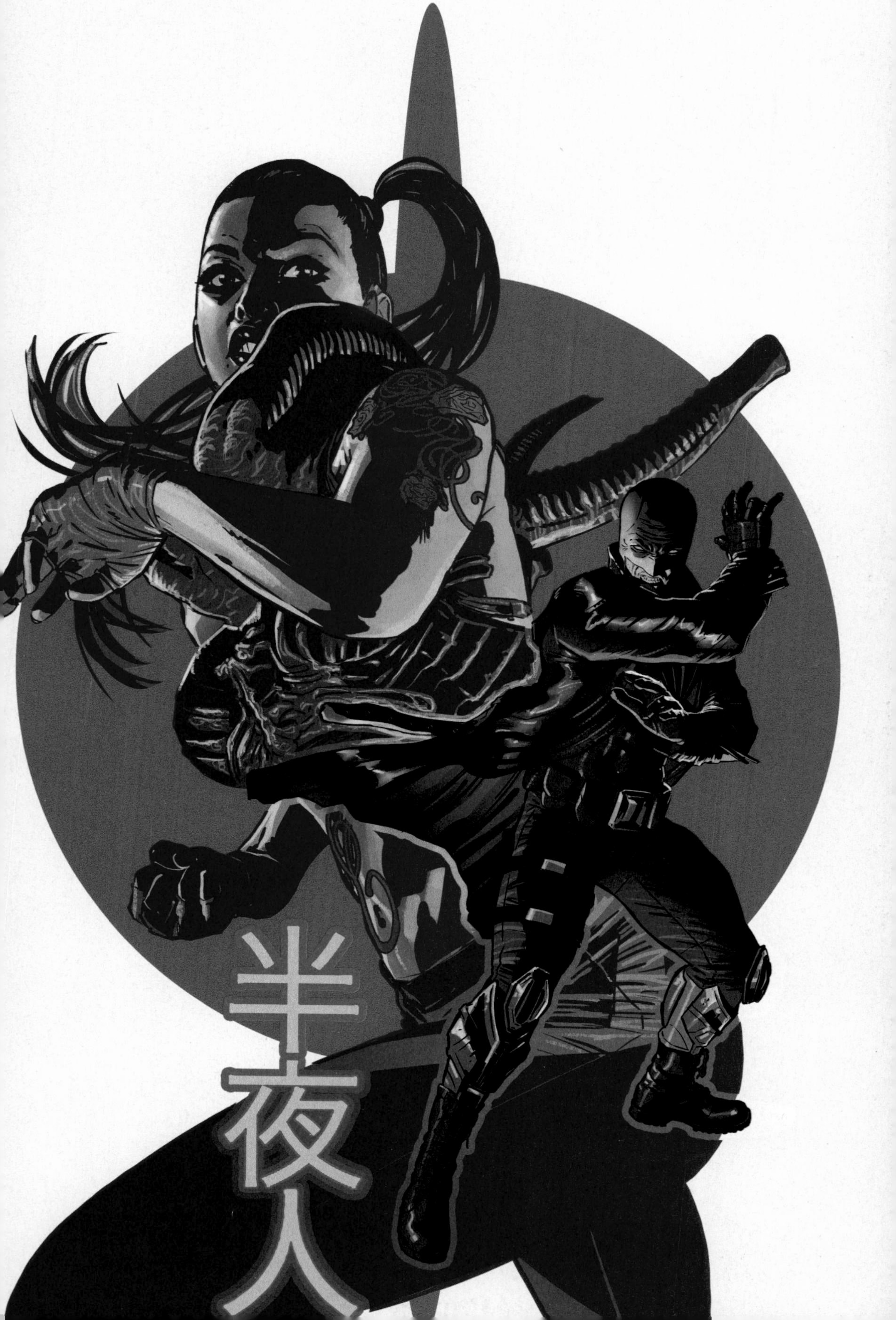
半夜人

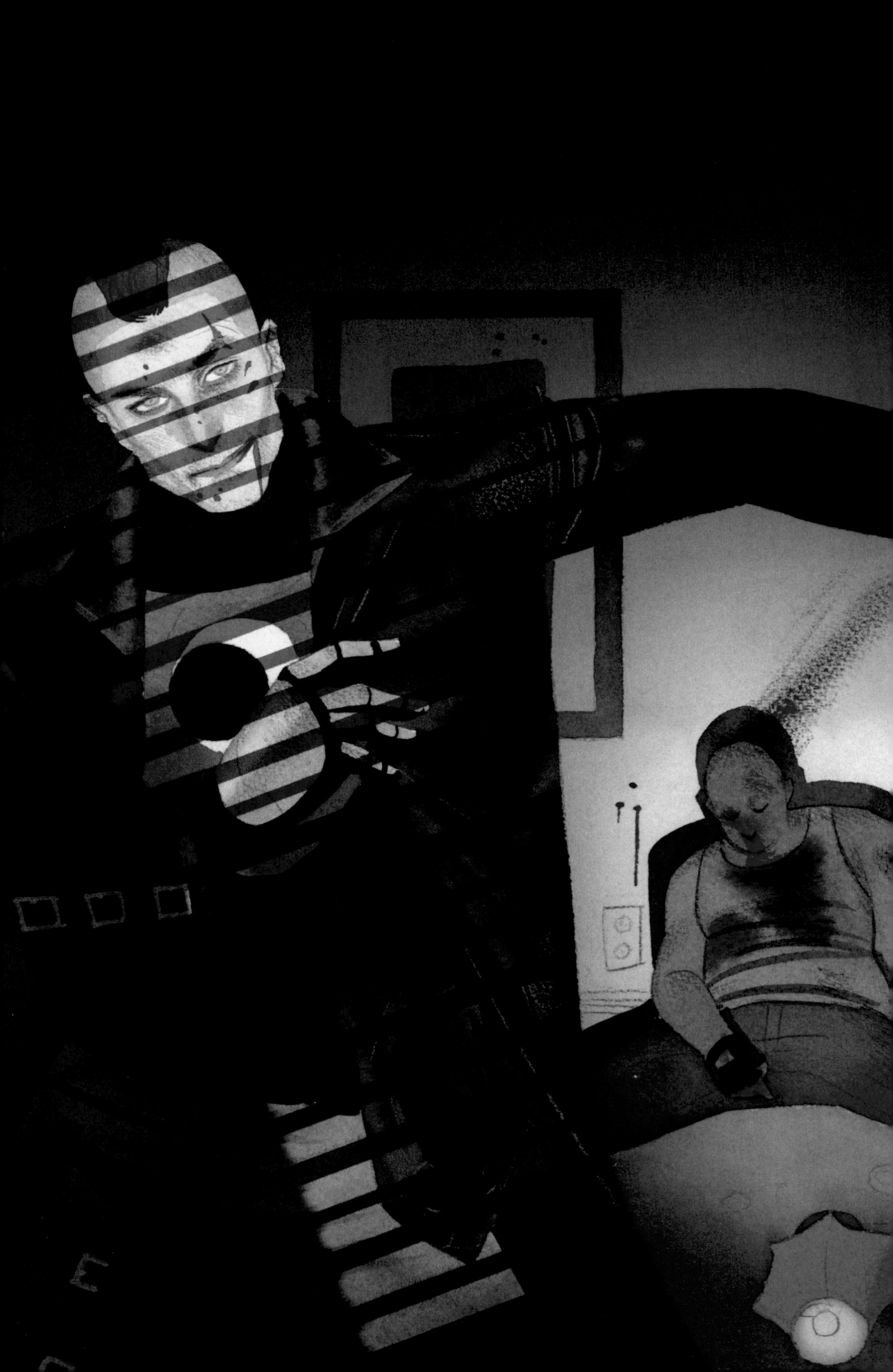

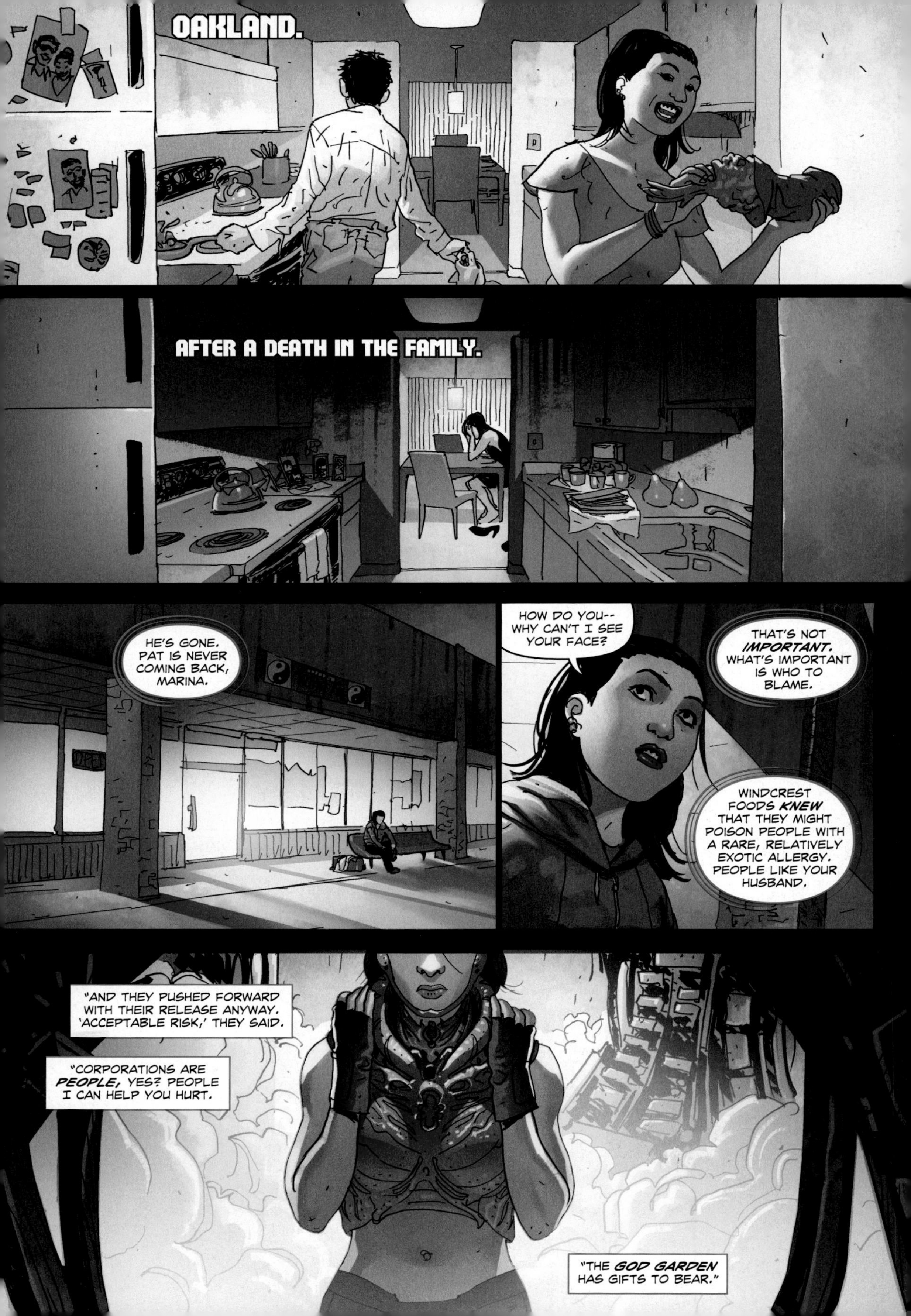
OAKLAND.
AFTER A DEATH IN THE FAMILY.
HE'S GONE. PAT IS NEVER COMING BACK, MARINA.
HOW DO YOU-- WHY CAN'T I SEE YOUR FACE?
THAT'S NOT *IMPORTANT.* WHAT'S IMPORTANT IS WHO TO BLAME.
WINDCREST FOODS *KNEW* THAT THEY MIGHT POISON PEOPLE WITH A RARE, RELATIVELY EXOTIC ALLERGY. PEOPLE LIKE YOUR HUSBAND.
"AND THEY PUSHED FORWARD WITH THEIR RELEASE ANYWAY. 'ACCEPTABLE RISK,' THEY SAID.
"CORPORATIONS ARE *PEOPLE,* YES? PEOPLE I CAN HELP YOU HURT.
"THE *GOD GARDEN* HAS GIFTS TO BEAR."

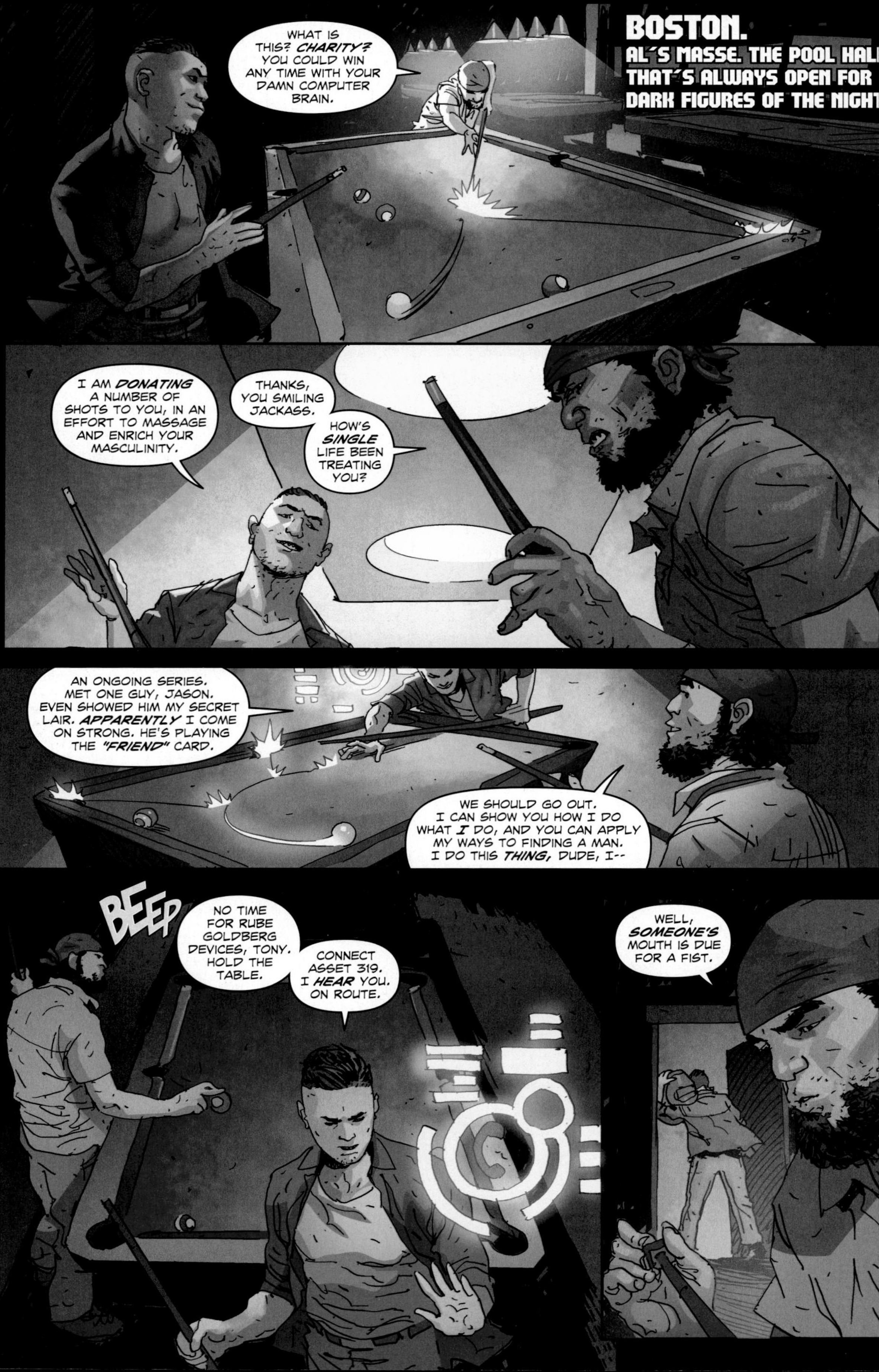
BOSTON.
AL´S MASSE. THE POOL HALL THAT´S ALWAYS OPEN FOR DARK FIGURES OF THE NIGHT
WHAT IS THIS? CHARITY? YOU COULD WIN ANY TIME WITH YOUR DAMN COMPUTER BRAIN.
I AM DONATING A NUMBER OF SHOTS TO YOU, IN AN EFFORT TO MASSAGE AND ENRICH YOUR MASCULINITY.
THANKS, YOU SMILING JACKASS.
HOW'S SINGLE LIFE BEEN TREATING YOU?
AN ONGOING SERIES. MET ONE GUY, JASON. EVEN SHOWED HIM MY SECRET LAIR. APPARENTLY I COME ON STRONG. HE'S PLAYING THE "FRIEND" CARD.
WE SHOULD GO OUT. I CAN SHOW YOU HOW I DO WHAT I DO, AND YOU CAN APPLY MY WAYS TO FINDING A MAN. I DO THIS THING, DUDE, I--
BEEP
NO TIME FOR RUBE GOLDBERG DEVICES, TONY. HOLD THE TABLE.
CONNECT ASSET 319. I HEAR YOU. ON ROUTE.
WELL, SOMEONE'S MOUTH IS DUE FOR A FIST.

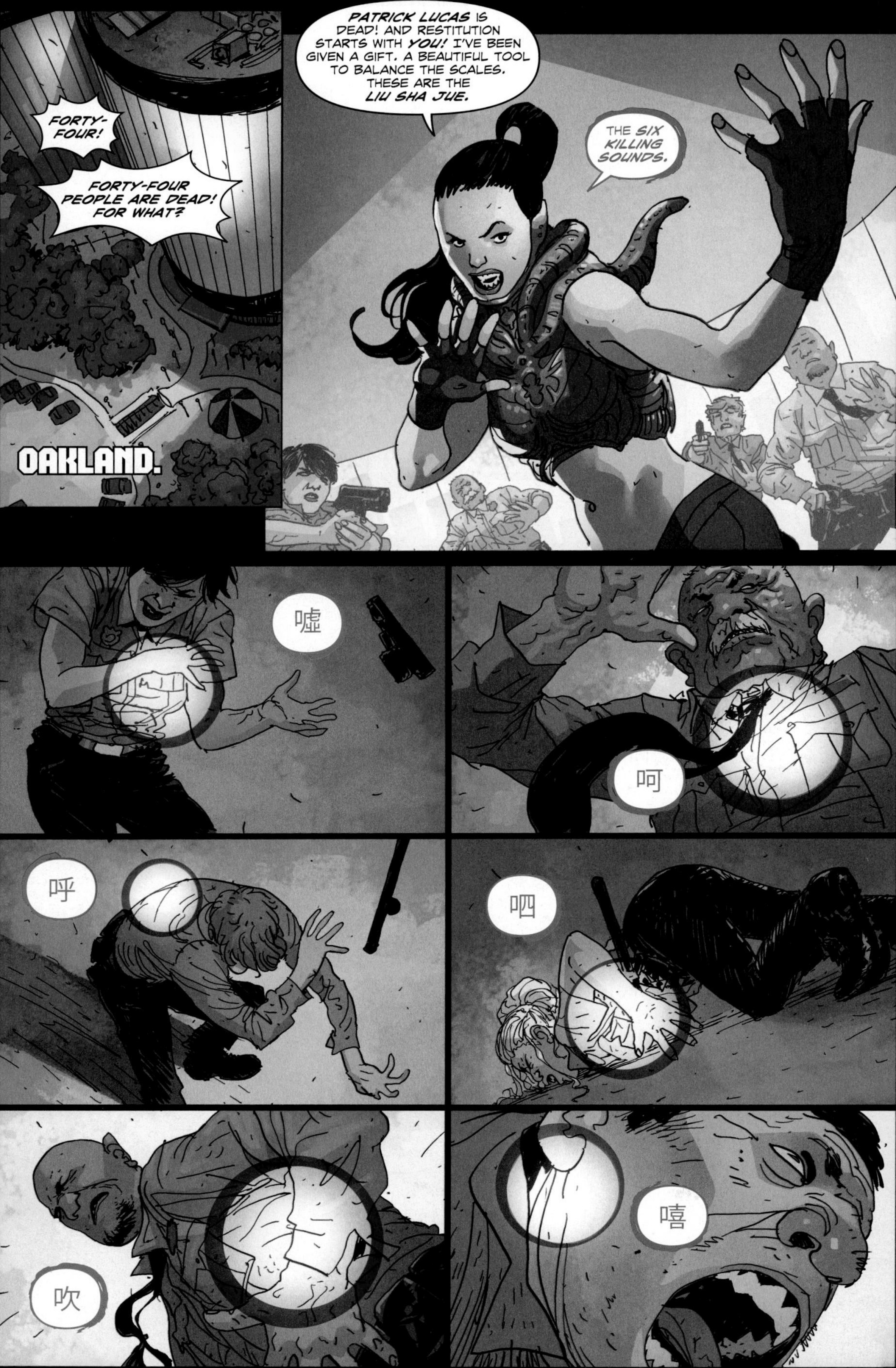
FORTY-FOUR!
FORTY-FOUR PEOPLE ARE DEAD! FOR WHAT?
OAKLAND.
PATRICK LUCAS IS DEAD! AND RESTITUTION STARTS WITH YOU! I'VE BEEN GIVEN A GIFT. A BEAUTIFUL TOOL TO BALANCE THE SCALES. THESE ARE THE LIU SHA JUE.
THE SIX KILLING SOUNDS.
噓
呵
呼
呬
吹
嘻

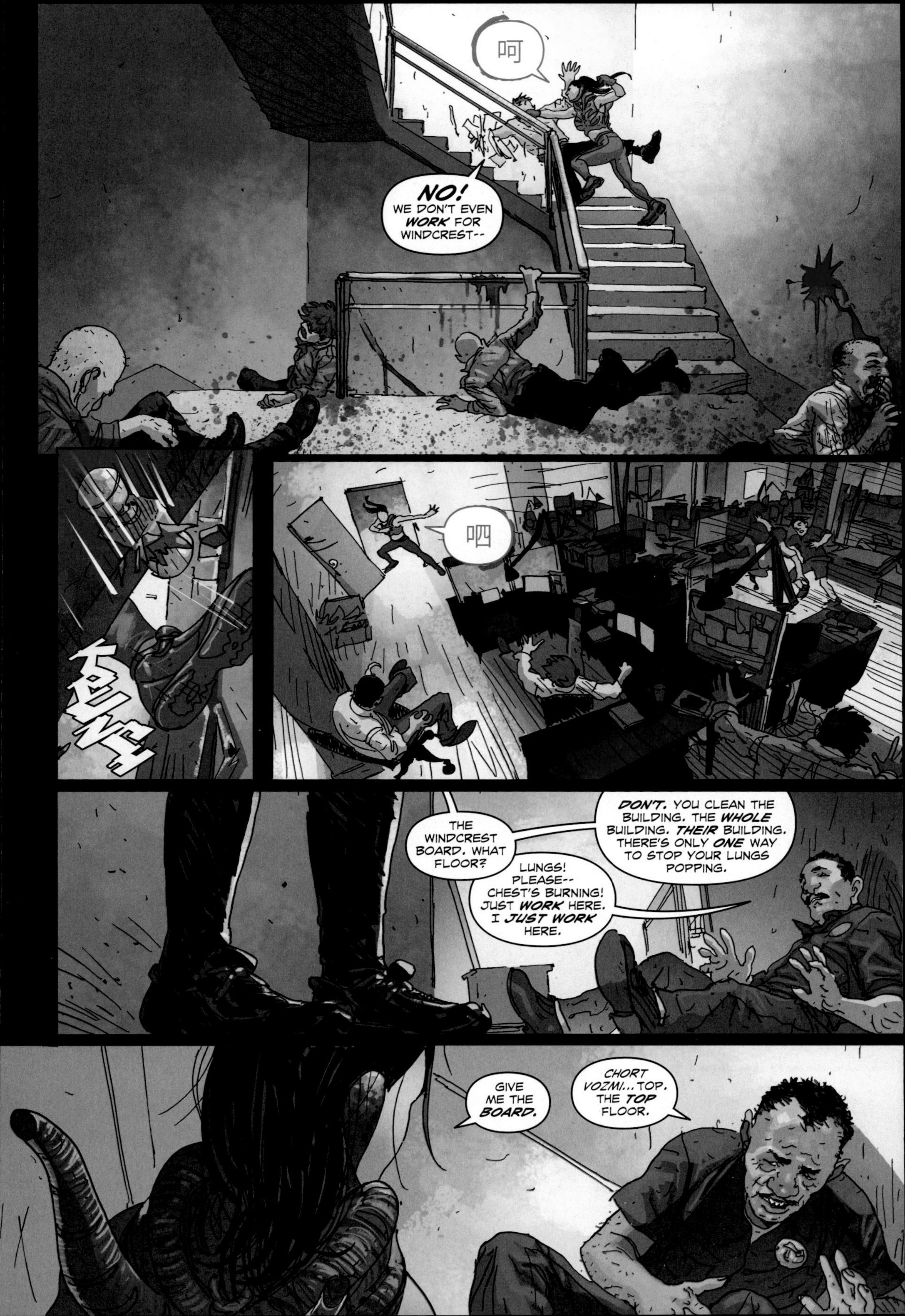

呵
NO! WE DON'T EVEN WORK FOR WINDCREST--
KRUNCH
呬
THE WINDCREST BOARD. WHAT FLOOR?
LUNGS! PLEASE-- CHEST'S BURNING! JUST WORK HERE. I JUST WORK HERE.
DON'T. YOU CLEAN THE BUILDING. THE WHOLE BUILDING. THEIR BUILDING. THERE'S ONLY ONE WAY TO STOP YOUR LUNGS POPPING.
GIVE ME THE BOARD.
CHORT VOZMI...TOP. THE TOP FLOOR.

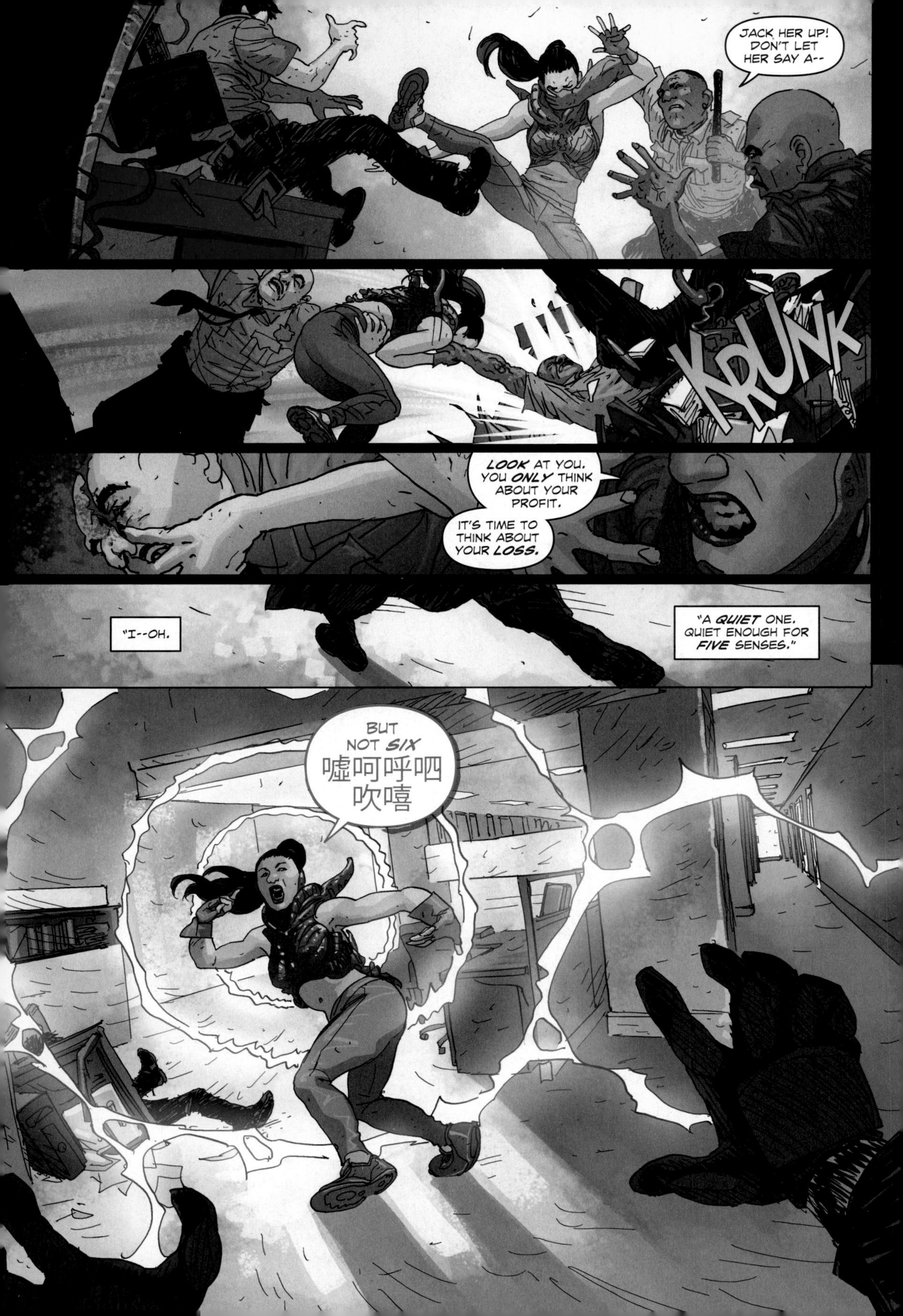
JACK HER UP! DON'T LET HER SAY A--
KRUNK
LOOK AT YOU. YOU ONLY THINK ABOUT YOUR PROFIT.
IT'S TIME TO THINK ABOUT YOUR LOSS.
"I--OH.
"A QUIET ONE. QUIET ENOUGH FOR FIVE SENSES."
BUT NOT SIX 噓呵呼呬吹嘻

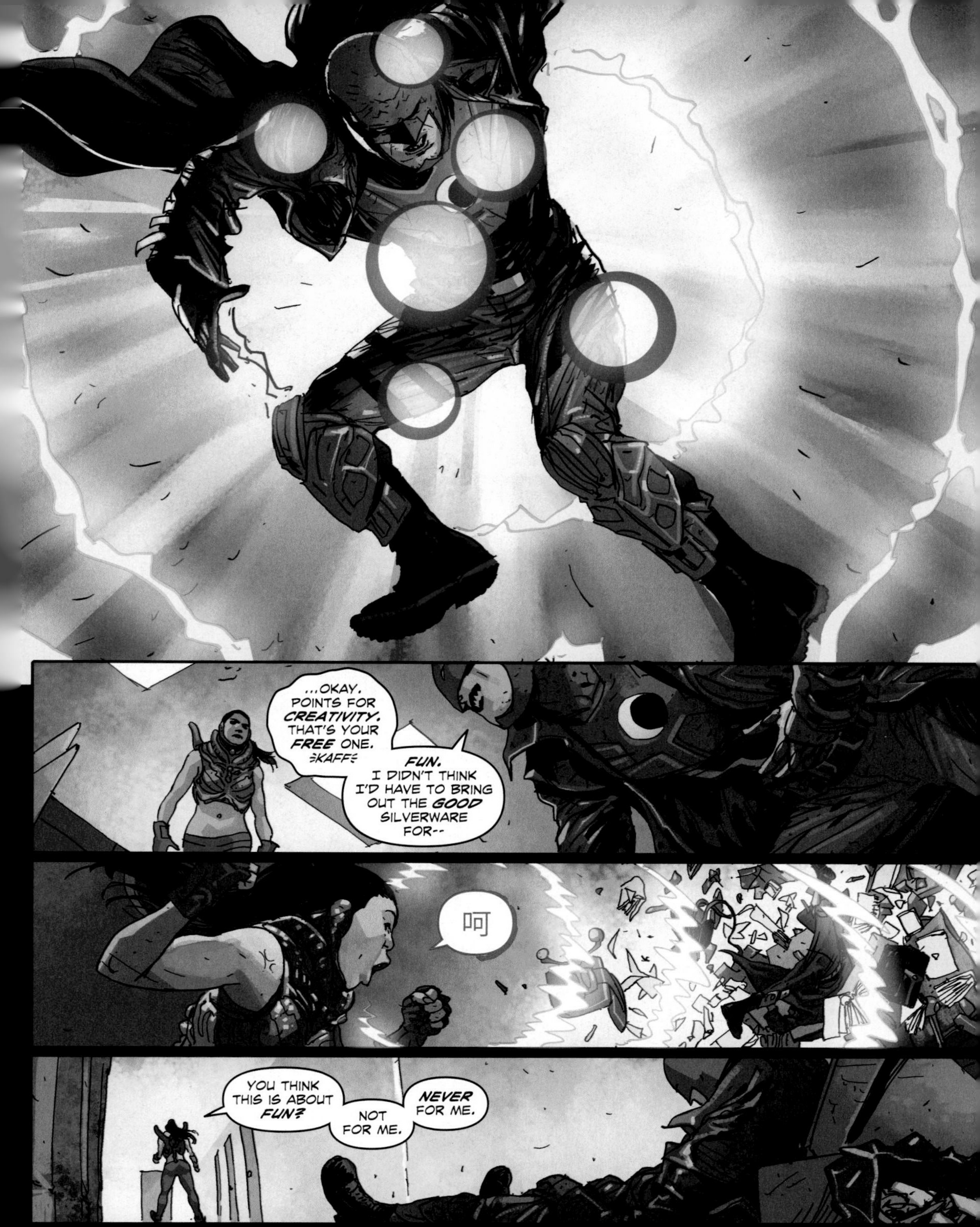

...OKAY. POINTS FOR *CREATIVITY.* THAT'S YOUR *FREE* ONE.
KAFF
FUN. I DIDN'T THINK I'D HAVE TO BRING OUT THE *GOOD* SILVERWARE FOR--
呵
YOU THINK THIS IS ABOUT *FUN?*
NOT FOR ME.
NEVER FOR ME.

MIDNIGHTER?

STEVE ORLANDO WRITER ALEC MORGAN ARTIST

ROMULO FAJARDO, JR. WITH ALLEN PASSALAQUA (PGS 16-20) COLORS JARED K. FLETCHER LETTERS ACO & ROMULO FAJARDO, JR. COVER KEVIN WADA VARIANT COVER

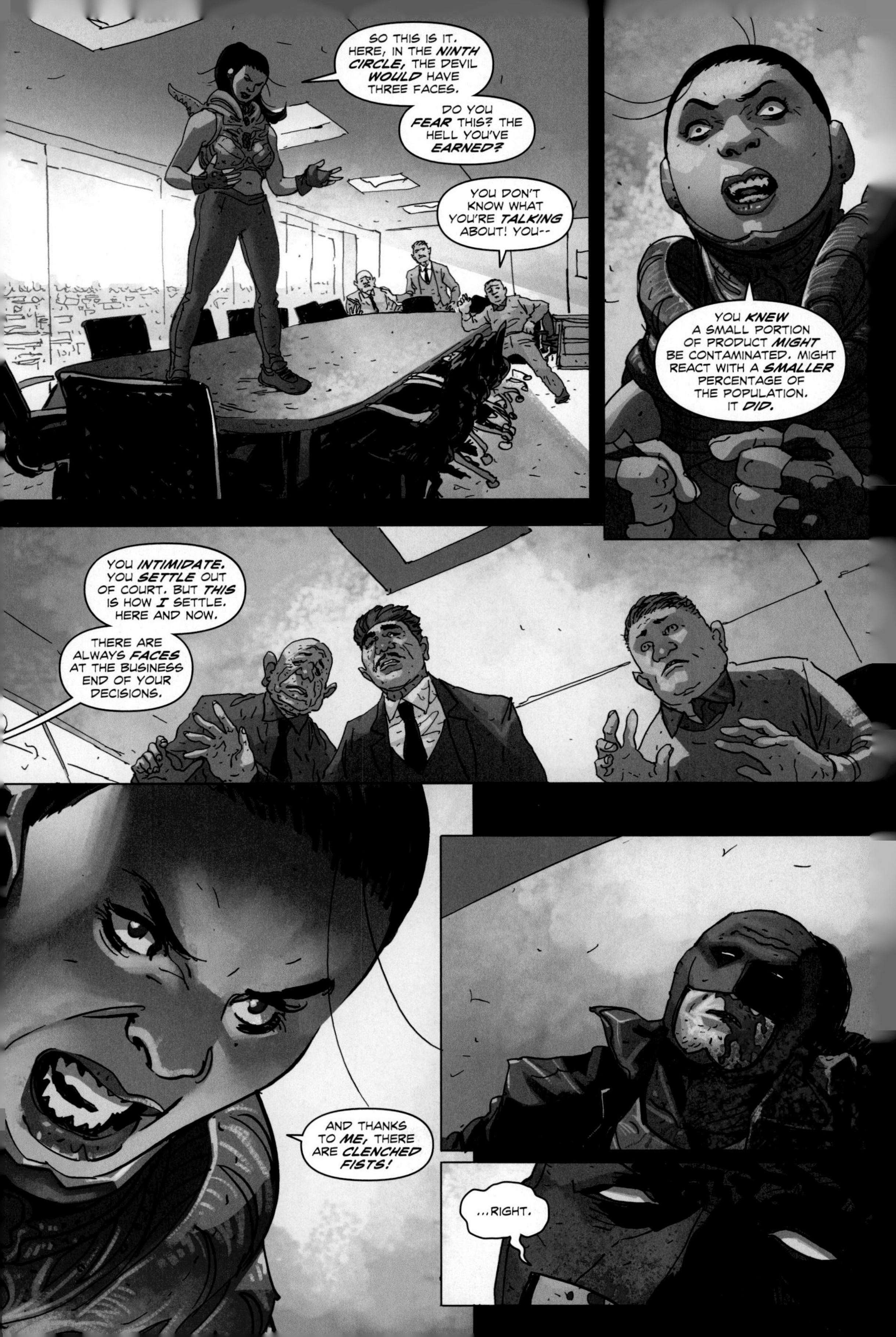
SO THIS IS IT. HERE, IN THE NINTH CIRCLE, THE DEVIL WOULD HAVE THREE FACES.
DO YOU FEAR THIS? THE HELL YOU'VE EARNED?
YOU DON'T KNOW WHAT YOU'RE TALKING ABOUT! YOU--
YOU KNEW A SMALL PORTION OF PRODUCT MIGHT BE CONTAMINATED. MIGHT REACT WITH A SMALLER PERCENTAGE OF THE POPULATION. IT DID.
YOU INTIMIDATE. YOU SETTLE OUT OF COURT. BUT THIS IS HOW I SETTLE. HERE AND NOW.
THERE ARE ALWAYS FACES AT THE BUSINESS END OF YOUR DECISIONS.
AND THANKS TO ME, THERE ARE CLENCHED FISTS!
...RIGHT.

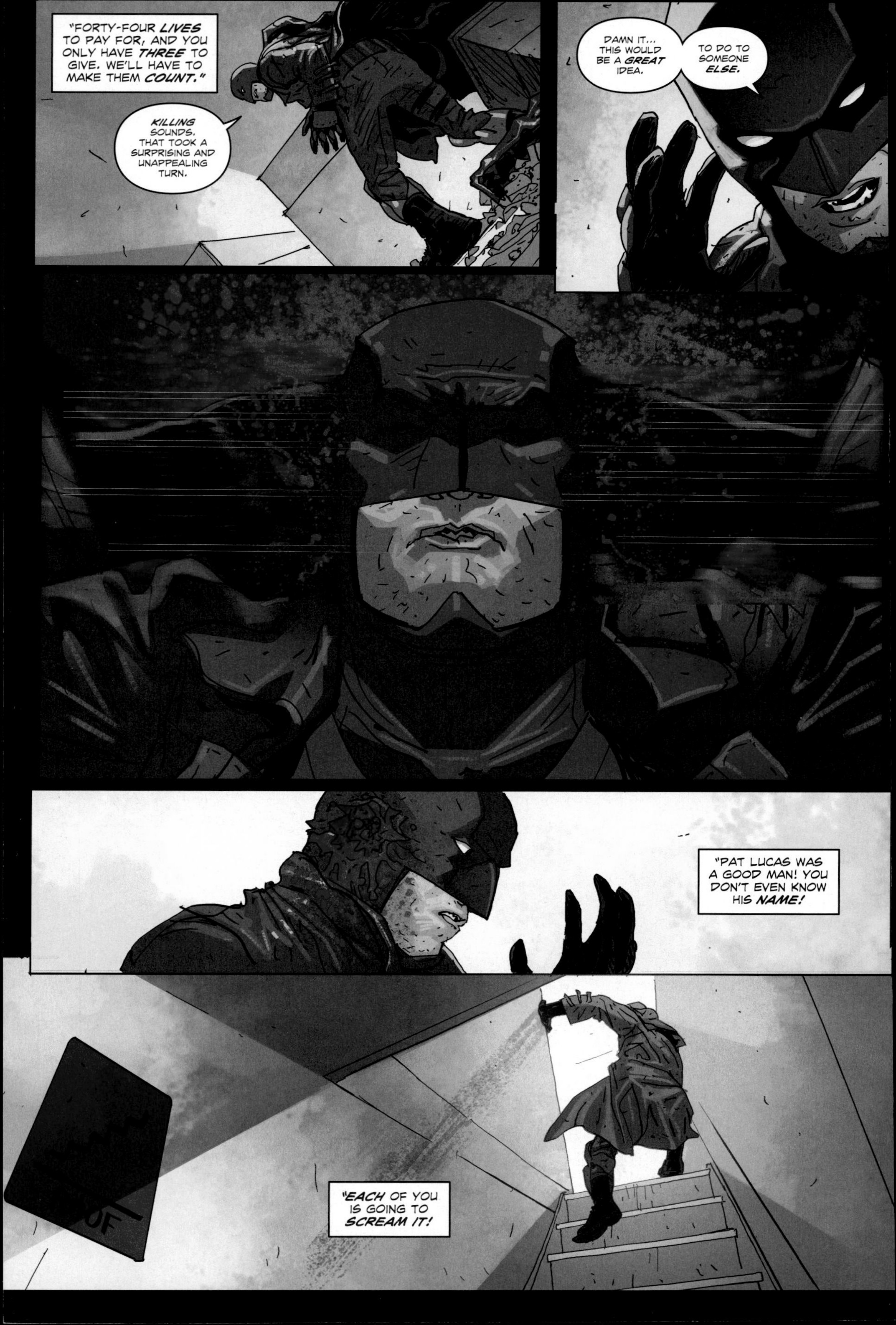
"FORTY-FOUR LIVES TO PAY FOR, AND YOU ONLY HAVE THREE TO GIVE. WE'LL HAVE TO MAKE THEM COUNT."
KILLING SOUNDS. THAT TOOK A SURPRISING AND UNAPPEALING TURN.
DAMN IT... THIS WOULD BE A GREAT IDEA.
TO DO TO SOMEONE ELSE.
"PAT LUCAS WAS A GOOD MAN! YOU DON'T EVEN KNOW HIS NAME!
"EACH OF YOU IS GOING TO SCREAM IT!
OF

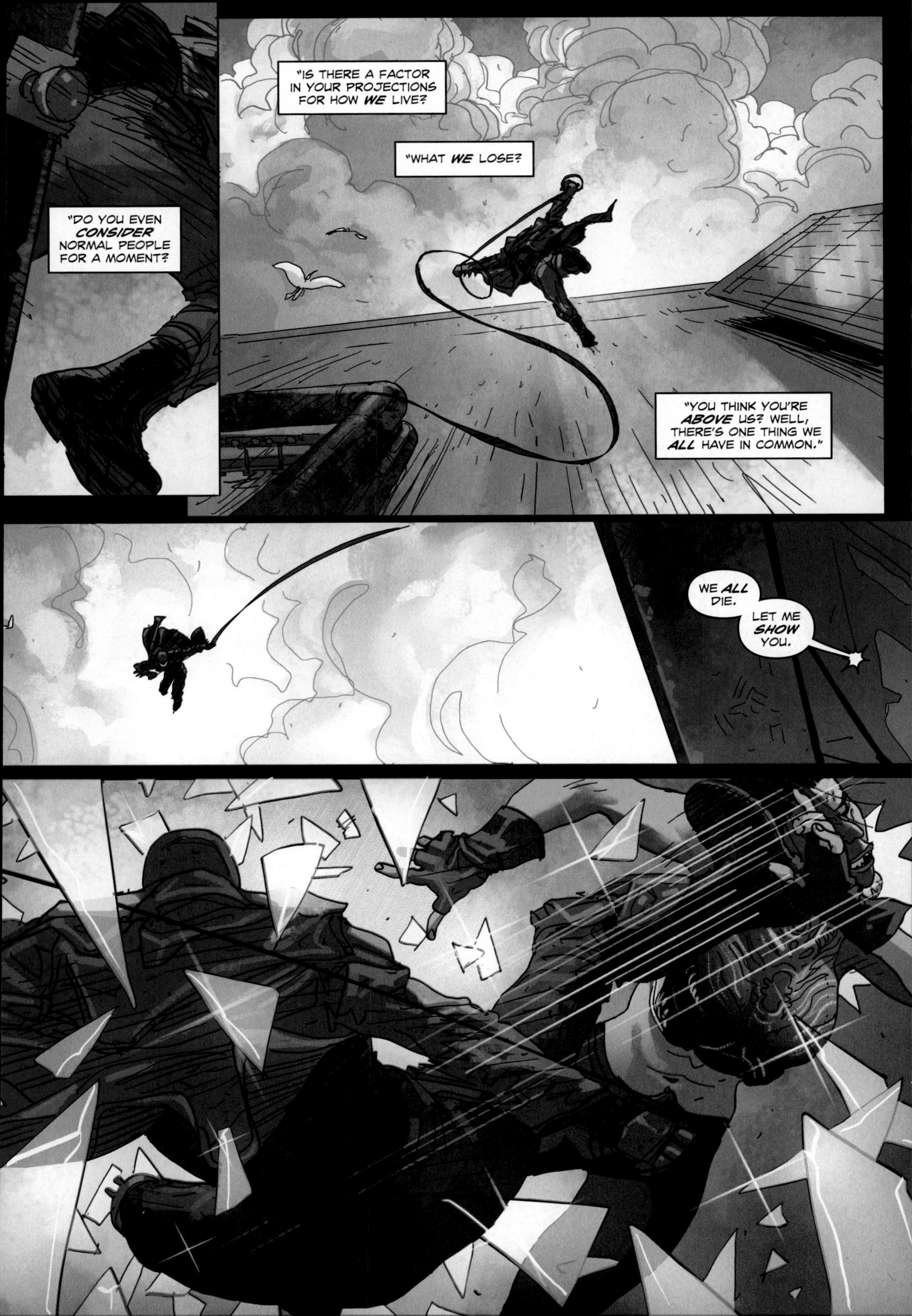
"IS THERE A FACTOR IN YOUR PROJECTIONS FOR HOW WE LIVE?
"WHAT WE LOSE?
"DO YOU EVEN CONSIDER NORMAL PEOPLE FOR A MOMENT?
"YOU THINK YOU'RE ABOVE US? WELL, THERE'S ONE THING WE ALL HAVE IN COMMON."
WE ALL DIE.
LET ME SHOW YOU.

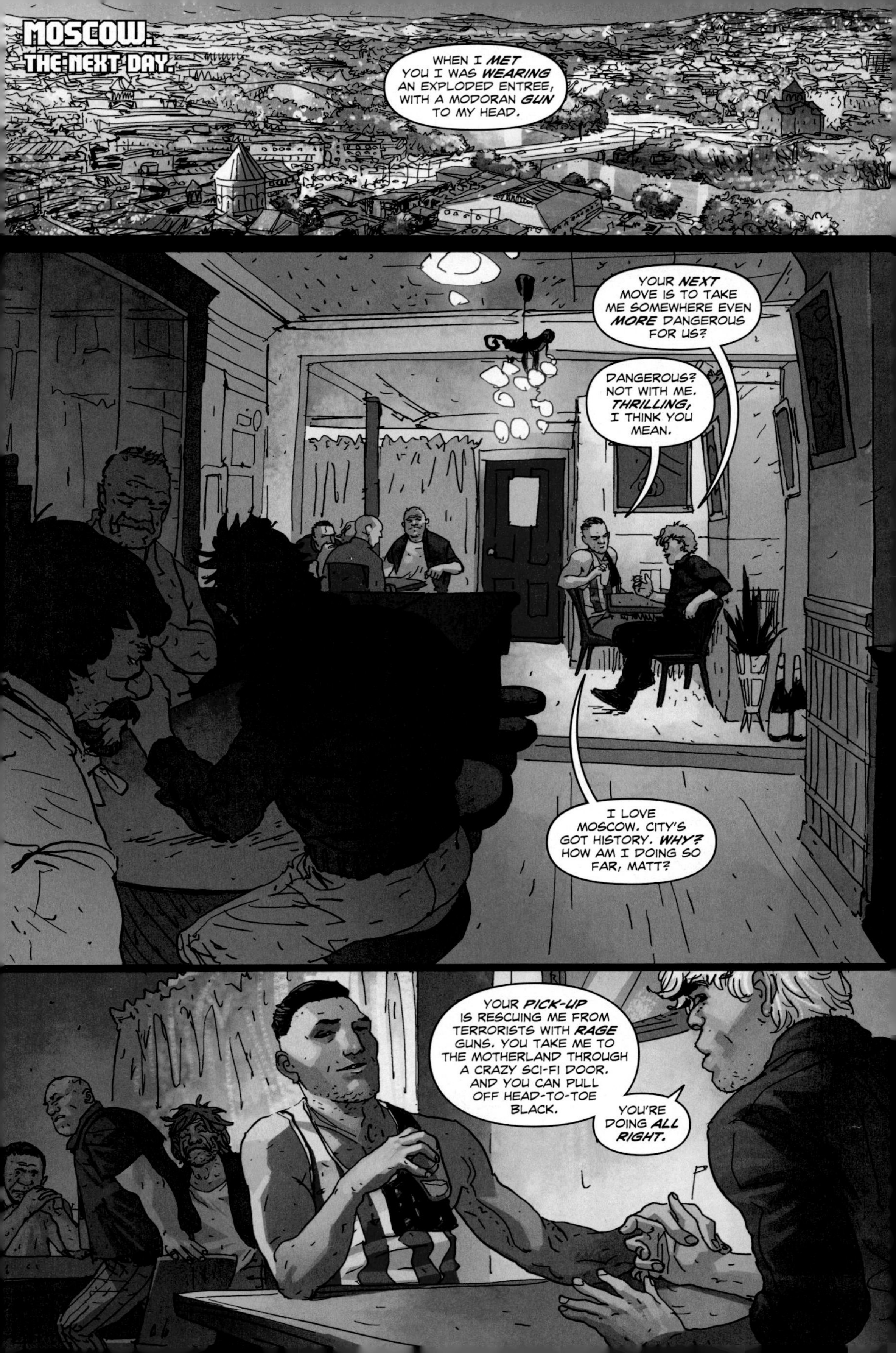
MOSCOW.
THE NEXT DAY.
WHEN I MET YOU I WAS WEARING AN EXPLODED ENTREE, WITH A MODORAN GUN TO MY HEAD.
YOUR NEXT MOVE IS TO TAKE ME SOMEWHERE EVEN MORE DANGEROUS FOR US?
DANGEROUS? NOT WITH ME. THRILLING, I THINK YOU MEAN.
I LOVE MOSCOW. CITY'S GOT HISTORY. WHY? HOW AM I DOING SO FAR, MATT?
YOUR PICK-UP IS RESCUING ME FROM TERRORISTS WITH RAGE GUNS. YOU TAKE ME TO THE MOTHERLAND THROUGH A CRAZY SCI-FI DOOR. AND YOU CAN PULL OFF HEAD-TO-TOE BLACK.
YOU'RE DOING ALL RIGHT.

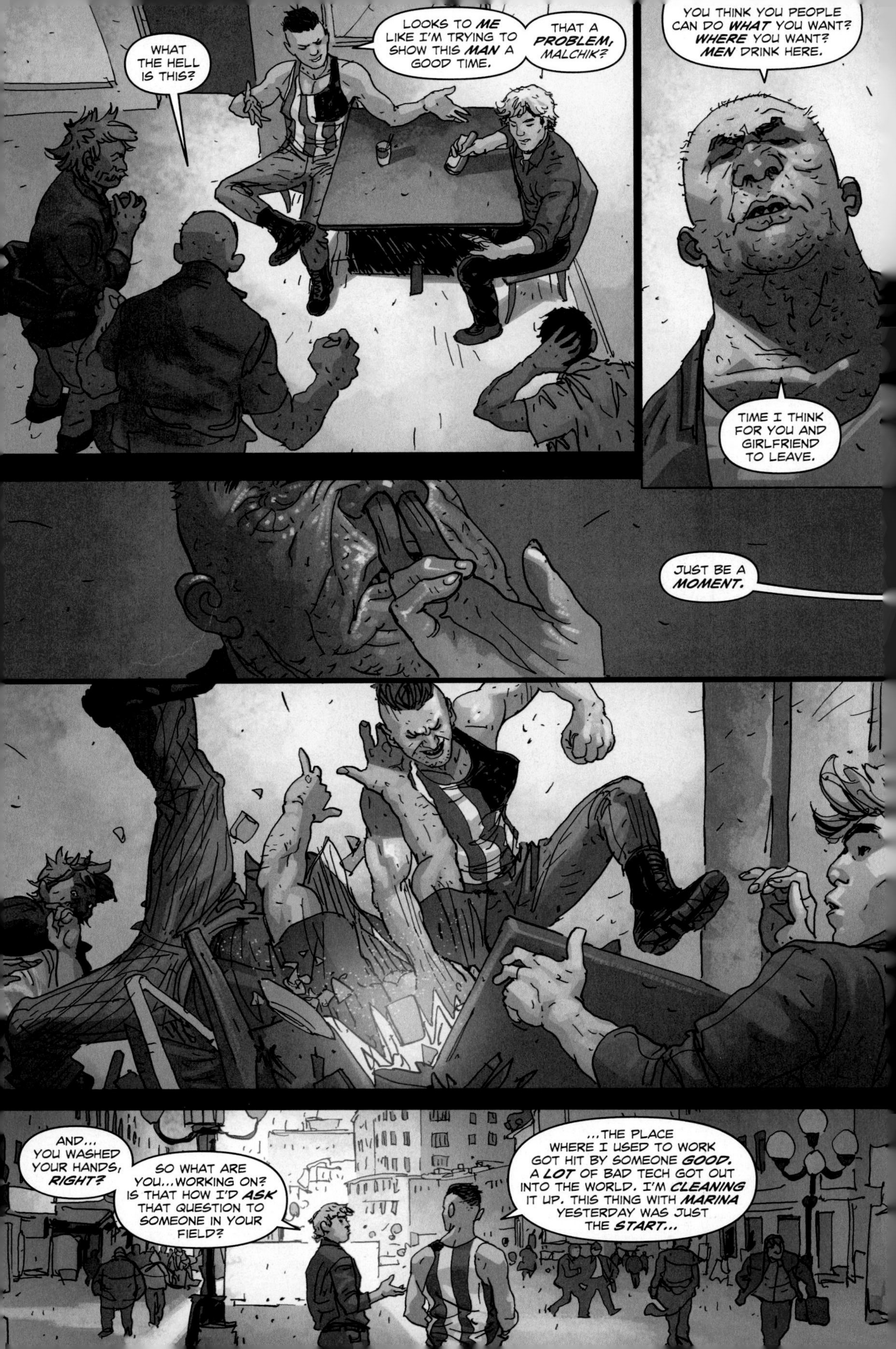
WHAT THE HELL IS THIS?
LOOKS TO ME LIKE I'M TRYING TO SHOW THIS MAN A GOOD TIME.
THAT A PROBLEM, MALCHIK?
YOU THINK YOU PEOPLE CAN DO WHAT YOU WANT? WHERE YOU WANT? MEN DRINK HERE.
TIME I THINK FOR YOU AND GIRLFRIEND TO LEAVE.
JUST BE A MOMENT.
AND... YOU WASHED YOUR HANDS, RIGHT?
SO WHAT ARE YOU...WORKING ON? IS THAT HOW I'D ASK THAT QUESTION TO SOMEONE IN YOUR FIELD?
...THE PLACE WHERE I USED TO WORK GOT HIT BY SOMEONE GOOD. A LOT OF BAD TECH GOT OUT INTO THE WORLD. I'M CLEANING IT UP. THIS THING WITH MARINA YESTERDAY WAS JUST THE START...

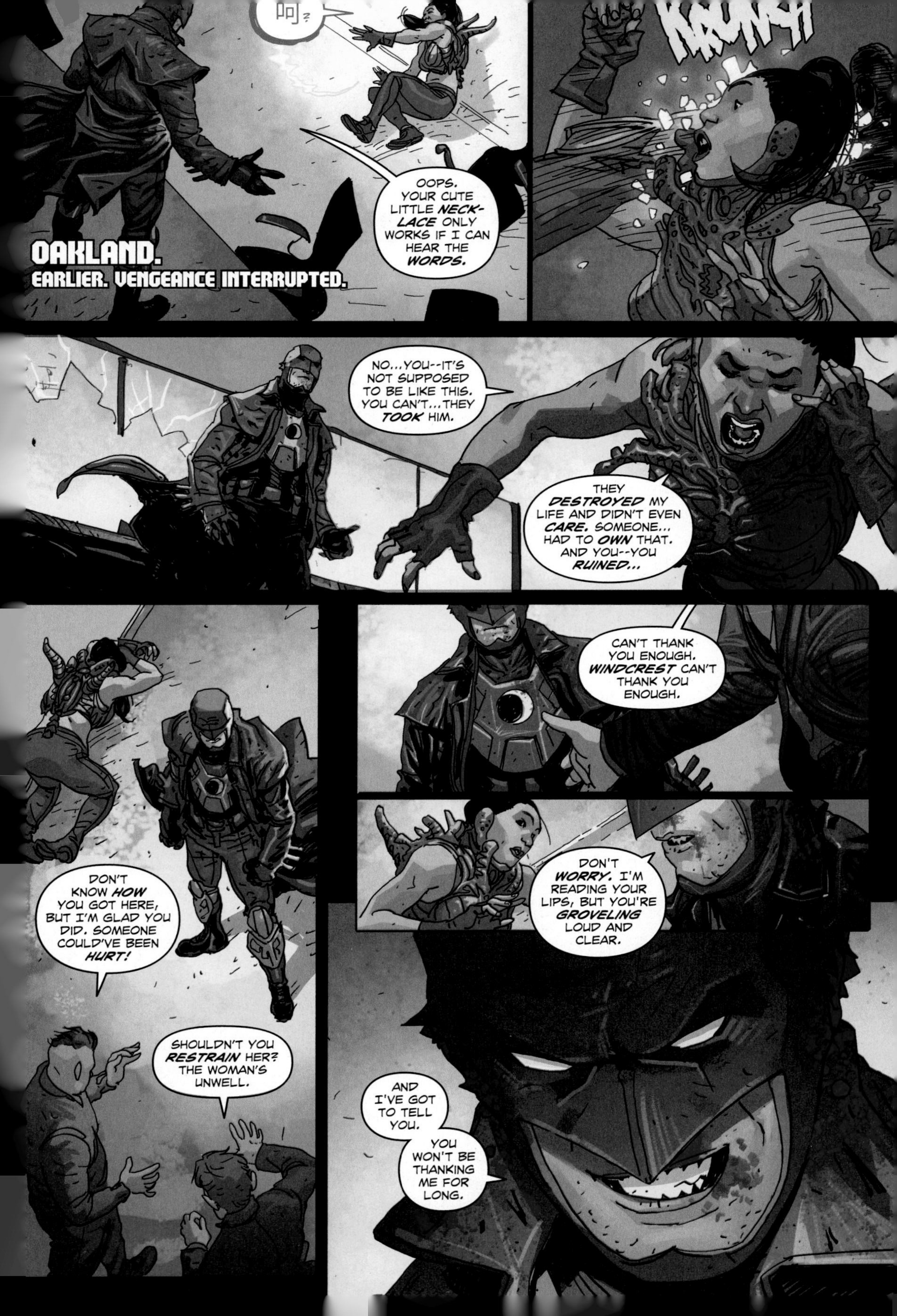
呵?
OOPS. YOUR CUTE LITTLE NECK-LACE ONLY WORKS IF I CAN HEAR THE WORDS.
OAKLAND.
EARLIER. VENGEANCE INTERRUPTED.
NO...YOU--IT'S NOT SUPPOSED TO BE LIKE THIS. YOU CAN'T...THEY TOOK HIM.
THEY DESTROYED MY LIFE AND DIDN'T EVEN CARE. SOMEONE... HAD TO OWN THAT. AND YOU--YOU RUINED...
DON'T KNOW HOW YOU GOT HERE, BUT I'M GLAD YOU DID. SOMEONE COULD'VE BEEN HURT!
SHOULDN'T YOU RESTRAIN HER? THE WOMAN'S UNWELL.
CAN'T THANK YOU ENOUGH. WINDCREST CAN'T THANK YOU ENOUGH.
DON'T WORRY. I'M READING YOUR LIPS, BUT YOU'RE GROVELING LOUD AND CLEAR.
AND I'VE GOT TO TELL YOU.
YOU WON'T BE THANKING ME FOR LONG.

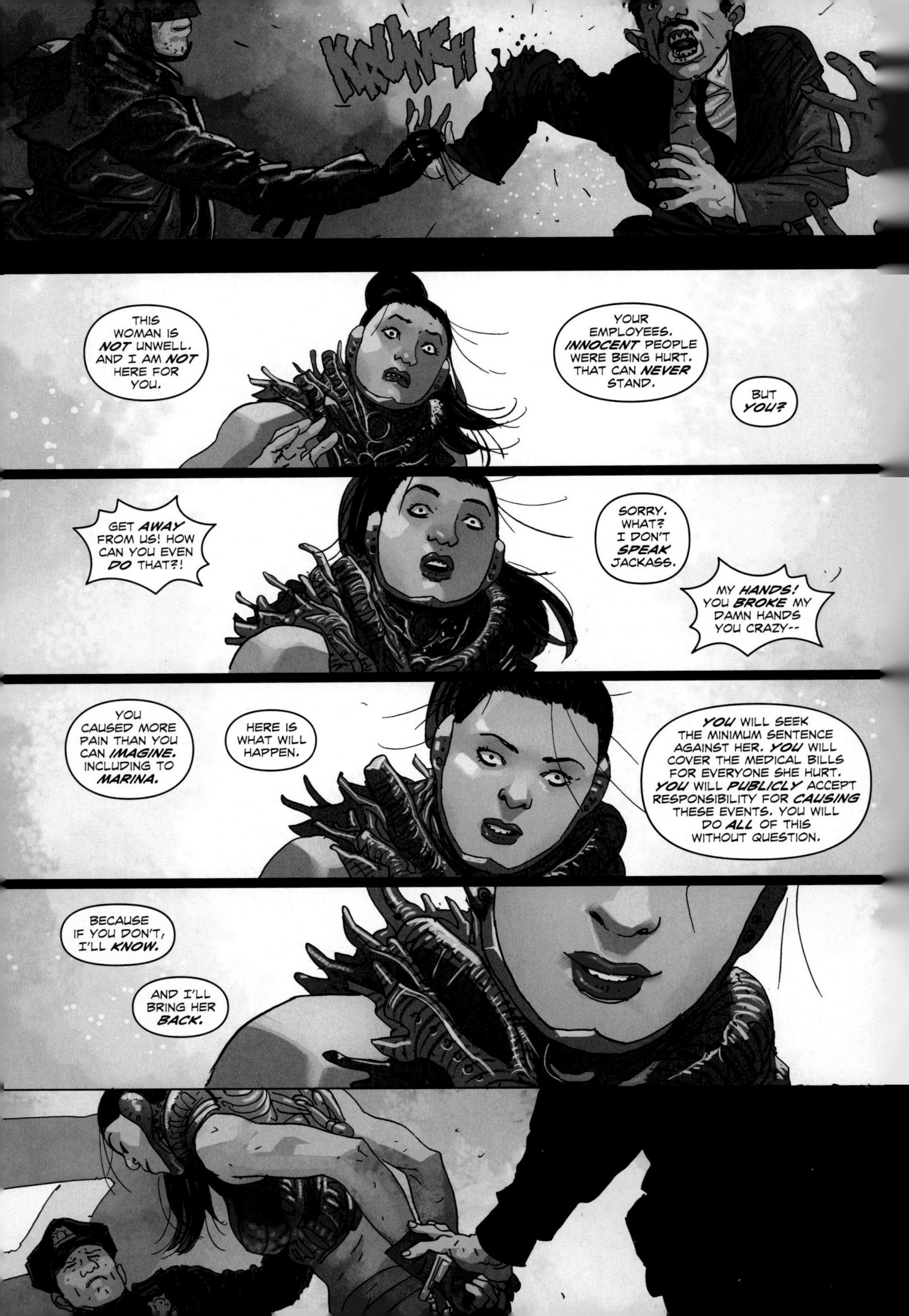
KRUNCH
THIS WOMAN IS NOT UNWELL. AND I AM NOT HERE FOR YOU.
YOUR EMPLOYEES. INNOCENT PEOPLE WERE BEING HURT. THAT CAN NEVER STAND.
BUT YOU?
GET AWAY FROM US! HOW CAN YOU EVEN DO THAT?!
SORRY. WHAT? I DON'T SPEAK JACKASS.
MY HANDS! YOU BROKE MY DAMN HANDS YOU CRAZY--
YOU CAUSED MORE PAIN THAN YOU CAN IMAGINE. INCLUDING TO MARINA.
HERE IS WHAT WILL HAPPEN.
YOU WILL SEEK THE MINIMUM SENTENCE AGAINST HER. YOU WILL COVER THE MEDICAL BILLS FOR EVERYONE SHE HURT. YOU WILL PUBLICLY ACCEPT RESPONSIBILITY FOR CAUSING THESE EVENTS. YOU WILL DO ALL OF THIS WITHOUT QUESTION.
BECAUSE IF YOU DON'T, I'LL KNOW.
AND I'LL BRING HER BACK.

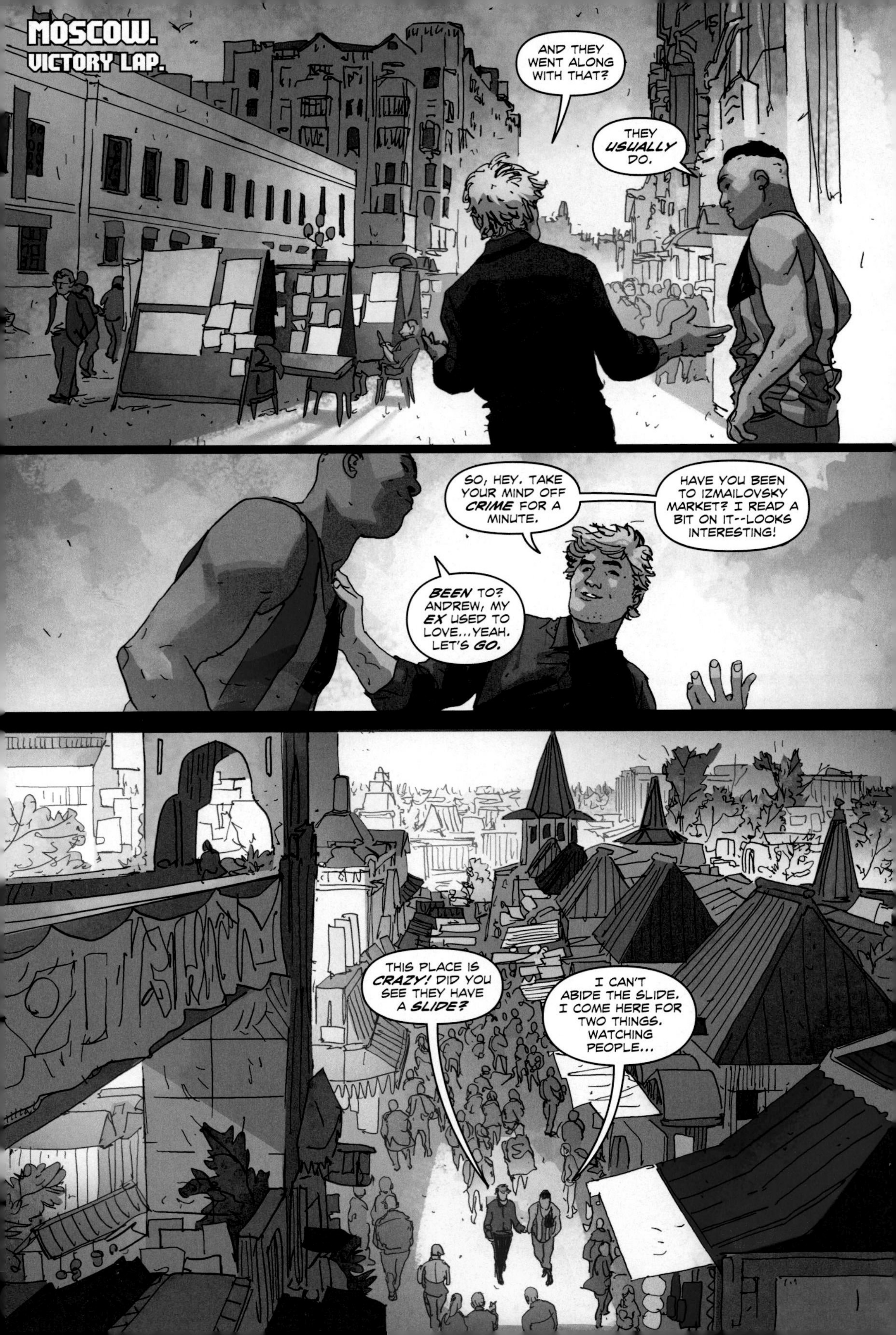
MOSCOW.
VICTORY LAP.
AND THEY WENT ALONG WITH THAT?
THEY *USUALLY* DO.
SO, HEY. TAKE YOUR MIND OFF *CRIME* FOR A MINUTE.
HAVE YOU BEEN TO IZMAILOVSKY MARKET? I READ A BIT ON IT--LOOKS INTERESTING!
BEEN TO? ANDREW, MY *EX* USED TO LOVE...YEAH. LET'S *GO.*
THIS PLACE IS *CRAZY!* DID YOU SEE THEY HAVE A *SLIDE?*
I CAN'T ABIDE THE SLIDE. I COME HERE FOR TWO THINGS. WATCHING PEOPLE...

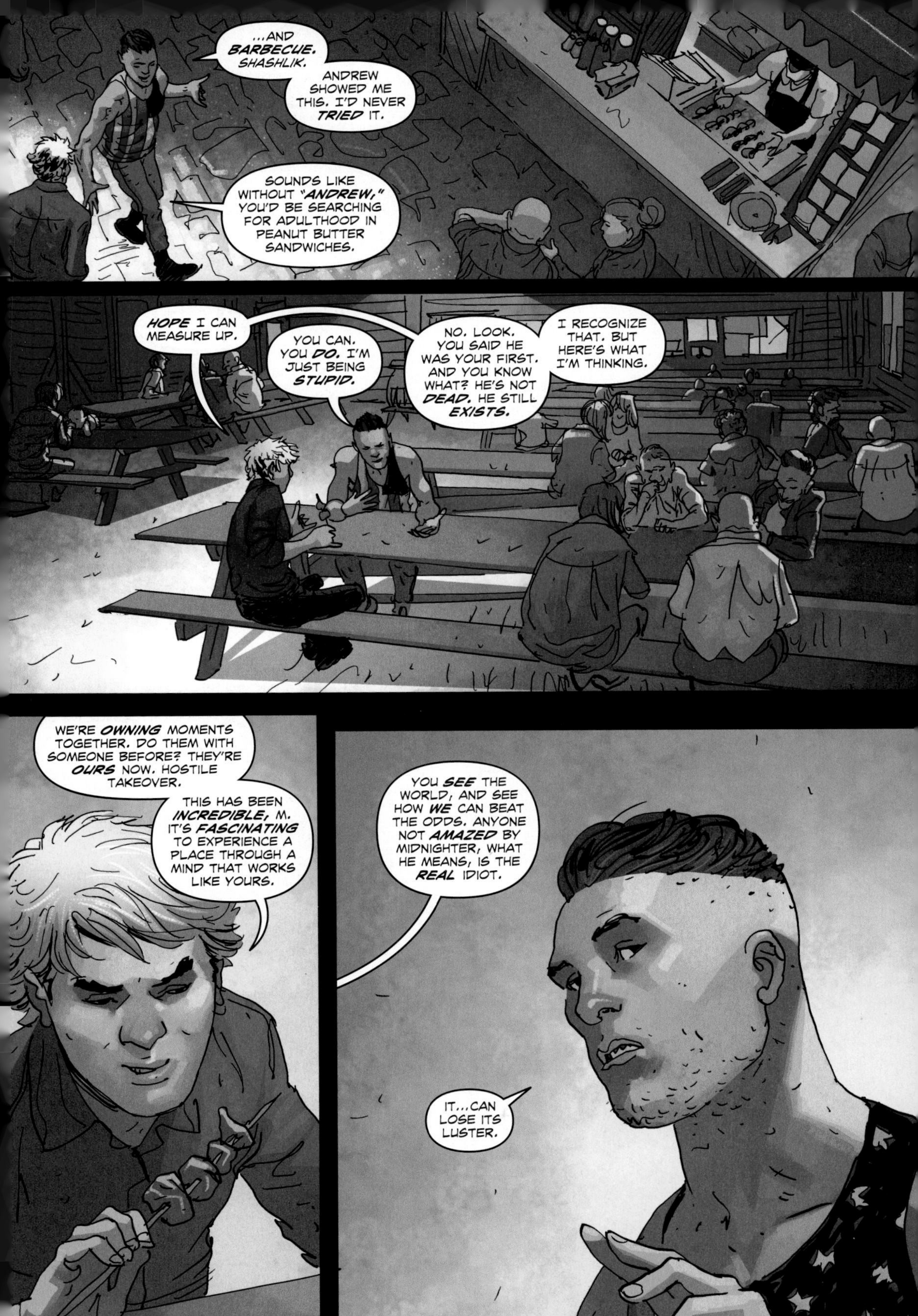
...AND BARBECUE. SHASHLIK.
ANDREW SHOWED ME THIS. I'D NEVER TRIED IT.
SOUNDS LIKE WITHOUT "ANDREW," YOU'D BE SEARCHING FOR ADULTHOOD IN PEANUT BUTTER SANDWICHES.
HOPE I CAN MEASURE UP.
YOU CAN. YOU DO. I'M JUST BEING STUPID.
NO. LOOK. YOU SAID HE WAS YOUR FIRST. AND YOU KNOW WHAT? HE'S NOT DEAD. HE STILL EXISTS.
I RECOGNIZE THAT. BUT HERE'S WHAT I'M THINKING.
WE'RE OWNING MOMENTS TOGETHER. DO THEM WITH SOMEONE BEFORE? THEY'RE OURS NOW. HOSTILE TAKEOVER.
THIS HAS BEEN INCREDIBLE, M. IT'S FASCINATING TO EXPERIENCE A PLACE THROUGH A MIND THAT WORKS LIKE YOURS.
YOU SEE THE WORLD, AND SEE HOW WE CAN BEAT THE ODDS. ANYONE NOT AMAZED BY MIDNIGHTER, WHAT HE MEANS, IS THE REAL IDIOT.
IT...CAN LOSE ITS LUSTER.

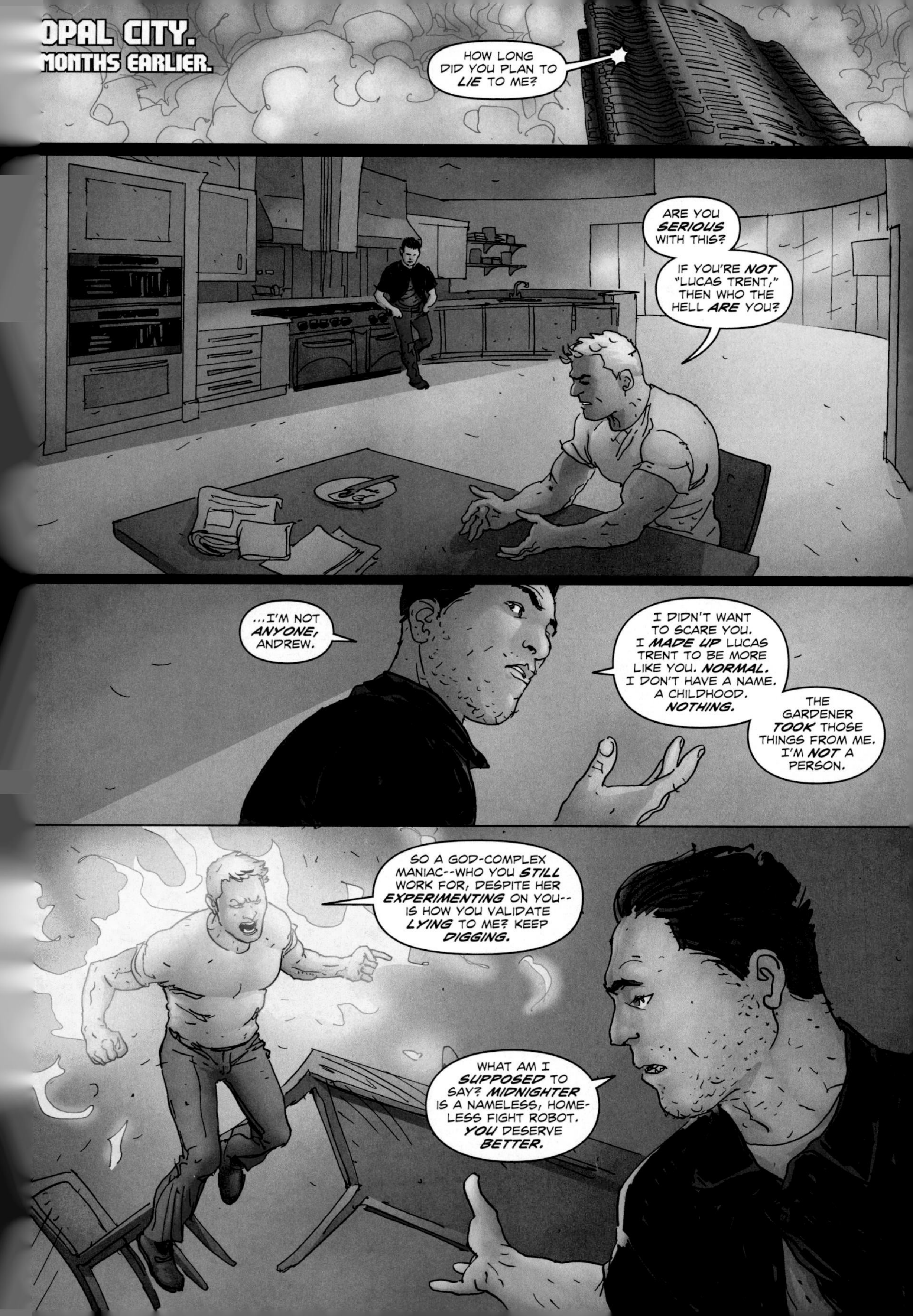
OPAL CITY.
MONTHS EARLIER.
HOW LONG DID YOU PLAN TO LIE TO ME?
ARE YOU SERIOUS WITH THIS?
IF YOU'RE NOT "LUCAS TRENT," THEN WHO THE HELL ARE YOU?
...I'M NOT ANYONE, ANDREW.
I DIDN'T WANT TO SCARE YOU. I MADE UP LUCAS TRENT TO BE MORE LIKE YOU. NORMAL. I DON'T HAVE A NAME. A CHILDHOOD. NOTHING.
THE GARDENER TOOK THOSE THINGS FROM ME. I'M NOT A PERSON.
SO A GOD-COMPLEX MANIAC--WHO YOU STILL WORK FOR, DESPITE HER EXPERIMENTING ON YOU--IS HOW YOU VALIDATE LYING TO ME? KEEP DIGGING.
WHAT AM I SUPPOSED TO SAY? MIDNIGHTER IS A NAMELESS, HOMELESS FIGHT ROBOT. YOU DESERVE BETTER.

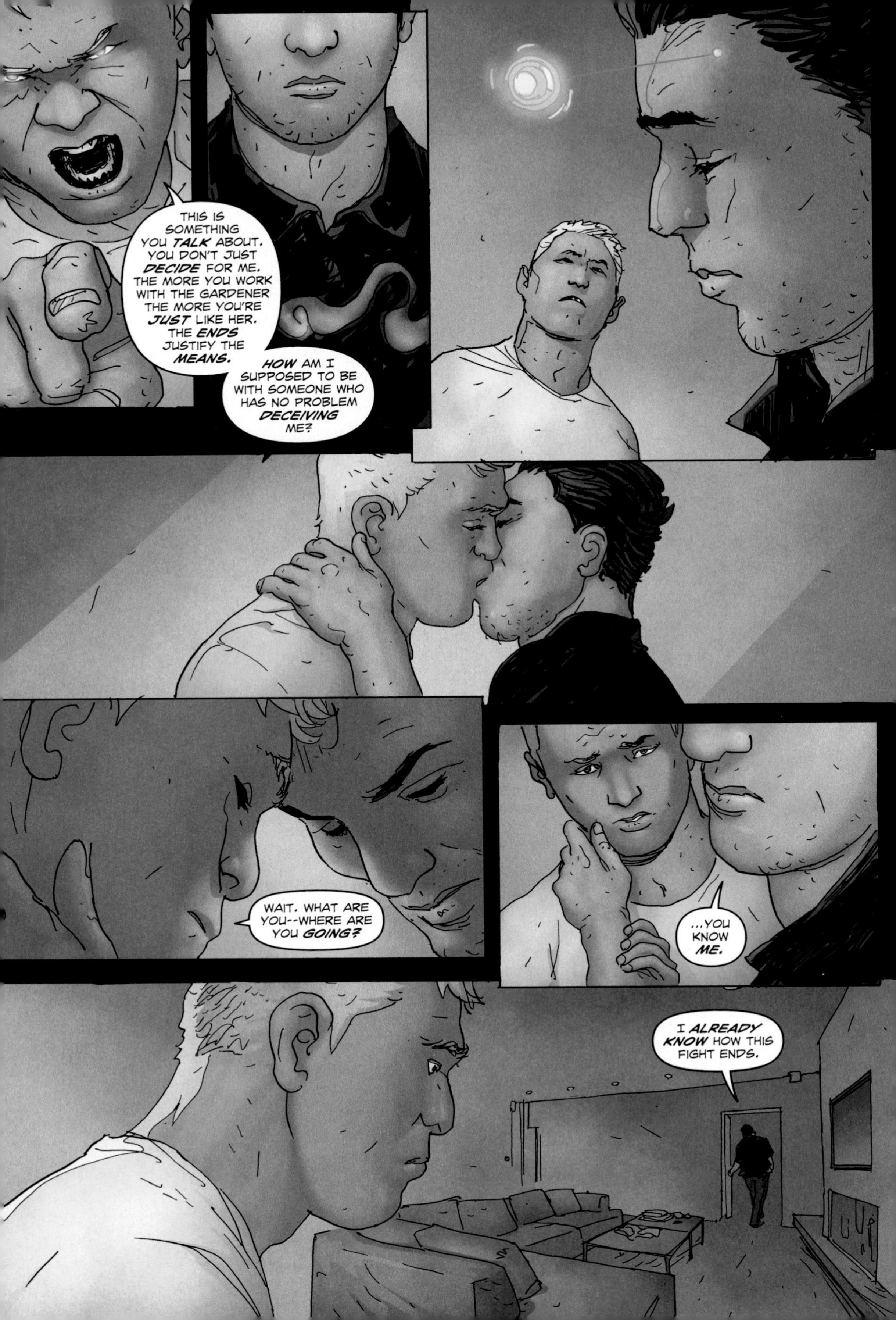
THIS IS SOMETHING YOU *TALK* ABOUT. YOU DON'T JUST *DECIDE* FOR ME. THE MORE YOU WORK WITH THE GARDENER THE MORE YOU'RE *JUST* LIKE HER. THE *ENDS* JUSTIFY THE *MEANS.*
HOW AM I SUPPOSED TO BE WITH SOMEONE WHO HAS NO PROBLEM *DECEIVING* ME?
WAIT. WHAT ARE YOU--WHERE ARE YOU *GOING?*
...YOU KNOW *ME.*
I *ALREADY KNOW* HOW THIS FIGHT ENDS.

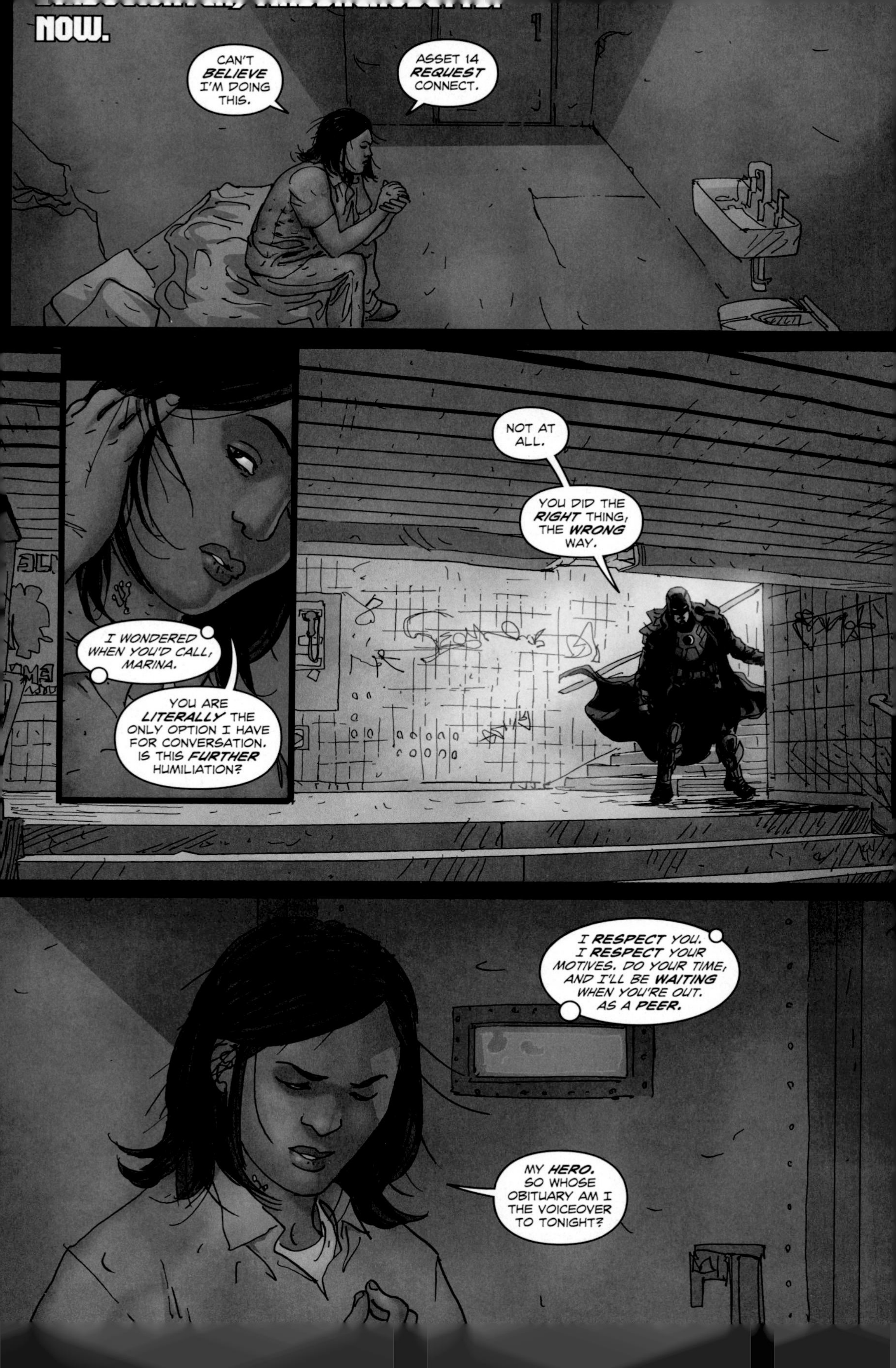
NOW.
CAN'T BELIEVE I'M DOING THIS.
ASSET 14 REQUEST CONNECT.
I WONDERED WHEN YOU'D CALL, MARINA.
YOU ARE LITERALLY THE ONLY OPTION I HAVE FOR CONVERSATION. IS THIS FURTHER HUMILIATION?
NOT AT ALL.
YOU DID THE RIGHT THING, THE WRONG WAY.
I RESPECT YOU. I RESPECT YOUR MOTIVES. DO YOUR TIME, AND I'LL BE WAITING WHEN YOU'RE OUT. AS A PEER.
MY HERO. SO WHOSE OBITUARY AM I THE VOICEOVER TO TONIGHT?

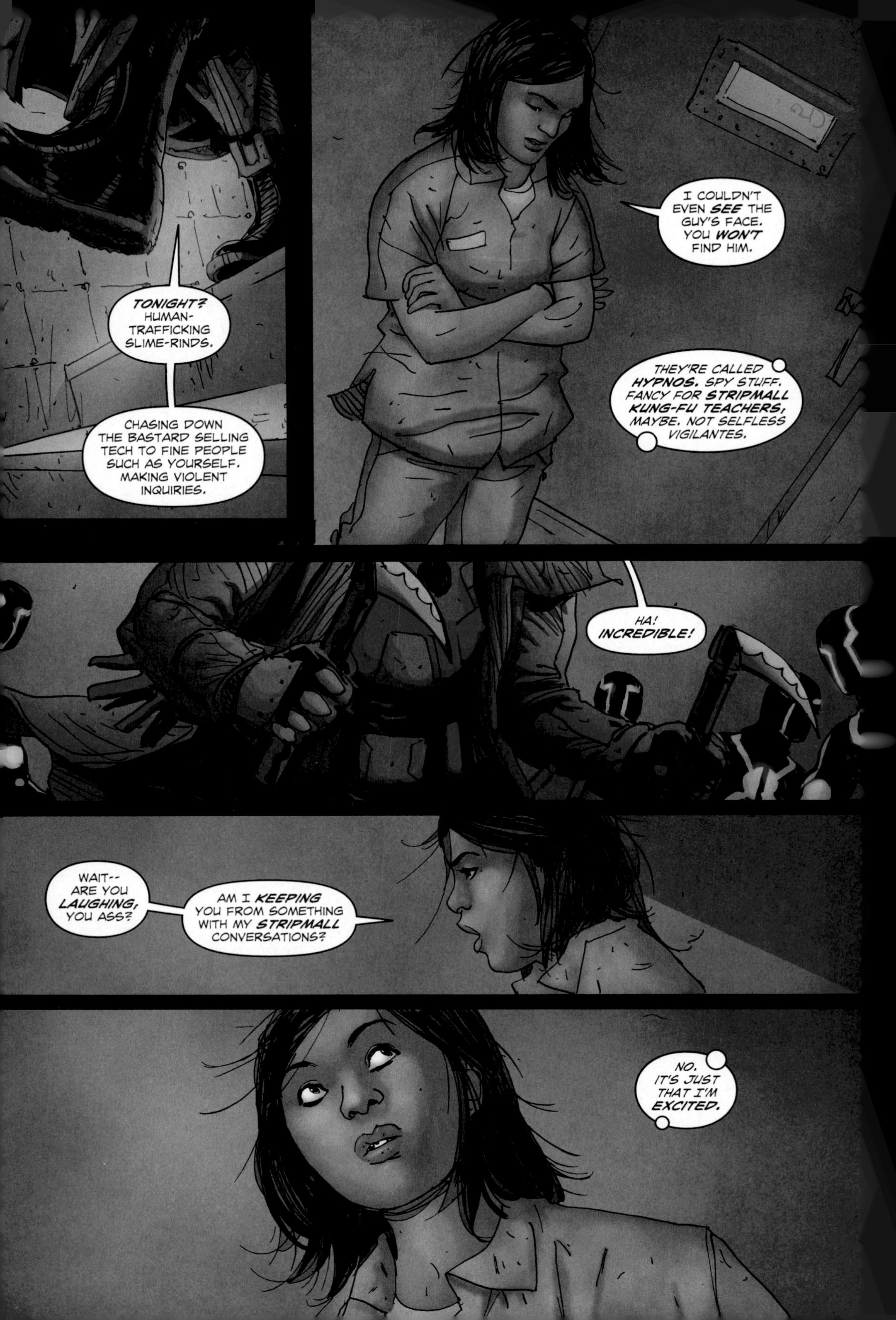
TONIGHT? HUMAN-TRAFFICKING SLIME-RINDS.
CHASING DOWN THE BASTARD SELLING TECH TO FINE PEOPLE SUCH AS YOURSELF. MAKING VIOLENT INQUIRIES.
I COULDN'T EVEN SEE THE GUY'S FACE. YOU WON'T FIND HIM.
THEY'RE CALLED HYPNOS. SPY STUFF. FANCY FOR STRIPMALL KUNG-FU TEACHERS, MAYBE. NOT SELFLESS VIGILANTES.
HA! INCREDIBLE!
WAIT-- ARE YOU LAUGHING, YOU ASS?
AM I KEEPING YOU FROM SOMETHING WITH MY STRIPMALL CONVERSATIONS?
NO. IT'S JUST THAT I'M EXCITED.

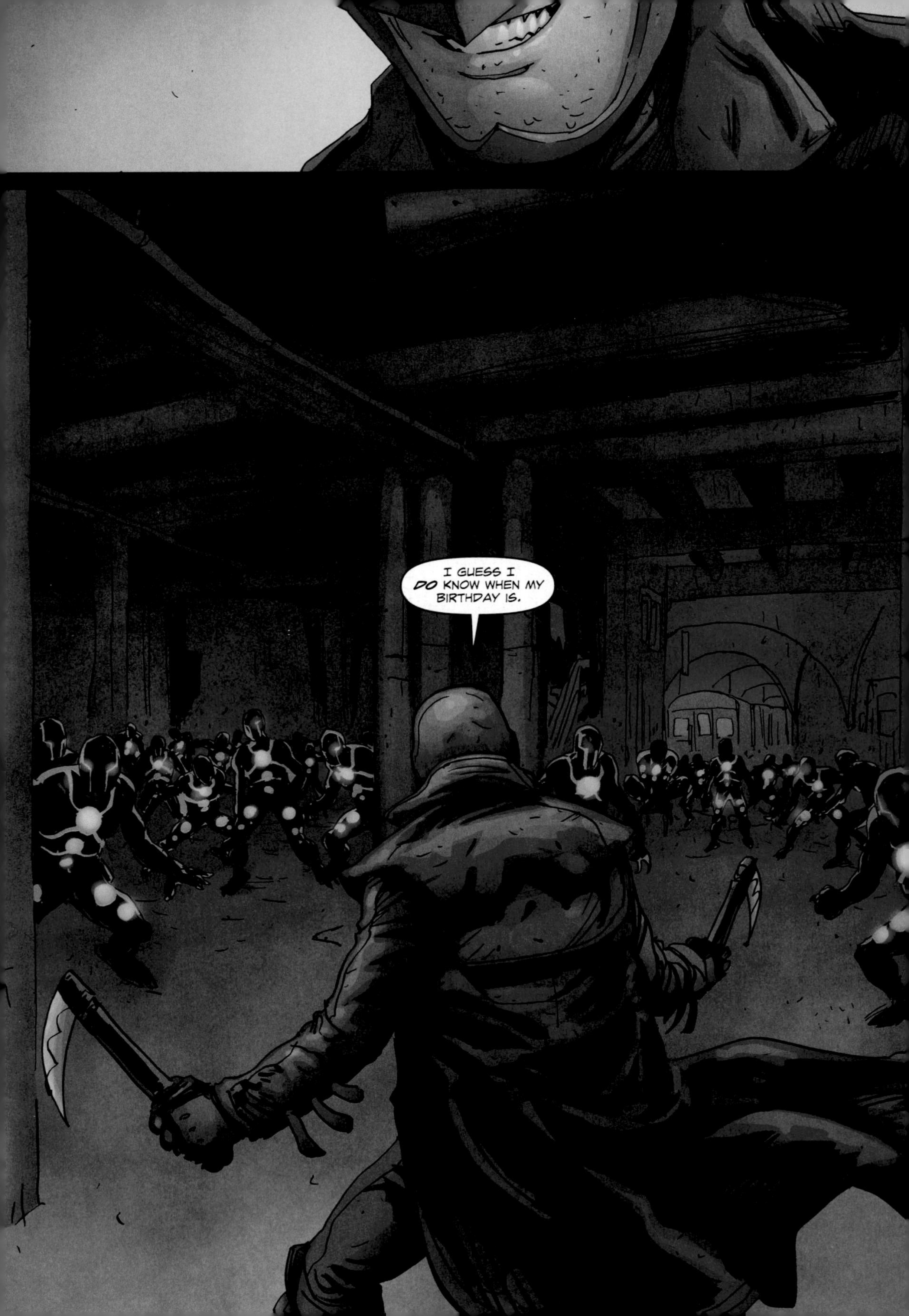
I GUESS I DO KNOW WHEN MY BIRTHDAY IS.

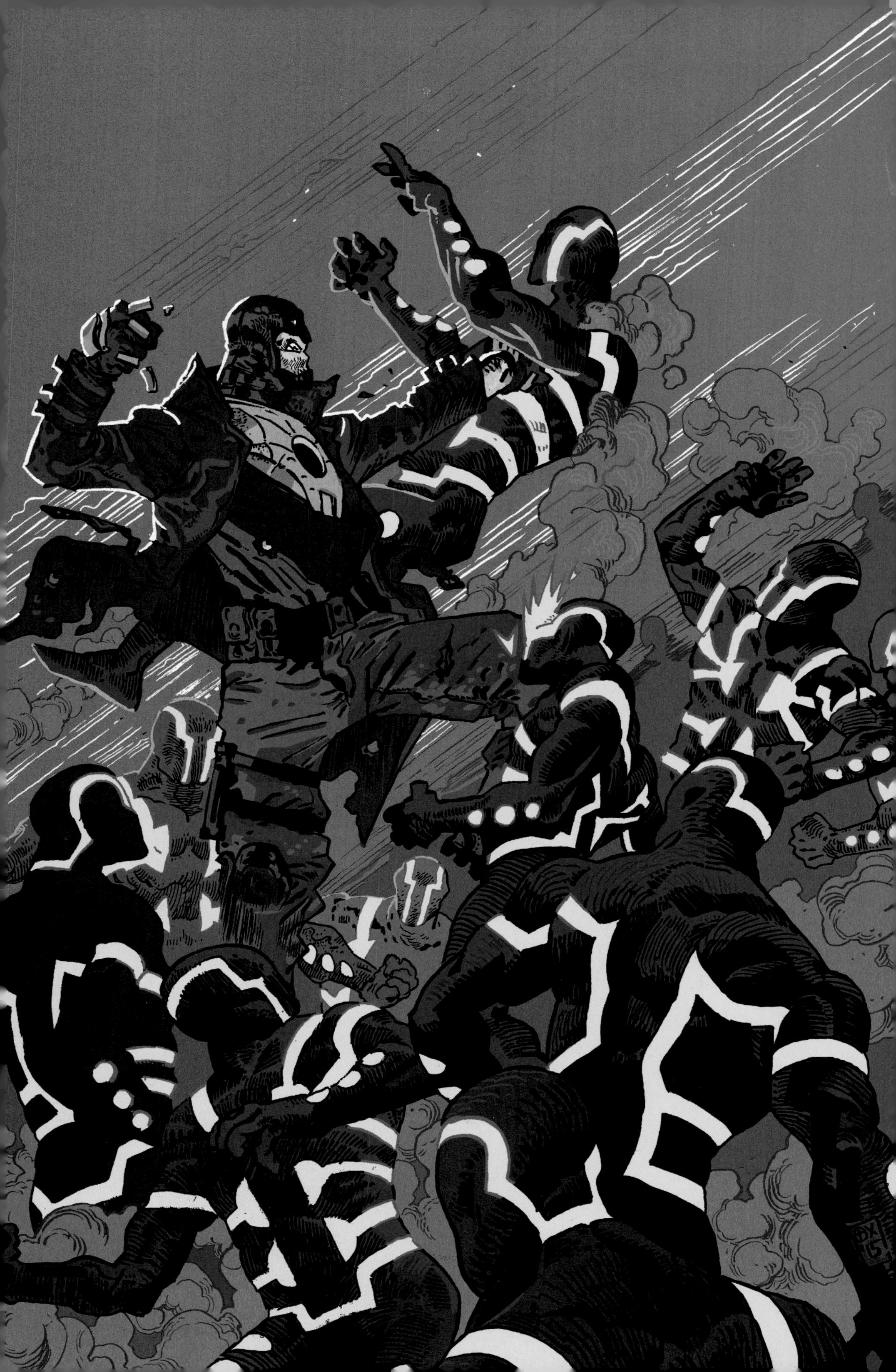

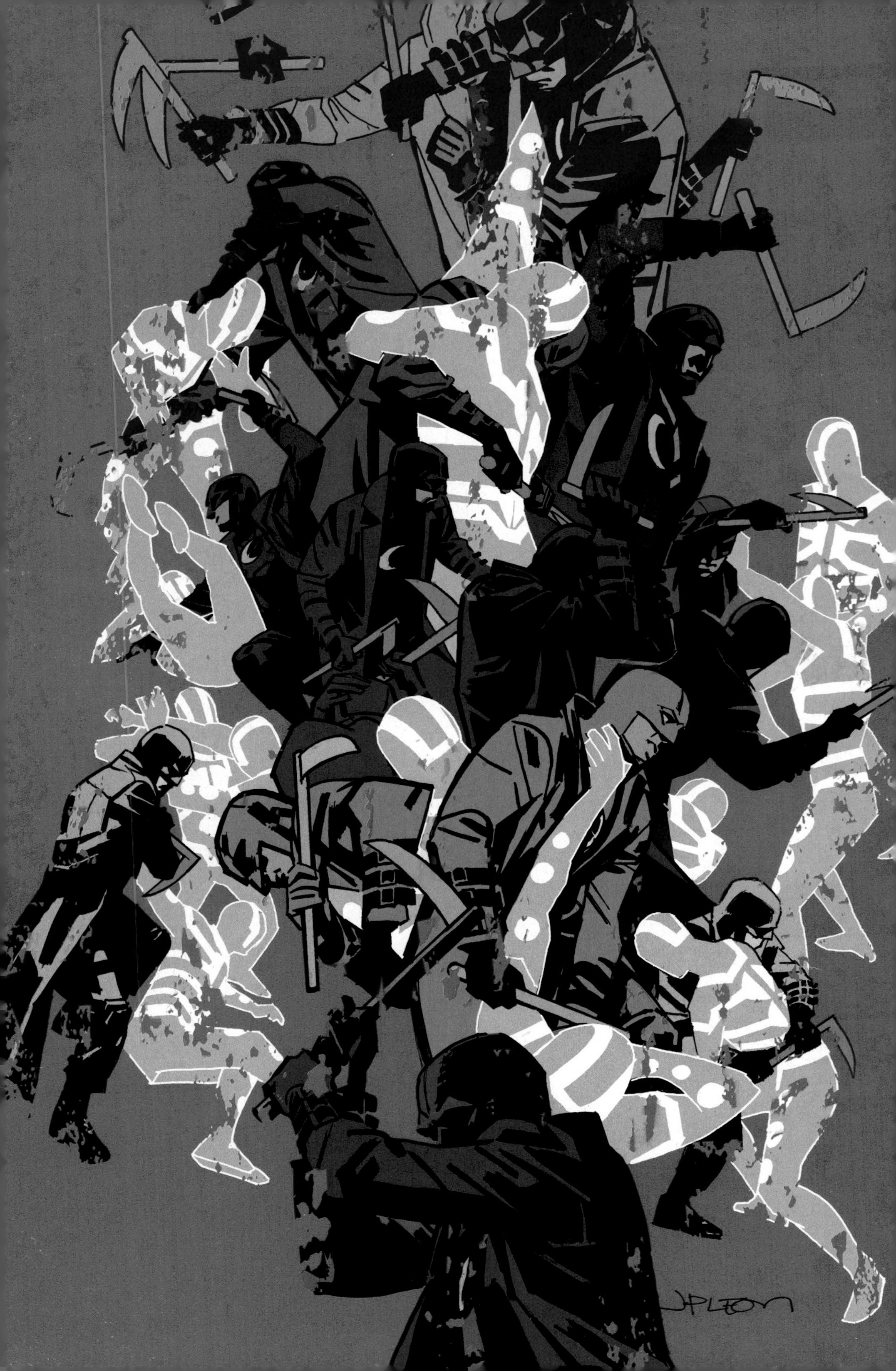

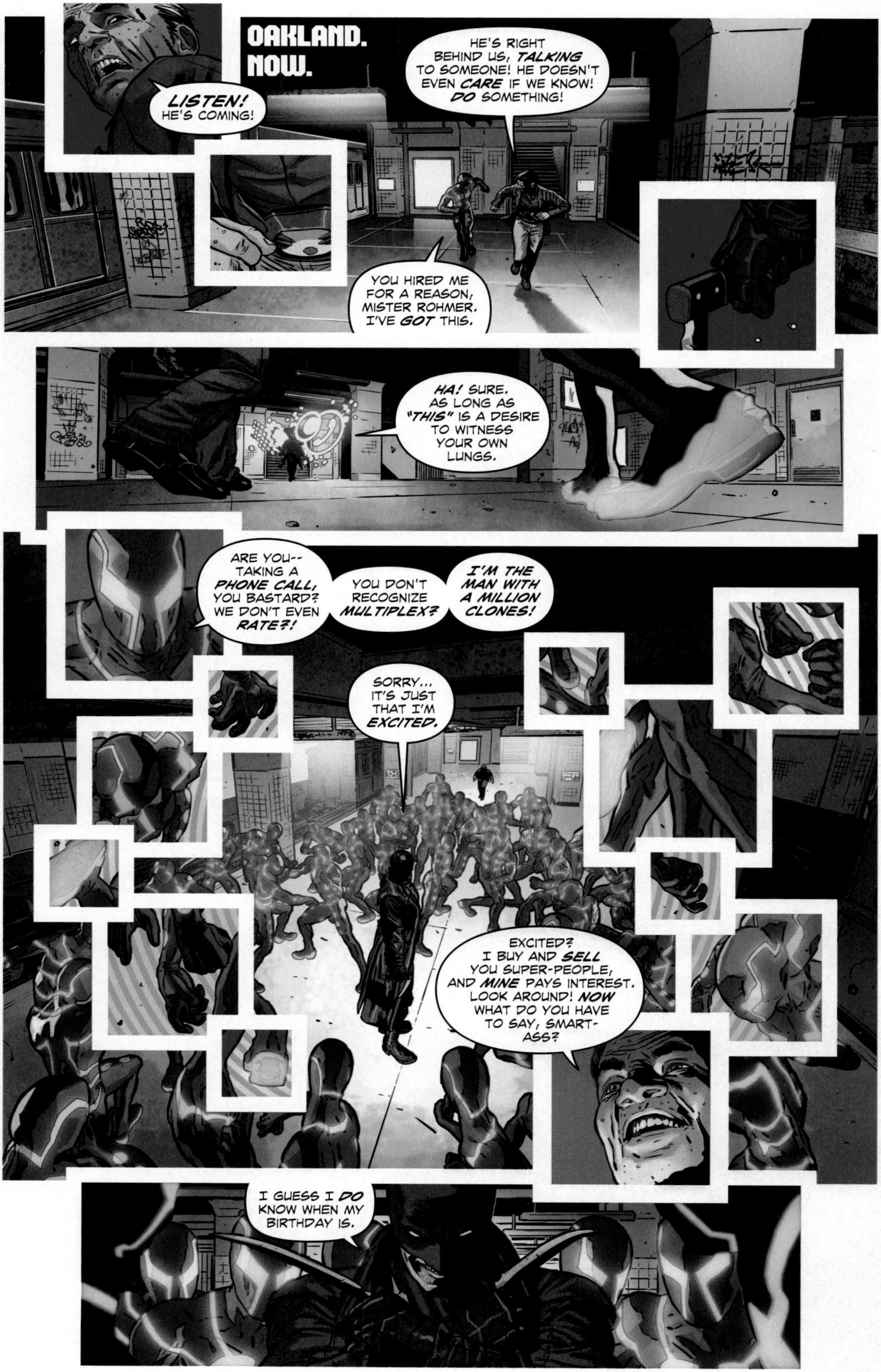
OAKLAND. NOW.
LISTEN! HE'S COMING!
HE'S RIGHT BEHIND US, TALKING TO SOMEONE! HE DOESN'T EVEN CARE IF WE KNOW! DO SOMETHING!
YOU HIRED ME FOR A REASON, MISTER ROHMER. I'VE GOT THIS.
HA! SURE. AS LONG AS "THIS" IS A DESIRE TO WITNESS YOUR OWN LUNGS.
ARE YOU-- TAKING A PHONE CALL, YOU BASTARD? WE DON'T EVEN RATE?!
YOU DON'T RECOGNIZE MULTIPLEX?
I'M THE MAN WITH A MILLION CLONES!
SORRY... IT'S JUST THAT I'M EXCITED.
EXCITED? I BUY AND SELL YOU SUPER-PEOPLE, AND MINE PAYS INTEREST. LOOK AROUND! NOW WHAT DO YOU HAVE TO SAY, SMART-ASS?
I GUESS I DO KNOW WHEN MY BIRTHDAY IS.

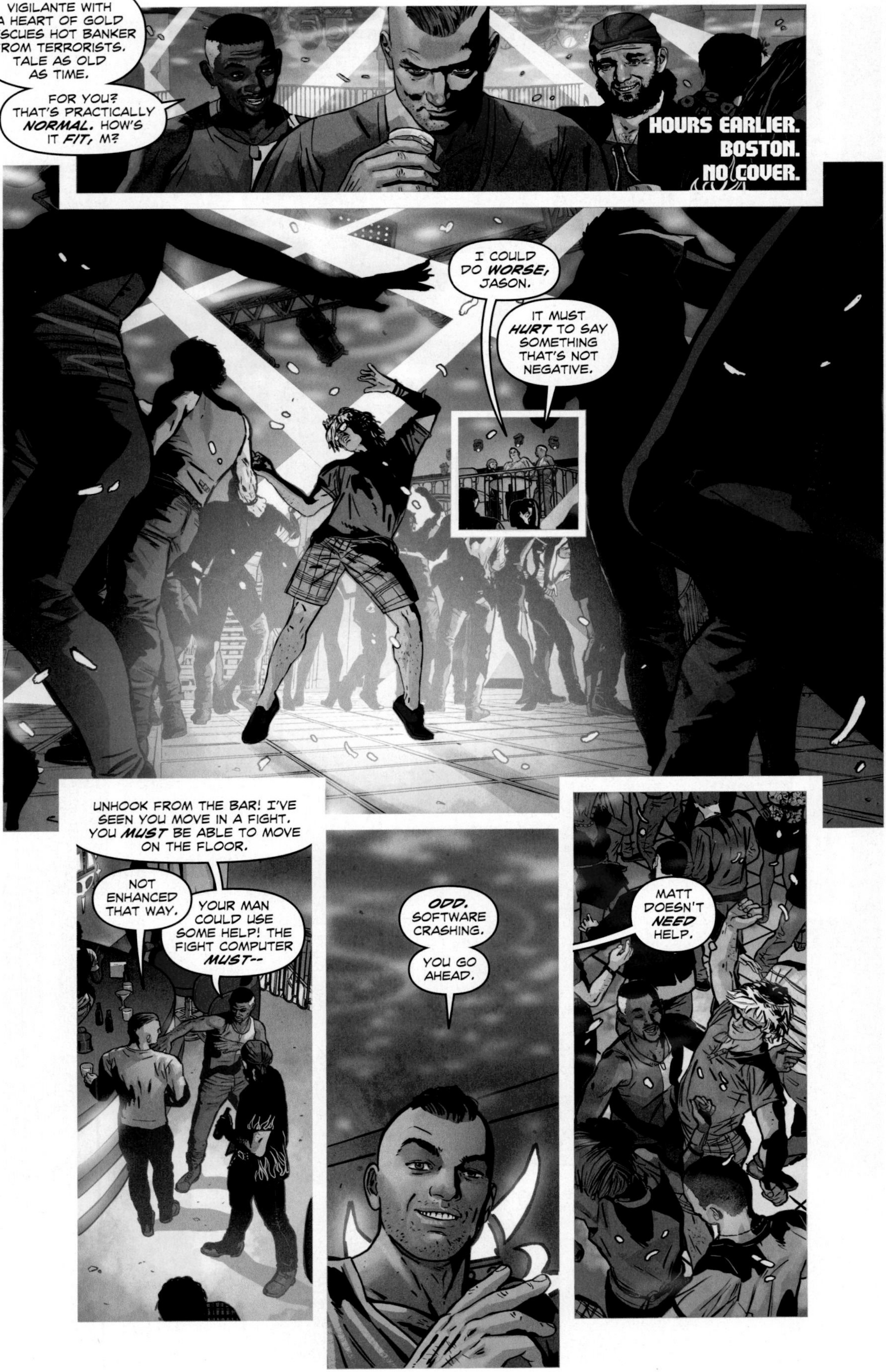
CRAZED VIGILANTE WITH A HEART OF GOLD RESCUES HOT BANKER FROM TERRORISTS. TALE AS OLD AS TIME.
FOR YOU? THAT'S PRACTICALLY NORMAL. HOW'S IT FIT, M?
HOURS EARLIER. BOSTON. NO COVER.
I COULD DO WORSE, JASON.
IT MUST HURT TO SAY SOMETHING THAT'S NOT NEGATIVE.
UNHOOK FROM THE BAR! I'VE SEEN YOU MOVE IN A FIGHT. YOU MUST BE ABLE TO MOVE ON THE FLOOR.
NOT ENHANCED THAT WAY.
YOUR MAN COULD USE SOME HELP! THE FIGHT COMPUTER MUST--
ODD. SOFTWARE CRASHING.
YOU GO AHEAD.
MATT DOESN'T NEED HELP.

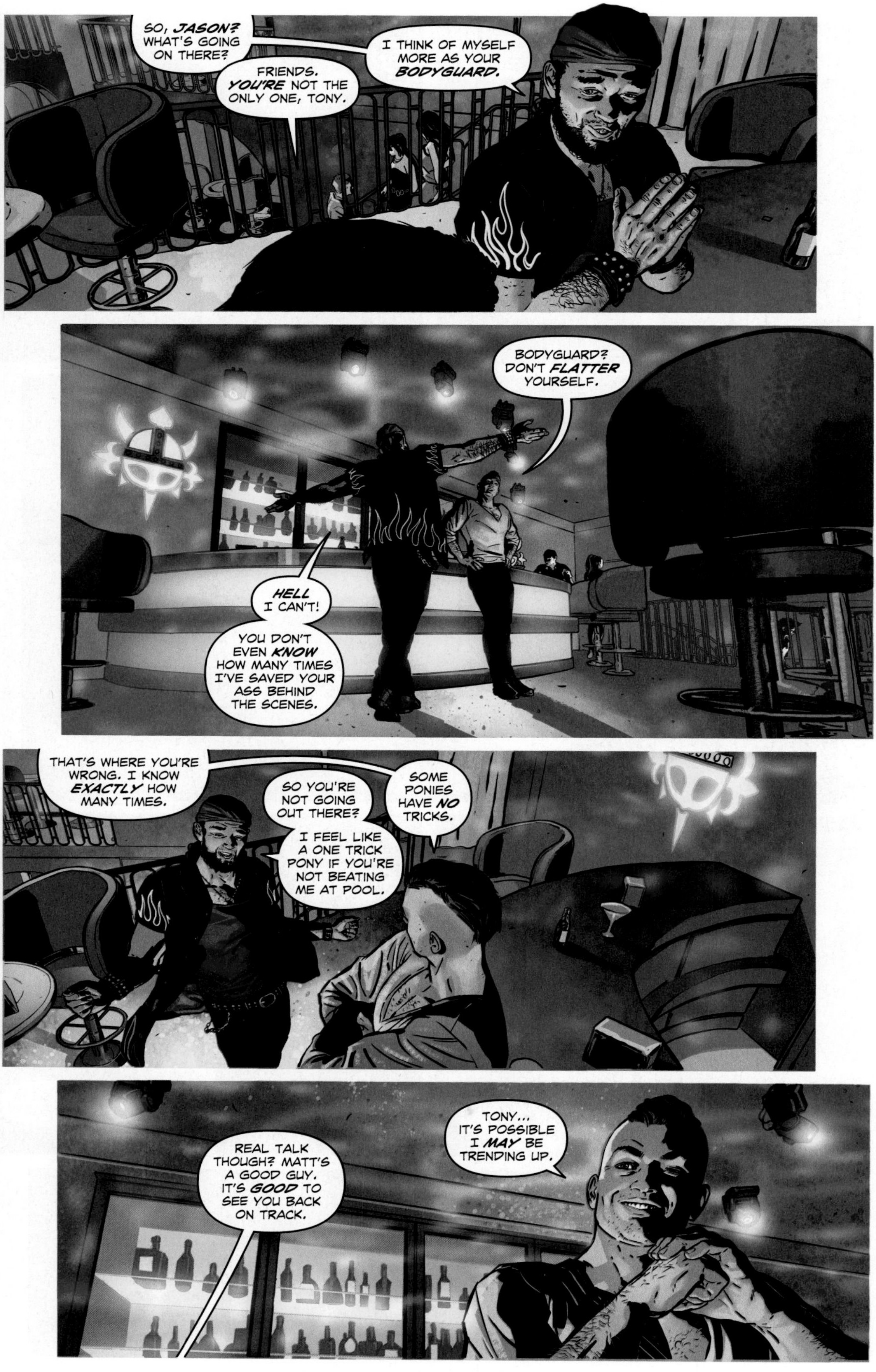

SO, JASON? WHAT'S GOING ON THERE?
FRIENDS. YOU'RE NOT THE ONLY ONE, TONY.
I THINK OF MYSELF MORE AS YOUR BODYGUARD.
BODYGUARD? DON'T FLATTER YOURSELF.
HELL I CAN'T!
YOU DON'T EVEN KNOW HOW MANY TIMES I'VE SAVED YOUR ASS BEHIND THE SCENES.
THAT'S WHERE YOU'RE WRONG. I KNOW EXACTLY HOW MANY TIMES.
SO YOU'RE NOT GOING OUT THERE?
I FEEL LIKE A ONE TRICK PONY IF YOU'RE NOT BEATING ME AT POOL.
SOME PONIES HAVE NO TRICKS.
REAL TALK THOUGH? MATT'S A GOOD GUY. IT'S GOOD TO SEE YOU BACK ON TRACK.
TONY... IT'S POSSIBLE I MAY BE TRENDING UP.

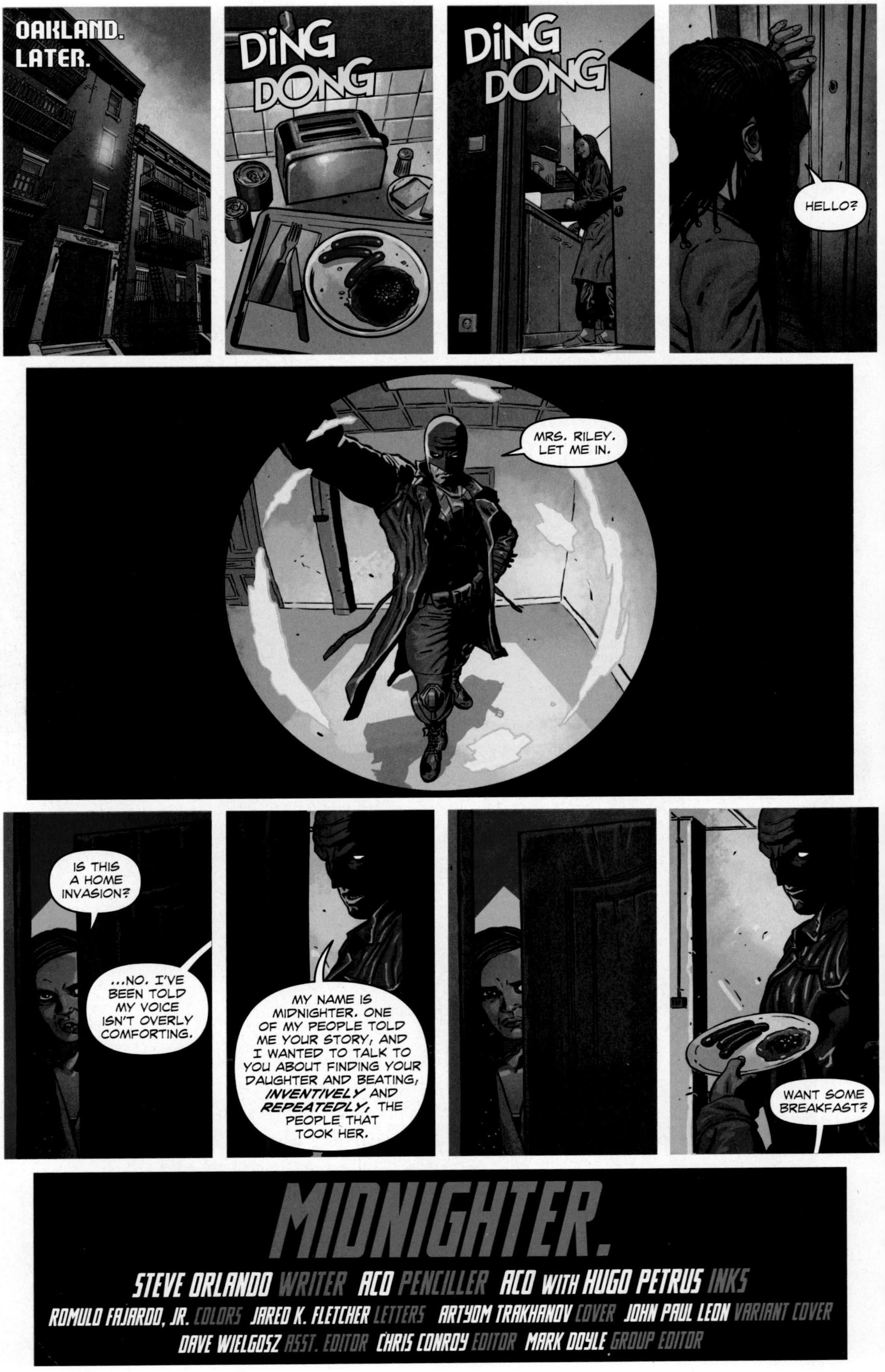
OAKLAND. LATER.
DiNG DONG
DiNG DONG
HELLO?
MRS. RILEY. LET ME IN.
IS THIS A HOME INVASION?
...NO. I'VE BEEN TOLD MY VOICE ISN'T OVERLY COMFORTING.
MY NAME IS MIDNIGHTER. ONE OF MY PEOPLE TOLD ME YOUR STORY, AND I WANTED TO TALK TO YOU ABOUT FINDING YOUR DAUGHTER AND BEATING, INVENTIVELY AND REPEATEDLY, THE PEOPLE THAT TOOK HER.
WANT SOME BREAKFAST?

MIDNIGHTER.

STEVE ORLANDO WRITER ACO PENCILLER ACO WITH HUGO PETRUS INKS
ROMULO FAJARDO, JR. COLORS JARED K. FLETCHER LETTERS ARTYOM TRAKHANOV COVER JOHN PAUL LEON VARIANT COVER
DAVE WIELGOSZ ASST. EDITOR CHRIS CONROY EDITOR MARK DOYLE GROUP EDITOR

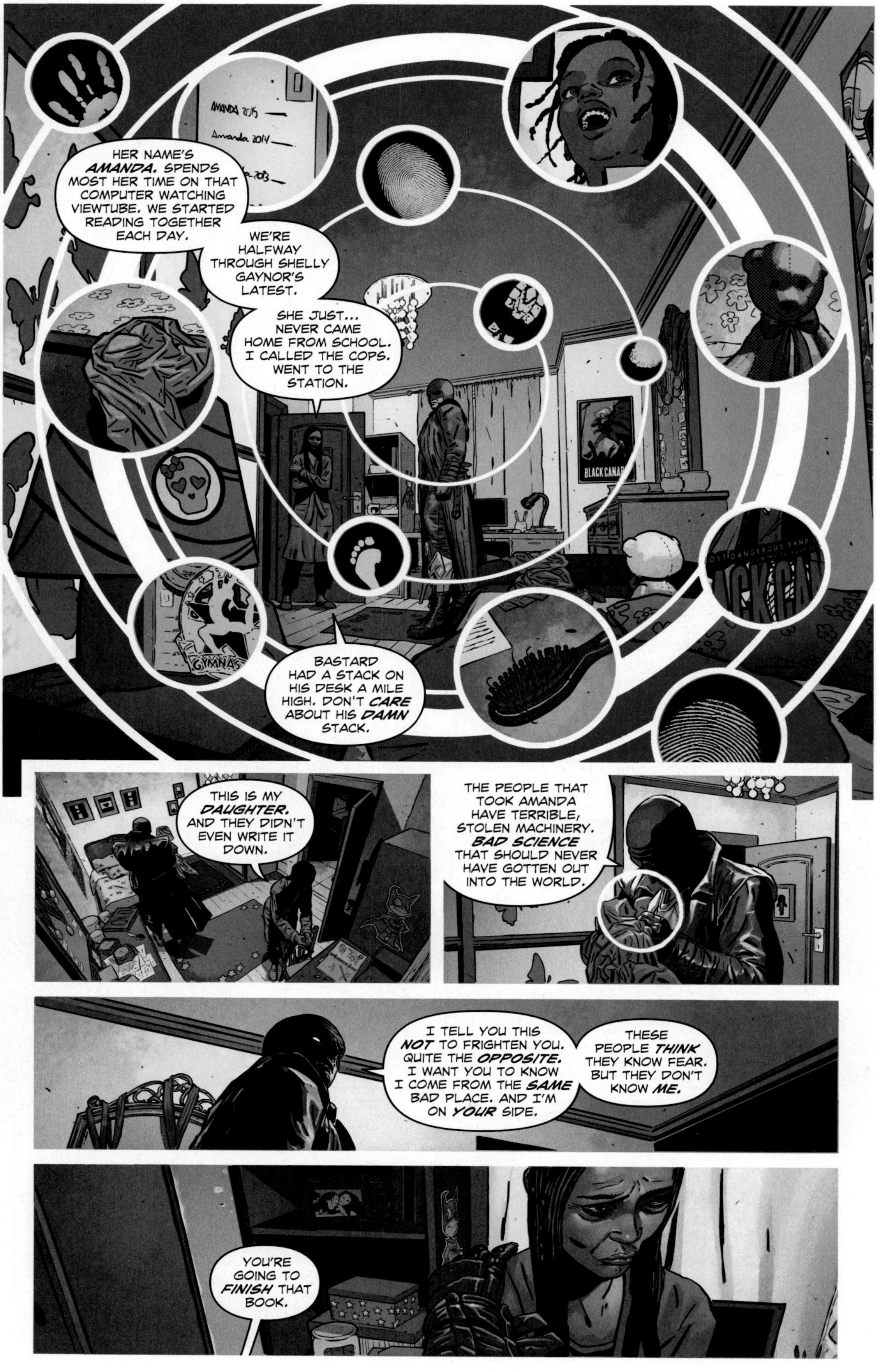

AMANDA 2015
Amanda 2014
HER NAME'S *AMANDA.* SPENDS MOST HER TIME ON THAT COMPUTER WATCHING VIEWTUBE. WE STARTED READING TOGETHER EACH DAY.
WE'RE HALFWAY THROUGH SHELLY GAYNOR'S LATEST.
SHE JUST... NEVER CAME HOME FROM SCHOOL. I CALLED THE COPS. WENT TO THE STATION.
BLACK CANA
BASTARD HAD A STACK ON HIS DESK A MILE HIGH. DON'T *CARE* ABOUT HIS *DAMN* STACK.
THIS IS MY *DAUGHTER.* AND THEY DIDN'T EVEN WRITE IT DOWN.
THE PEOPLE THAT TOOK AMANDA HAVE TERRIBLE, STOLEN MACHINERY. *BAD SCIENCE* THAT SHOULD NEVER HAVE GOTTEN OUT INTO THE WORLD.
I TELL YOU THIS *NOT* TO FRIGHTEN YOU. QUITE THE *OPPOSITE.* I WANT YOU TO KNOW I COME FROM THE *SAME* BAD PLACE. AND I'M ON *YOUR* SIDE.
THESE PEOPLE *THINK* THEY KNOW FEAR. BUT THEY DON'T KNOW *ME.*
YOU'RE GOING TO *FINISH* THAT BOOK.

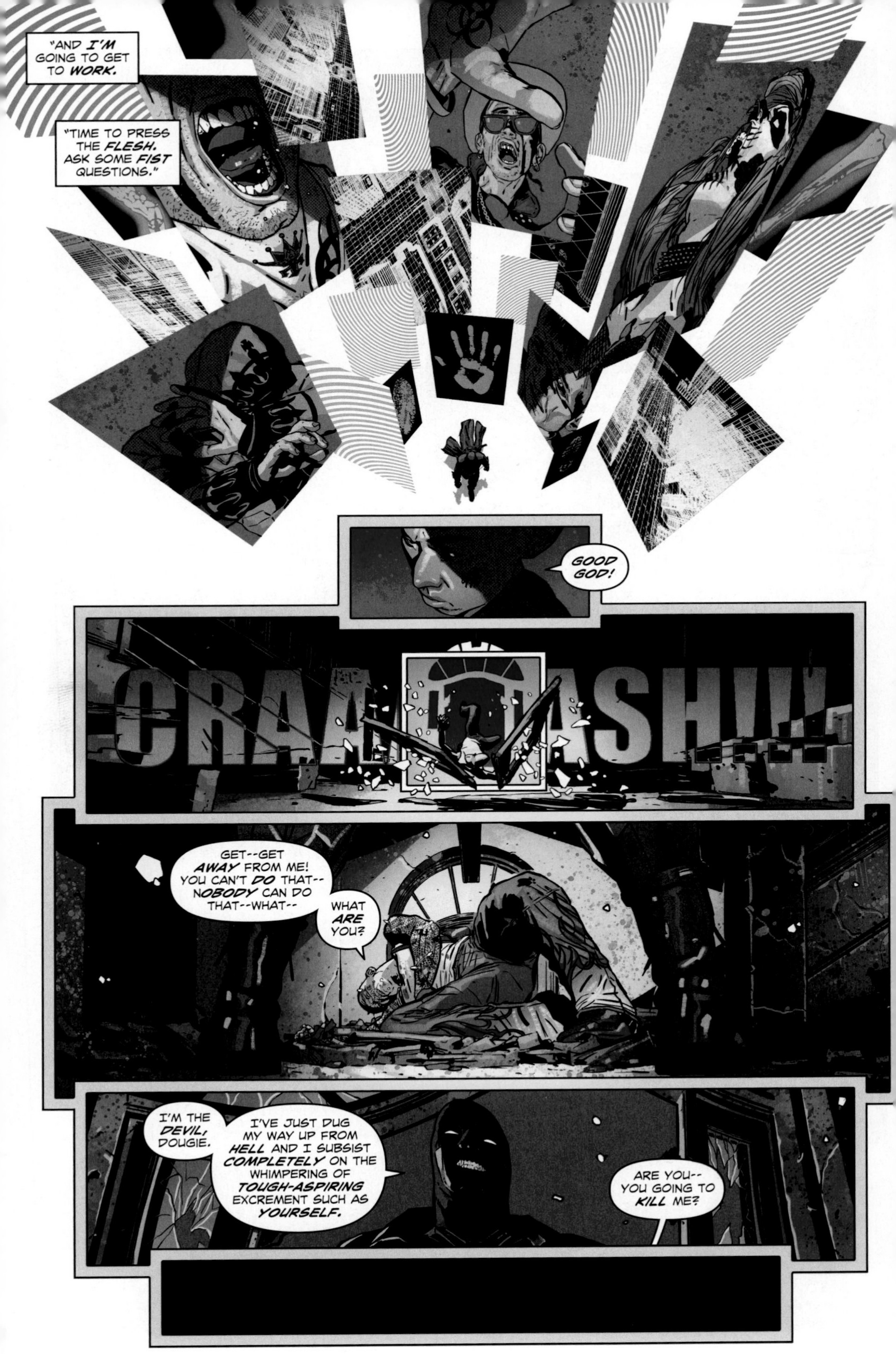
"AND I'M GOING TO GET TO WORK.
"TIME TO PRESS THE FLESH. ASK SOME FIST QUESTIONS."
GOOD GOD!
CRAA ASH!!
GET--GET AWAY FROM ME! YOU CAN'T DO THAT--NOBODY CAN DO THAT--WHAT--
WHAT ARE YOU?
I'M THE DEVIL, DOUGIE.
I'VE JUST DUG MY WAY UP FROM HELL AND I SUBSIST COMPLETELY ON THE WHIMPERING OF TOUGH-ASPIRING EXCREMENT SUCH AS YOURSELF.
ARE YOU--YOU GOING TO KILL ME?

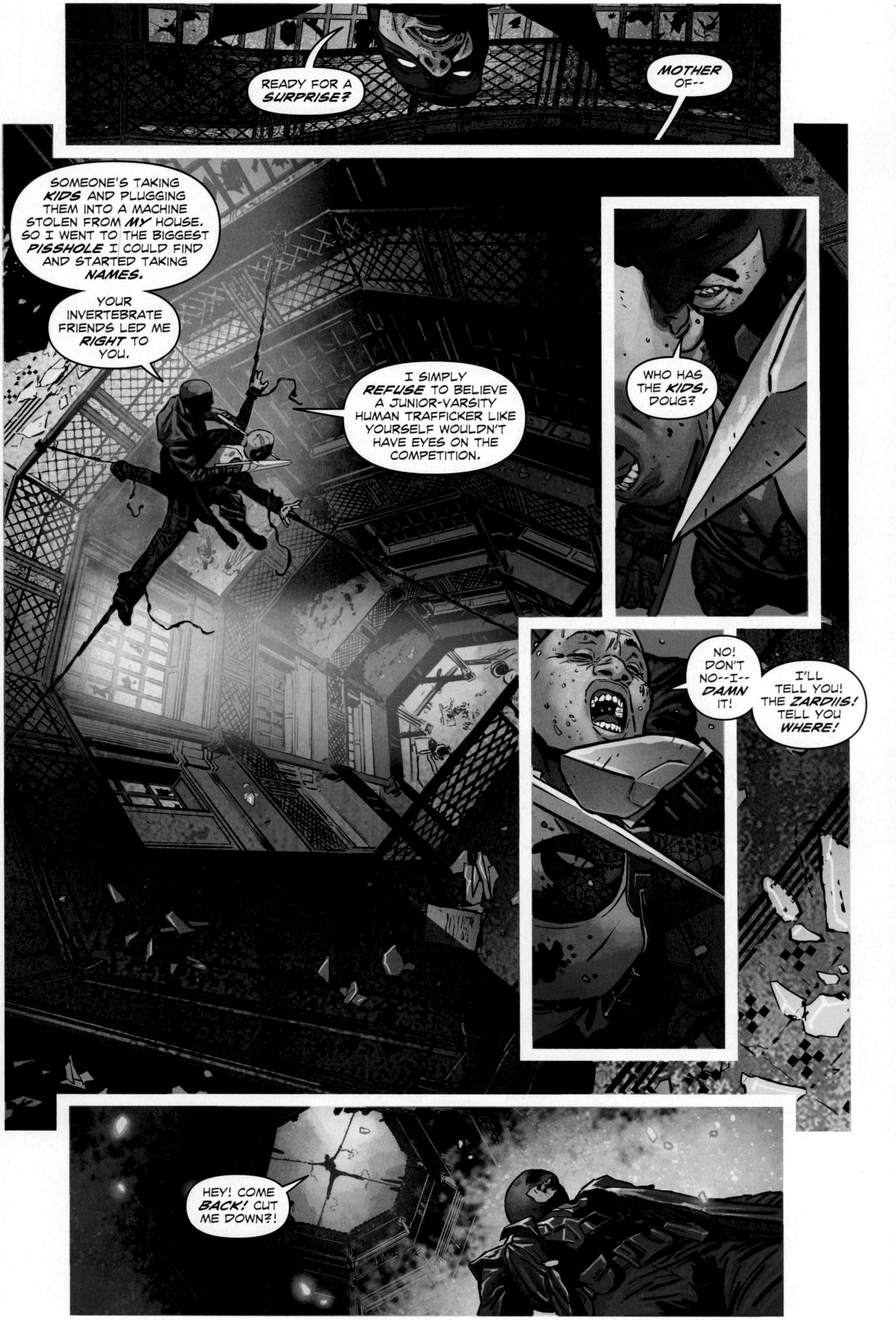
READY FOR A SURPRISE?
MOTHER OF--
SOMEONE'S TAKING KIDS AND PLUGGING THEM INTO A MACHINE STOLEN FROM MY HOUSE. SO I WENT TO THE BIGGEST PISSHOLE I COULD FIND AND STARTED TAKING NAMES.
YOUR INVERTEBRATE FRIENDS LED ME RIGHT TO YOU.
I SIMPLY REFUSE TO BELIEVE A JUNIOR-VARSITY HUMAN TRAFFICKER LIKE YOURSELF WOULDN'T HAVE EYES ON THE COMPETITION.
WHO HAS THE KIDS, DOUG?
NO! DON'T NO--I--DAMN IT!
I'LL TELL YOU! THE ZARDIIS! TELL YOU WHERE!
HEY! COME BACK! CUT ME DOWN?!

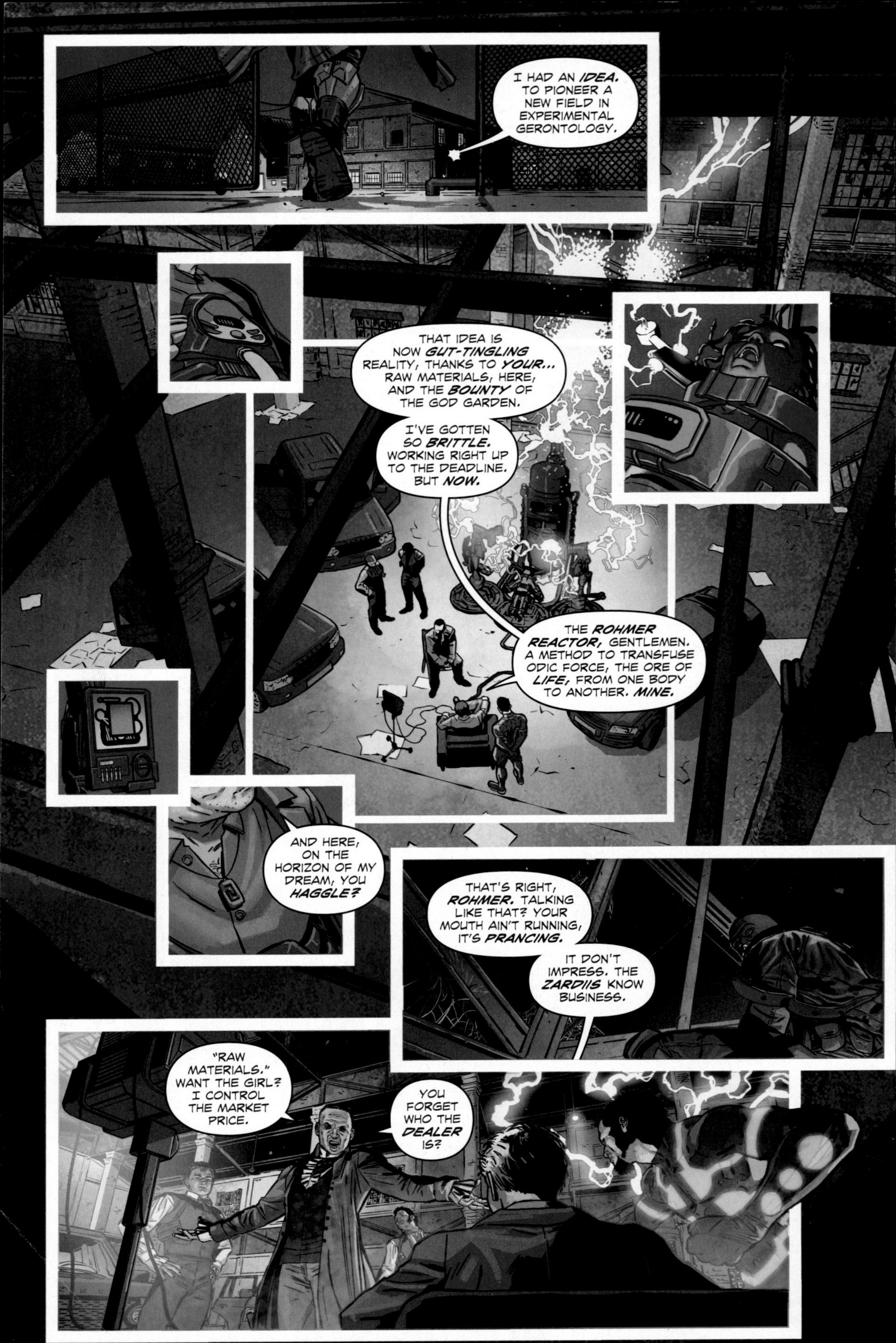
I HAD AN IDEA. TO PIONEER A NEW FIELD IN EXPERIMENTAL GERONTOLOGY.
THAT IDEA IS NOW GUT-TINGLING REALITY, THANKS TO YOUR... RAW MATERIALS, HERE, AND THE BOUNTY OF THE GOD GARDEN.
I'VE GOTTEN SO BRITTLE. WORKING RIGHT UP TO THE DEADLINE. BUT NOW.
THE ROHMER REACTOR, GENTLEMEN. A METHOD TO TRANSFUSE ODIC FORCE, THE ORE OF LIFE, FROM ONE BODY TO ANOTHER. MINE.
AND HERE, ON THE HORIZON OF MY DREAM, YOU HAGGLE?
THAT'S RIGHT, ROHMER. TALKING LIKE THAT? YOUR MOUTH AIN'T RUNNING, IT'S PRANCING.
IT DON'T IMPRESS. THE ZARDIIS KNOW BUSINESS.
"RAW MATERIALS." WANT THE GIRL? I CONTROL THE MARKET PRICE.
YOU FORGET WHO THE DEALER IS?

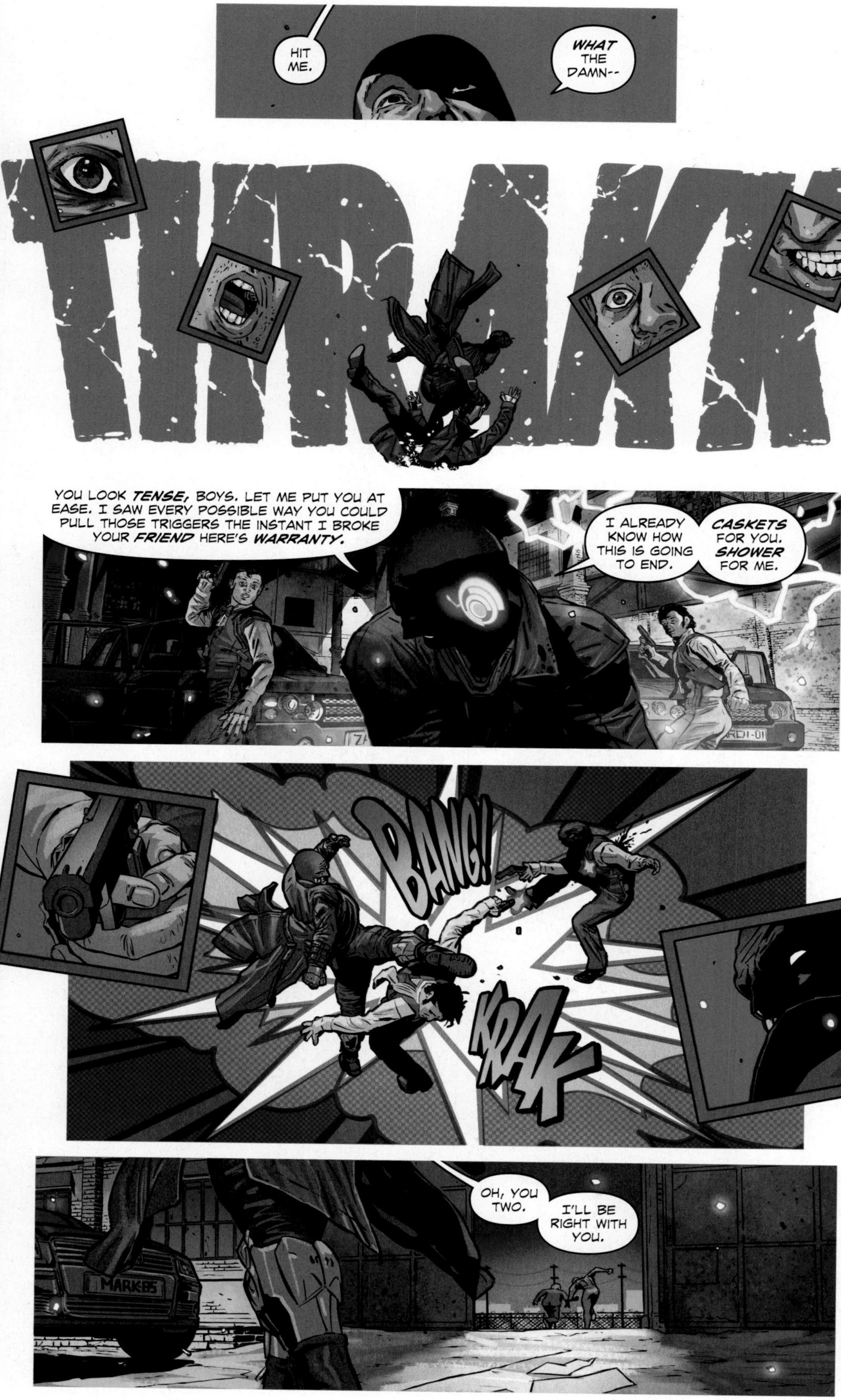

HIT ME.
WHAT THE DAMN--
THRAKK
YOU LOOK TENSE, BOYS. LET ME PUT YOU AT EASE. I SAW EVERY POSSIBLE WAY YOU COULD PULL THOSE TRIGGERS THE INSTANT I BROKE YOUR FRIEND HERE'S WARRANTY.
I ALREADY KNOW HOW THIS IS GOING TO END.
CASKETS FOR YOU. SHOWER FOR ME.
BANG!
KRAK
OH, YOU TWO.
I'LL BE RIGHT WITH YOU.

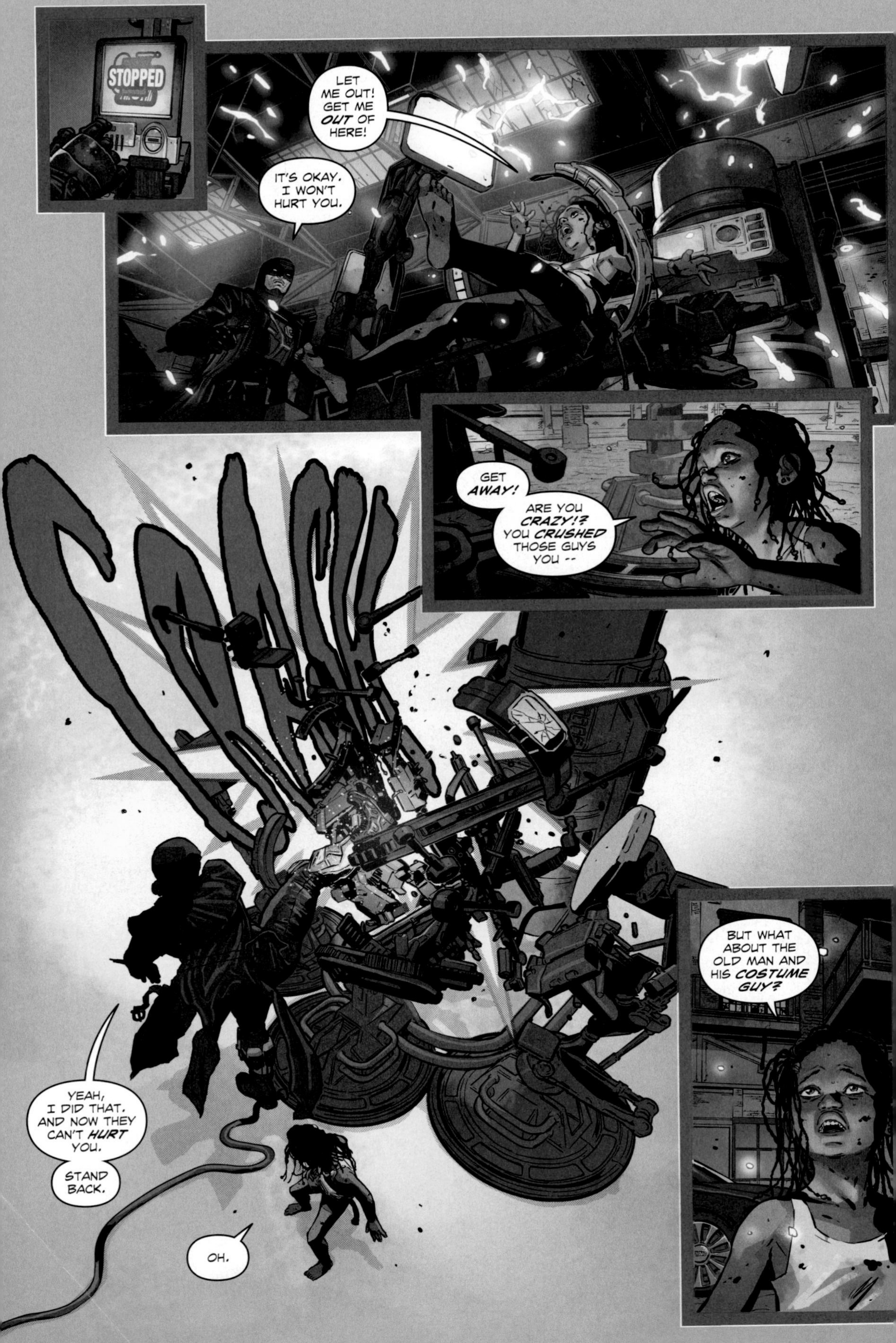
STOPPED
LET ME OUT! GET ME OUT OF HERE!
IT'S OKAY. I WON'T HURT YOU.
GET AWAY!
ARE YOU CRAZY!? YOU CRUSHED THOSE GUYS YOU --
YEAH, I DID THAT. AND NOW THEY CAN'T HURT YOU.
STAND BACK.
OH.
BUT WHAT ABOUT THE OLD MAN AND HIS COSTUME GUY?

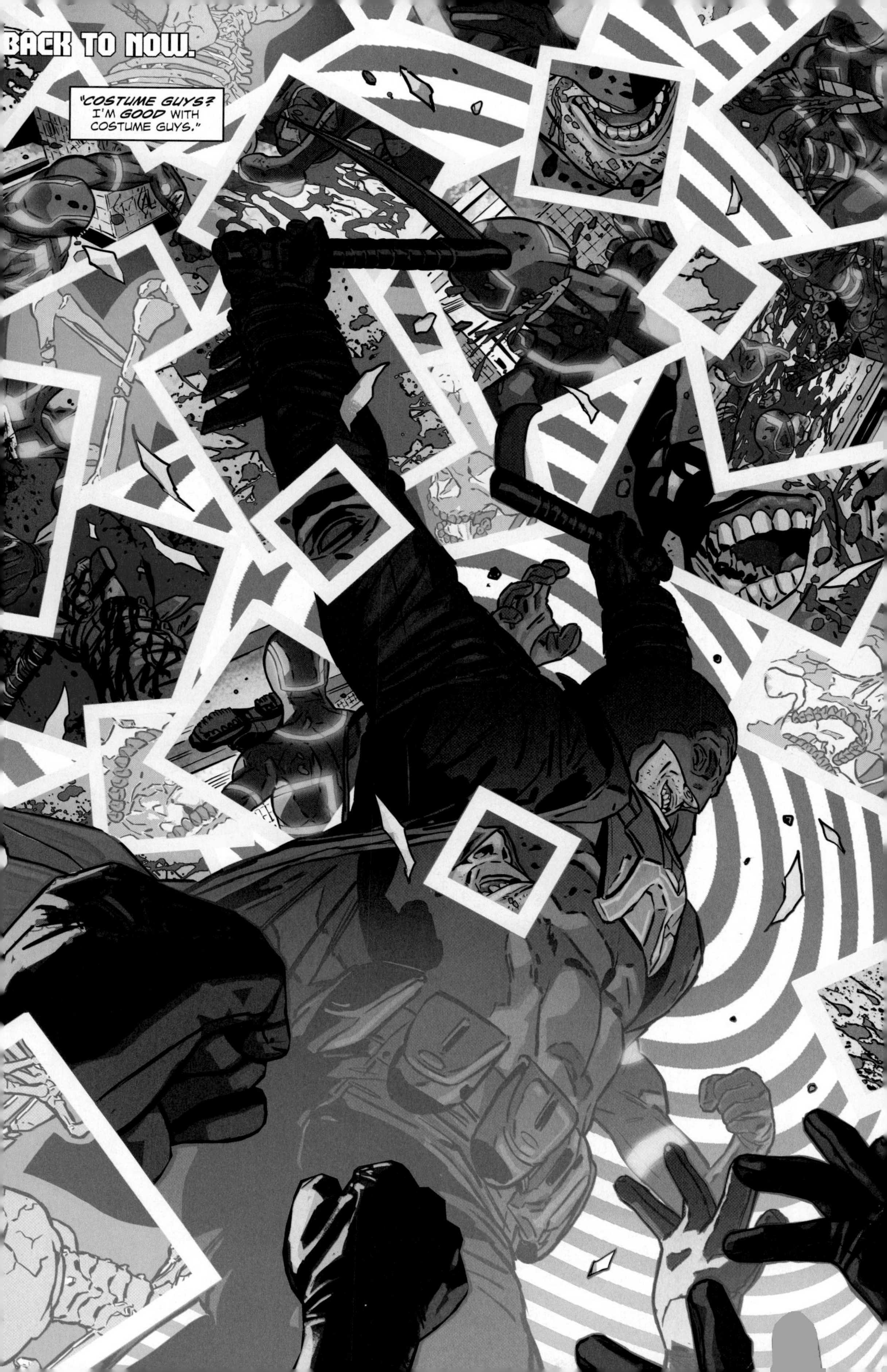
BACK TO NOW.
"COSTUME GUYS? I'M GOOD WITH COSTUME GUYS."

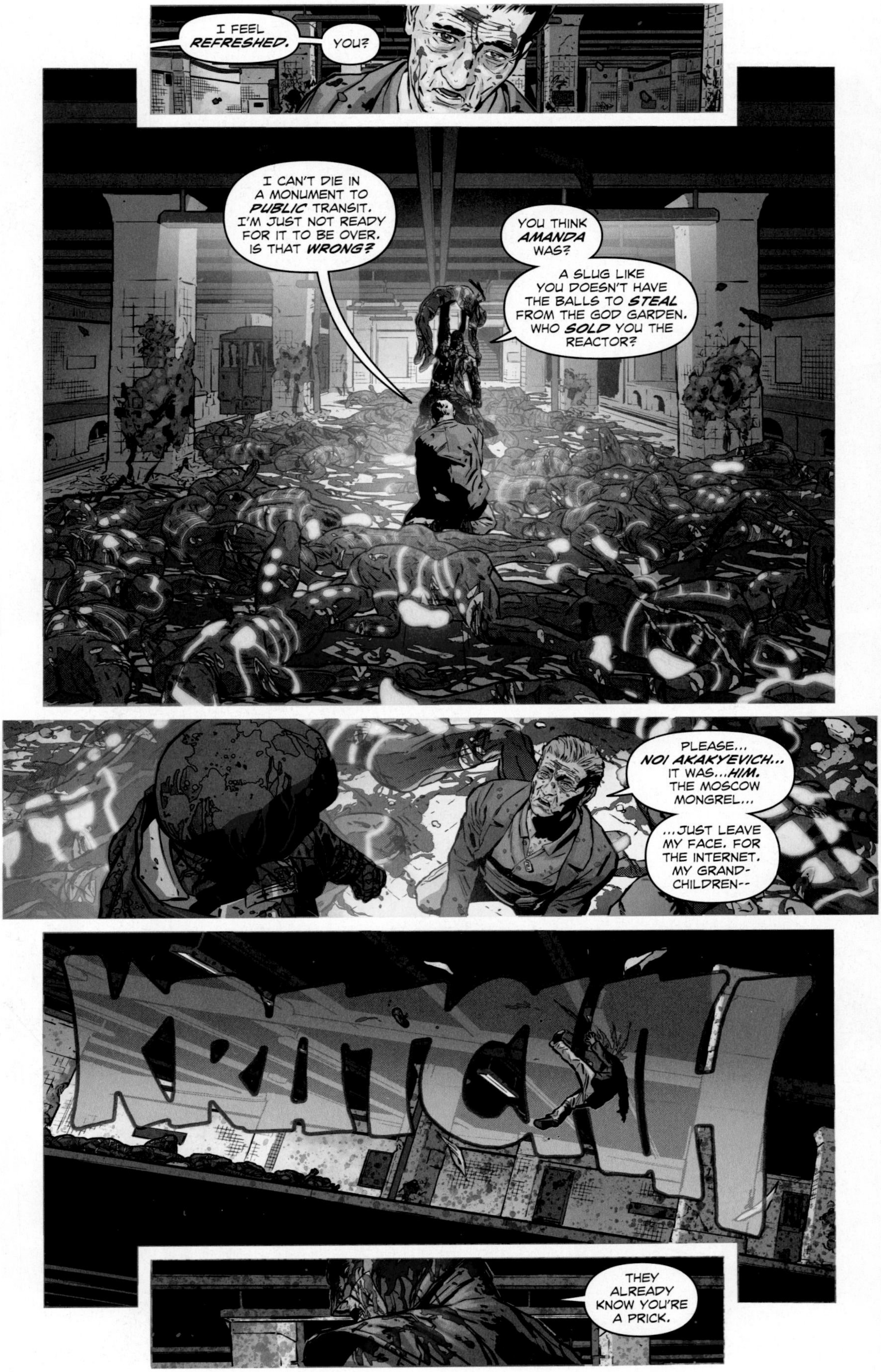
I FEEL REFRESHED.
YOU?
I CAN'T DIE IN A MONUMENT TO PUBLIC TRANSIT. I'M JUST NOT READY FOR IT TO BE OVER. IS THAT WRONG?
YOU THINK AMANDA WAS?
A SLUG LIKE YOU DOESN'T HAVE THE BALLS TO STEAL FROM THE GOD GARDEN. WHO SOLD YOU THE REACTOR?
PLEASE... NOI AKAKYEVICH... IT WAS...HIM. THE MOSCOW MONGREL...
...JUST LEAVE MY FACE. FOR THE INTERNET. MY GRAND-CHILDREN--
THEY ALREADY KNOW YOU'RE A PRICK.

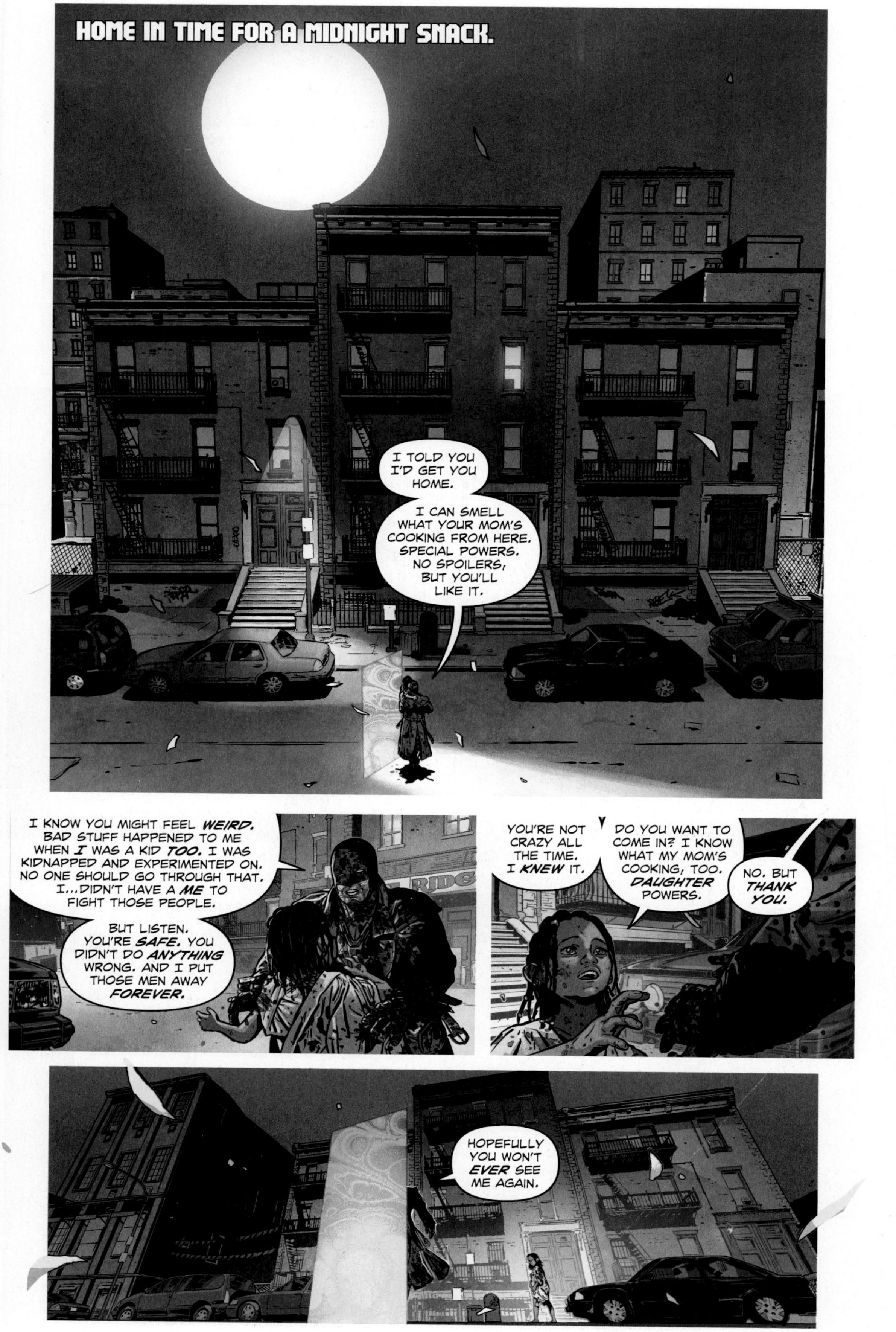
HOME IN TIME FOR A MIDNIGHT SNACK.
I TOLD YOU I'D GET YOU HOME.
I CAN SMELL WHAT YOUR MOM'S COOKING FROM HERE. SPECIAL POWERS. NO SPOILERS, BUT YOU'LL LIKE IT.
I KNOW YOU MIGHT FEEL WEIRD. BAD STUFF HAPPENED TO ME WHEN I WAS A KID TOO. I WAS KIDNAPPED AND EXPERIMENTED ON. NO ONE SHOULD GO THROUGH THAT. I...DIDN'T HAVE A ME TO FIGHT THOSE PEOPLE.
BUT LISTEN. YOU'RE SAFE. YOU DIDN'T DO ANYTHING WRONG. AND I PUT THOSE MEN AWAY FOREVER.
YOU'RE NOT CRAZY ALL THE TIME. I KNEW IT.
DO YOU WANT TO COME IN? I KNOW WHAT MY MOM'S COOKING, TOO. DAUGHTER POWERS.
NO. BUT THANK YOU.
HOPEFULLY YOU WON'T EVER SEE ME AGAIN.

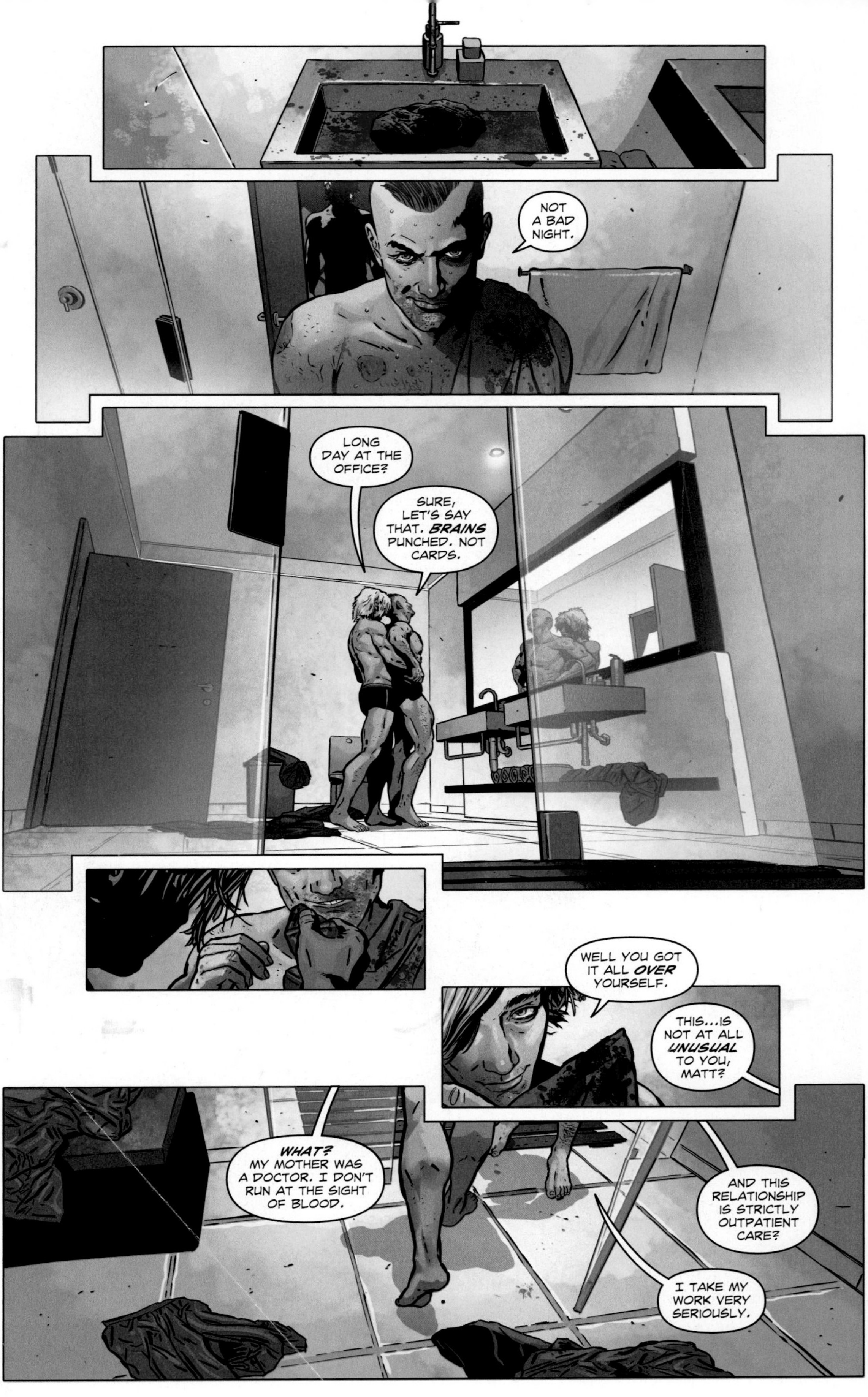
NOT A BAD NIGHT.
LONG DAY AT THE OFFICE?
SURE, LET'S SAY THAT. *BRAINS* PUNCHED. NOT CARDS.
WELL YOU GOT IT ALL *OVER* YOURSELF.
THIS...IS NOT AT ALL *UNUSUAL* TO YOU, MATT?
WHAT? MY MOTHER WAS A DOCTOR. I DON'T RUN AT THE SIGHT OF BLOOD.
AND THIS RELATIONSHIP IS STRICTLY OUTPATIENT CARE?
I TAKE MY WORK VERY SERIOUSLY.

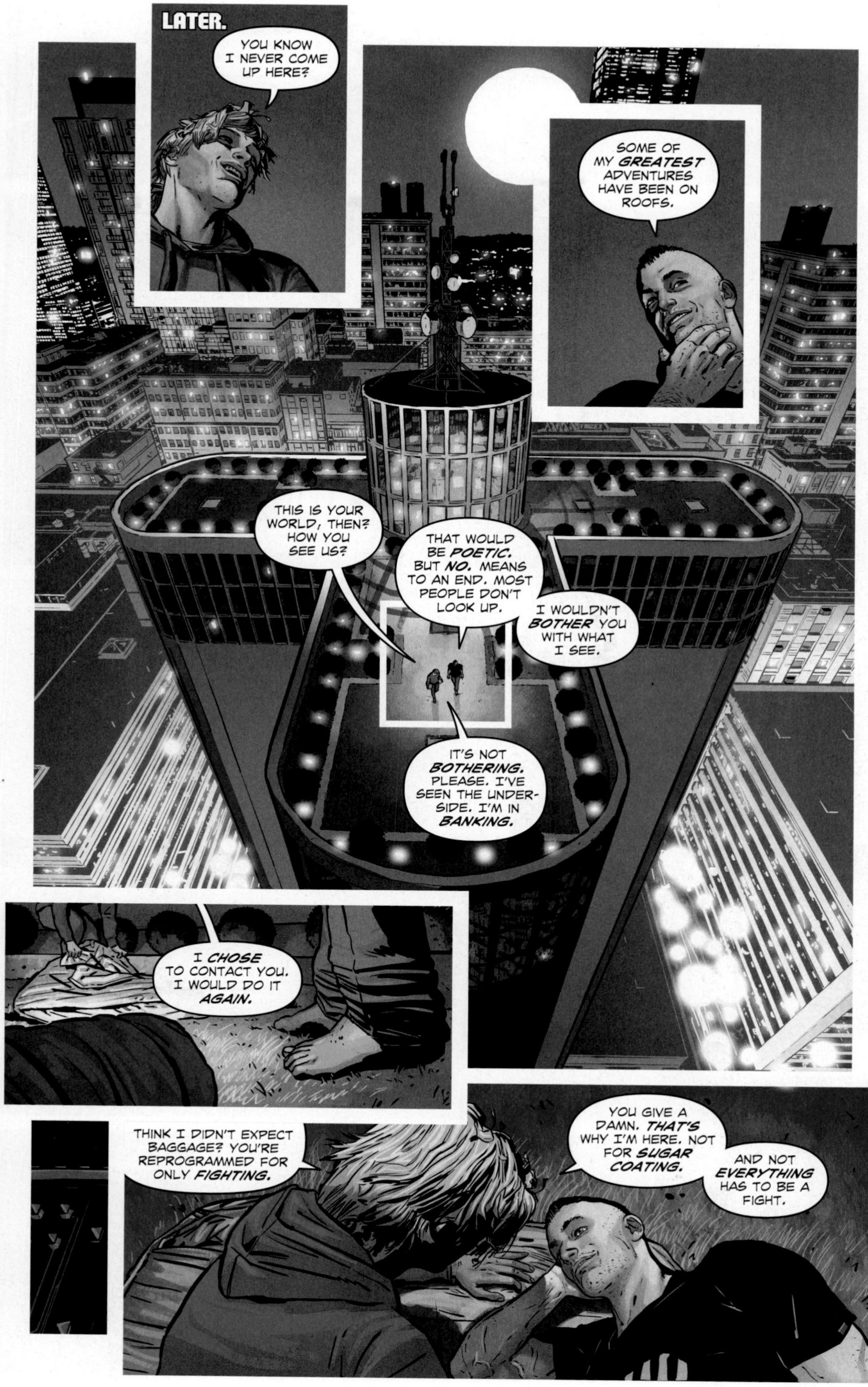
LATER.
YOU KNOW I NEVER COME UP HERE?
SOME OF MY GREATEST ADVENTURES HAVE BEEN ON ROOFS.
THIS IS YOUR WORLD, THEN? HOW YOU SEE US?
THAT WOULD BE POETIC. BUT NO. MEANS TO AN END. MOST PEOPLE DON'T LOOK UP.
I WOULDN'T BOTHER YOU WITH WHAT I SEE.
IT'S NOT BOTHERING. PLEASE. I'VE SEEN THE UNDER-SIDE. I'M IN BANKING.
I CHOSE TO CONTACT YOU. I WOULD DO IT AGAIN.
THINK I DIDN'T EXPECT BAGGAGE? YOU'RE REPROGRAMMED FOR ONLY FIGHTING.
YOU GIVE A DAMN. THAT'S WHY I'M HERE. NOT FOR SUGAR COATING.
AND NOT EVERYTHING HAS TO BE A FIGHT.

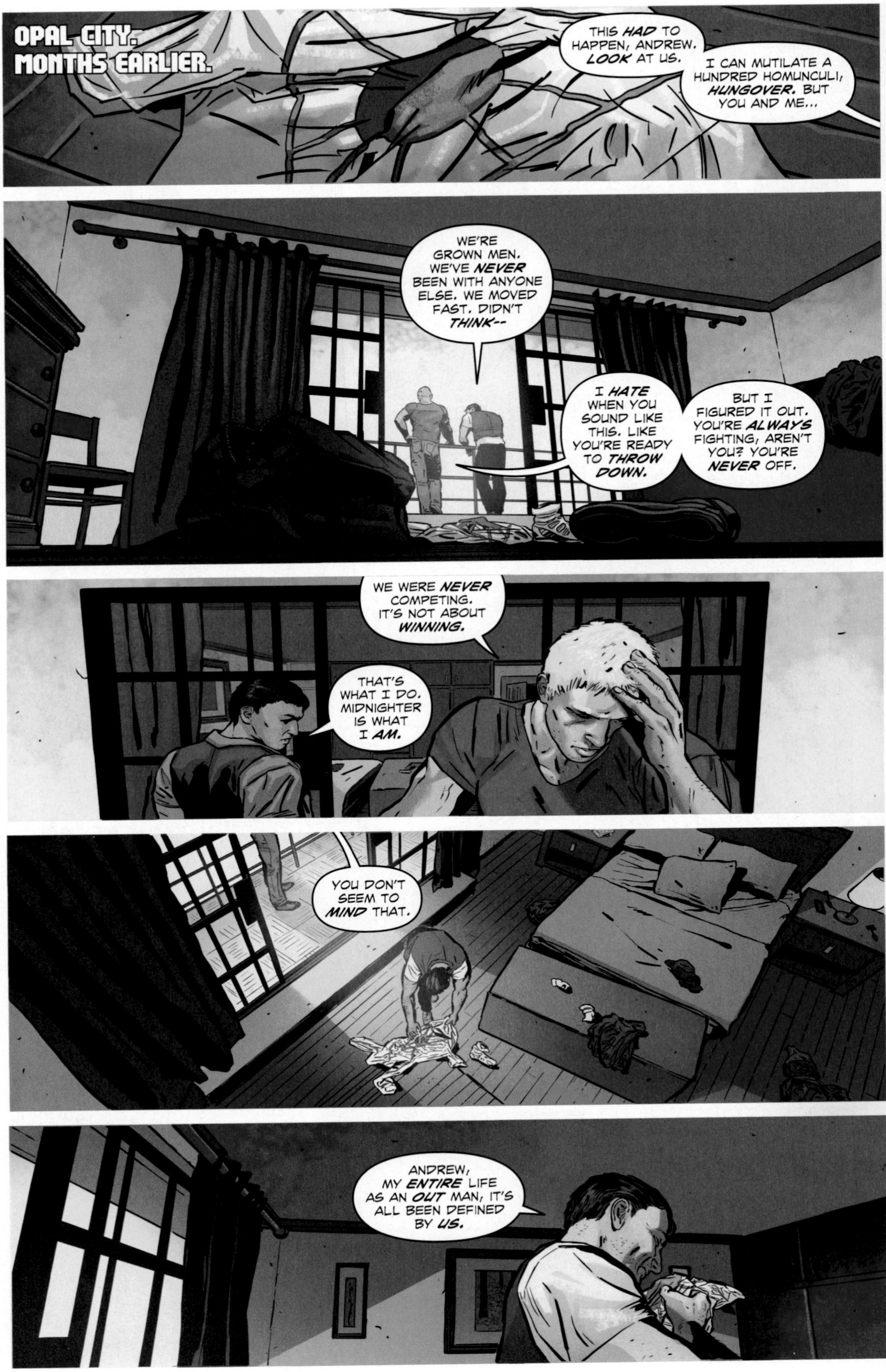
OPAL CITY.
MONTHS EARLIER.
THIS HAD TO HAPPEN, ANDREW. LOOK AT US.
I CAN MUTILATE A HUNDRED HOMUNCULI, HUNGOVER. BUT YOU AND ME...
WE'RE GROWN MEN. WE'VE NEVER BEEN WITH ANYONE ELSE. WE MOVED FAST. DIDN'T THINK--
I HATE WHEN YOU SOUND LIKE THIS. LIKE YOU'RE READY TO THROW DOWN.
BUT I FIGURED IT OUT. YOU'RE ALWAYS FIGHTING, AREN'T YOU? YOU'RE NEVER OFF.
WE WERE NEVER COMPETING. IT'S NOT ABOUT WINNING.
THAT'S WHAT I DO. MIDNIGHTER IS WHAT I AM.
YOU DON'T SEEM TO MIND THAT.
ANDREW, MY ENTIRE LIFE AS AN OUT MAN, IT'S ALL BEEN DEFINED BY US.

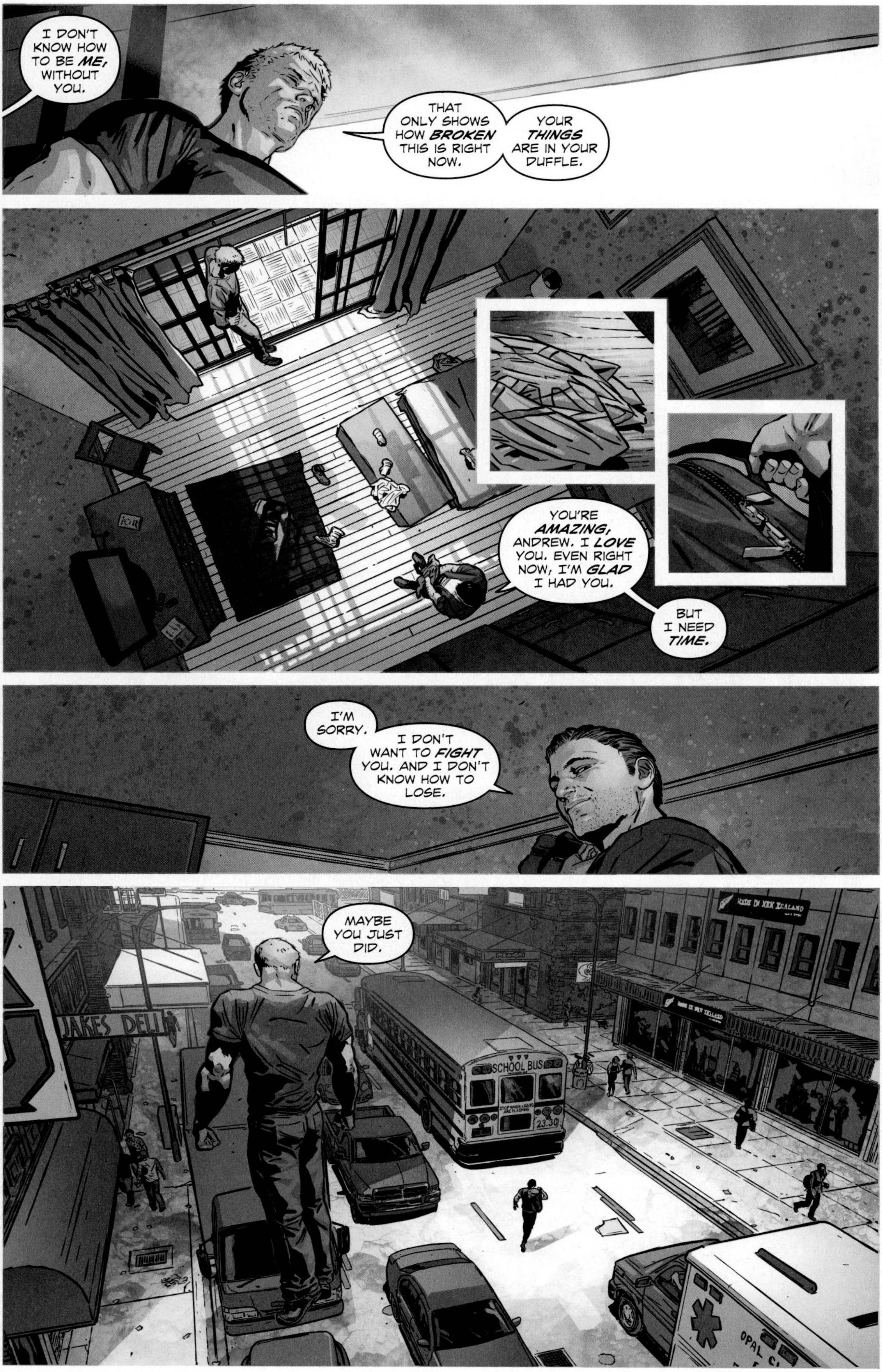
I DON'T KNOW HOW TO BE *ME,* WITHOUT YOU.
THAT ONLY SHOWS HOW *BROKEN* THIS IS RIGHT NOW.
YOUR *THINGS* ARE IN YOUR DUFFLE.
YOU'RE *AMAZING,* ANDREW. I *LOVE* YOU. EVEN RIGHT NOW, I'M *GLAD* I HAD YOU.
BUT I NEED *TIME.*
I'M SORRY.
I DON'T WANT TO *FIGHT* YOU. AND I DON'T KNOW HOW TO LOSE.
MAYBE YOU JUST DID.
JAKES DELI
SCHOOL BUS
23.30

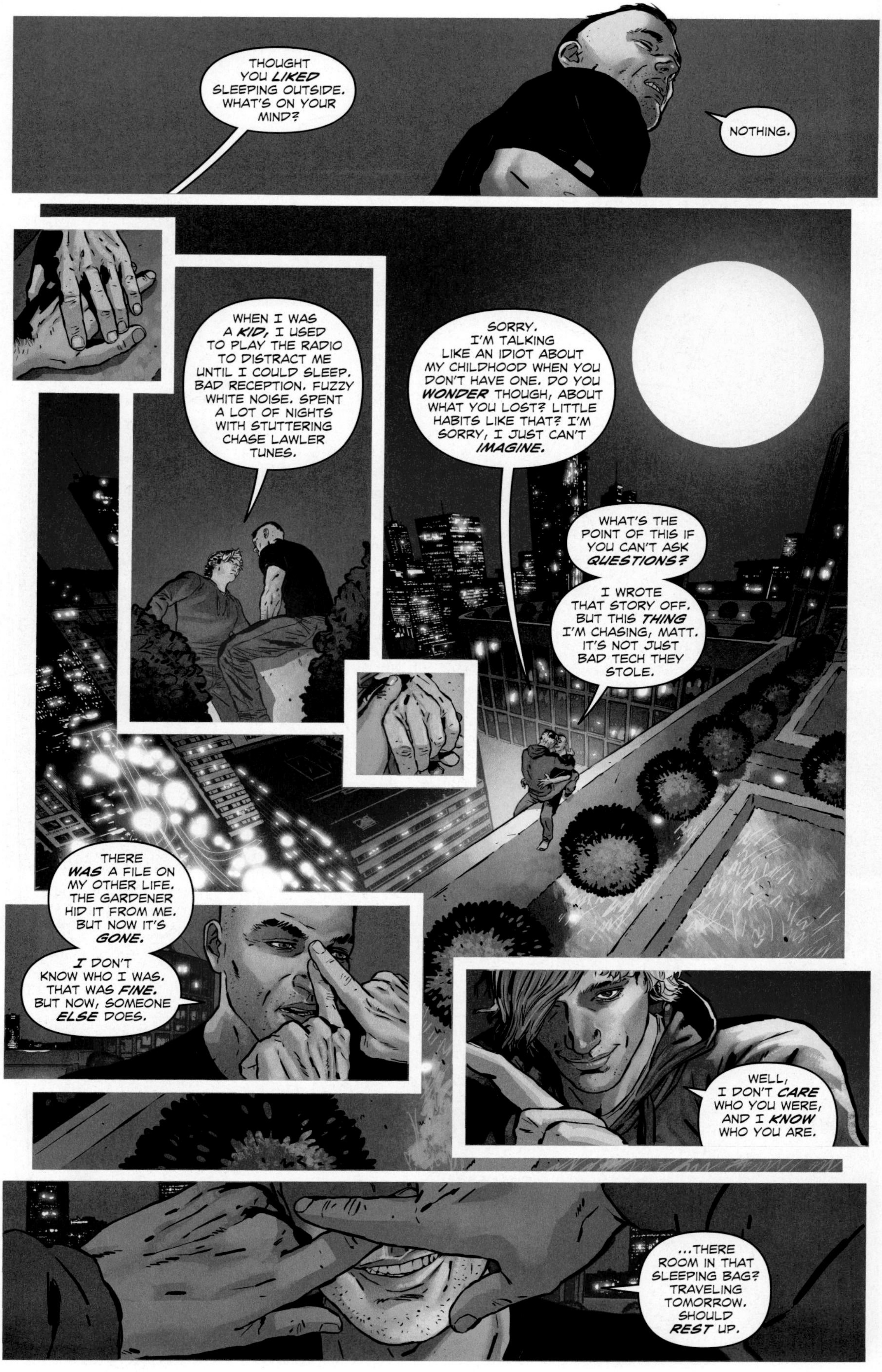
THOUGHT YOU *LIKED* SLEEPING OUTSIDE. WHAT'S ON YOUR MIND?
NOTHING.
WHEN I WAS A *KID,* I USED TO PLAY THE RADIO TO DISTRACT ME UNTIL I COULD SLEEP. BAD RECEPTION. FUZZY WHITE NOISE. SPENT A LOT OF NIGHTS WITH STUTTERING CHASE LAWLER TUNES.
SORRY. I'M TALKING LIKE AN IDIOT ABOUT MY CHILDHOOD WHEN YOU DON'T HAVE ONE. DO YOU *WONDER* THOUGH, ABOUT WHAT YOU LOST? LITTLE HABITS LIKE THAT? I'M SORRY, I JUST CAN'T *IMAGINE.*
WHAT'S THE POINT OF THIS IF YOU CAN'T ASK *QUESTIONS?*
I WROTE THAT STORY OFF. BUT THIS *THING* I'M CHASING, MATT. IT'S NOT JUST BAD TECH THEY STOLE.
THERE *WAS* A FILE ON MY OTHER LIFE. THE GARDENER HID IT FROM ME. BUT NOW IT'S *GONE.*
I DON'T KNOW WHO I WAS. THAT WAS *FINE.* BUT NOW, SOMEONE *ELSE* DOES.
WELL, I DON'T *CARE* WHO YOU WERE, AND I *KNOW* WHO YOU ARE.
...THERE ROOM IN THAT SLEEPING BAG? TRAVELING TOMORROW. SHOULD *REST* UP.

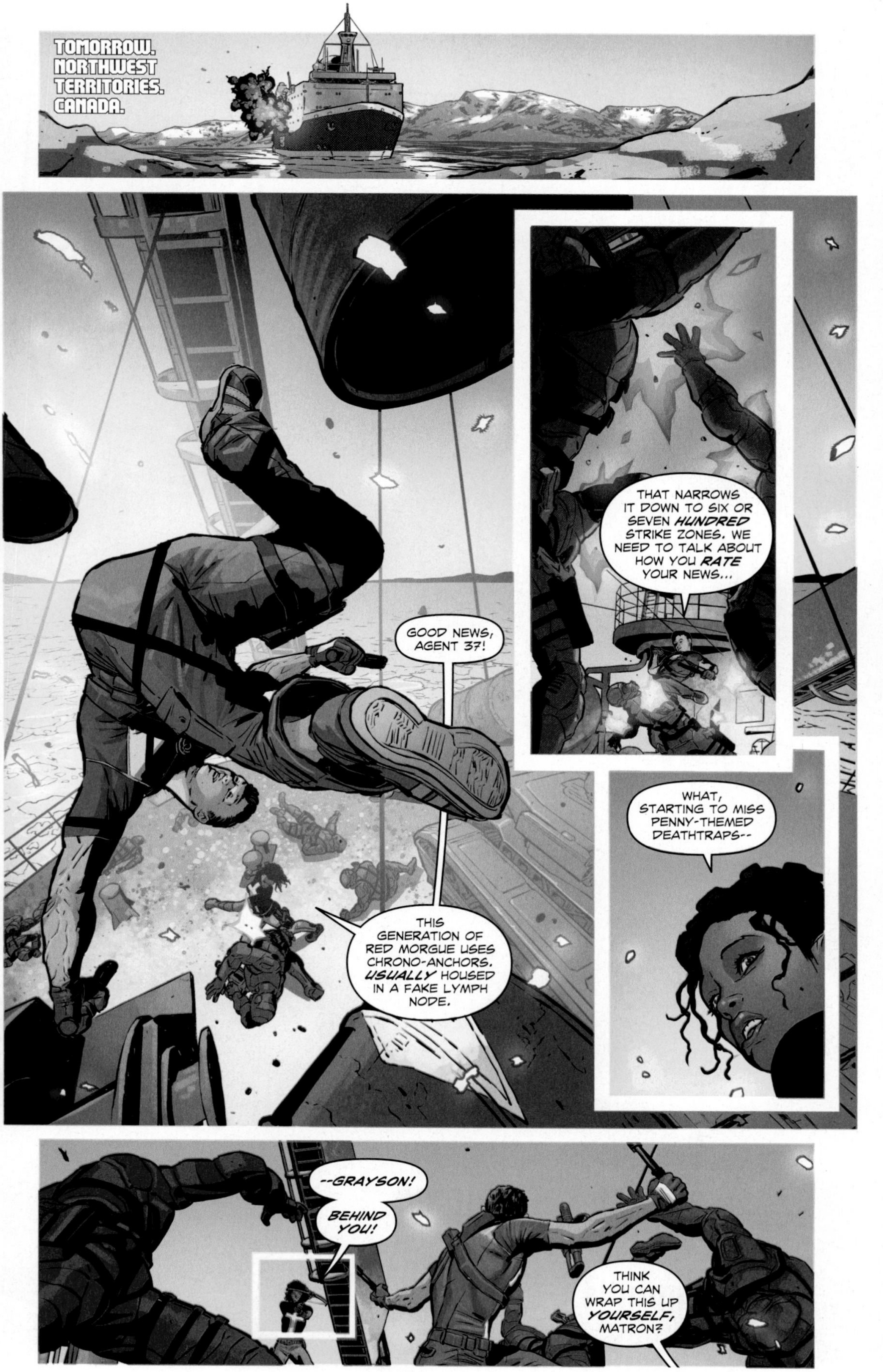

TOMORROW. NORTHWEST TERRITORIES. CANADA.
GOOD NEWS, AGENT 37!
THIS GENERATION OF RED MORGUE USES CHRONO-ANCHORS. *USUALLY* HOUSED IN A FAKE LYMPH NODE.
THAT NARROWS IT DOWN TO SIX OR SEVEN *HUNDRED* STRIKE ZONES. WE NEED TO TALK ABOUT HOW YOU *RATE* YOUR NEWS...
WHAT, STARTING TO MISS PENNY-THEMED DEATHTRAPS--
--GRAYSON!
BEHIND YOU!
THINK YOU CAN WRAP THIS UP *YOURSELF,* MATRON?

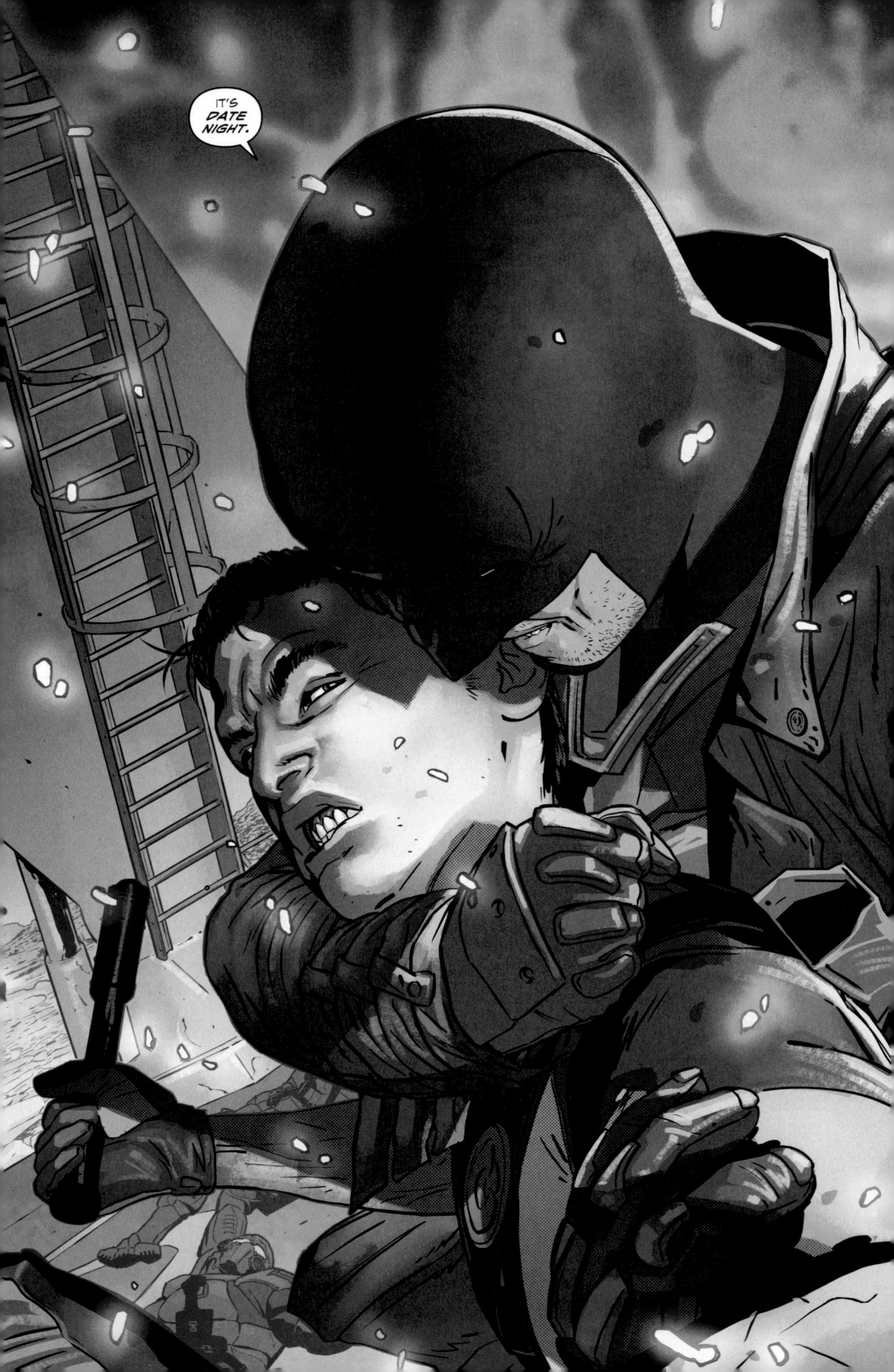
IT'S *DATE NIGHT.*

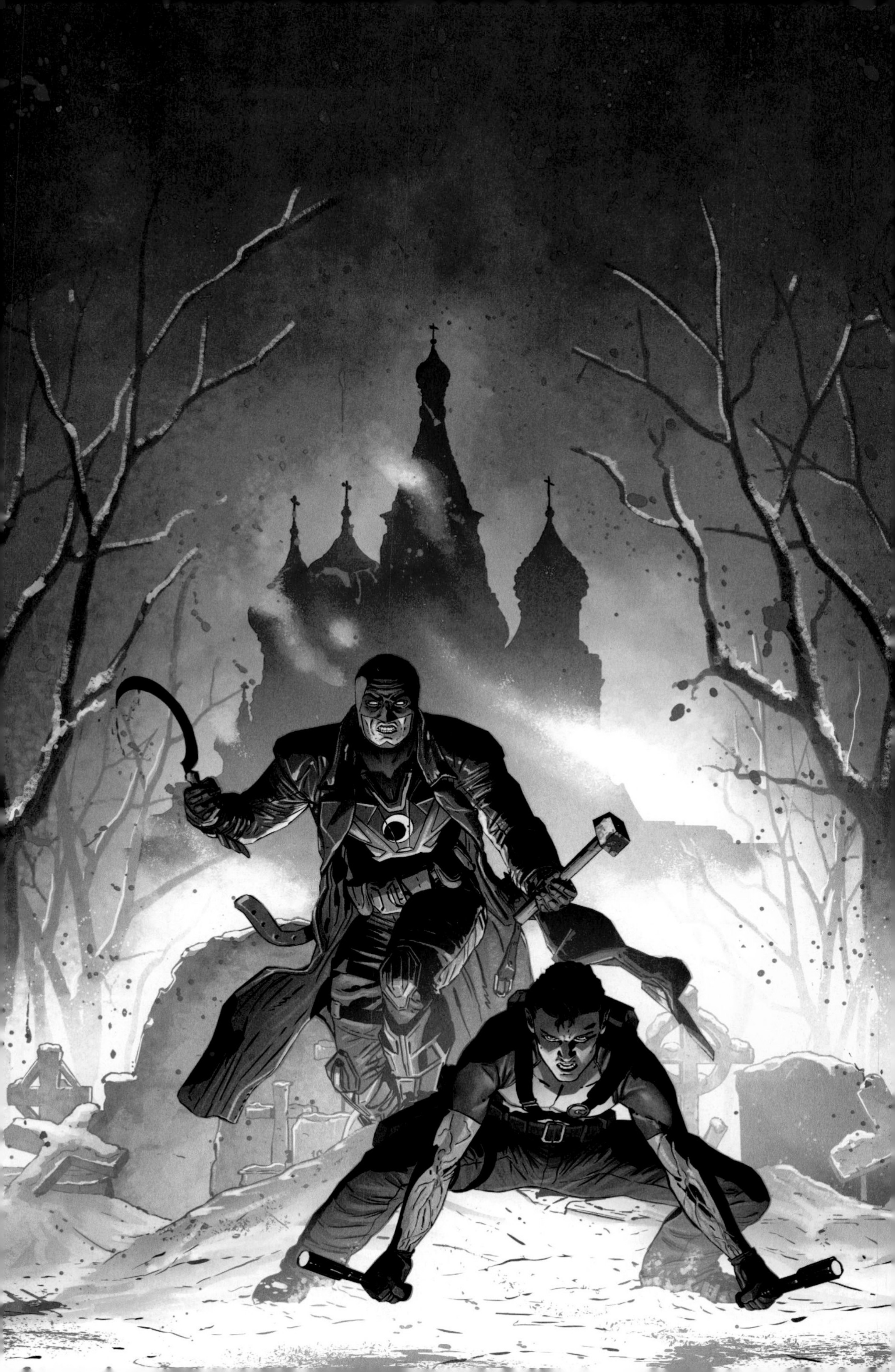

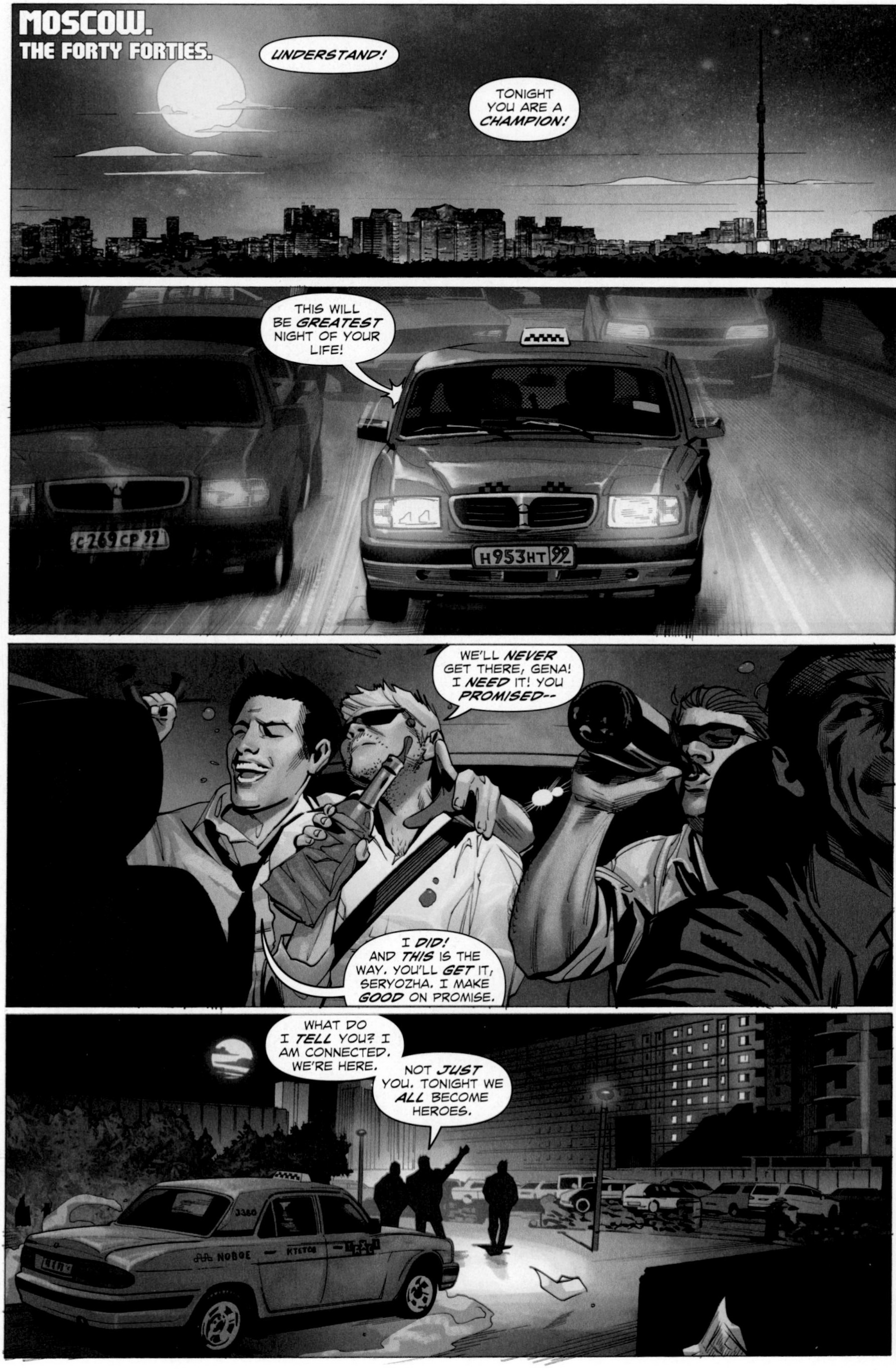
MOSCOW.
THE FORTY FORTIES.
UNDERSTAND!
TONIGHT YOU ARE A CHAMPION!
THIS WILL BE GREATEST NIGHT OF YOUR LIFE!
WE'LL NEVER GET THERE, GENA! I NEED IT! YOU PROMISED--
I DID! AND THIS IS THE WAY. YOU'LL GET IT, SERYOZHA. I MAKE GOOD ON PROMISE.
WHAT DO I TELL YOU? I AM CONNECTED. WE'RE HERE.
NOT JUST YOU. TONIGHT WE ALL BECOME HEROES.

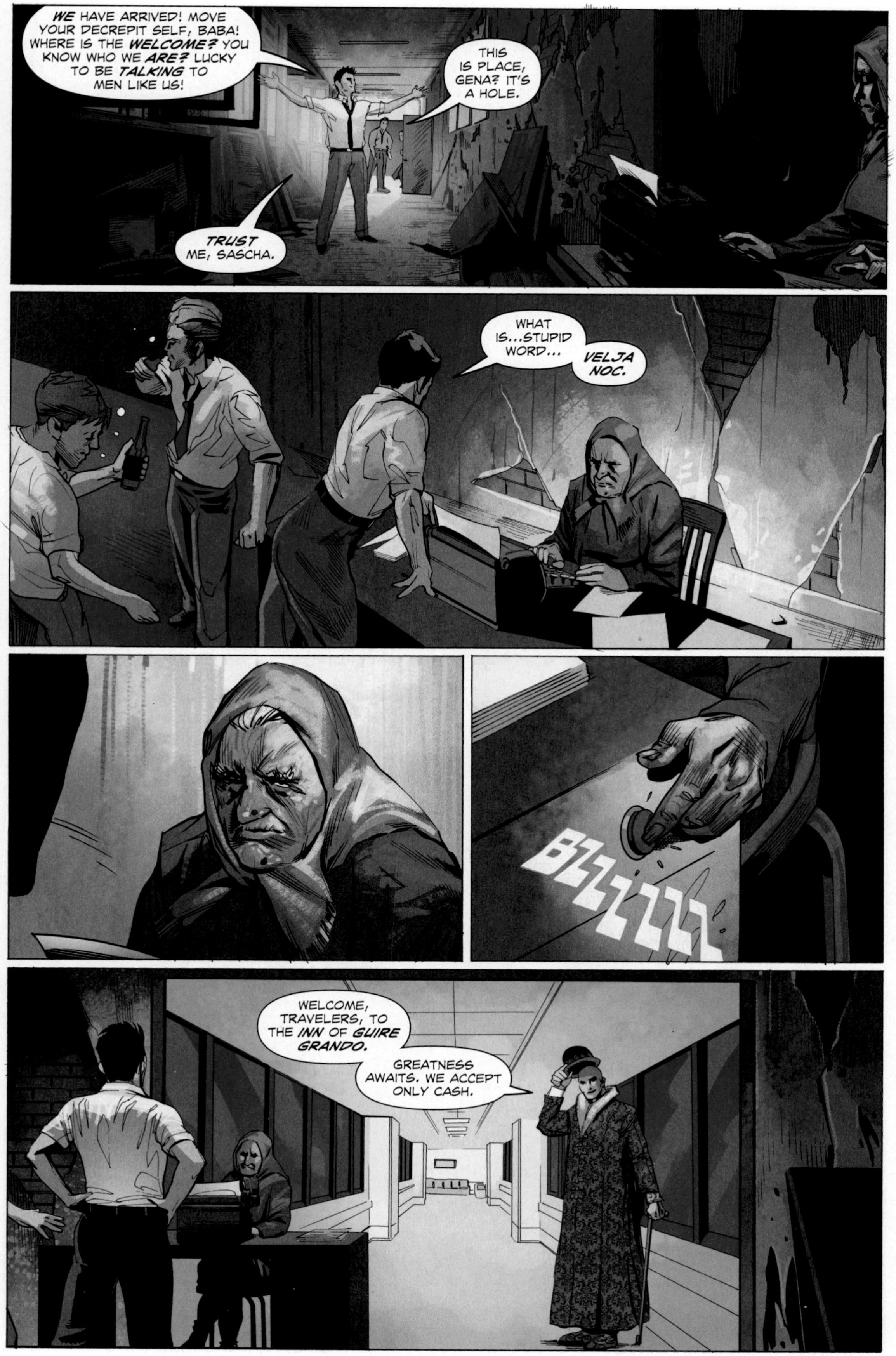
WE HAVE ARRIVED! MOVE YOUR DECREPIT SELF, BABA! WHERE IS THE WELCOME? YOU KNOW WHO WE ARE? LUCKY TO BE TALKING TO MEN LIKE US!
THIS IS PLACE, GENA? IT'S A HOLE.
TRUST ME, SASCHA.
WHAT IS...STUPID WORD... VELJA NOC.
BZZZZZZ
WELCOME, TRAVELERS, TO THE INN OF GUIRE GRANDO.
GREATNESS AWAITS. WE ACCEPT ONLY CASH.

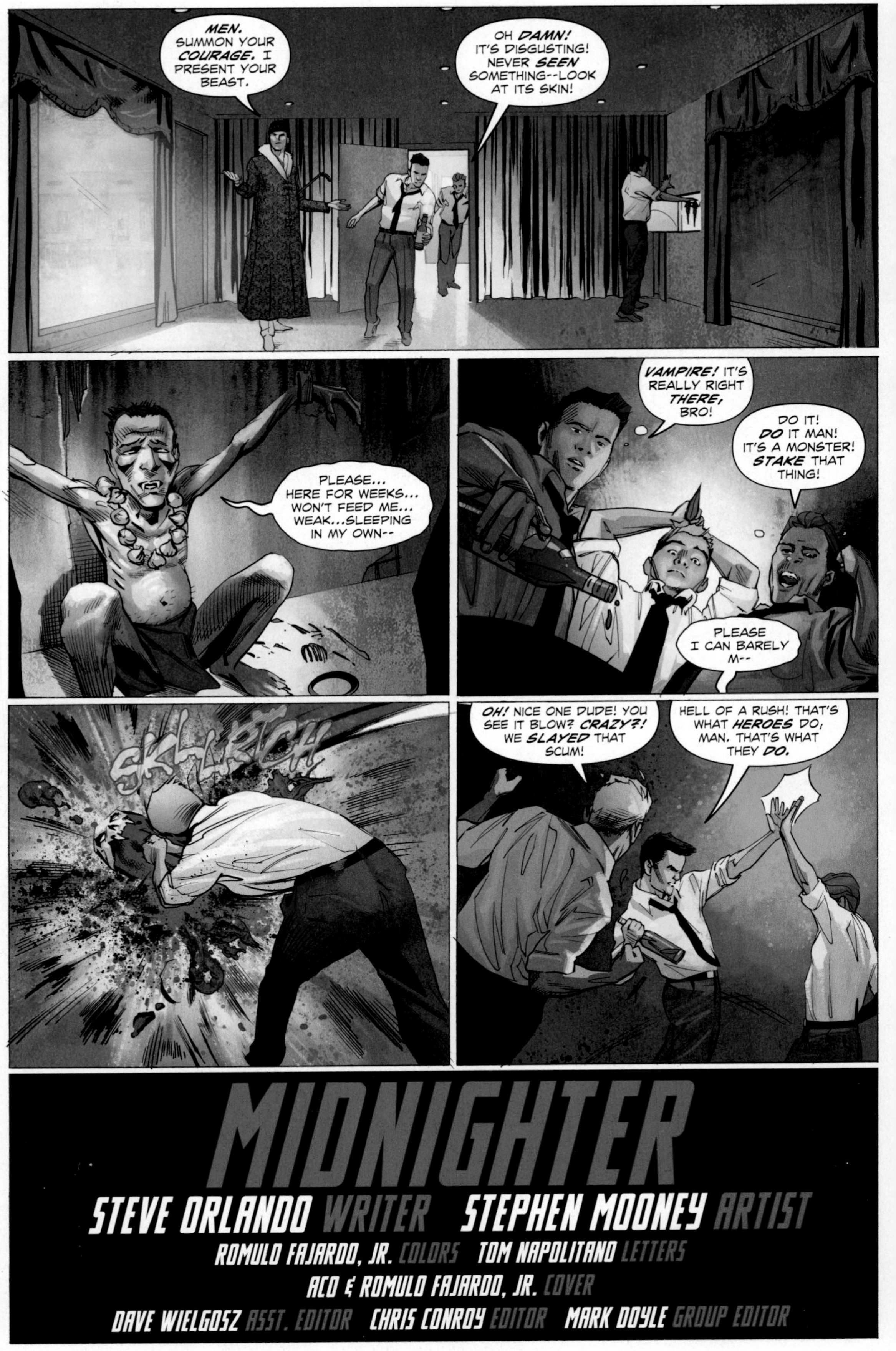
MEN. SUMMON YOUR COURAGE. I PRESENT YOUR BEAST.
OH DAMN! IT'S DISGUSTING! NEVER SEEN SOMETHING--LOOK AT ITS SKIN!
PLEASE... HERE FOR WEEKS... WON'T FEED ME... WEAK...SLEEPING IN MY OWN--
VAMPIRE! IT'S REALLY RIGHT THERE, BRO!
DO IT! DO IT MAN! IT'S A MONSTER! STAKE THAT THING!
PLEASE I CAN BARELY M--
SKHLRCH
OH! NICE ONE DUDE! YOU SEE IT BLOW? CRAZY?! WE SLAYED THAT SCUM!
HELL OF A RUSH! THAT'S WHAT HEROES DO, MAN. THAT'S WHAT THEY DO.

MIDNIGHTER

STEVE ORLANDO WRITER STEPHEN MOONEY ARTIST

ROMULO FAJARDO, JR. COLORS TOM NAPOLITANO LETTERS

ACO & ROMULO FAJARDO, JR. COVER

DAVE WIELGOSZ ASST. EDITOR CHRIS CONROY EDITOR MARK DOYLE GROUP EDITOR

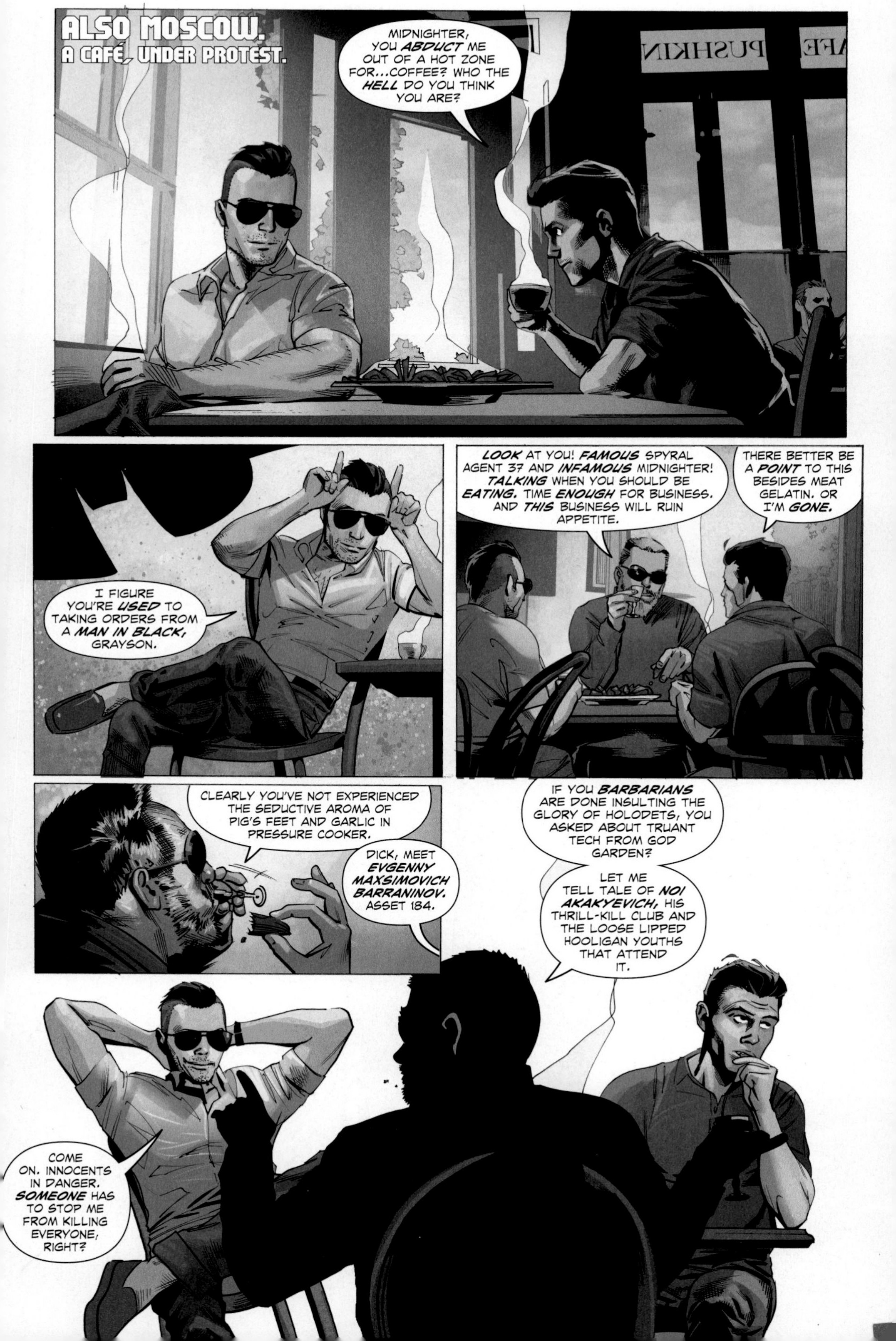
ALSO MOSCOW.
A CAFÉ, UNDER PROTEST.
MIDNIGHTER, YOU ABDUCT ME OUT OF A HOT ZONE FOR...COFFEE? WHO THE HELL DO YOU THINK YOU ARE?
PUSHKIN
I FIGURE YOU'RE USED TO TAKING ORDERS FROM A MAN IN BLACK, GRAYSON.
LOOK AT YOU! FAMOUS SPYRAL AGENT 37 AND INFAMOUS MIDNIGHTER! TALKING WHEN YOU SHOULD BE EATING. TIME ENOUGH FOR BUSINESS. AND THIS BUSINESS WILL RUIN APPETITE.
THERE BETTER BE A POINT TO THIS BESIDES MEAT GELATIN. OR I'M GONE.
CLEARLY YOU'VE NOT EXPERIENCED THE SEDUCTIVE AROMA OF PIG'S FEET AND GARLIC IN PRESSURE COOKER.
DICK, MEET EVGENNY MAXSIMOVICH BARRANINOV. ASSET 184.
IF YOU BARBARIANS ARE DONE INSULTING THE GLORY OF HOLODETS, YOU ASKED ABOUT TRUANT TECH FROM GOD GARDEN?
LET ME TELL TALE OF NOI AKAKYEVICH, HIS THRILL-KILL CLUB AND THE LOOSE LIPPED HOOLIGAN YOUTHS THAT ATTEND IT.
COME ON. INNOCENTS IN DANGER. SOMEONE HAS TO STOP ME FROM KILLING EVERYONE, RIGHT?

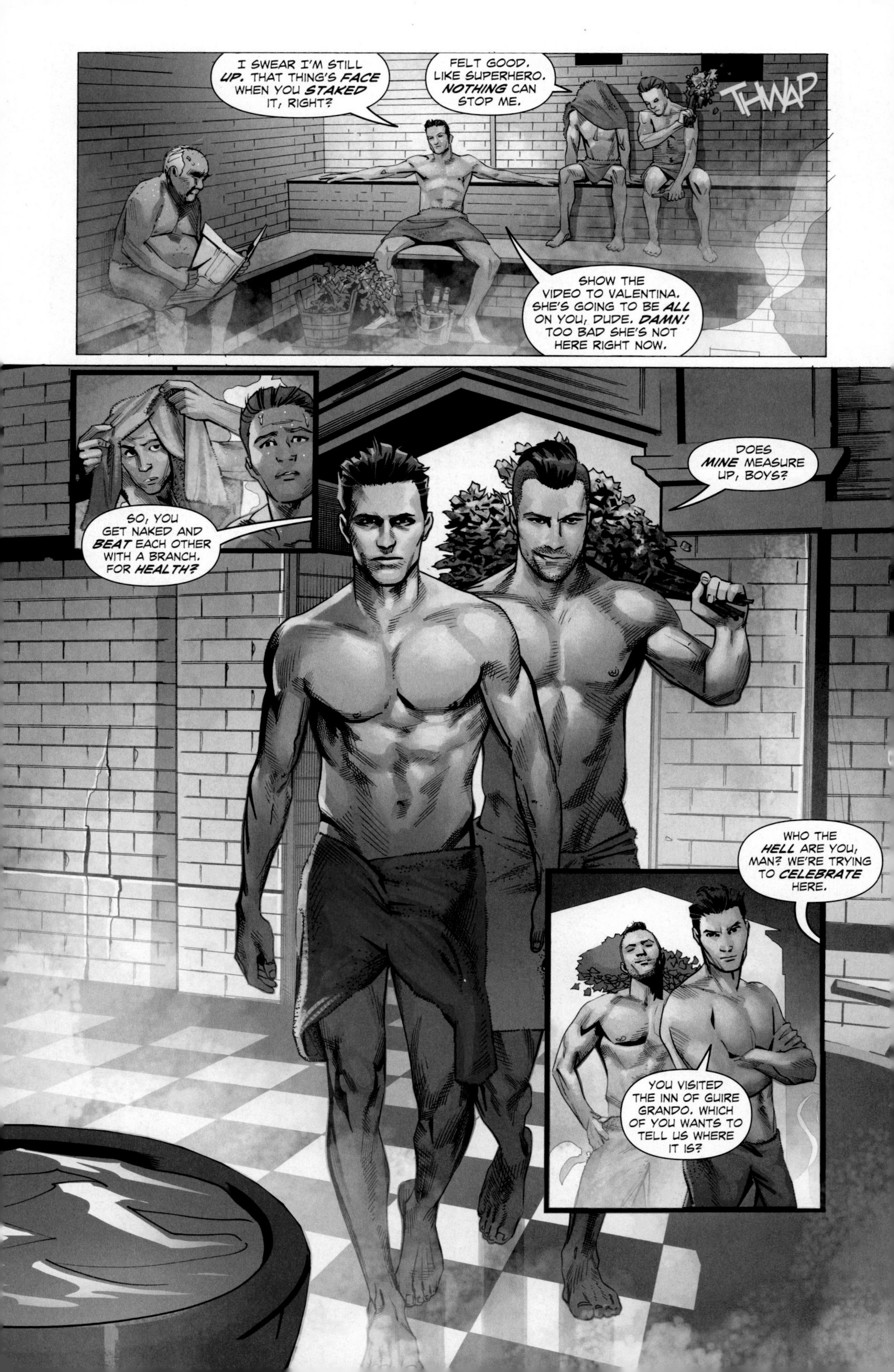
I SWEAR I'M STILL UP. THAT THING'S FACE WHEN YOU STAKED IT, RIGHT?
FELT GOOD. LIKE SUPERHERO. NOTHING CAN STOP ME.
THWAP
SHOW THE VIDEO TO VALENTINA. SHE'S GOING TO BE ALL ON YOU, DUDE. DAMN! TOO BAD SHE'S NOT HERE RIGHT NOW.
SO, YOU GET NAKED AND BEAT EACH OTHER WITH A BRANCH. FOR HEALTH?
DOES MINE MEASURE UP, BOYS?
WHO THE HELL ARE YOU, MAN? WE'RE TRYING TO CELEBRATE HERE.
YOU VISITED THE INN OF GUIRE GRANDO. WHICH OF YOU WANTS TO TELL US WHERE IT IS?

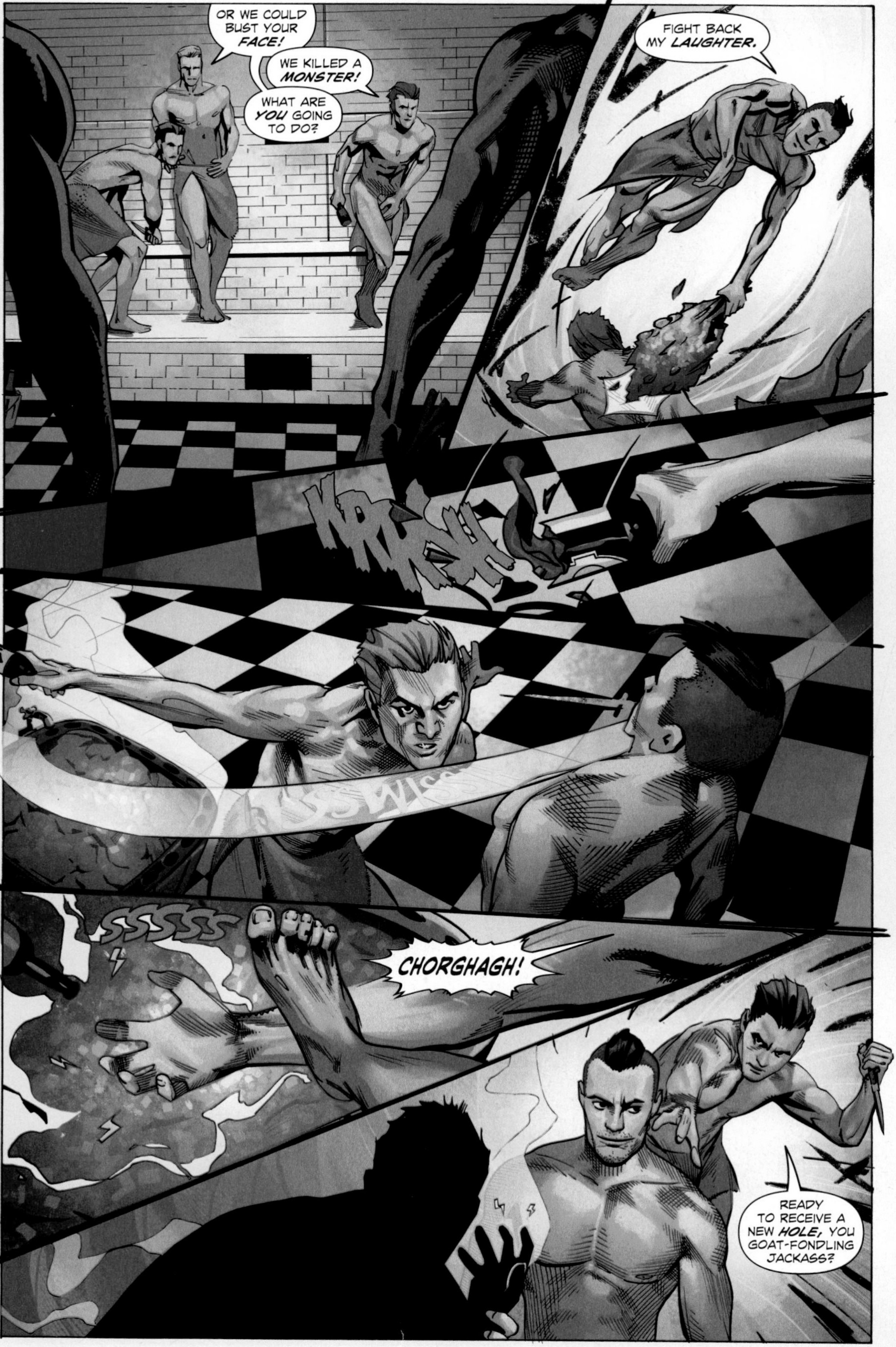

OR WE COULD BUST YOUR *FACE!*
WE KILLED A *MONSTER!*
WHAT ARE *YOU* GOING TO DO?
FIGHT BACK MY *LAUGHTER.*
KRUSH
SSSSS
CHORGHAGH!
READY TO RECEIVE A NEW *HOLE,* YOU GOAT-FONDLING JACKASS?

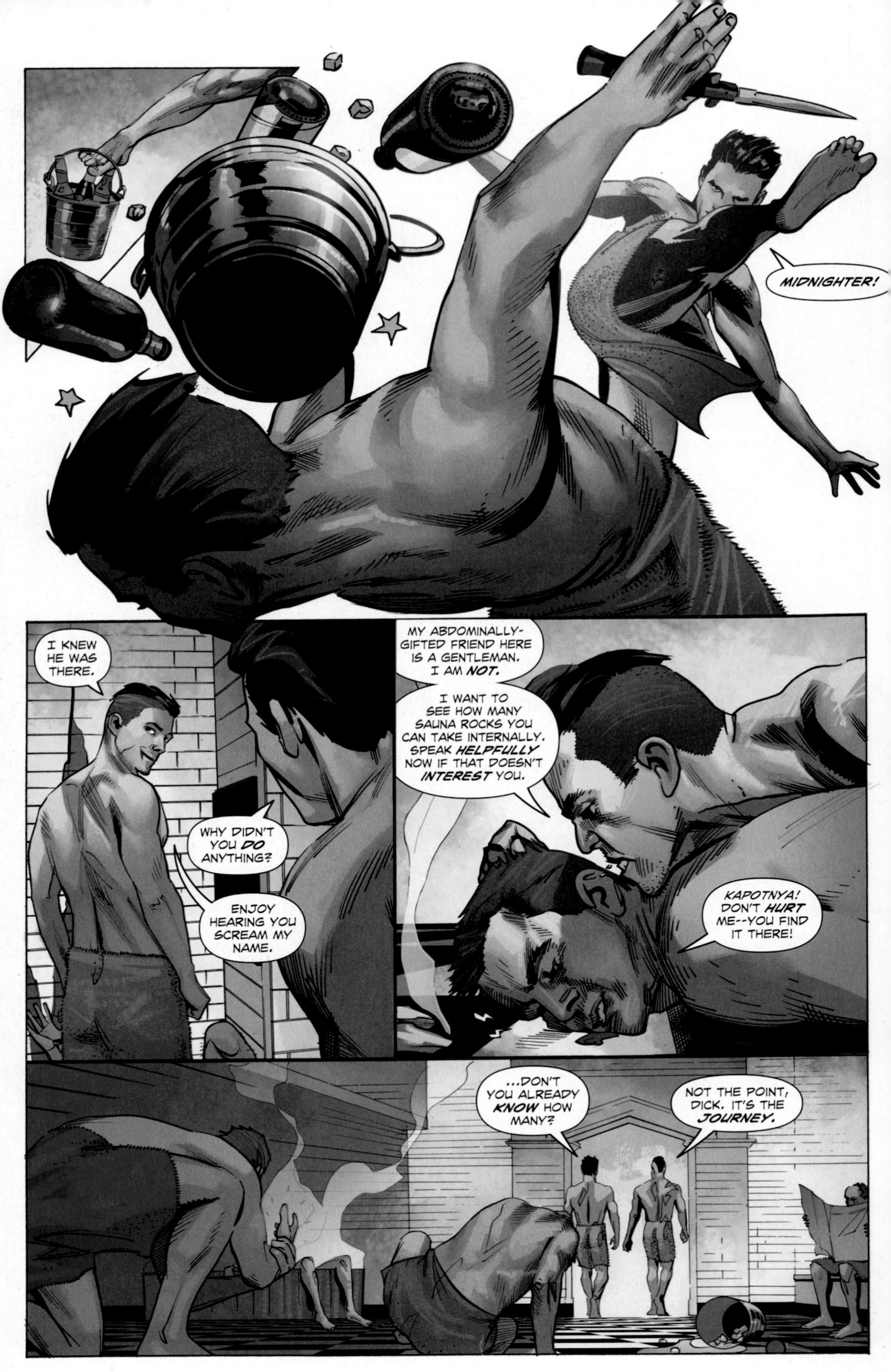
MIDNIGHTER!
I KNEW HE WAS THERE.
WHY DIDN'T YOU DO ANYTHING?
ENJOY HEARING YOU SCREAM MY NAME.
MY ABDOMINALLY-GIFTED FRIEND HERE IS A GENTLEMAN. I AM NOT.
I WANT TO SEE HOW MANY SAUNA ROCKS YOU CAN TAKE INTERNALLY. SPEAK HELPFULLY NOW IF THAT DOESN'T INTEREST YOU.
KAPOTNYA! DON'T HURT ME--YOU FIND IT THERE!
...DON'T YOU ALREADY KNOW HOW MANY?
NOT THE POINT, DICK. IT'S THE JOURNEY.

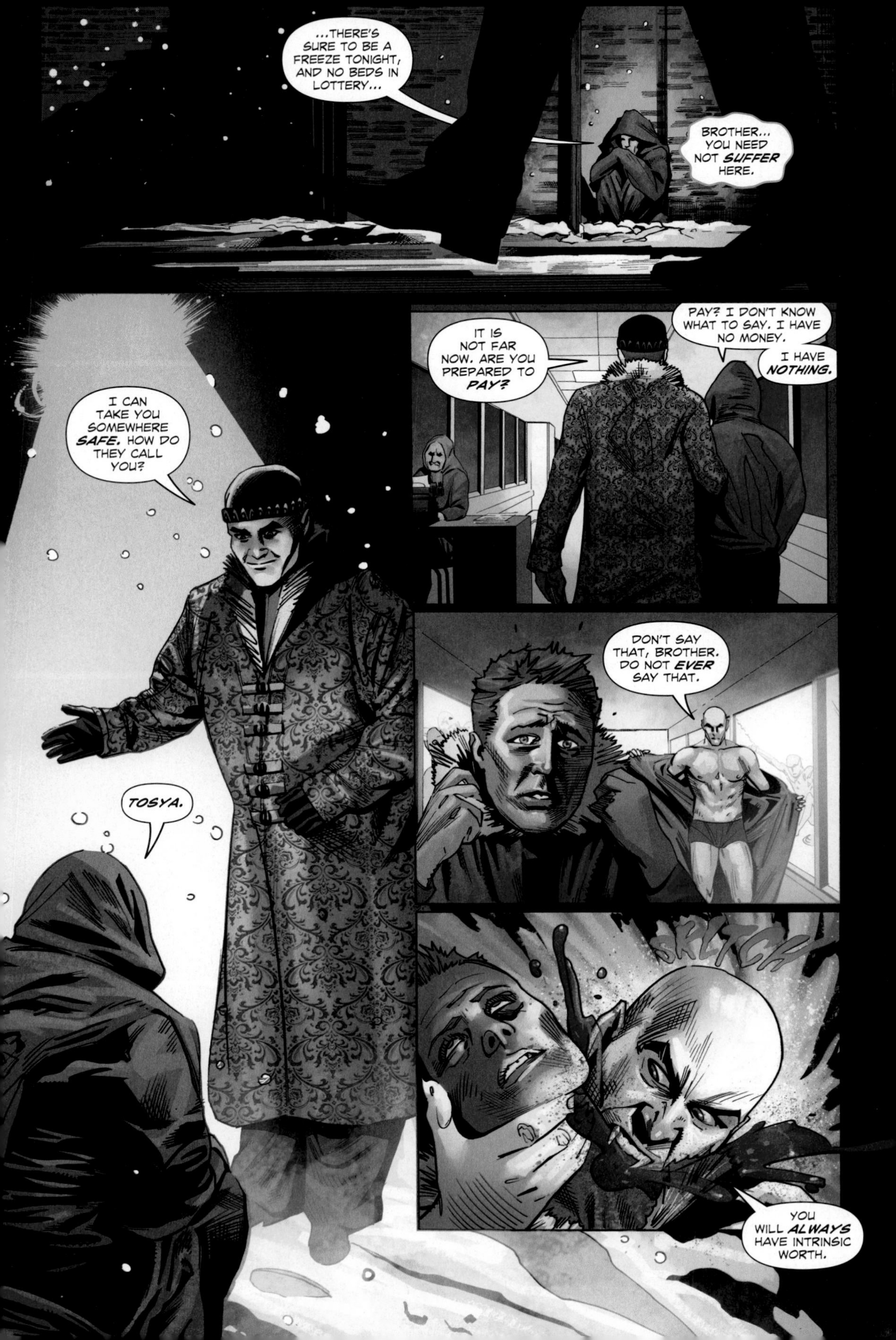
...THERE'S SURE TO BE A FREEZE TONIGHT, AND NO BEDS IN LOTTERY...
BROTHER... YOU NEED NOT SUFFER HERE.
I CAN TAKE YOU SOMEWHERE SAFE. HOW DO THEY CALL YOU?
TOSYA.
IT IS NOT FAR NOW. ARE YOU PREPARED TO PAY?
PAY? I DON'T KNOW WHAT TO SAY. I HAVE NO MONEY.
I HAVE NOTHING.
DON'T SAY THAT, BROTHER. DO NOT EVER SAY THAT.
SRLTCH
YOU WILL ALWAYS HAVE INTRINSIC WORTH.

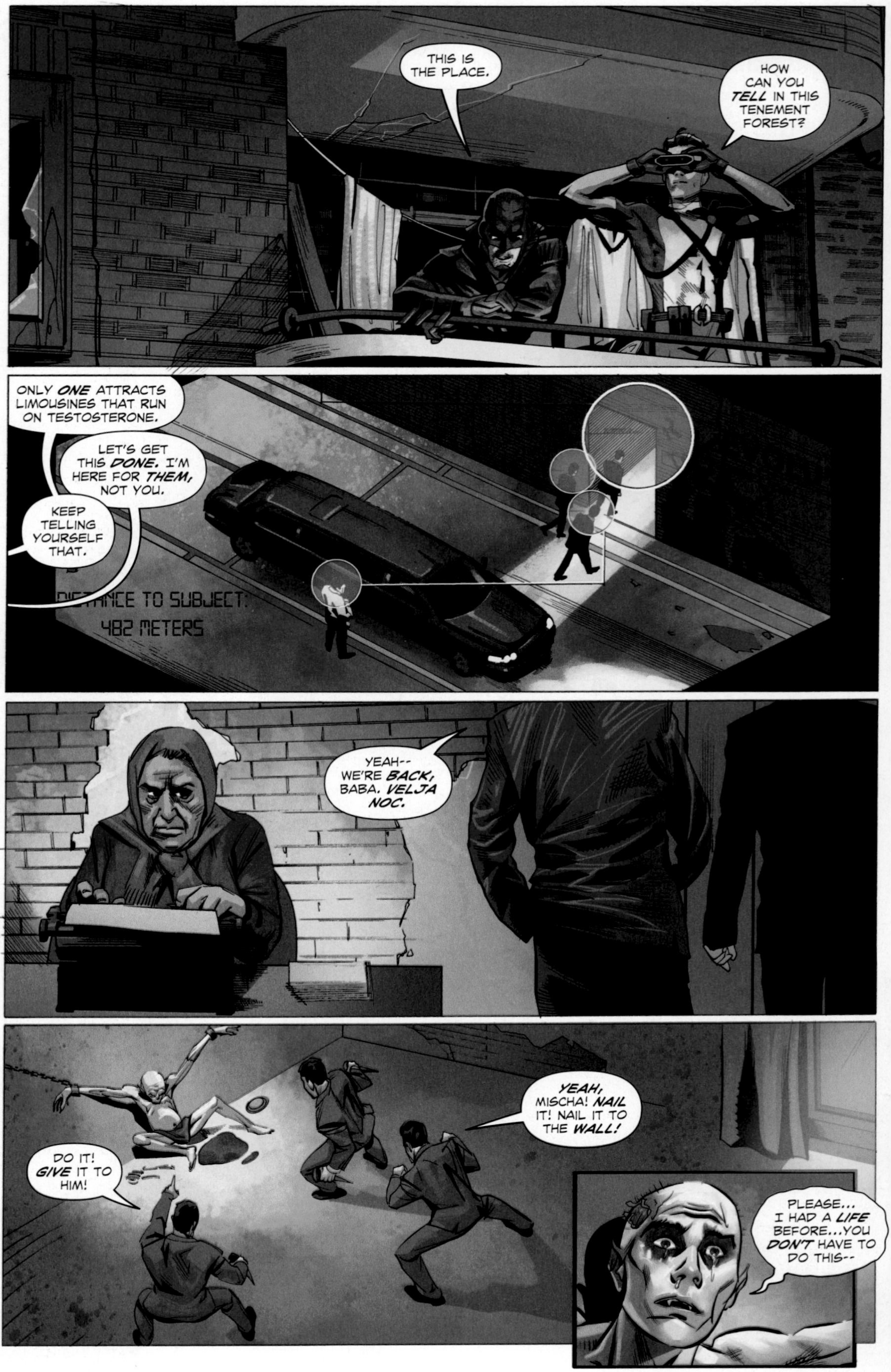
THIS IS THE PLACE.
HOW CAN YOU TELL IN THIS TENEMENT FOREST?
ONLY ONE ATTRACTS LIMOUSINES THAT RUN ON TESTOSTERONE.
LET'S GET THIS DONE. I'M HERE FOR THEM, NOT YOU.
KEEP TELLING YOURSELF THAT.
DISTANCE TO SUBJECT:
482 METERS
YEAH-- WE'RE BACK, BABA. VELJA NOC.
YEAH, MISCHA! NAIL IT! NAIL IT TO THE WALL!
DO IT! GIVE IT TO HIM!
PLEASE... I HAD A LIFE BEFORE...YOU DON'T HAVE TO DO THIS--

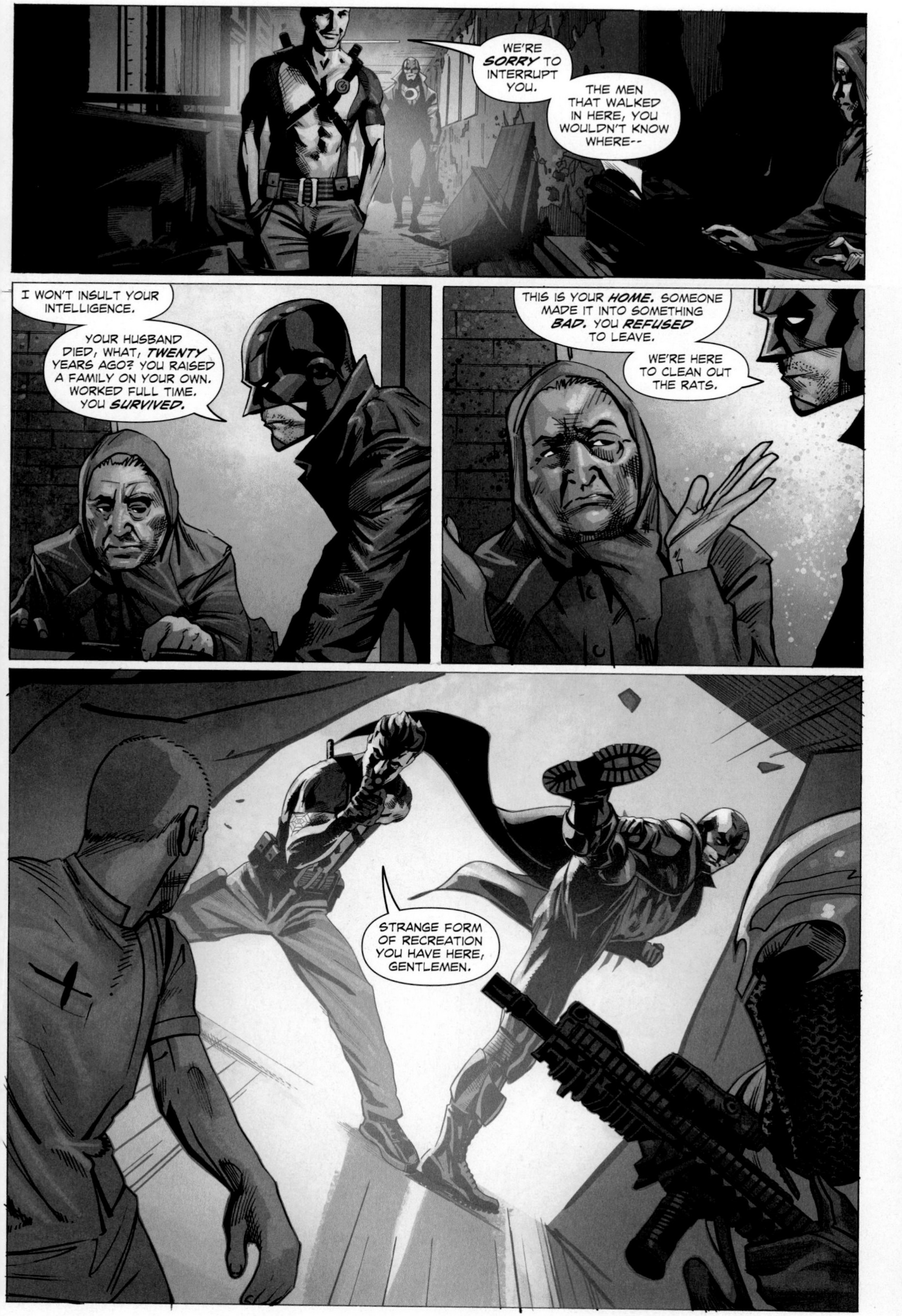
WE'RE SORRY TO INTERRUPT YOU.
THE MEN THAT WALKED IN HERE, YOU WOULDN'T KNOW WHERE--
I WON'T INSULT YOUR INTELLIGENCE.
YOUR HUSBAND DIED, WHAT, TWENTY YEARS AGO? YOU RAISED A FAMILY ON YOUR OWN. WORKED FULL TIME. YOU SURVIVED.
THIS IS YOUR HOME. SOMEONE MADE IT INTO SOMETHING BAD. YOU REFUSED TO LEAVE.
WE'RE HERE TO CLEAN OUT THE RATS.
STRANGE FORM OF RECREATION YOU HAVE HERE, GENTLEMEN.

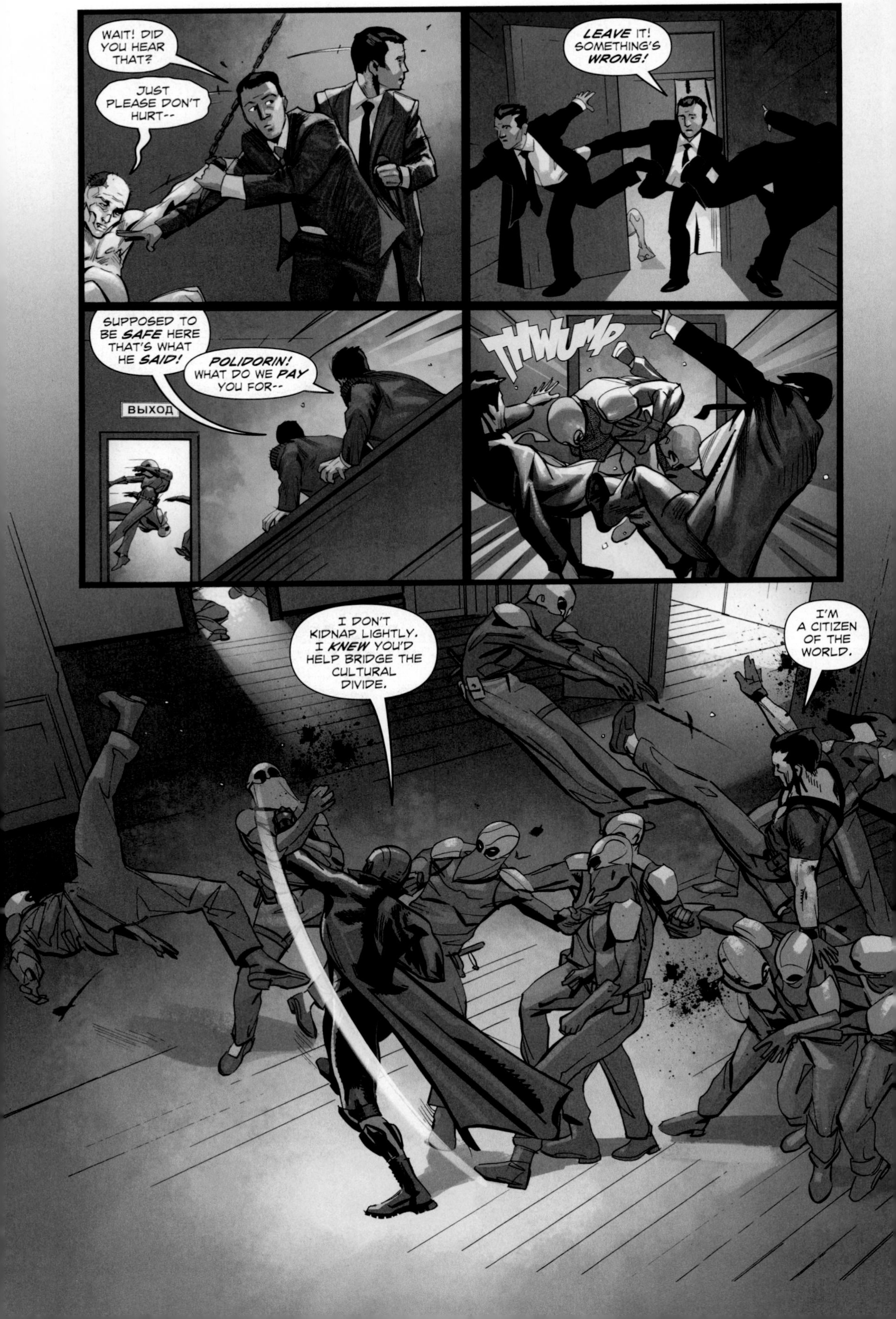
WAIT! DID YOU HEAR THAT?
JUST PLEASE DON'T HURT--
LEAVE IT! SOMETHING'S WRONG!
SUPPOSED TO BE SAFE HERE THAT'S WHAT HE SAID!
POLIDORIN! WHAT DO WE PAY YOU FOR--
ВЫХОД
THWUMP
I DON'T KIDNAP LIGHTLY. I KNEW YOU'D HELP BRIDGE THE CULTURAL DIVIDE.
I'M A CITIZEN OF THE WORLD.

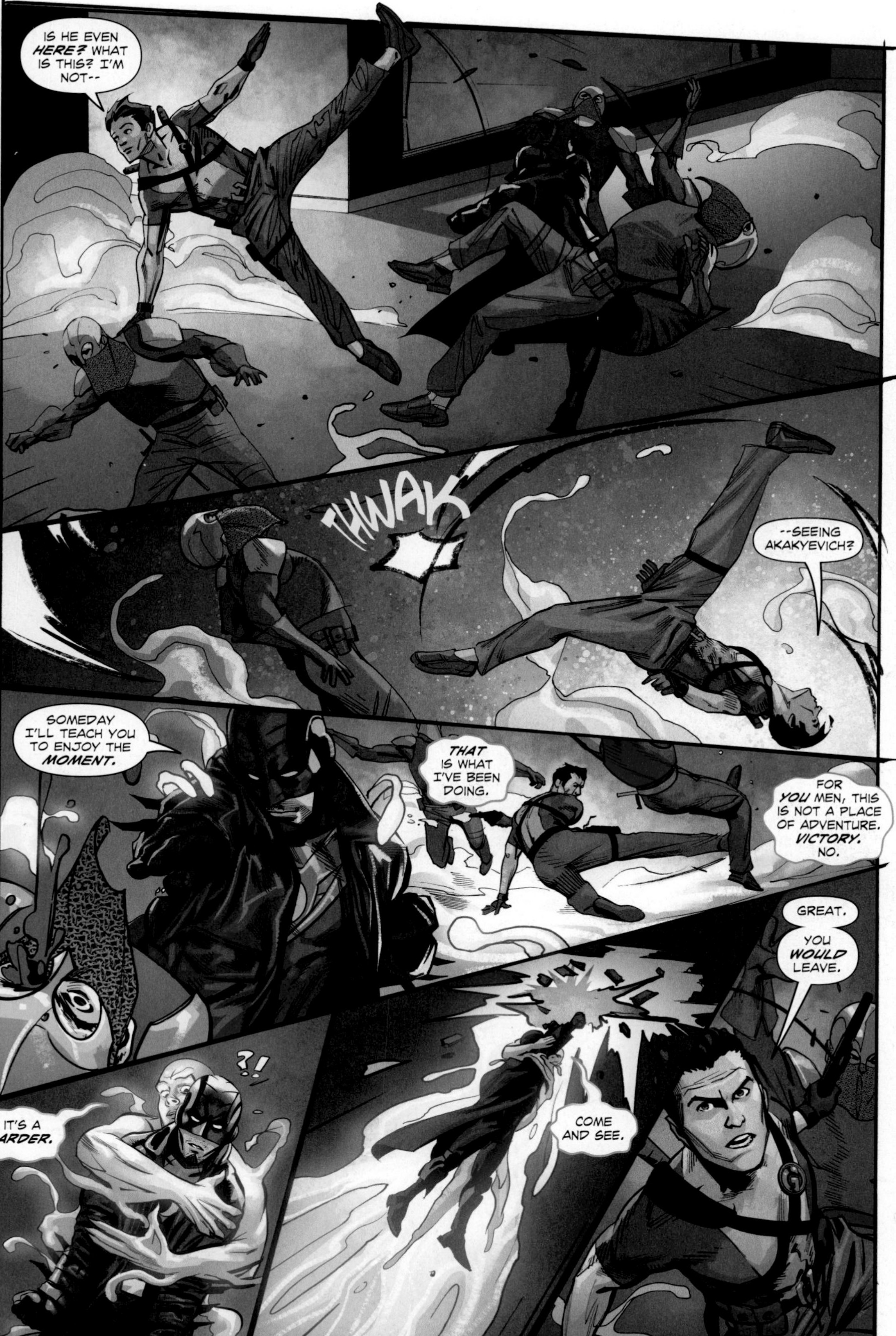
IS HE EVEN HERE? WHAT IS THIS? I'M NOT--
THWAK
--SEEING AKAKYEVICH?
SOMEDAY I'LL TEACH YOU TO ENJOY THE MOMENT.
THAT IS WHAT I'VE BEEN DOING.
FOR YOU MEN, THIS IS NOT A PLACE OF ADVENTURE. VICTORY. NO.
GREAT.
YOU WOULD LEAVE.
?!
IT'S A LARDER.
COME AND SEE.

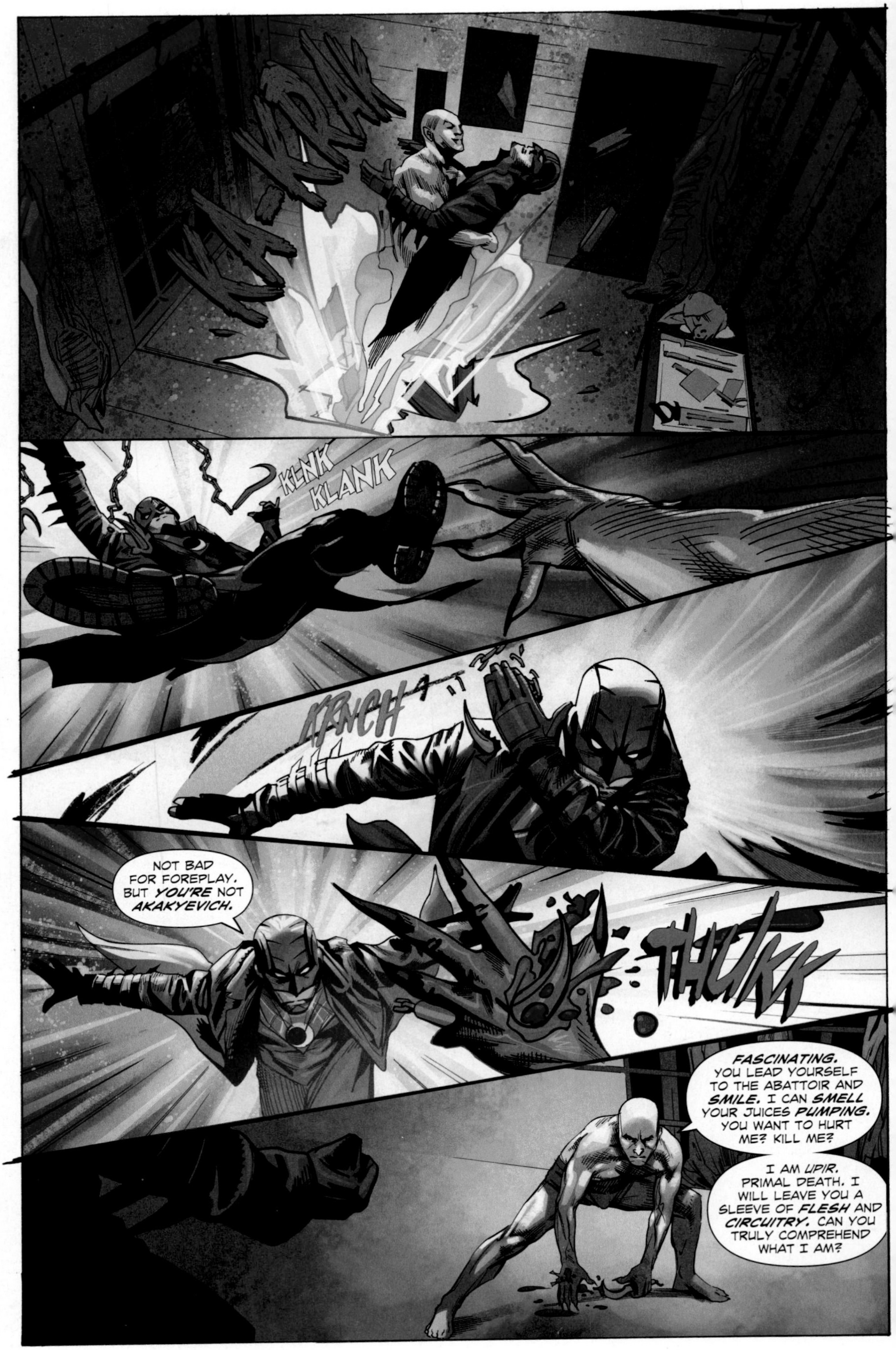

KRAKK
KLNK
KLANK
KRNCH
NOT BAD FOR FOREPLAY. BUT YOU'RE NOT AKAKYEVICH.
THUKK
FASCINATING. YOU LEAD YOURSELF TO THE ABATTOIR AND SMILE. I CAN SMELL YOUR JUICES PUMPING. YOU WANT TO HURT ME? KILL ME?
I AM UPIR. PRIMAL DEATH. I WILL LEAVE YOU A SLEEVE OF FLESH AND CIRCUITRY. CAN YOU TRULY COMPREHEND WHAT I AM?

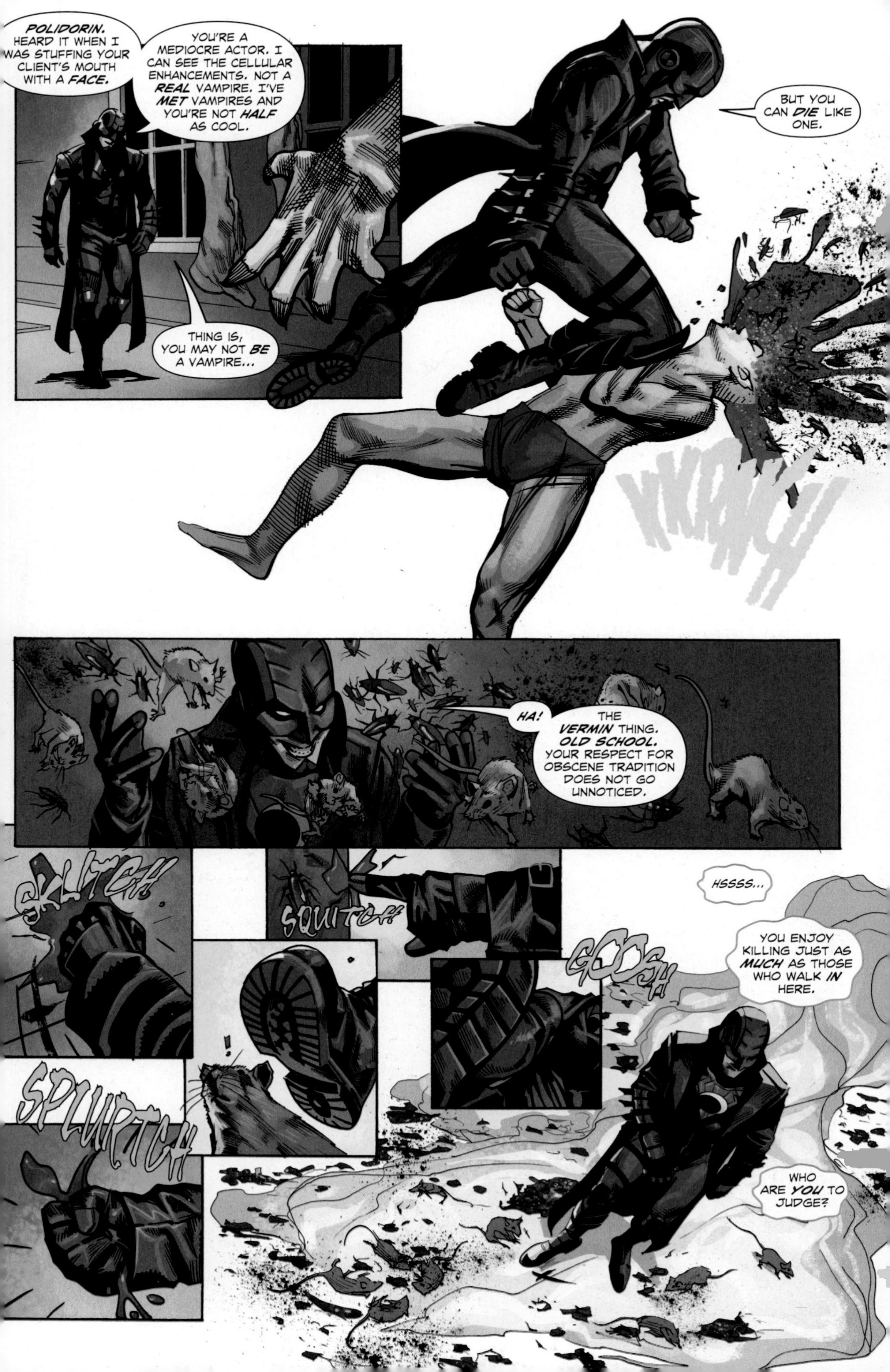
POLIDORIN. HEARD IT WHEN I WAS STUFFING YOUR CLIENT'S MOUTH WITH A FACE.
YOU'RE A MEDIOCRE ACTOR. I CAN SEE THE CELLULAR ENHANCEMENTS. NOT A REAL VAMPIRE. I'VE MET VAMPIRES AND YOU'RE NOT HALF AS COOL.
THING IS, YOU MAY NOT BE A VAMPIRE...
BUT YOU CAN DIE LIKE ONE.
YKRAKH
HA!
THE VERMIN THING. OLD SCHOOL. YOUR RESPECT FOR OBSCENE TRADITION DOES NOT GO UNNOTICED.
SKLITCH
SQUITCH
GOOSH
!
SPLURTCH
HSSSS...
YOU ENJOY KILLING JUST AS MUCH AS THOSE WHO WALK IN HERE.
WHO ARE YOU TO JUDGE?

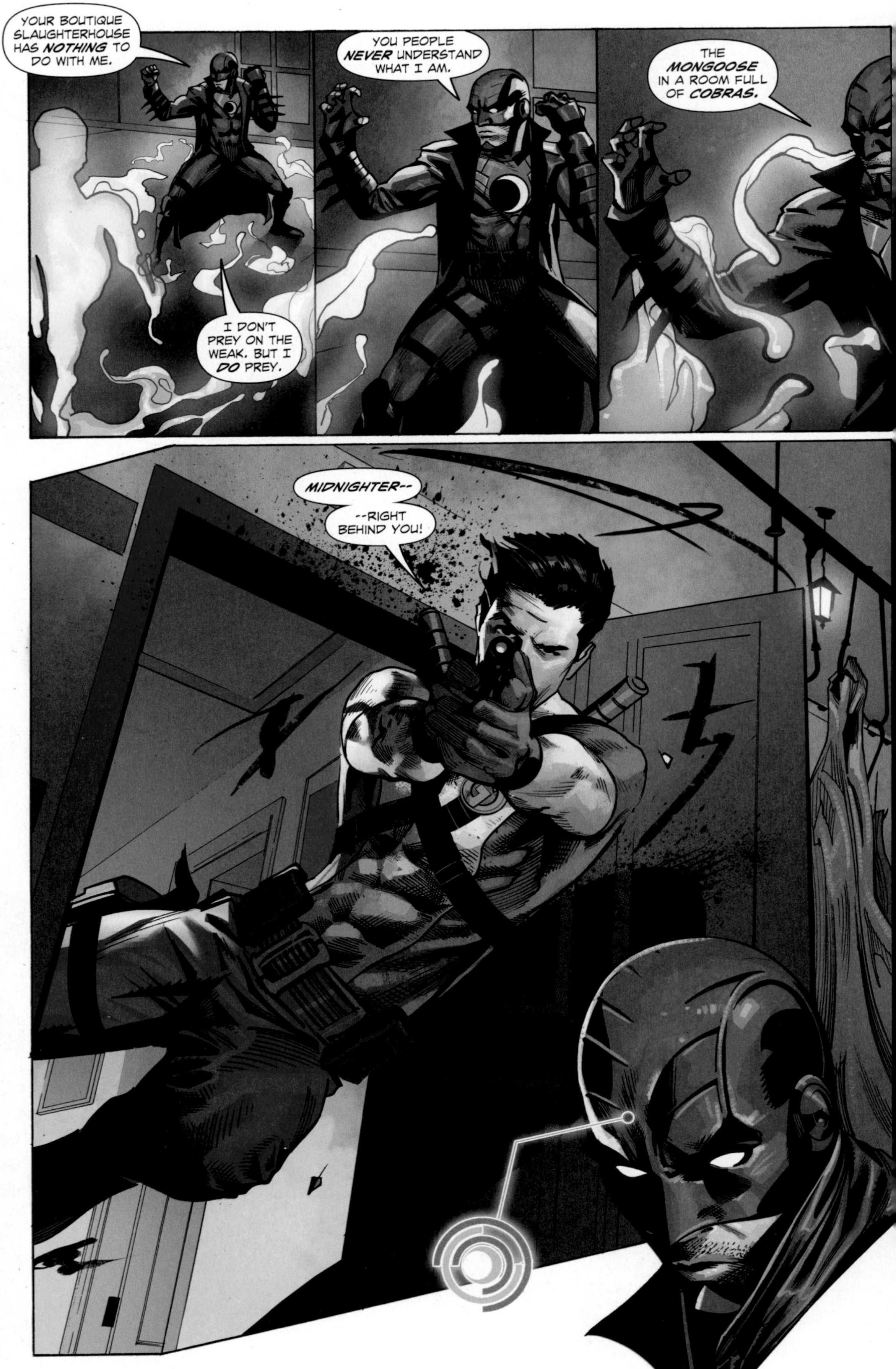

YOUR BOUTIQUE SLAUGHTERHOUSE HAS *NOTHING* TO DO WITH ME.
I DON'T PREY ON THE WEAK. BUT I *DO* PREY.
YOU PEOPLE *NEVER* UNDERSTAND WHAT I AM.
THE *MONGOOSE* IN A ROOM FULL OF *COBRAS.*
MIDNIGHTER--
--RIGHT BEHIND YOU!

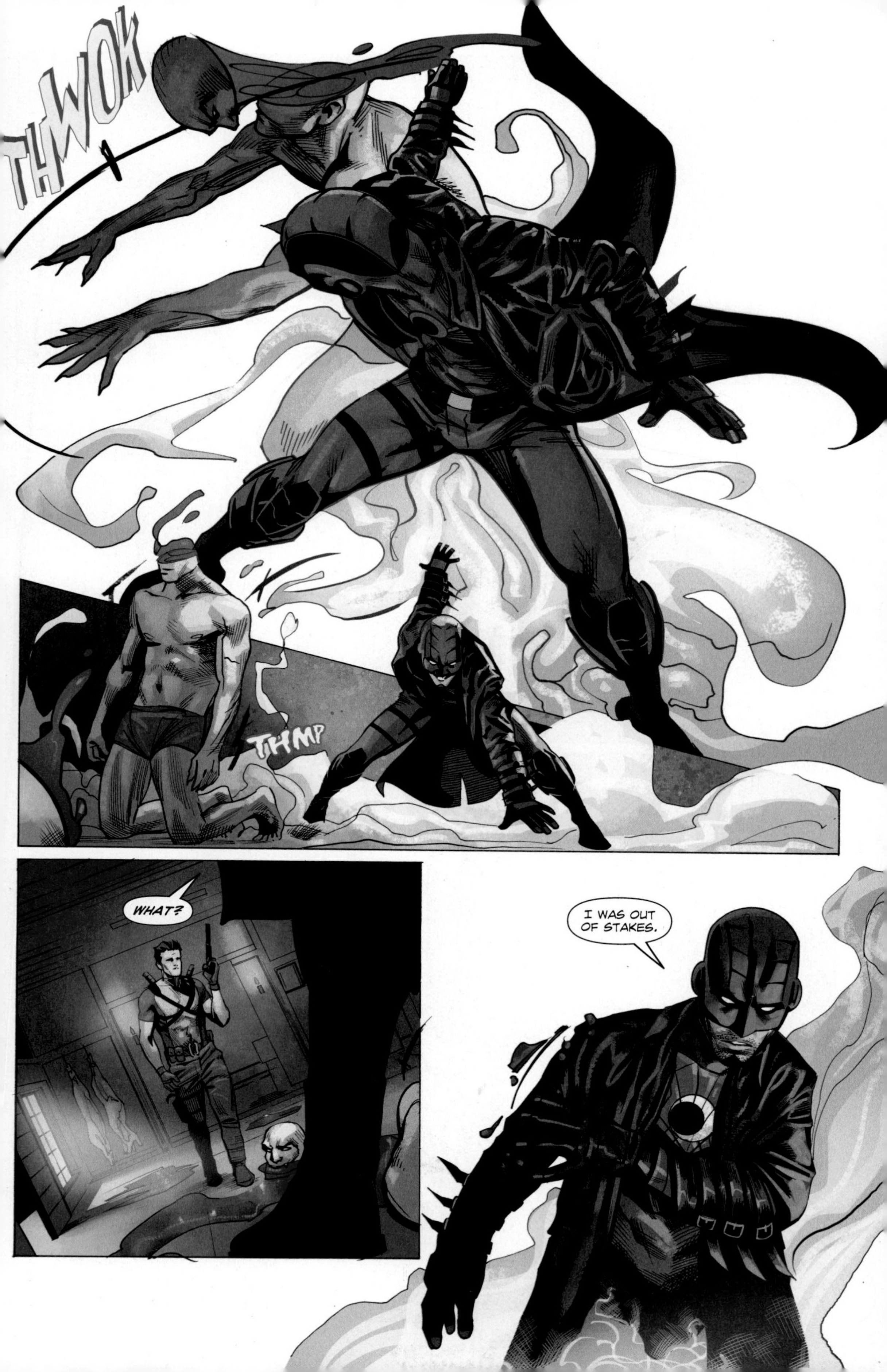
THWOK
THMP
WHAT?
I WAS OUT OF STAKES.

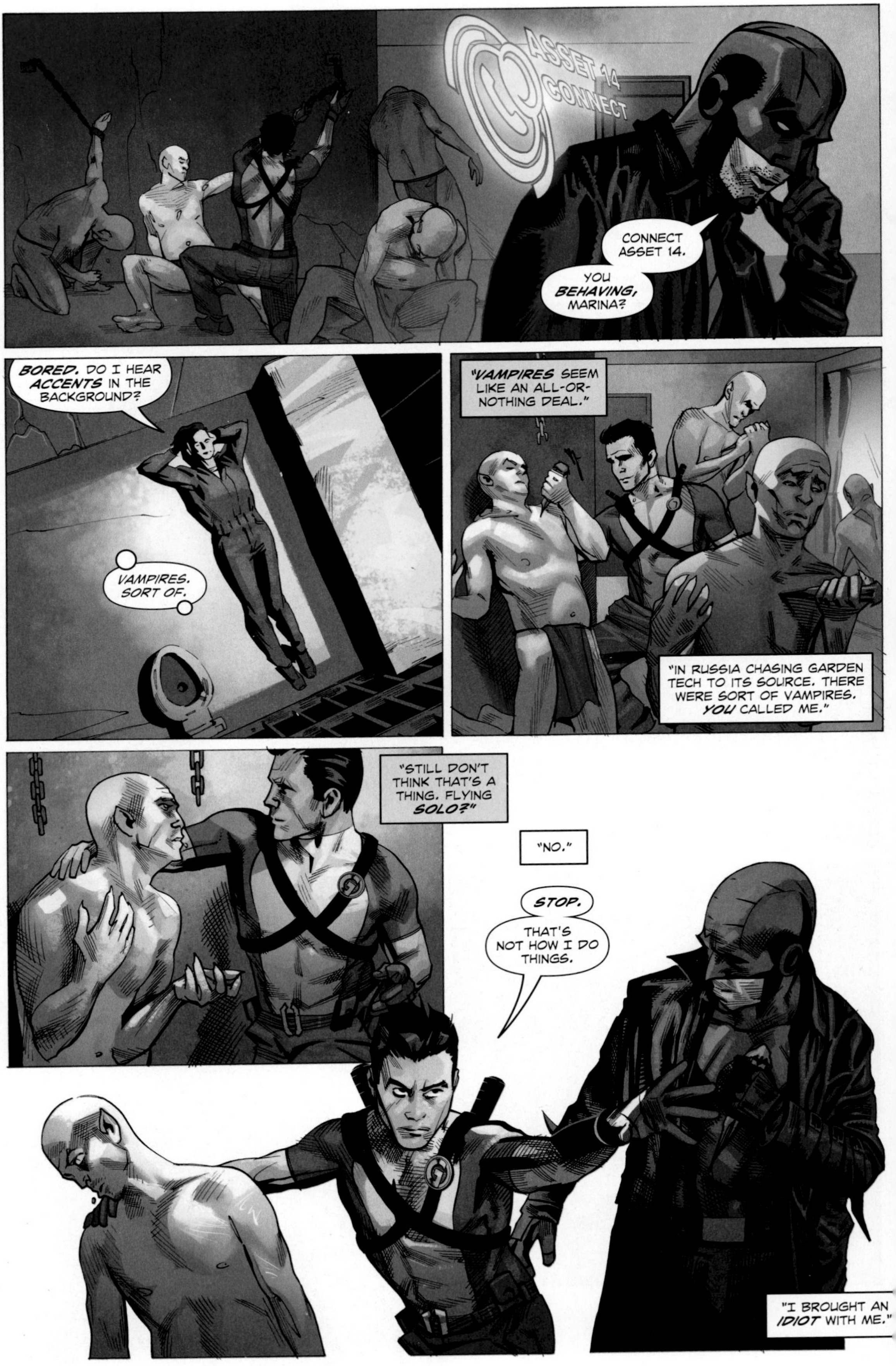
ASSET 14 CONNECT
CONNECT ASSET 14.
YOU BEHAVING, MARINA?
BORED. DO I HEAR ACCENTS IN THE BACKGROUND?
VAMPIRES. SORT OF.
"VAMPIRES SEEM LIKE AN ALL-OR-NOTHING DEAL."
"IN RUSSIA CHASING GARDEN TECH TO ITS SOURCE. THERE WERE SORT OF VAMPIRES. YOU CALLED ME."
"STILL DON'T THINK THAT'S A THING. FLYING SOLO?"
"NO."
STOP.
THAT'S NOT HOW I DO THINGS.
"I BROUGHT AN IDIOT WITH ME."

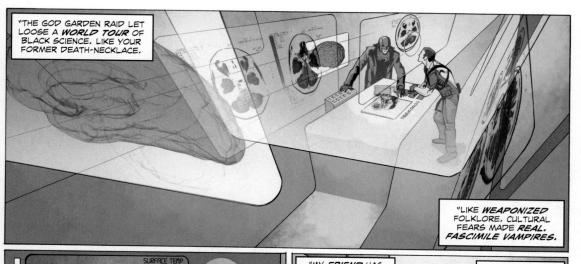

"THE GOD GARDEN RAID LET LOOSE A *WORLD TOUR* OF BLACK SCIENCE. LIKE YOUR FORMER DEATH-NECKLACE.

"LIKE *WEAPONIZED* FOLKLORE. CULTURAL FEARS MADE *REAL.* FASCIMILE VAMPIRES.

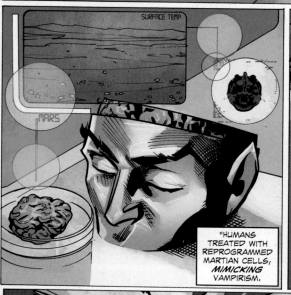

SURFACE TEMP

MARS

"HUMANS TREATED WITH REPROGRAMMED MARTIAN CELLS, *MIMICKING* VAMPIRISM.

"MY *FRIEND* HAS CONNECTIONS. *SPY* SCIENCE. THOUGHT HE COULD *REVERSE* THE GENE THERAPY.

"BUT THE CELLS WEREN'T JUST REPROGRAMMED."

≥HHHCH≤

NNNAAAHH!

"THEY WERE *BOOBYTRAPPED.*

"THIS IS THE TYPE OF THING THAT MAKES MY FRIEND UNHAPPY."

"SOUNDS LIKE YOU'VE GOT MORE *WORK* TO DO."

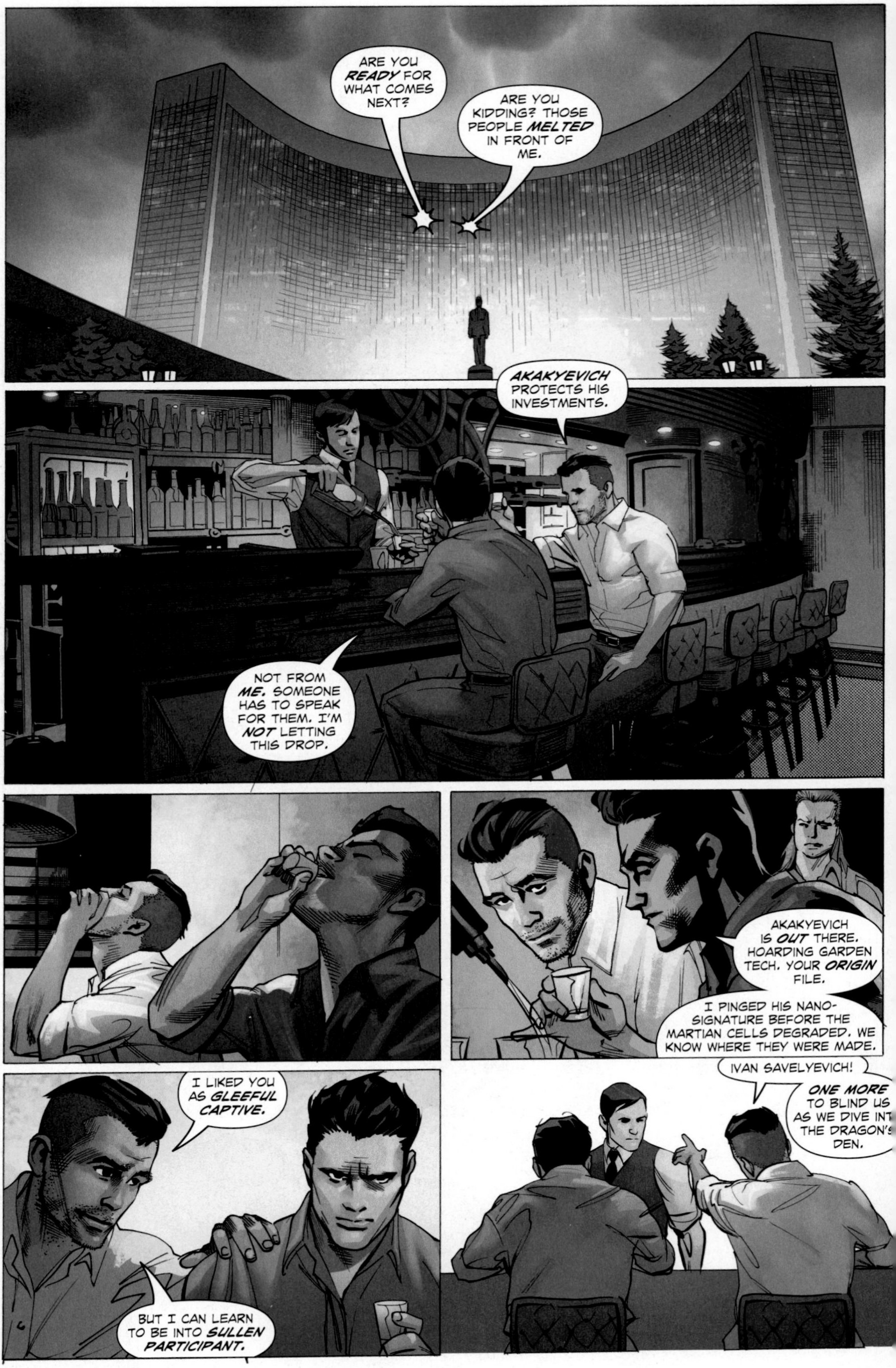
ARE YOU READY FOR WHAT COMES NEXT?
ARE YOU KIDDING? THOSE PEOPLE MELTED IN FRONT OF ME.
AKAKYEVICH PROTECTS HIS INVESTMENTS.
NOT FROM ME. SOMEONE HAS TO SPEAK FOR THEM. I'M NOT LETTING THIS DROP.
AKAKYEVICH IS OUT THERE. HOARDING GARDEN TECH. YOUR ORIGIN FILE.
I PINGED HIS NANO-SIGNATURE BEFORE THE MARTIAN CELLS DEGRADED. WE KNOW WHERE THEY WERE MADE.
I LIKED YOU AS GLEEFUL CAPTIVE.
BUT I CAN LEARN TO BE INTO SULLEN PARTICIPANT.
IVAN SAVELYEVICH!
ONE MORE TO BLIND US AS WE DIVE INT THE DRAGON'S DEN.

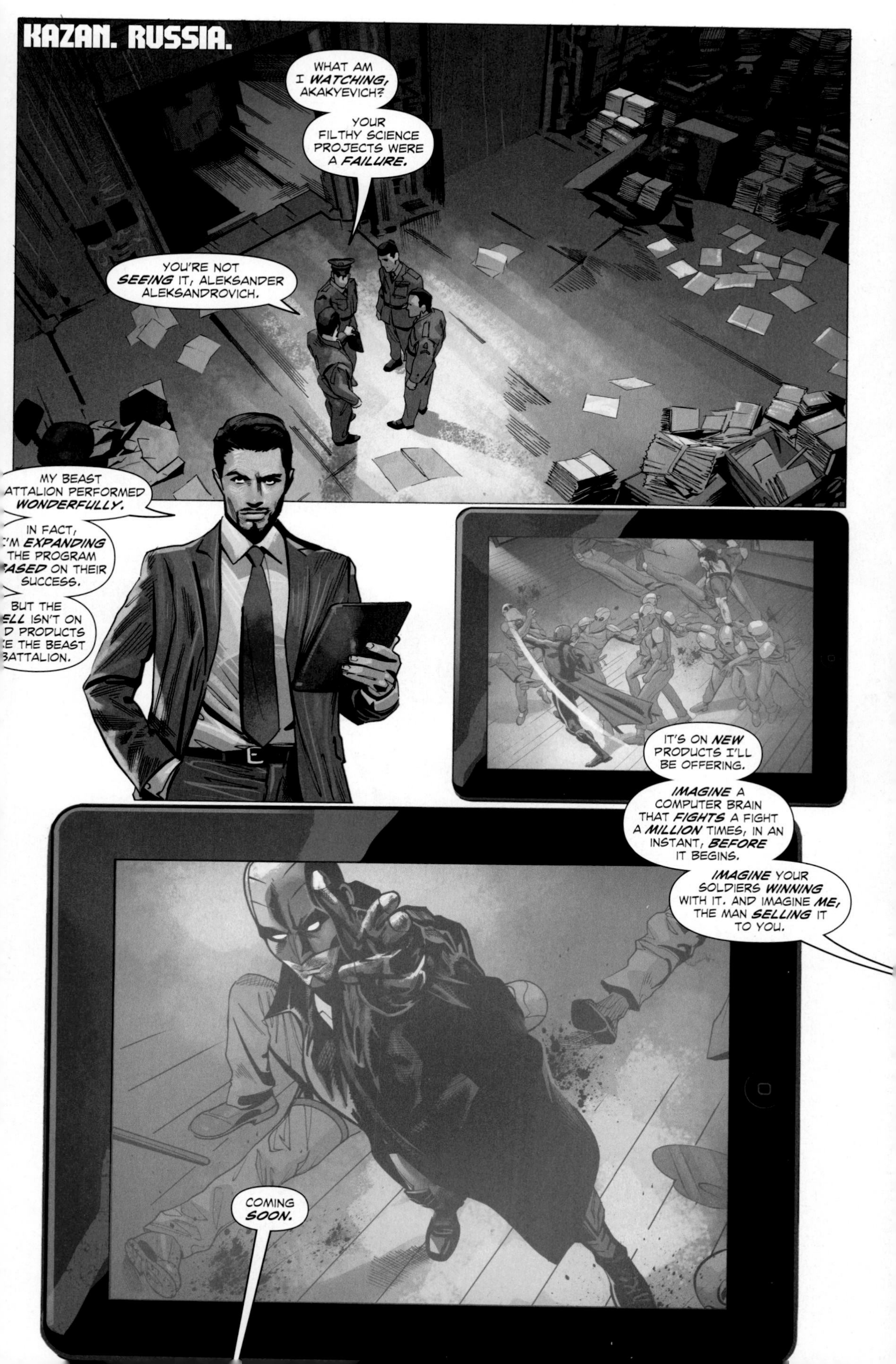
KAZAN. RUSSIA.
WHAT AM I WATCHING, AKAKYEVICH?
YOUR FILTHY SCIENCE PROJECTS WERE A FAILURE.
YOU'RE NOT SEEING IT, ALEKSANDER ALEKSANDROVICH.
MY BEAST ATTALION PERFORMED WONDERFULLY.
IN FACT, 'M EXPANDING THE PROGRAM ASED ON THEIR SUCCESS.
BUT THE ELL ISN'T ON D PRODUCTS E THE BEAST BATTALION.
IT'S ON NEW PRODUCTS I'LL BE OFFERING.
IMAGINE A COMPUTER BRAIN THAT FIGHTS A FIGHT A MILLION TIMES, IN AN INSTANT, BEFORE IT BEGINS.
IMAGINE YOUR SOLDIERS WINNING WITH IT. AND IMAGINE ME, THE MAN SELLING IT TO YOU.
COMING SOON.

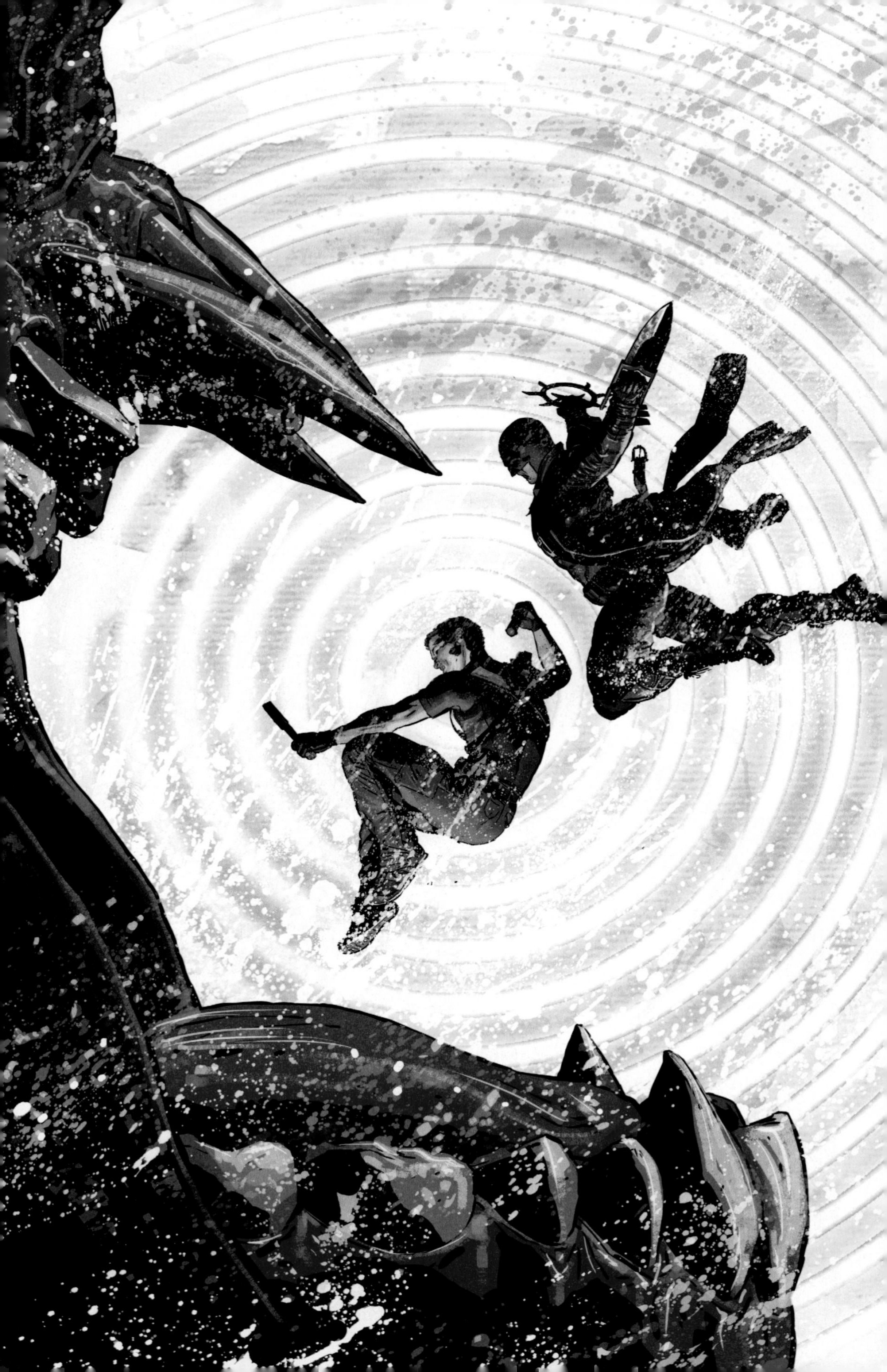

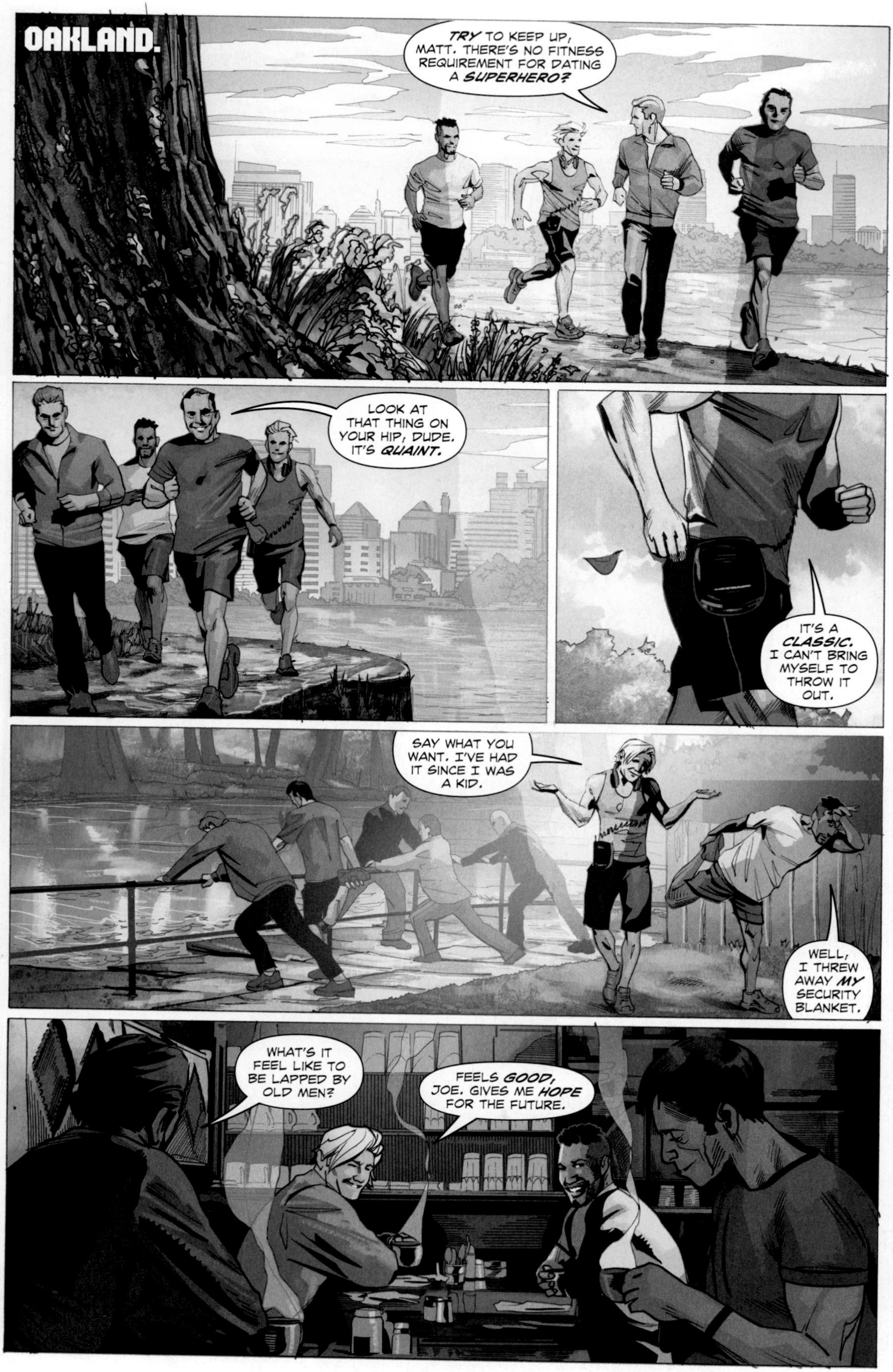
OAKLAND.
TRY TO KEEP UP, MATT. THERE'S NO FITNESS REQUIREMENT FOR DATING A SUPERHERO?
LOOK AT THAT THING ON YOUR HIP, DUDE. IT'S QUAINT.
IT'S A CLASSIC. I CAN'T BRING MYSELF TO THROW IT OUT.
SAY WHAT YOU WANT. I'VE HAD IT SINCE I WAS A KID.
WELL, I THREW AWAY MY SECURITY BLANKET.
WHAT'S IT FEEL LIKE TO BE LAPPED BY OLD MEN?
FEELS GOOD, JOE. GIVES ME HOPE FOR THE FUTURE.

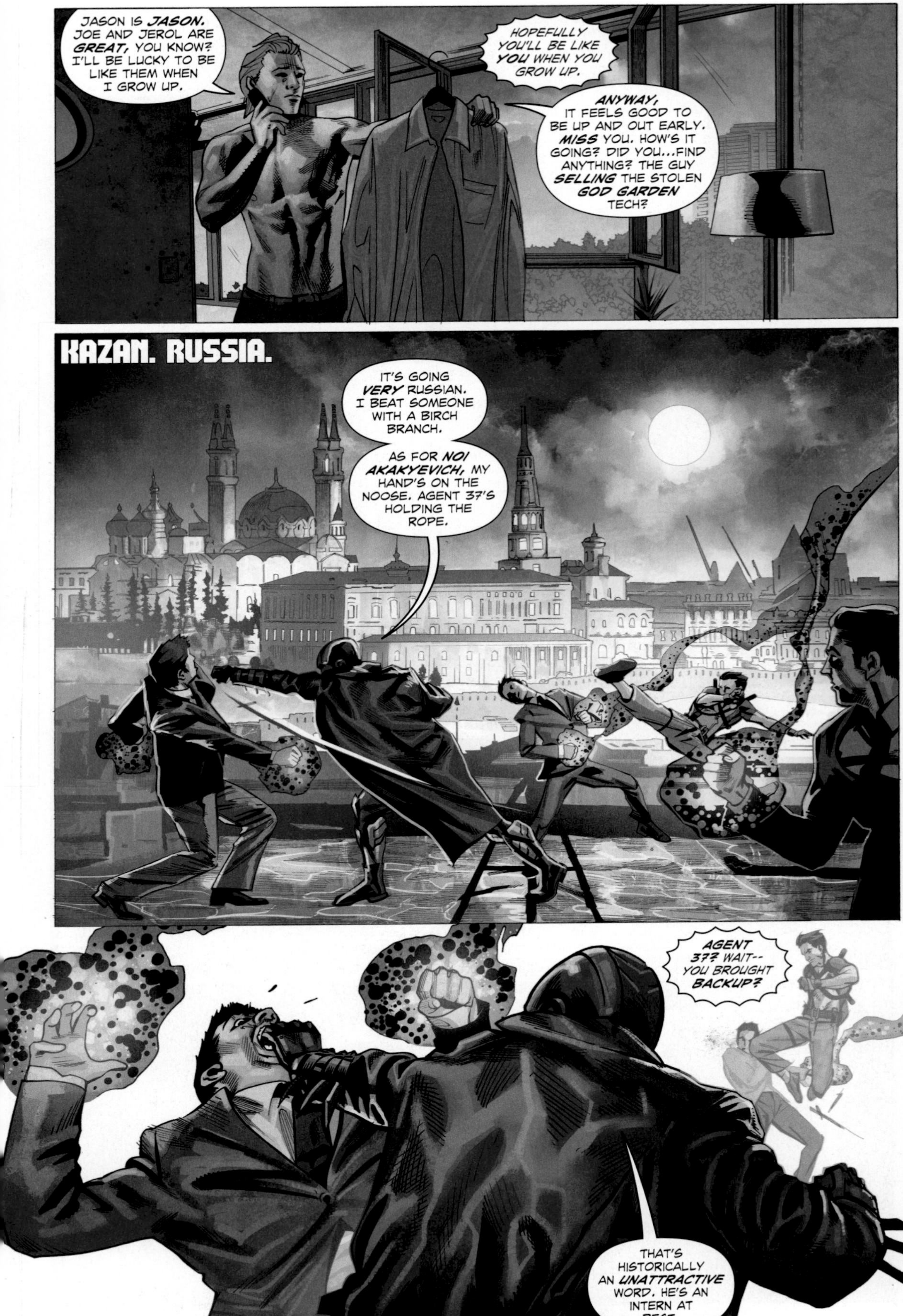
JASON IS JASON. JOE AND JEROL ARE GREAT, YOU KNOW? I'LL BE LUCKY TO BE LIKE THEM WHEN I GROW UP.
HOPEFULLY YOU'LL BE LIKE YOU WHEN YOU GROW UP.
ANYWAY, IT FEELS GOOD TO BE UP AND OUT EARLY. MISS YOU. HOW'S IT GOING? DID YOU...FIND ANYTHING? THE GUY SELLING THE STOLEN GOD GARDEN TECH?
KAZAN. RUSSIA.
IT'S GOING VERY RUSSIAN. I BEAT SOMEONE WITH A BIRCH BRANCH.
AS FOR NOI AKAKYEVICH, MY HAND'S ON THE NOOSE. AGENT 37'S HOLDING THE ROPE.
AGENT 37? WAIT-- YOU BROUGHT BACKUP?
THAT'S HISTORICALLY AN UNATTRACTIVE WORD. HE'S AN INTERN AT BEST.

⟨YOU DON'T WANT *ME* TO COOK, NO!?⟩*

⟨WHAT? OF *COURSE* NOT. I'VE BEEN COOKING *BLINI* SINCE I WAS A CHILD.⟩

*TRANSLATED FROM RUSSIAN.

⟨I DIDN'T THINK *YOU'D* WASTE TIME IN THE KITCHEN.⟩

⟨YOUR PROJECTS--⟩

⟨--ARE *MOVING*, ZINOCHKA. WE MUST *ALWAYS* MAKE TIME FOR TRADITION. EVEN AS WE CHAMPION PROGRESS.⟩

⟨A *TRUE* MAN PROVIDES IN ALL WAYS.⟩

"⟨TOMORROW, BY DESIGN...⟩"

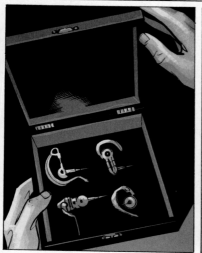

"⟨...IS RIPPED FROM THE CAUL OF YESTERDAY.⟩"

ZZZTT

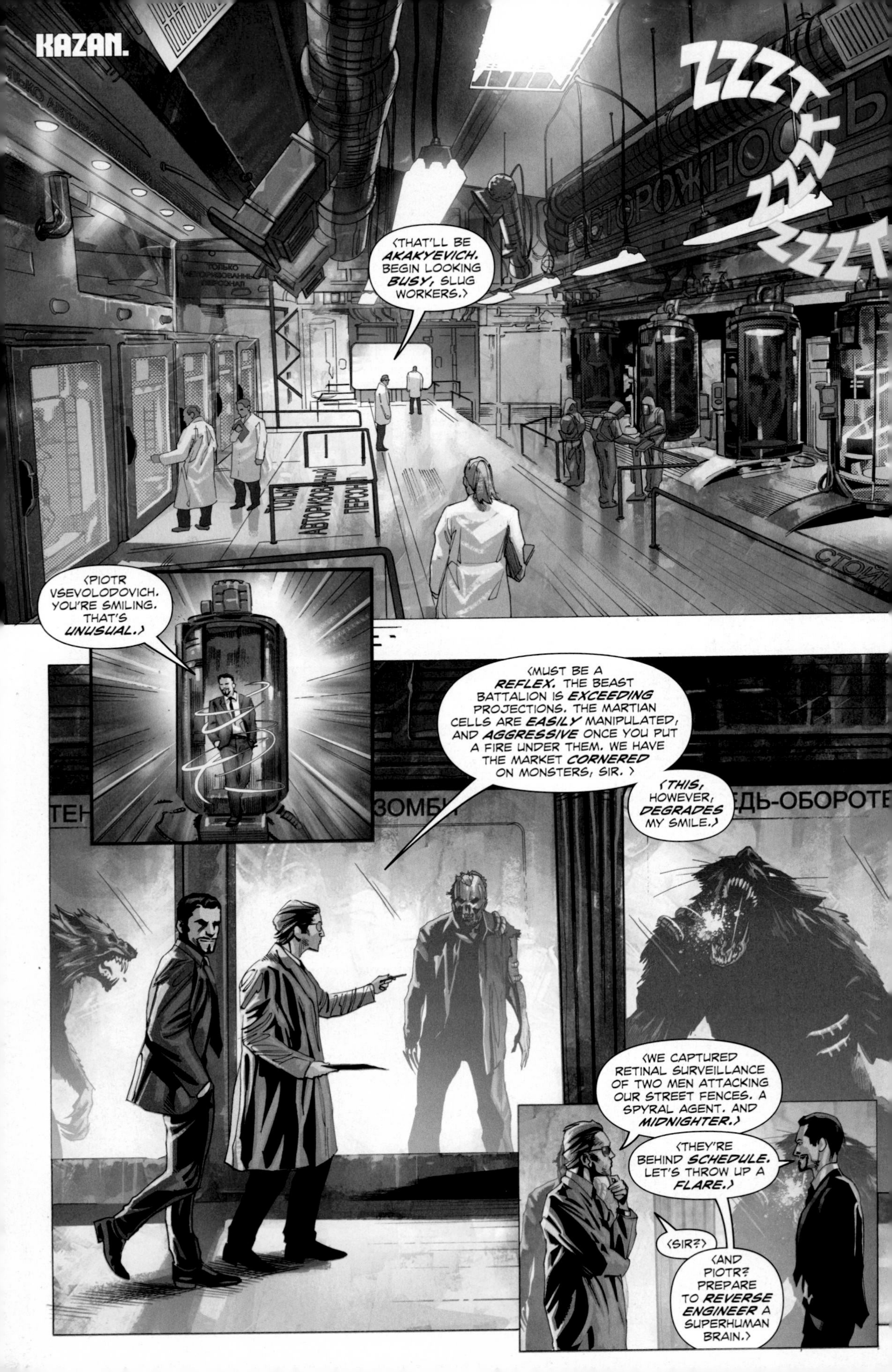

KAZAN.
ZZZT ZZZT ZZZT
‹THAT'LL BE AKAKYEVICH. BEGIN LOOKING BUSY, SLUG WORKERS.›
‹PIOTR VSEVOLODOVICH. YOU'RE SMILING. THAT'S UNUSUAL.›
‹MUST BE A REFLEX. THE BEAST BATTALION IS EXCEEDING PROJECTIONS. THE MARTIAN CELLS ARE EASILY MANIPULATED, AND AGGRESSIVE ONCE YOU PUT A FIRE UNDER THEM. WE HAVE THE MARKET CORNERED ON MONSTERS, SIR.›
‹THIS, HOWEVER, DEGRADES MY SMILE.›
‹WE CAPTURED RETINAL SURVEILLANCE OF TWO MEN ATTACKING OUR STREET FENCES. A SPYRAL AGENT. AND MIDNIGHTER.›
‹THEY'RE BEHIND SCHEDULE. LET'S THROW UP A FLARE.›
‹SIR?›
‹AND PIOTR? PREPARE TO REVERSE ENGINEER A SUPERHUMAN BRAIN.›

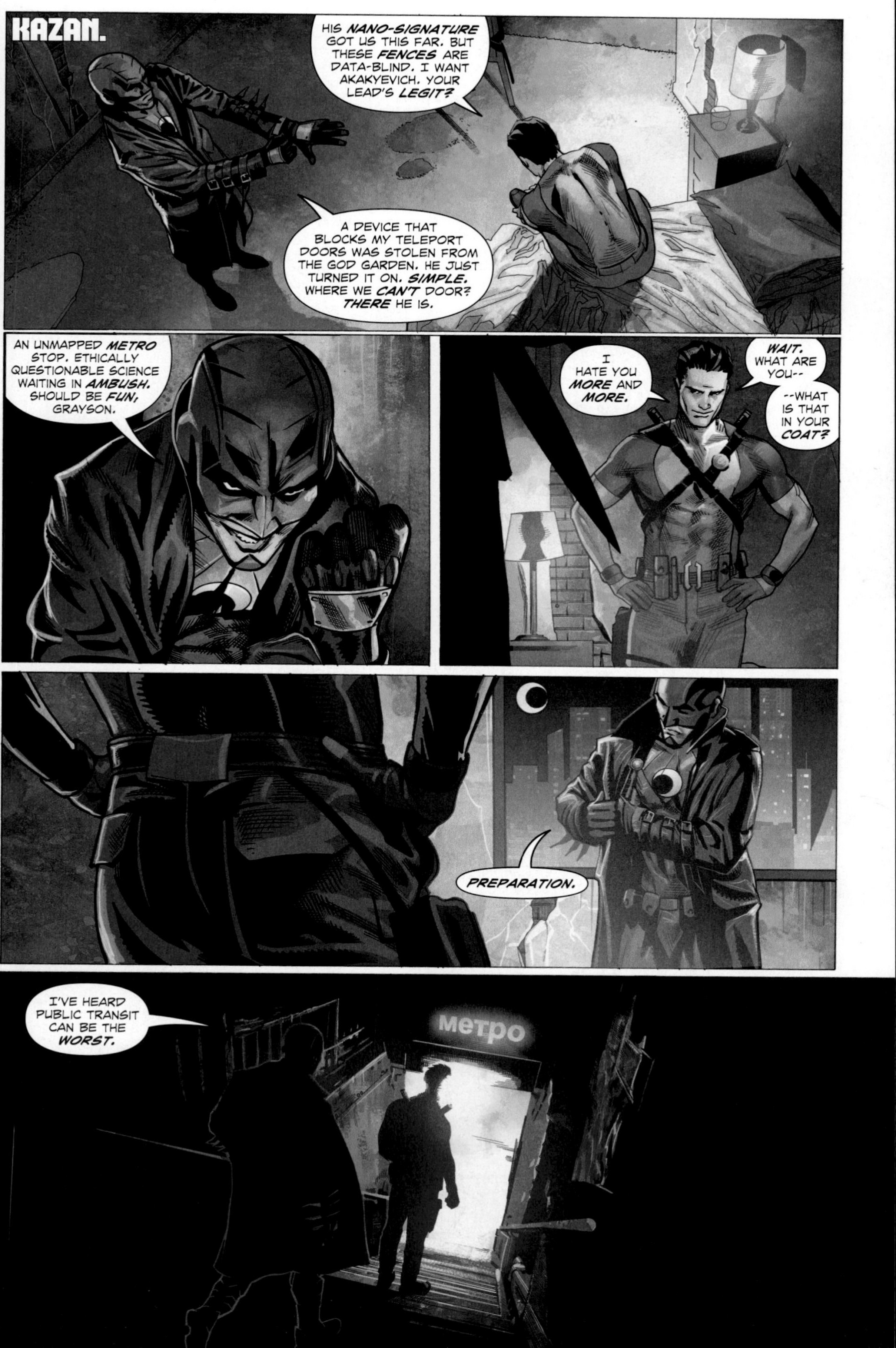
KAZAN.
HIS NANO-SIGNATURE GOT US THIS FAR. BUT THESE FENCES ARE DATA-BLIND. I WANT AKAKYEVICH. YOUR LEAD'S LEGIT?
A DEVICE THAT BLOCKS MY TELEPORT DOORS WAS STOLEN FROM THE GOD GARDEN. HE JUST TURNED IT ON. SIMPLE. WHERE WE CAN'T DOOR? THERE HE IS.
AN UNMAPPED METRO STOP. ETHICALLY QUESTIONABLE SCIENCE WAITING IN AMBUSH. SHOULD BE FUN, GRAYSON.
I HATE YOU MORE AND MORE.
WAIT. WHAT ARE YOU--
--WHAT IS THAT IN YOUR COAT?
PREPARATION.
I'VE HEARD PUBLIC TRANSIT CAN BE THE WORST.
МЕТРО

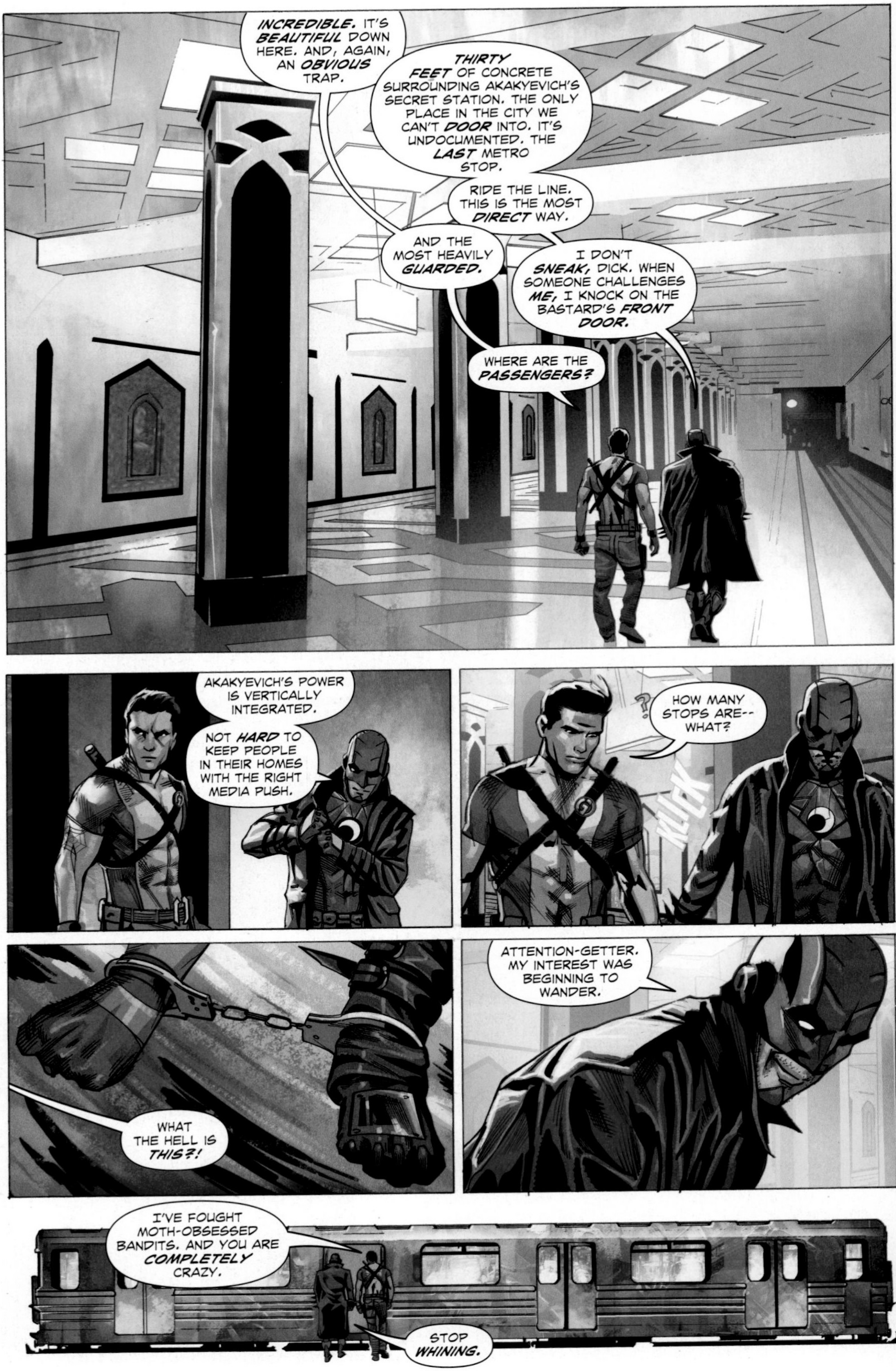
INCREDIBLE. IT'S BEAUTIFUL DOWN HERE. AND, AGAIN, AN OBVIOUS TRAP.
THIRTY FEET OF CONCRETE SURROUNDING AKAKYEVICH'S SECRET STATION. THE ONLY PLACE IN THE CITY WE CAN'T DOOR INTO. IT'S UNDOCUMENTED. THE LAST METRO STOP.
RIDE THE LINE. THIS IS THE MOST DIRECT WAY.
AND THE MOST HEAVILY GUARDED.
I DON'T SNEAK, DICK. WHEN SOMEONE CHALLENGES ME, I KNOCK ON THE BASTARD'S FRONT DOOR.
WHERE ARE THE PASSENGERS?
AKAKYEVICH'S POWER IS VERTICALLY INTEGRATED.
NOT HARD TO KEEP PEOPLE IN THEIR HOMES WITH THE RIGHT MEDIA PUSH.
?
HOW MANY STOPS ARE-- WHAT?
KLICK
WHAT THE HELL IS THIS?!
ATTENTION-GETTER. MY INTEREST WAS BEGINNING TO WANDER.
I'VE FOUGHT MOTH-OBSESSED BANDITS. AND YOU ARE COMPLETELY CRAZY.
STOP WHINING.

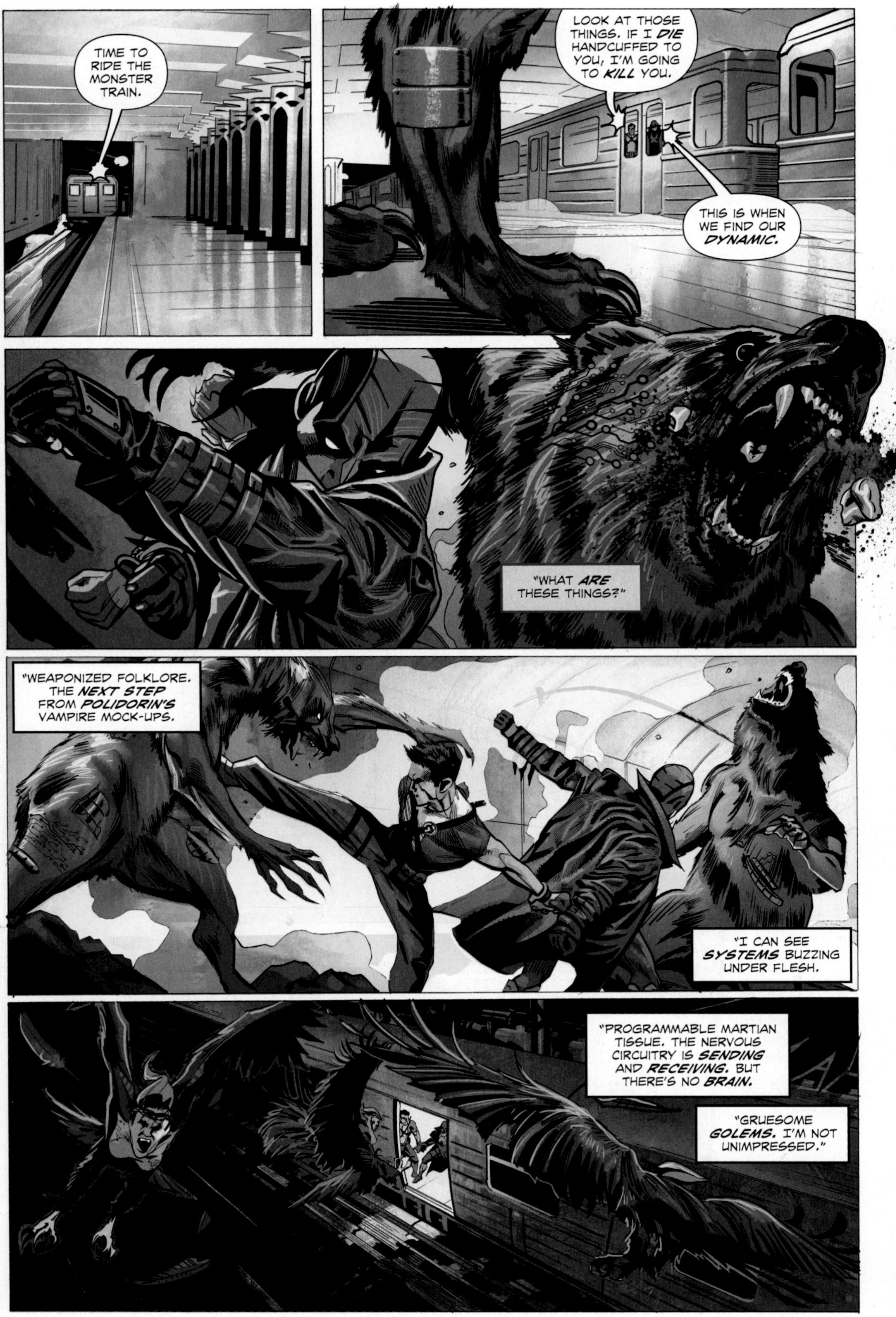
TIME TO RIDE THE MONSTER TRAIN.
LOOK AT THOSE THINGS. IF I DIE HANDCUFFED TO YOU, I'M GOING TO KILL YOU.
THIS IS WHEN WE FIND OUR DYNAMIC.
"WHAT ARE THESE THINGS?"
"WEAPONIZED FOLKLORE. THE NEXT STEP FROM POLIDORIN'S VAMPIRE MOCK-UPS.
"I CAN SEE SYSTEMS BUZZING UNDER FLESH.
"PROGRAMMABLE MARTIAN TISSUE. THE NERVOUS CIRCUITRY IS SENDING AND RECEIVING. BUT THERE'S NO BRAIN.
"GRUESOME GOLEMS. I'M NOT UNIMPRESSED."

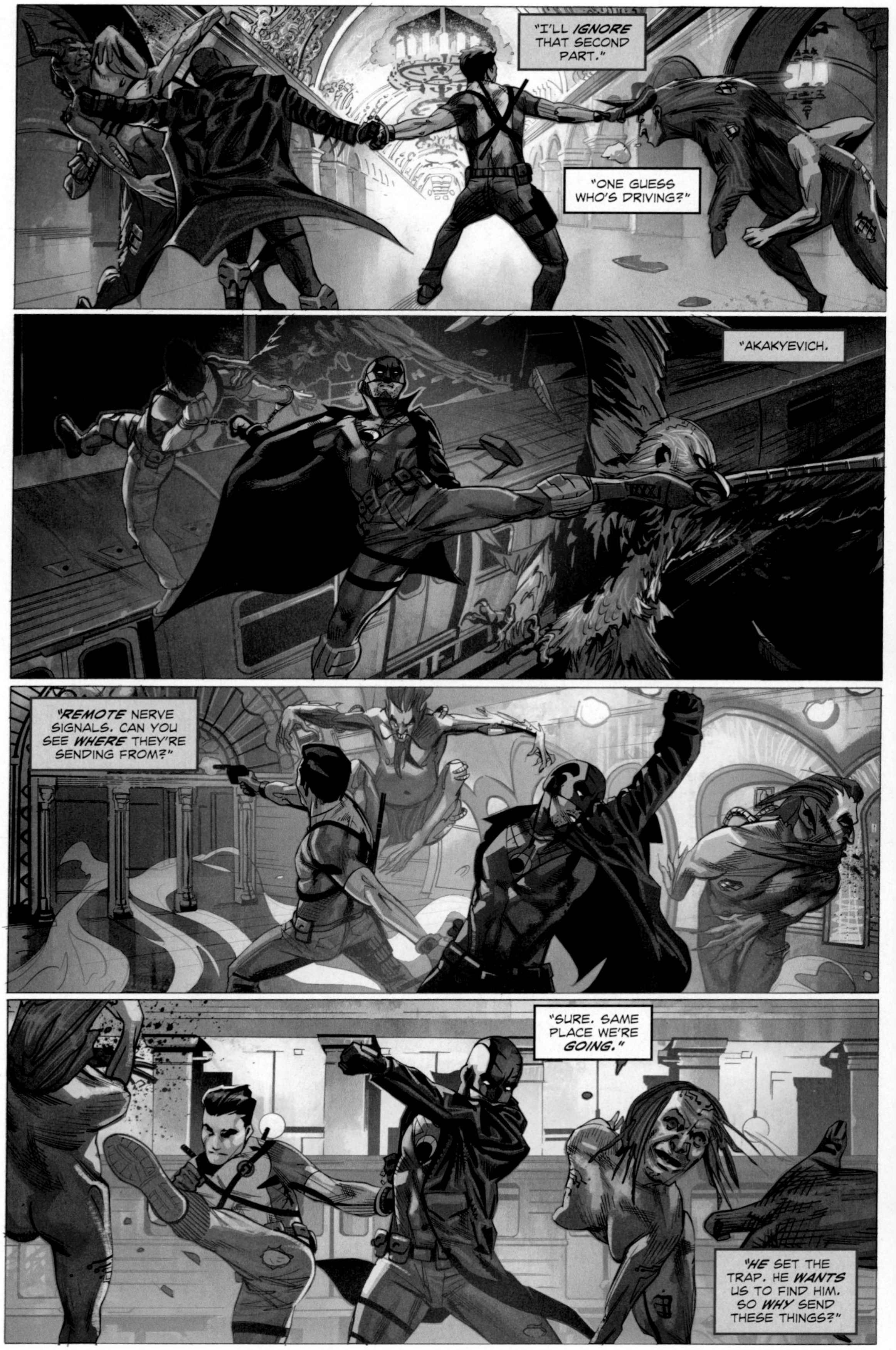
"I'LL *IGNORE* THAT SECOND PART."
"ONE GUESS WHO'S DRIVING?"
"AKAKYEVICH.
"*REMOTE* NERVE SIGNALS. CAN YOU SEE *WHERE* THEY'RE SENDING FROM?"
"SURE. SAME PLACE WE'RE *GOING.*"
"*HE* SET THE TRAP. HE *WANTS* US TO FIND HIM. SO *WHY* SEND THESE THINGS?"

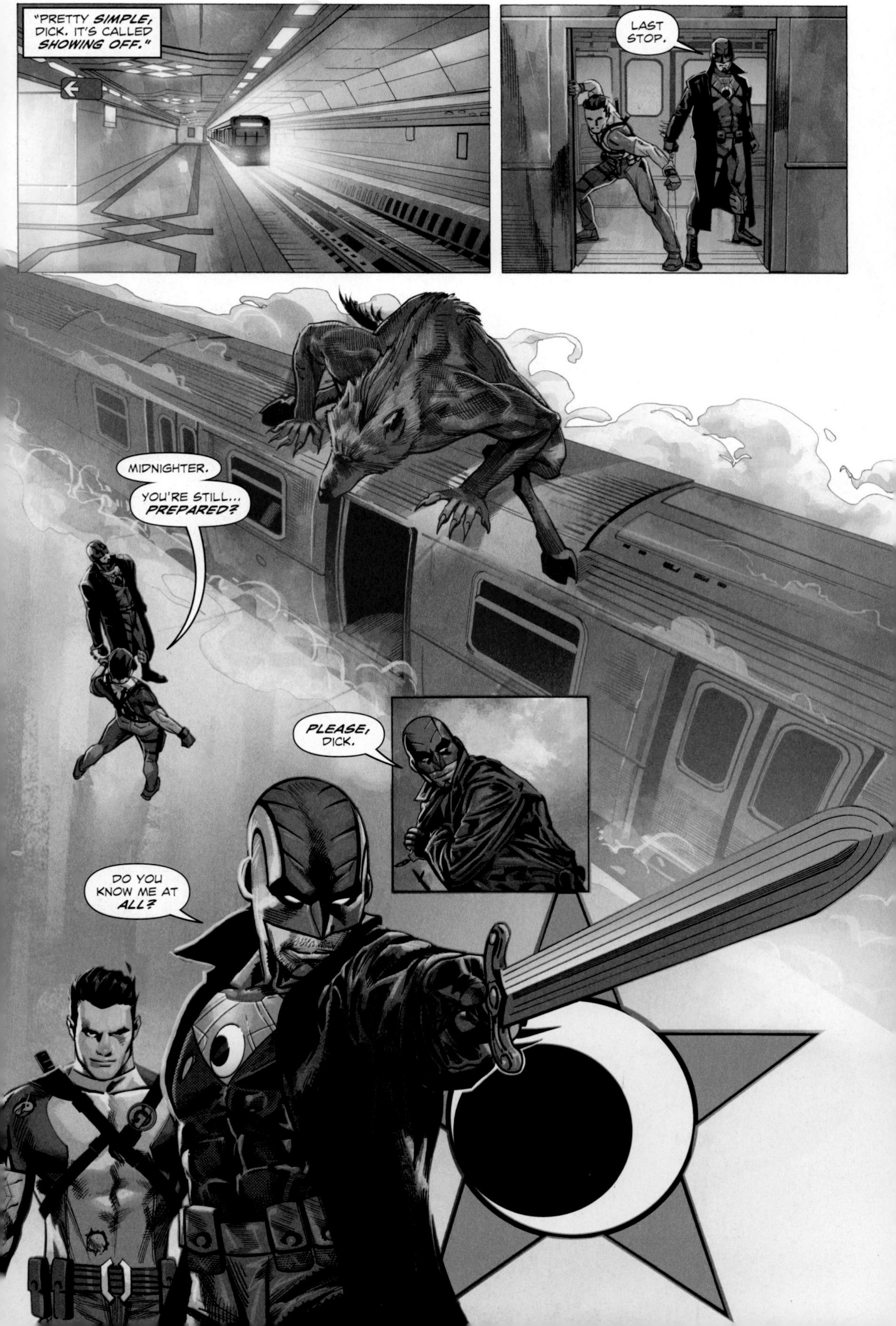
"PRETTY SIMPLE, DICK. IT'S CALLED SHOWING OFF."
LAST STOP.
MIDNIGHTER.
YOU'RE STILL... PREPARED?
PLEASE, DICK.
DO YOU KNOW ME AT ALL?

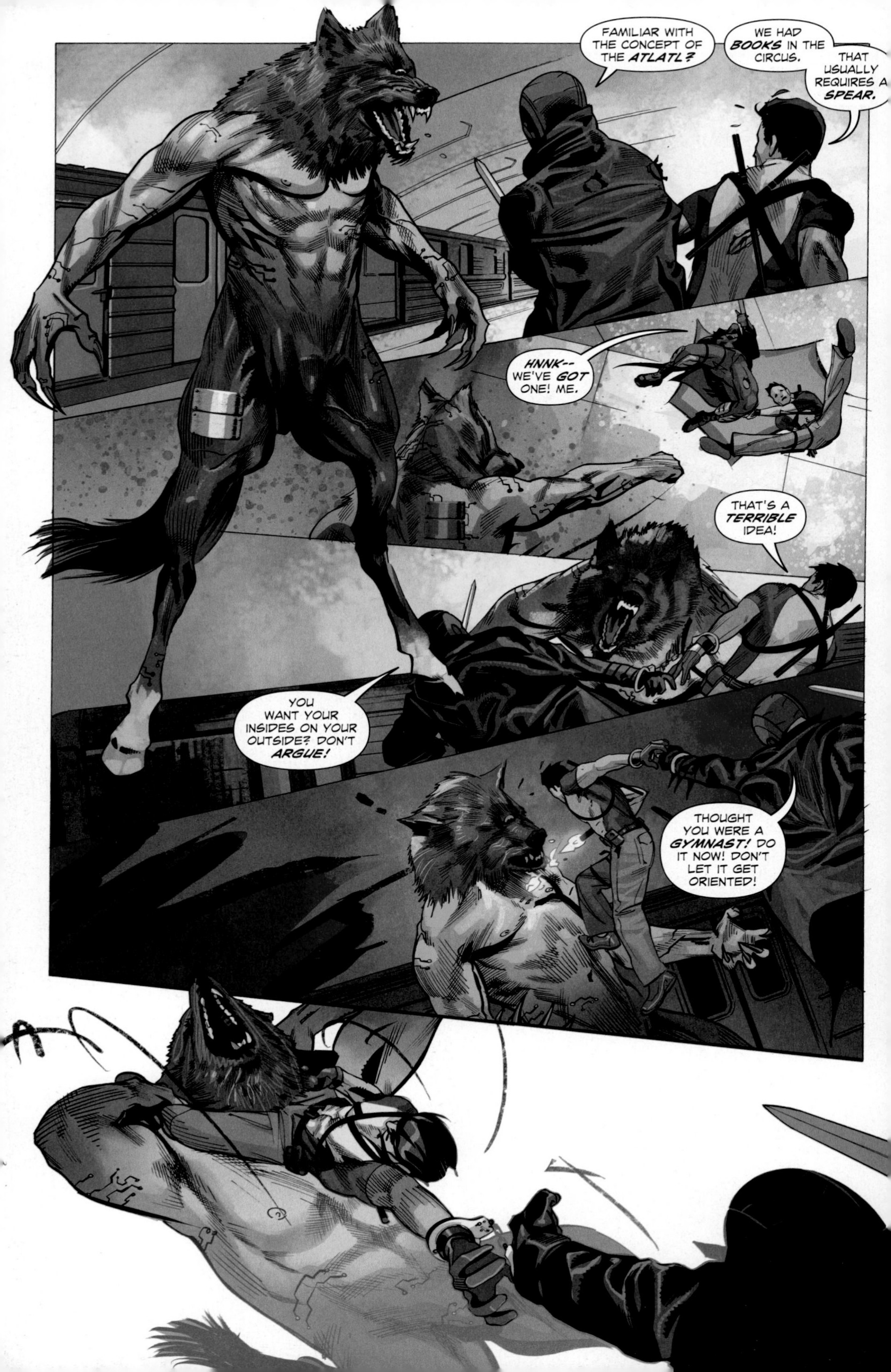
FAMILIAR WITH THE CONCEPT OF THE *ATLATL?*
WE HAD *BOOKS* IN THE CIRCUS.
THAT USUALLY REQUIRES A *SPEAR.*
HNNK-- WE'VE *GOT* ONE! ME.
THAT'S A *TERRIBLE* IDEA!
YOU WANT YOUR INSIDES ON YOUR OUTSIDE? DON'T *ARGUE!*
THOUGHT YOU WERE A *GYMNAST!* DO IT NOW! DON'T LET IT GET ORIENTED!

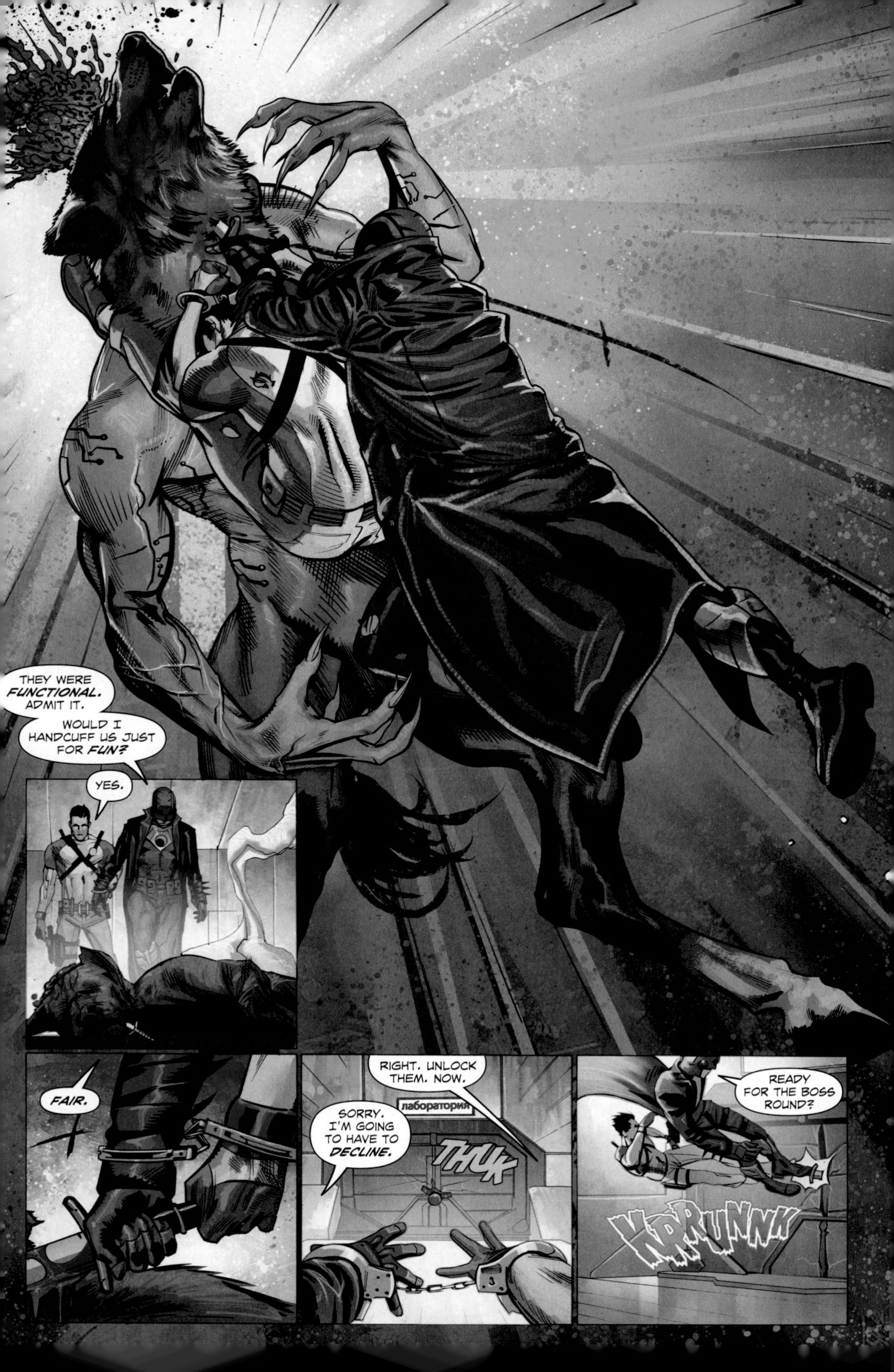

THEY WERE FUNCTIONAL. ADMIT IT.
WOULD I HANDCUFF US JUST FOR FUN?
YES.
FAIR.
RIGHT. UNLOCK THEM. NOW.
лаборатория
SORRY. I'M GOING TO HAVE TO DECLINE.
THUK
READY FOR THE BOSS ROUND?
KRRUNNK

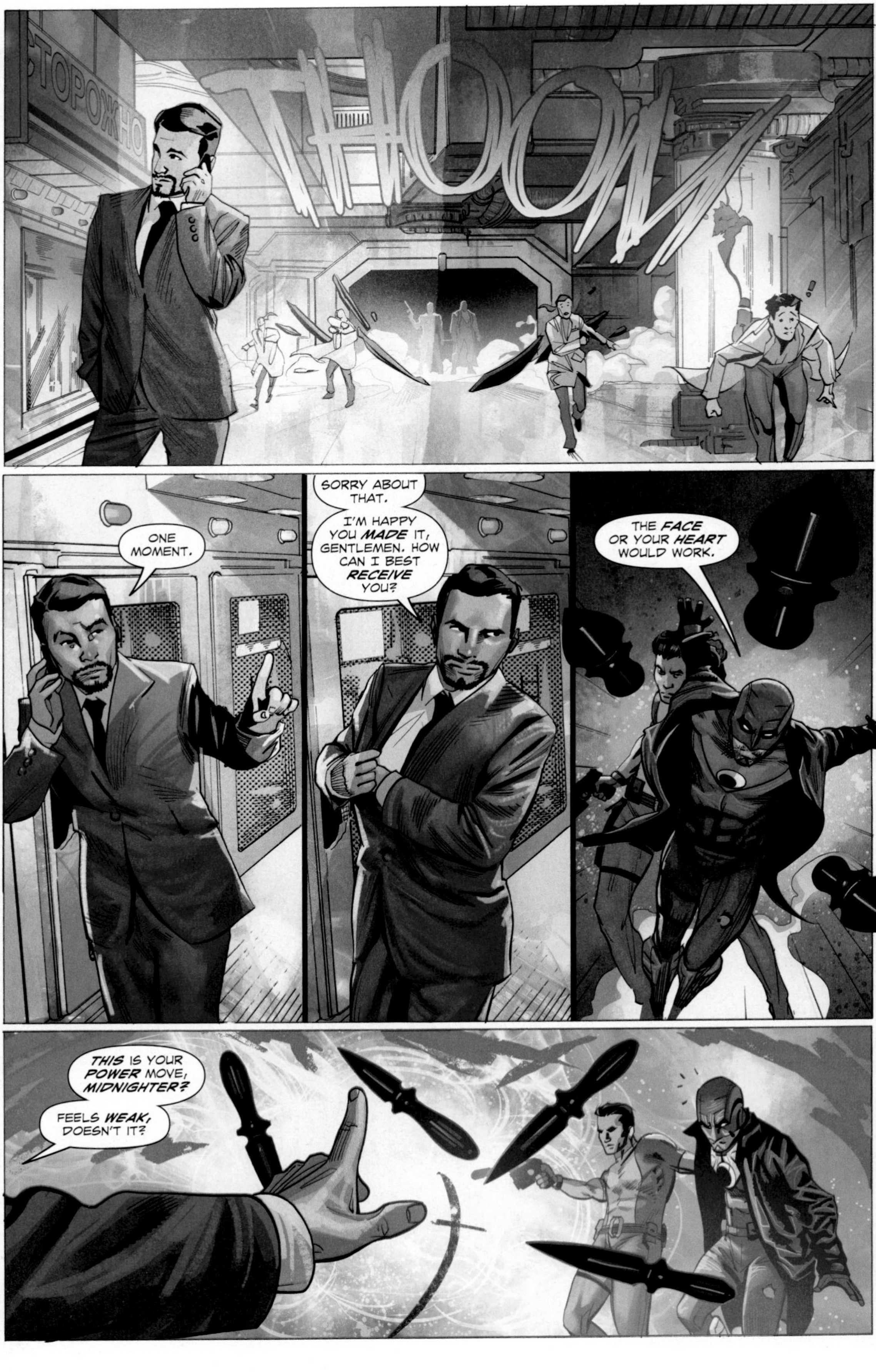
THOOM
ONE MOMENT.
SORRY ABOUT THAT.
I'M HAPPY YOU MADE IT, GENTLEMEN. HOW CAN I BEST RECEIVE YOU?
THE FACE OR YOUR HEART WOULD WORK.
THIS IS YOUR POWER MOVE, MIDNIGHTER?
FEELS WEAK, DOESN'T IT?

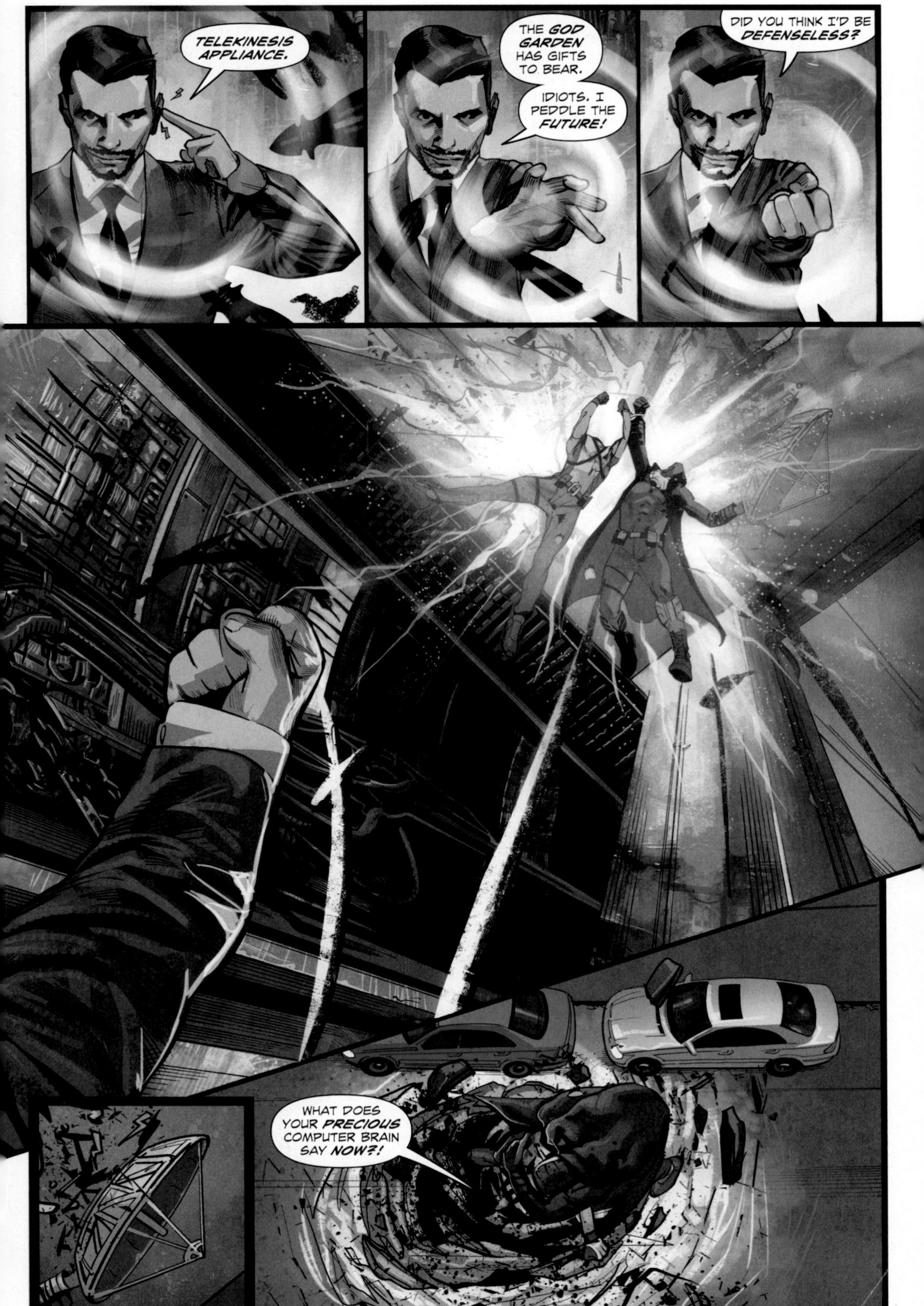
TELEKINESIS APPLIANCE.
THE GOD GARDEN HAS GIFTS TO BEAR.
IDIOTS. I PEDDLE THE FUTURE!
DID YOU THINK I'D BE DEFENSELESS?
WHAT DOES YOUR PRECIOUS COMPUTER BRAIN SAY NOW?!

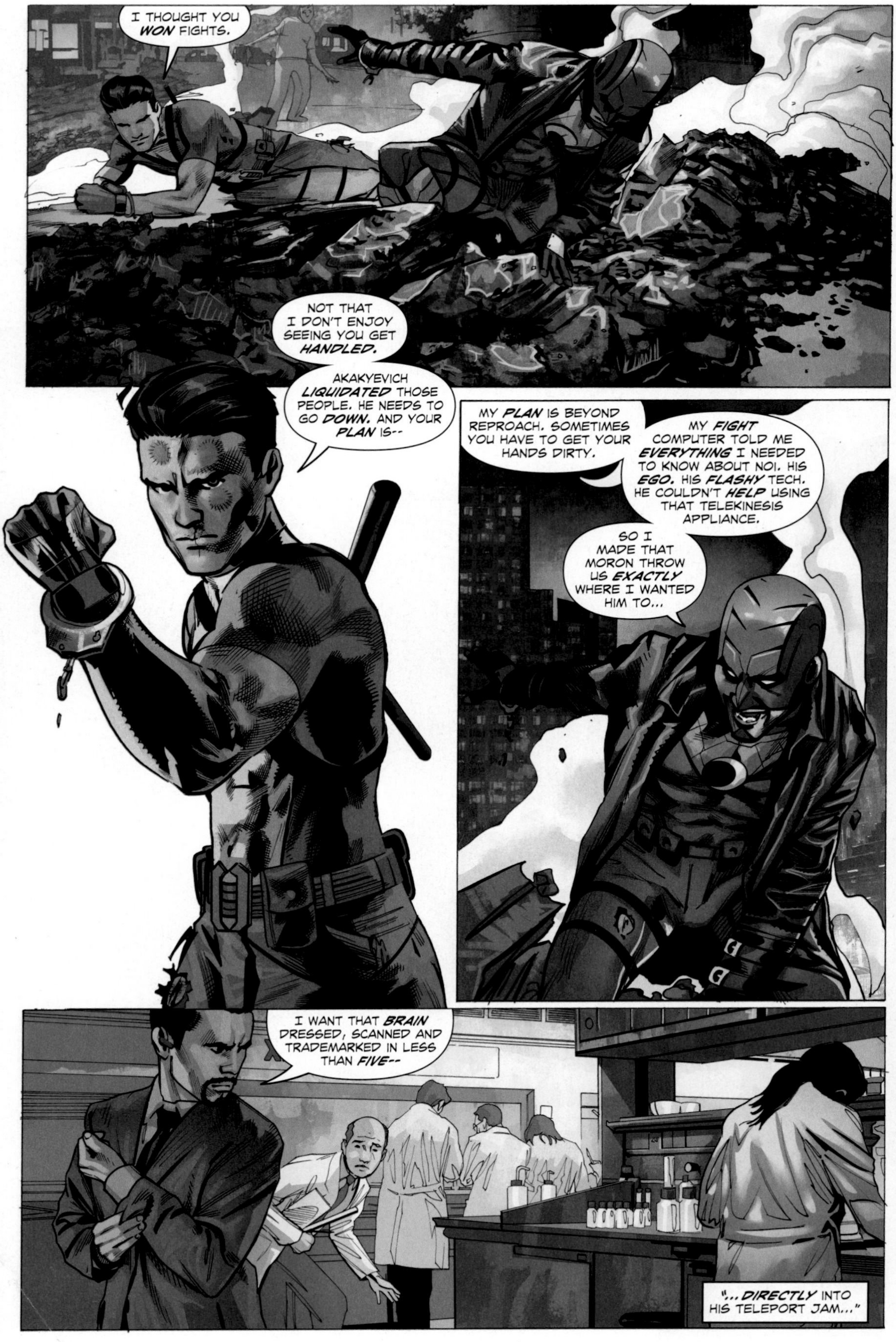
I THOUGHT YOU WON FIGHTS.
NOT THAT I DON'T ENJOY SEEING YOU GET HANDLED.
AKAKYEVICH LIQUIDATED THOSE PEOPLE. HE NEEDS TO GO DOWN. AND YOUR PLAN IS--
MY PLAN IS BEYOND REPROACH. SOMETIMES YOU HAVE TO GET YOUR HANDS DIRTY.
MY FIGHT COMPUTER TOLD ME EVERYTHING I NEEDED TO KNOW ABOUT NOI. HIS EGO. HIS FLASHY TECH. HE COULDN'T HELP USING THAT TELEKINESIS APPLIANCE.
SO I MADE THAT MORON THROW US EXACTLY WHERE I WANTED HIM TO...
I WANT THAT BRAIN DRESSED, SCANNED AND TRADEMARKED IN LESS THAN FIVE--
"...DIRECTLY INTO HIS TELEPORT JAM..."

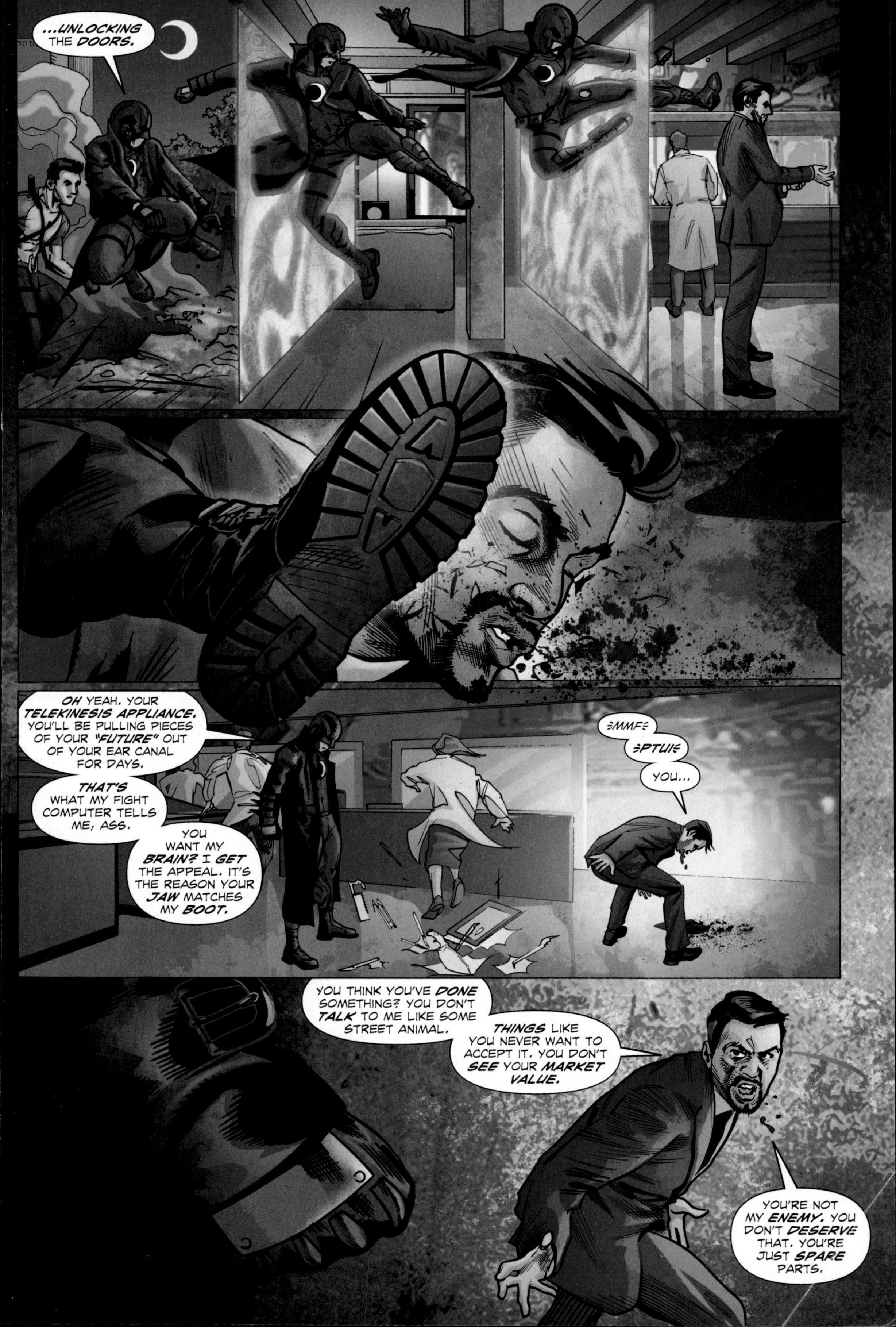

...UNLOCKING THE DOORS.
OH YEAH. YOUR TELEKINESIS APPLIANCE. YOU'LL BE PULLING PIECES OF YOUR "FUTURE" OUT OF YOUR EAR CANAL FOR DAYS.
THAT'S WHAT MY FIGHT COMPUTER TELLS ME, ASS.
YOU WANT MY BRAIN? I GET THE APPEAL. IT'S THE REASON YOUR JAW MATCHES MY BOOT.
MMF
PTUI
YOU...
YOU THINK YOU'VE DONE SOMETHING? YOU DON'T TALK TO ME LIKE SOME STREET ANIMAL.
THINGS LIKE YOU NEVER WANT TO ACCEPT IT. YOU DON'T SEE YOUR MARKET VALUE.
YOU'RE NOT MY ENEMY. YOU DON'T DESERVE THAT. YOU'RE JUST SPARE PARTS.

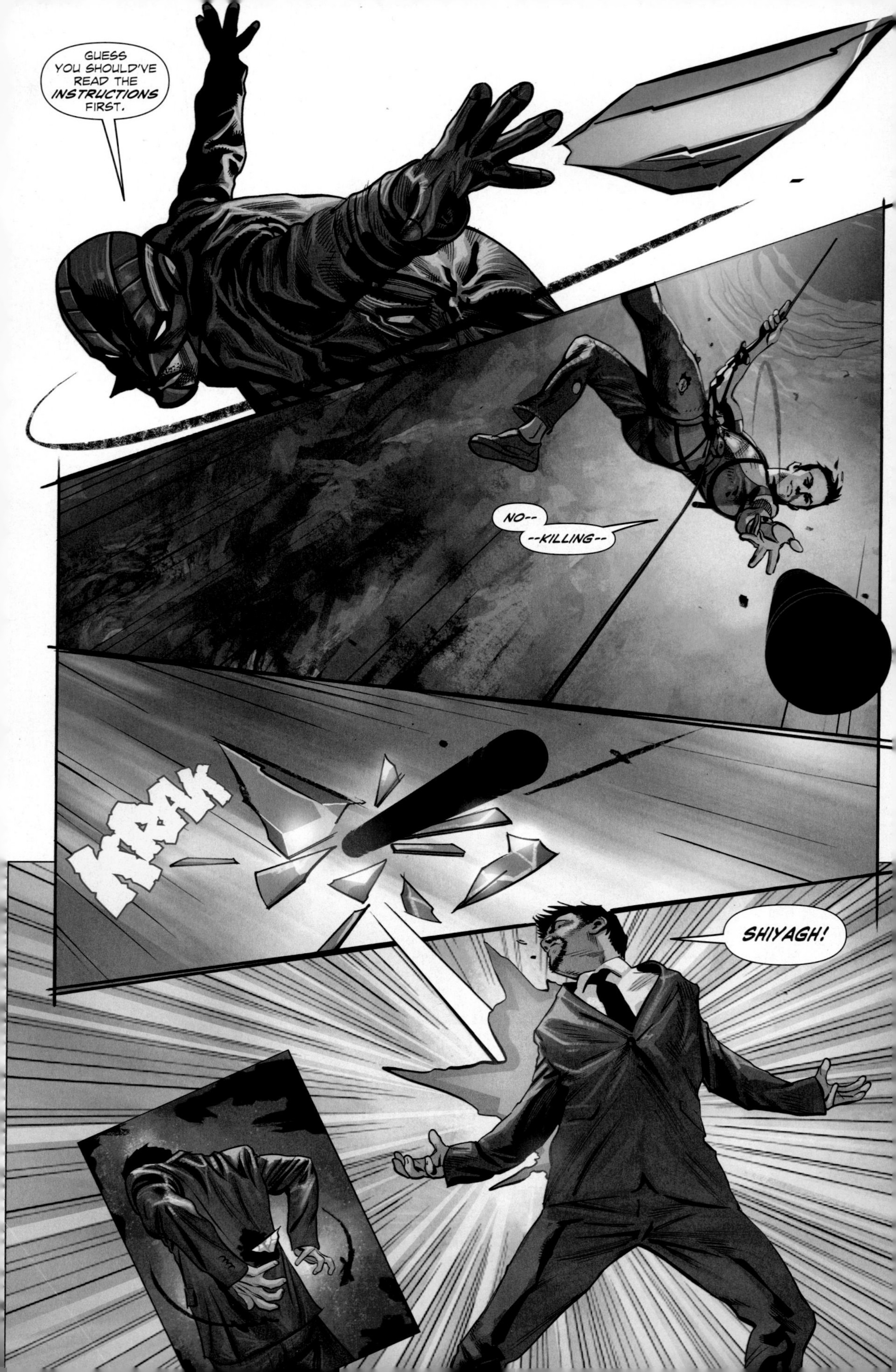
GUESS YOU SHOULD'VE READ THE *INSTRUCTIONS* FIRST.
NO--
--KILLING--
KRAK
SHIYAGH!

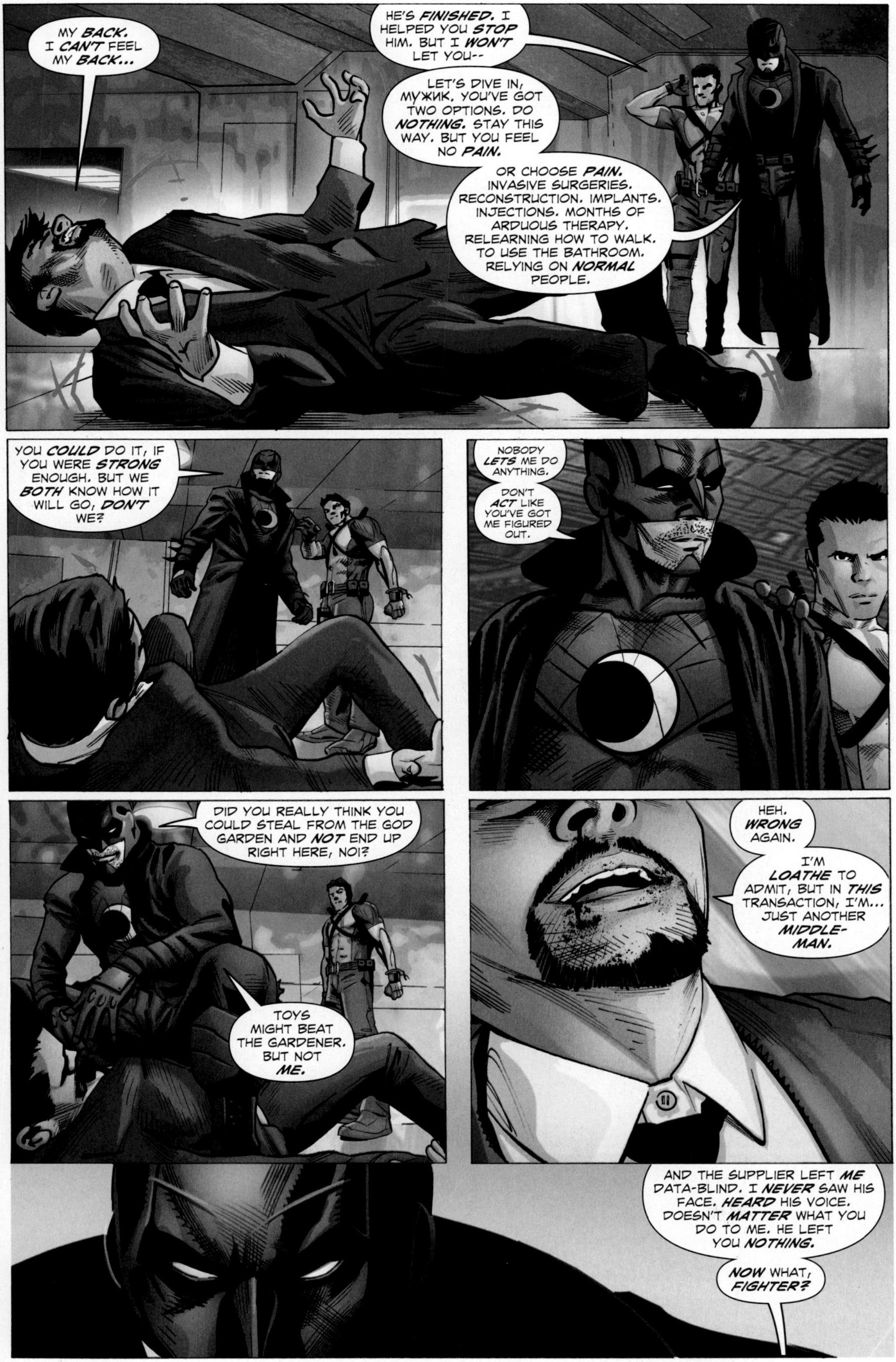
MY BACK. I CAN'T FEEL MY BACK...
HE'S FINISHED. I HELPED YOU STOP HIM. BUT I WON'T LET YOU--
LET'S DIVE IN, МУЖИК. YOU'VE GOT TWO OPTIONS. DO NOTHING. STAY THIS WAY. BUT YOU FEEL NO PAIN.
OR CHOOSE PAIN. INVASIVE SURGERIES. RECONSTRUCTION. IMPLANTS. INJECTIONS. MONTHS OF ARDUOUS THERAPY. RELEARNING HOW TO WALK. TO USE THE BATHROOM. RELYING ON NORMAL PEOPLE.
YOU COULD DO IT, IF YOU WERE STRONG ENOUGH. BUT WE BOTH KNOW HOW IT WILL GO, DON'T WE?
NOBODY LETS ME DO ANYTHING.
DON'T ACT LIKE YOU'VE GOT ME FIGURED OUT.
DID YOU REALLY THINK YOU COULD STEAL FROM THE GOD GARDEN AND NOT END UP RIGHT HERE, NOI?
TOYS MIGHT BEAT THE GARDENER. BUT NOT ME.
HEH. WRONG AGAIN.
I'M LOATHE TO ADMIT, BUT IN THIS TRANSACTION, I'M... JUST ANOTHER MIDDLE-MAN.
AND THE SUPPLIER LEFT ME DATA-BLIND. I NEVER SAW HIS FACE. HEARD HIS VOICE. DOESN'T MATTER WHAT YOU DO TO ME. HE LEFT YOU NOTHING.
NOW WHAT, FIGHTER?

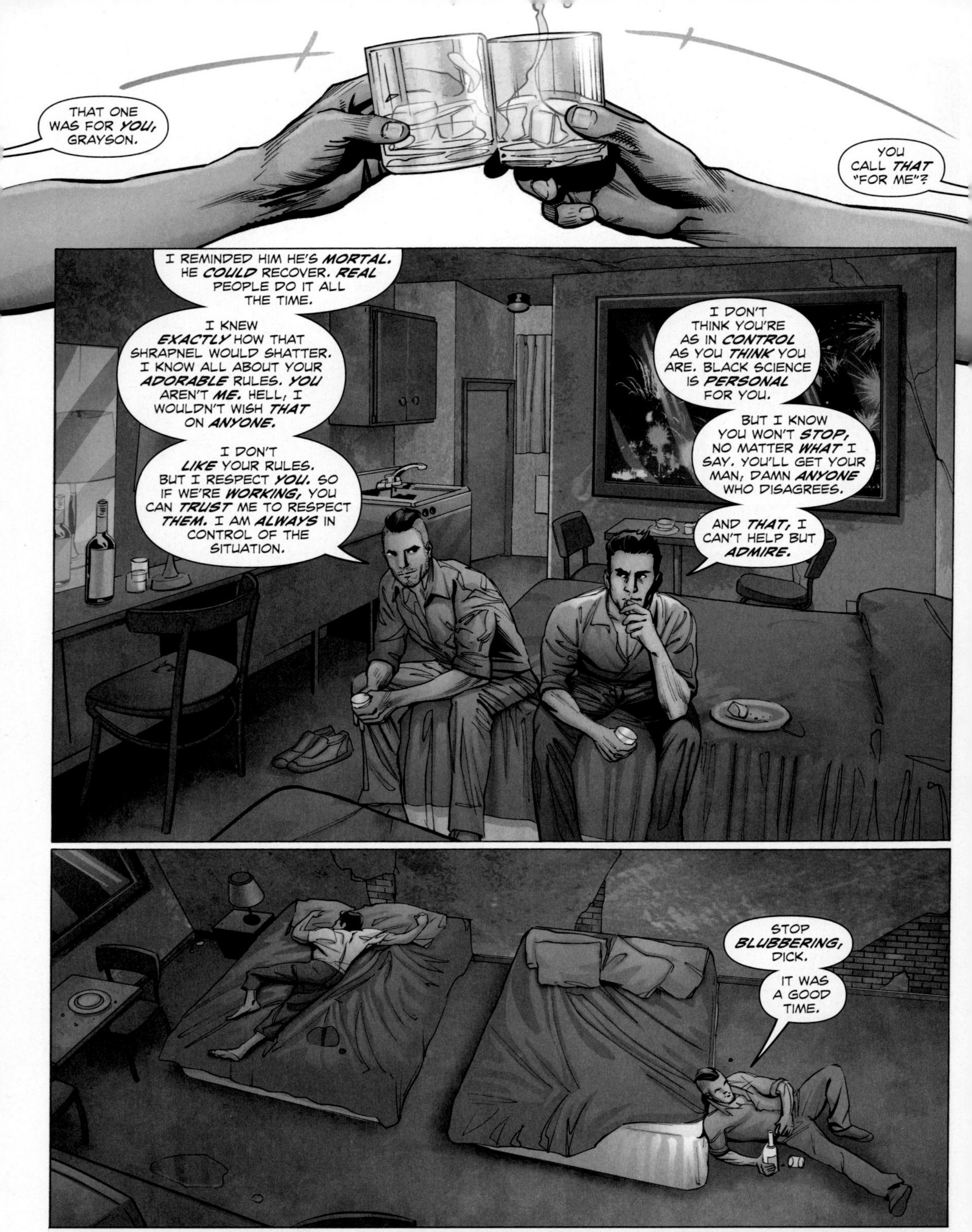
THAT ONE WAS FOR YOU, GRAYSON.
YOU CALL THAT "FOR ME"?
I REMINDED HIM HE'S MORTAL. HE COULD RECOVER. REAL PEOPLE DO IT ALL THE TIME.
I KNEW EXACTLY HOW THAT SHRAPNEL WOULD SHATTER. I KNOW ALL ABOUT YOUR ADORABLE RULES. YOU AREN'T ME. HELL, I WOULDN'T WISH THAT ON ANYONE.
I DON'T LIKE YOUR RULES. BUT I RESPECT YOU. SO IF WE'RE WORKING, YOU CAN TRUST ME TO RESPECT THEM. I AM ALWAYS IN CONTROL OF THE SITUATION.
I DON'T THINK YOU'RE AS IN CONTROL AS YOU THINK YOU ARE. BLACK SCIENCE IS PERSONAL FOR YOU.
BUT I KNOW YOU WON'T STOP, NO MATTER WHAT I SAY. YOU'LL GET YOUR MAN, DAMN ANYONE WHO DISAGREES.
AND THAT, I CAN'T HELP BUT ADMIRE.
STOP BLUBBERING, DICK.
IT WAS A GOOD TIME.

ПОЛУНОЧНИК

STEVE ORLANDO WRITER STEPHEN MOONEY ARTIST

ROMULO FAJARDO, JR. WITH JEREMY COX (PGS 15,17-20) COLORS TOM NAPOLITANO LETTERS

ACO & ROMULO FAJARDO, JR. COVER

DAVE WIELGOSZ ASST. EDITOR CHRIS CONROY EDITOR MARK DOYLE GROUP EDITOR

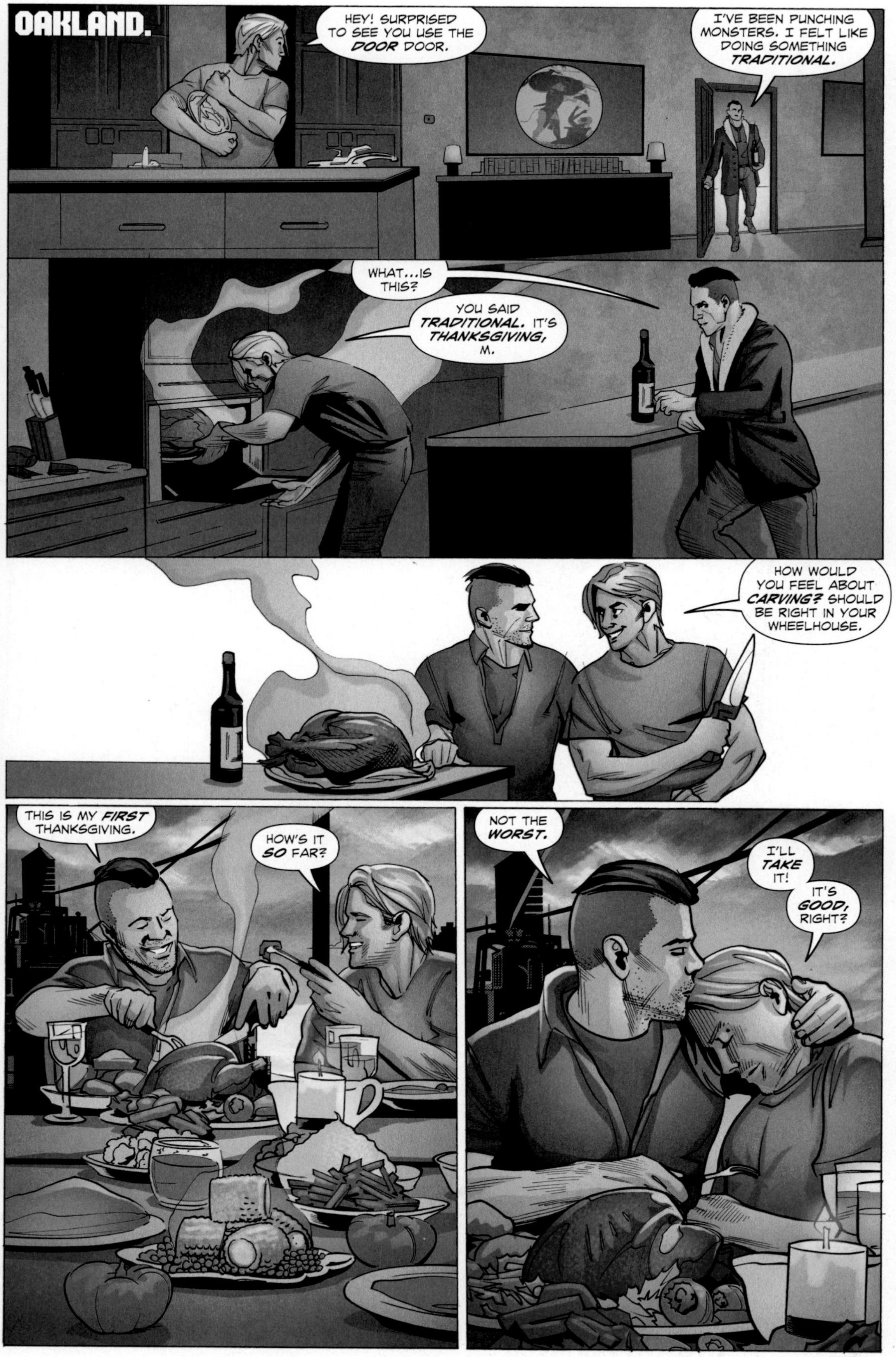
OAKLAND.
HEY! SURPRISED TO SEE YOU USE THE DOOR DOOR.
I'VE BEEN PUNCHING MONSTERS. I FELT LIKE DOING SOMETHING TRADITIONAL.
WHAT...IS THIS?
YOU SAID TRADITIONAL. IT'S THANKSGIVING, M.
HOW WOULD YOU FEEL ABOUT CARVING? SHOULD BE RIGHT IN YOUR WHEELHOUSE.
THIS IS MY FIRST THANKSGIVING.
HOW'S IT SO FAR?
NOT THE WORST.
I'LL TAKE IT!
IT'S GOOD, RIGHT?

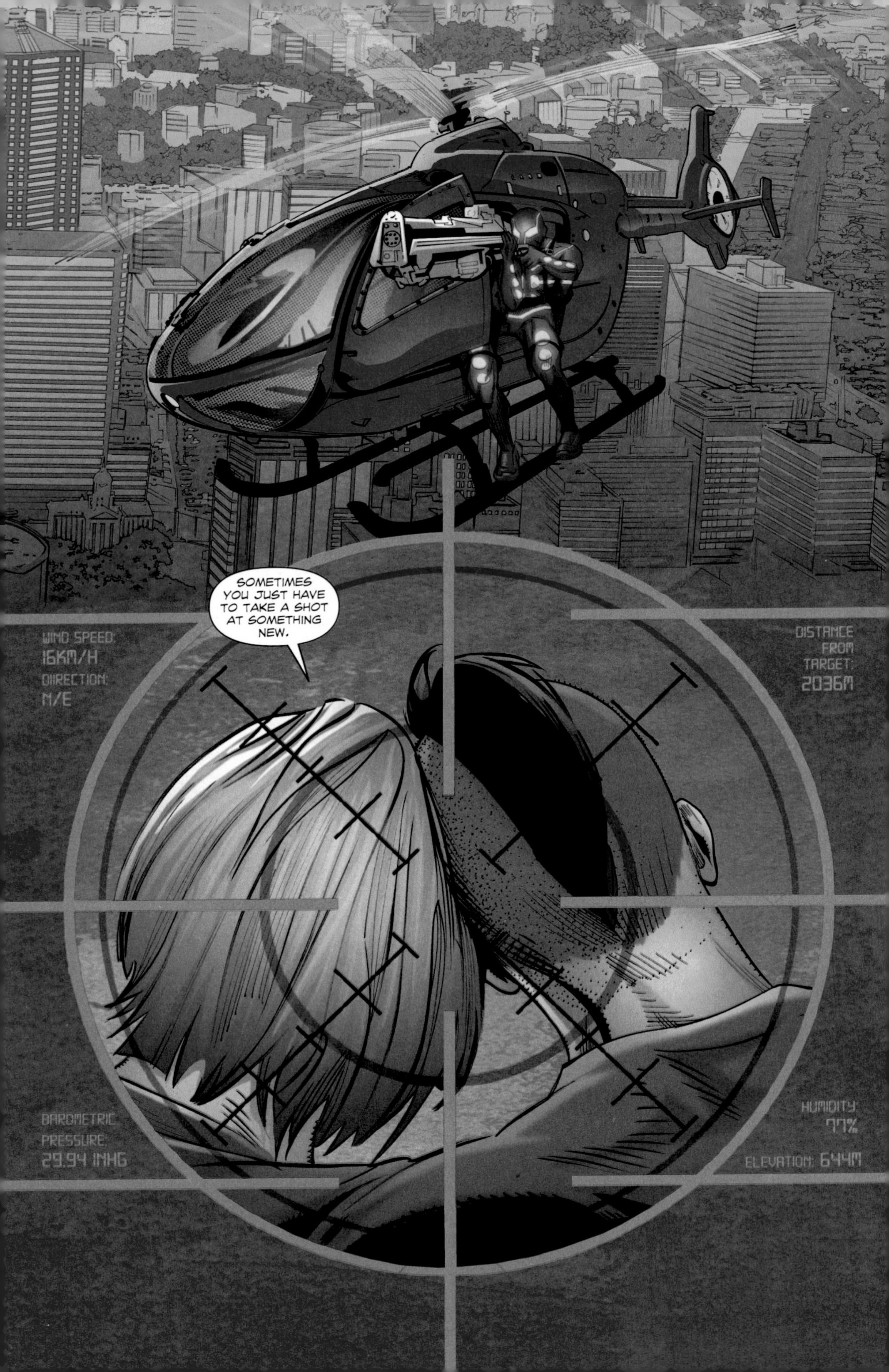
SOMETIMES YOU JUST HAVE TO TAKE A SHOT AT SOMETHING NEW.
WIND SPEED: 16KM/H
DIIRECTION: N/E
DISTANCE FROM TARGET: 2036M
BAROMETRIC PRESSURE: 29.94 INHG
HUMIDITY: 77%
ELEVATION: 644M

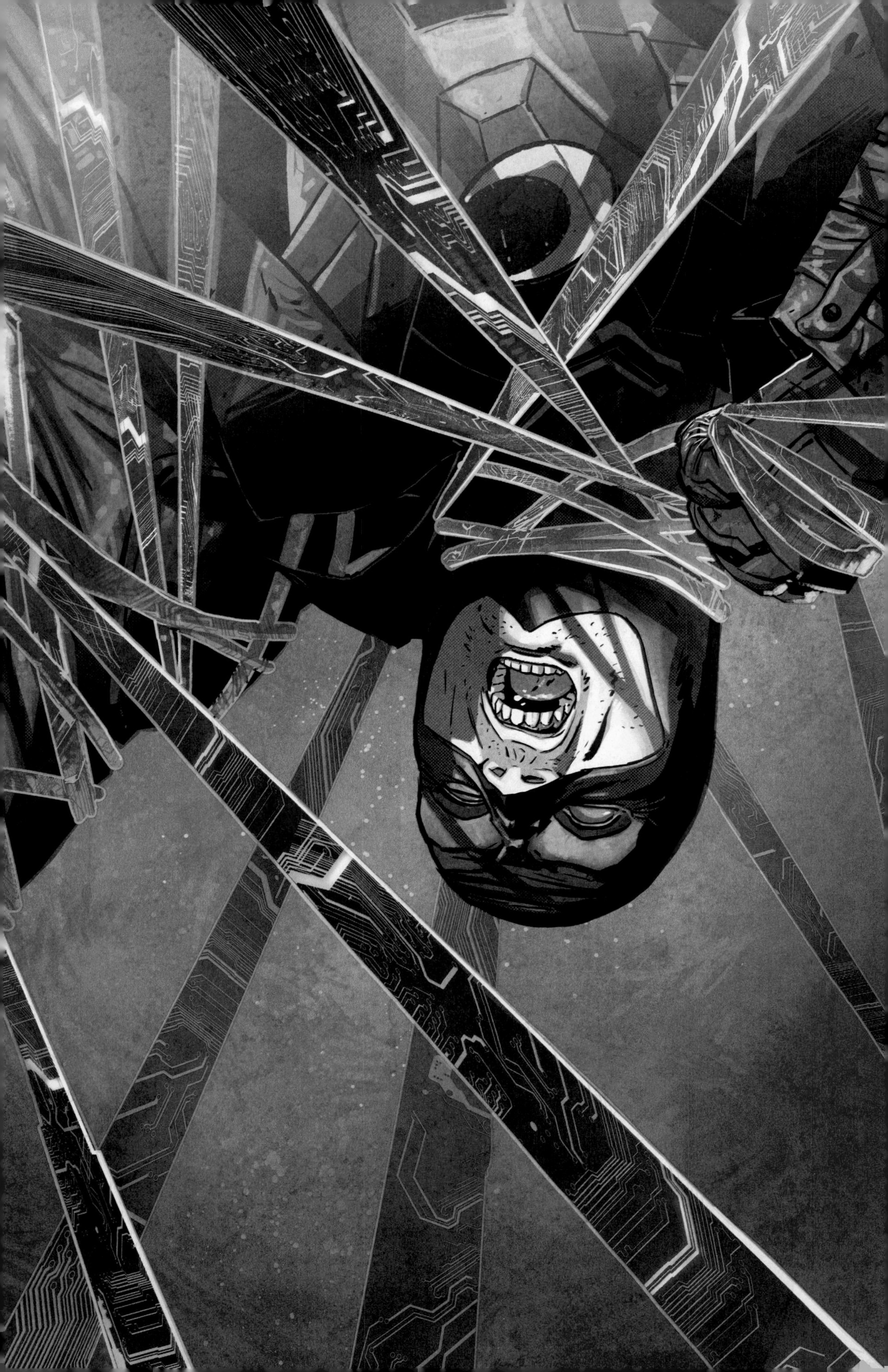

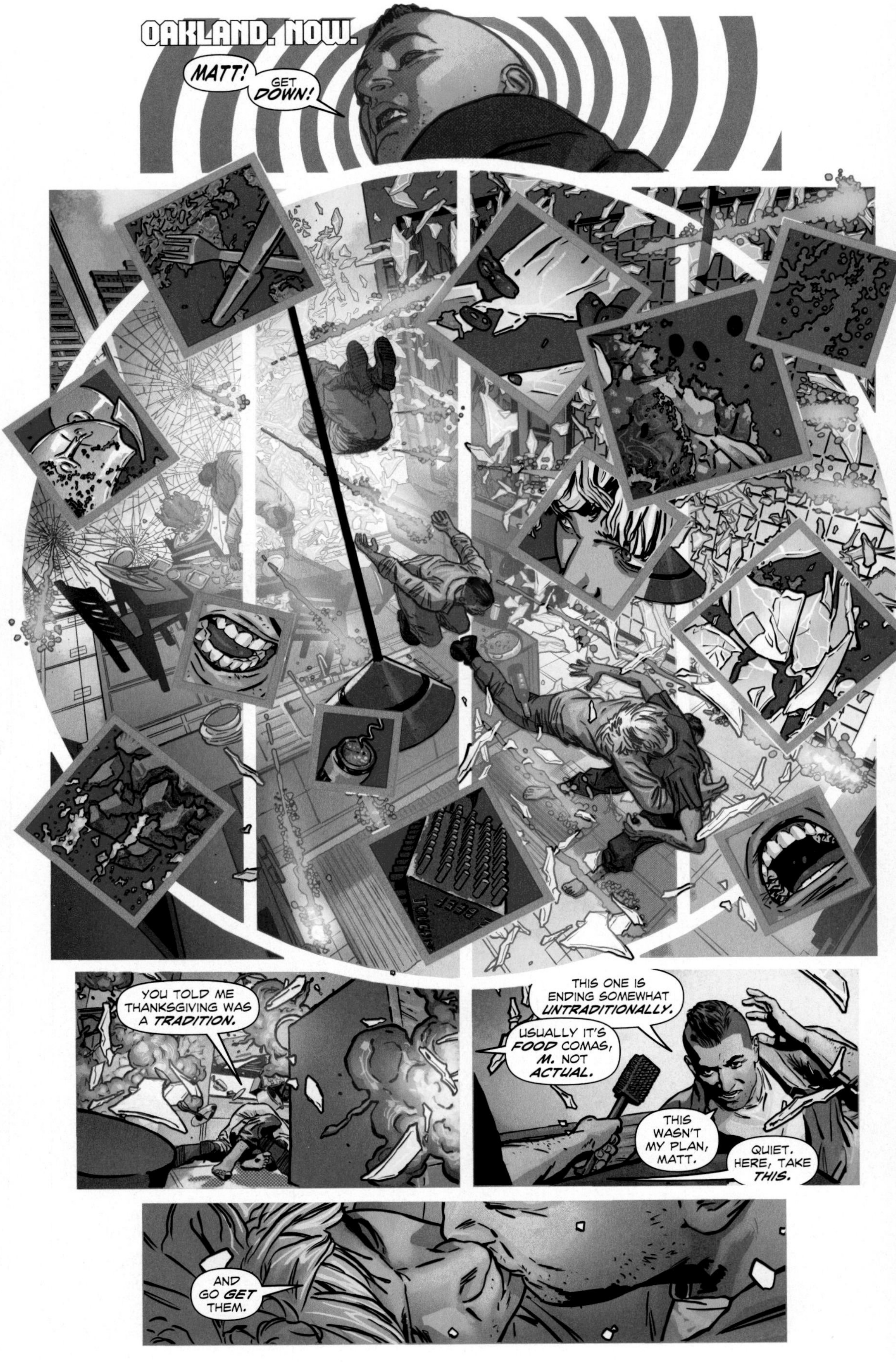
OAKLAND. NOW.
MATT!
GET DOWN!
YOU TOLD ME THANKSGIVING WAS A TRADITION.
THIS ONE IS ENDING SOMEWHAT UNTRADITIONALLY.
USUALLY IT'S FOOD COMAS, M. NOT ACTUAL.
THIS WASN'T MY PLAN, MATT.
QUIET. HERE, TAKE THIS.
AND GO GET THEM.

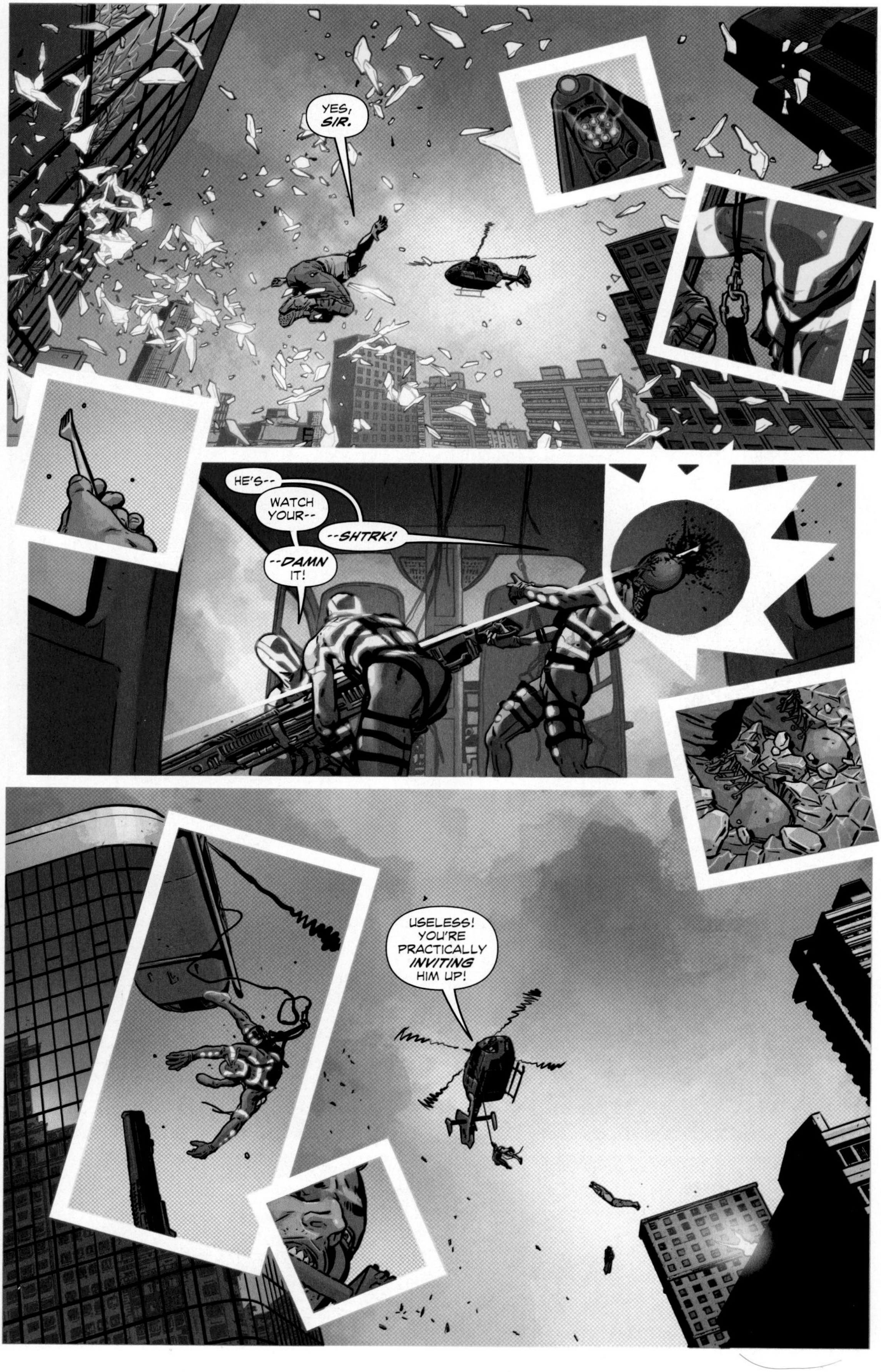
YES, SIR.
HE'S--
WATCH YOUR--
--SHTRK!
--DAMN IT!
USELESS! YOU'RE PRACTICALLY INVITING HIM UP!

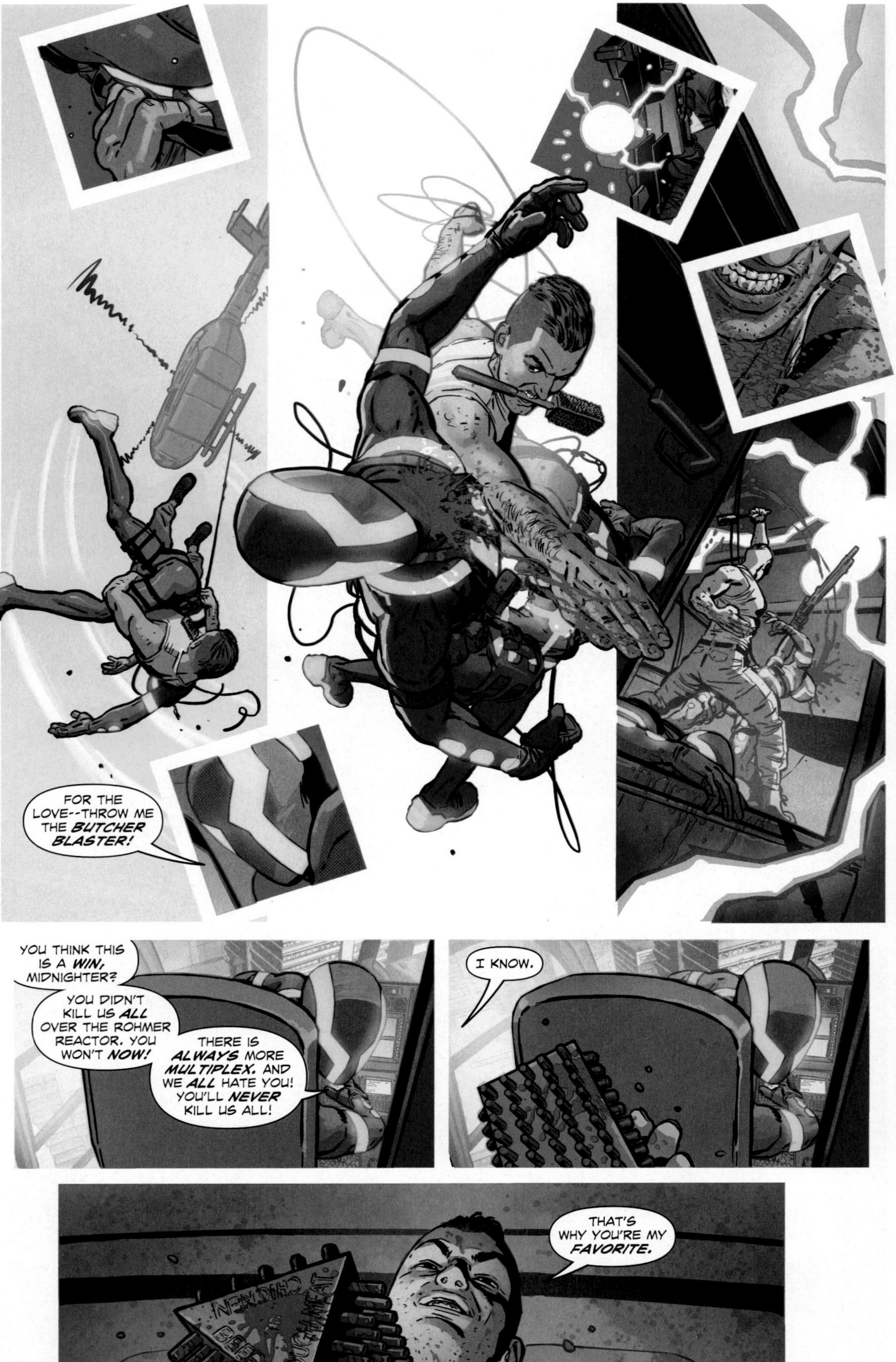
FOR THE LOVE--THROW ME THE BUTCHER BLASTER!
YOU THINK THIS IS A WIN, MIDNIGHTER?
YOU DIDN'T KILL US ALL OVER THE ROHMER REACTOR. YOU WON'T NOW!
THERE IS ALWAYS MORE MULTIPLEX. AND WE ALL HATE YOU! YOU'LL NEVER KILL US ALL!
I KNOW.
THAT'S WHY YOU'RE MY FAVORITE.

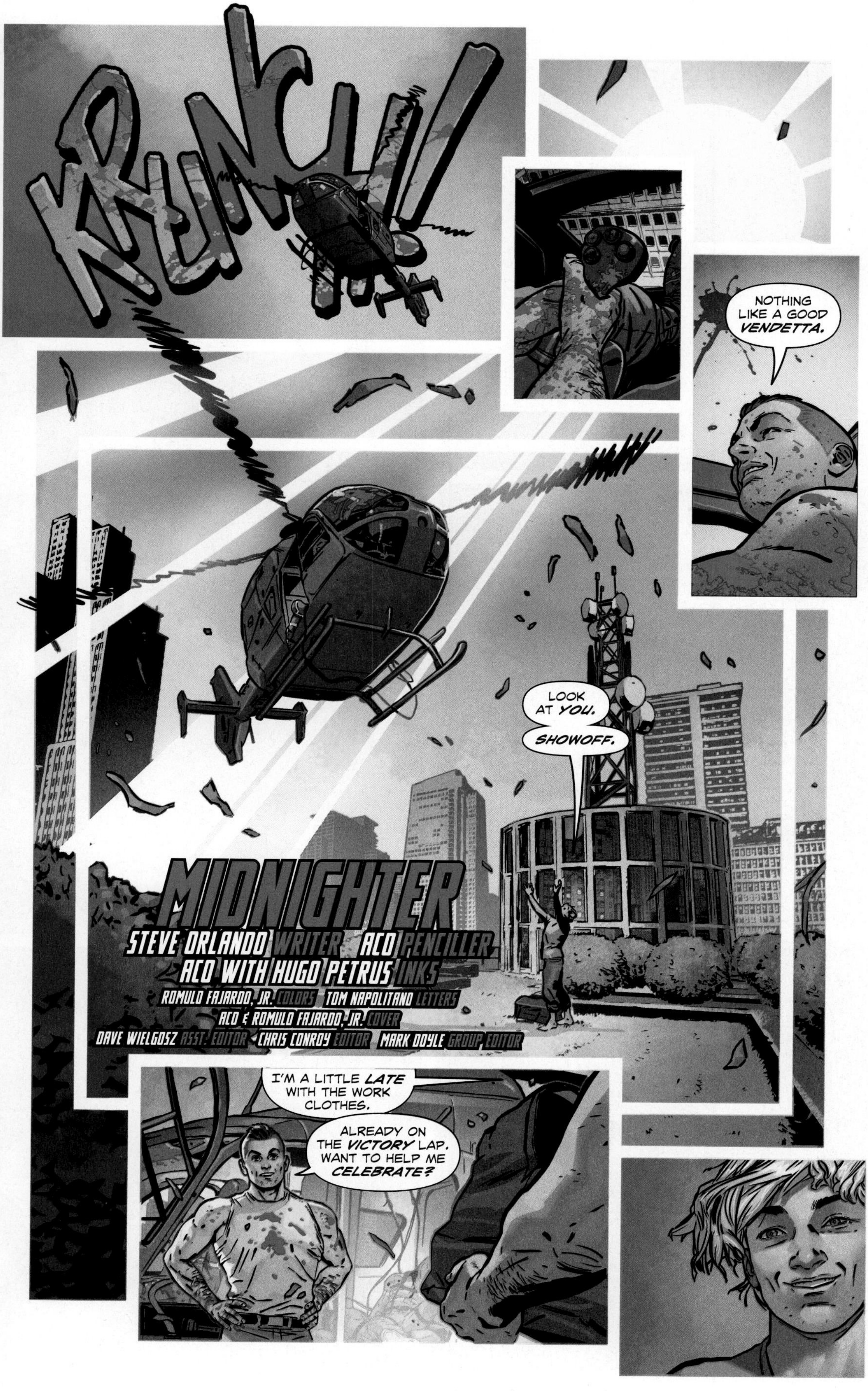
KRUNCH!!
NOTHING LIKE A GOOD VENDETTA.
LOOK AT YOU.
SHOWOFF.
MIDNIGHTER
STEVE ORLANDO WRITER ACO PENCILLER
ACO WITH HUGO PETRUS INKS
ROMULO FAJARDO, JR. COLORS TOM NAPOLITANO LETTERS
ACO & ROMULO FAJARDO, JR. COVER
DAVE WIELGOSZ ASST. EDITOR CHRIS CONROY EDITOR MARK DOYLE GROUP EDITOR
I'M A LITTLE LATE WITH THE WORK CLOTHES.
ALREADY ON THE VICTORY LAP. WANT TO HELP ME CELEBRATE?

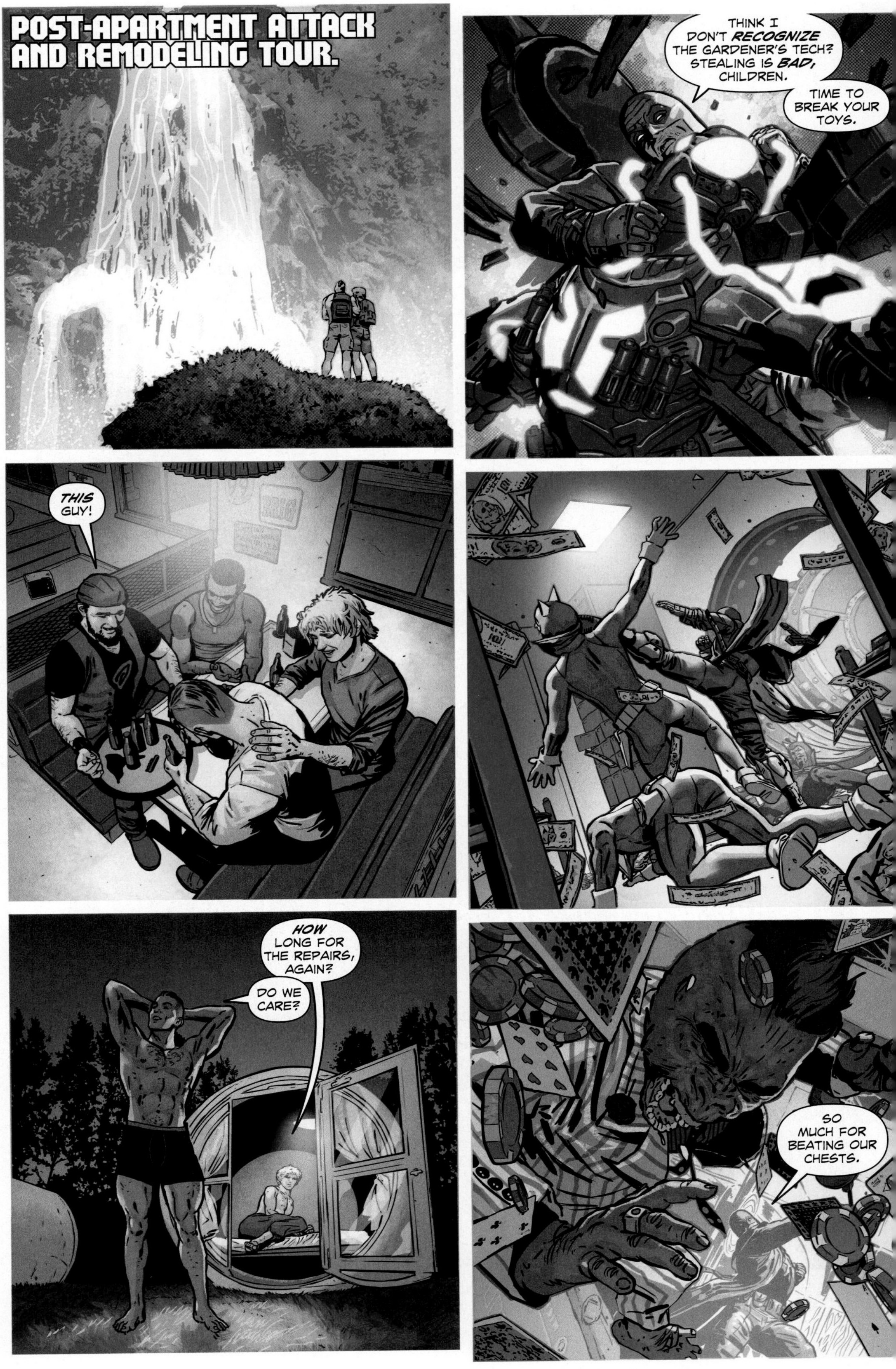
POST-APARTMENT ATTACK AND REMODELING TOUR.
THINK I DON'T RECOGNIZE THE GARDENER'S TECH? STEALING IS BAD, CHILDREN.
TIME TO BREAK YOUR TOYS.
THIS GUY!
HOW LONG FOR THE REPAIRS, AGAIN?
DO WE CARE?
SO MUCH FOR BEATING OUR CHESTS.

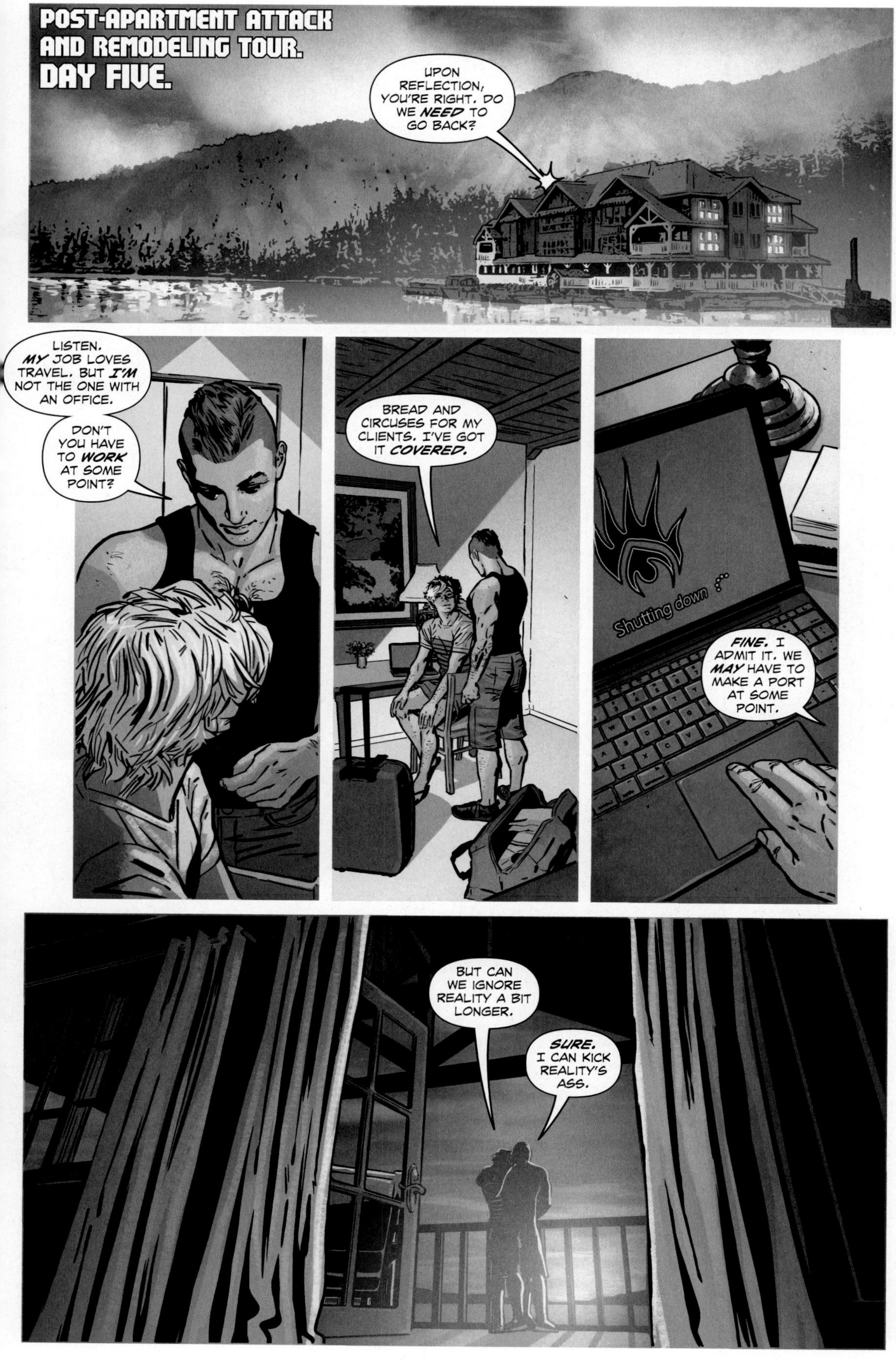
POST-APARTMENT ATTACK AND REMODELING TOUR. DAY FIVE.
UPON REFLECTION, YOU'RE RIGHT. DO WE NEED TO GO BACK?
LISTEN. MY JOB LOVES TRAVEL. BUT I'M NOT THE ONE WITH AN OFFICE.
DON'T YOU HAVE TO WORK AT SOME POINT?
BREAD AND CIRCUSES FOR MY CLIENTS. I'VE GOT IT COVERED.
Shutting down
FINE. I ADMIT IT. WE MAY HAVE TO MAKE A PORT AT SOME POINT.
BUT CAN WE IGNORE REALITY A BIT LONGER.
SURE. I CAN KICK REALITY'S ASS.

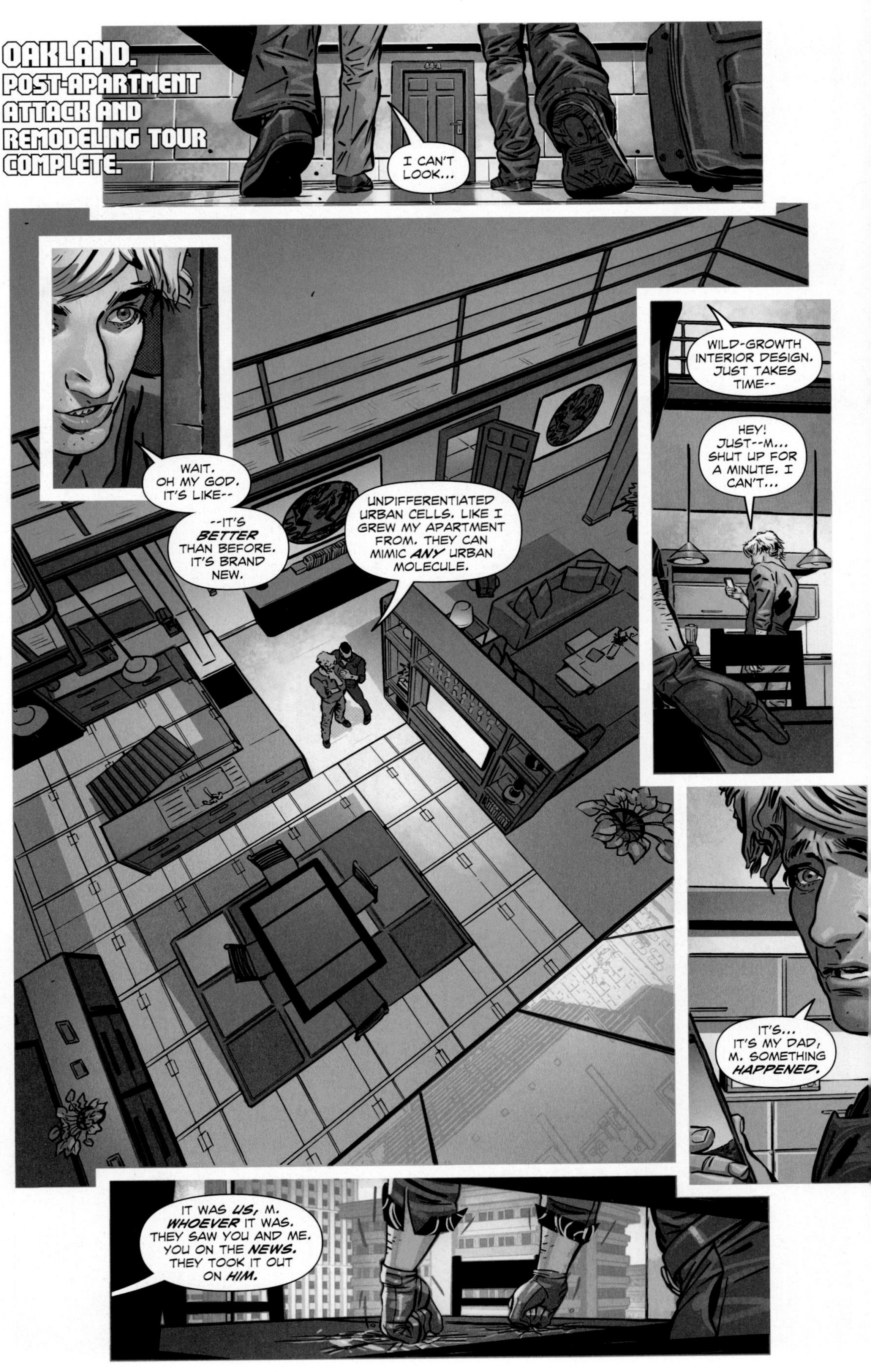
OAKLAND. POST-APARTMENT ATTACK AND REMODELING TOUR COMPLETE.
I CAN'T LOOK...
WAIT. OH MY GOD. IT'S LIKE--
--IT'S BETTER THAN BEFORE. IT'S BRAND NEW.
UNDIFFERENTIATED URBAN CELLS. LIKE I GREW MY APARTMENT FROM. THEY CAN MIMIC ANY URBAN MOLECULE.
WILD-GROWTH INTERIOR DESIGN. JUST TAKES TIME--
HEY! JUST--M... SHUT UP FOR A MINUTE. I CAN'T...
IT'S... IT'S MY DAD, M. SOMETHING HAPPENED.
IT WAS US, M. WHOEVER IT WAS. THEY SAW YOU AND ME. YOU ON THE NEWS. THEY TOOK IT OUT ON HIM.

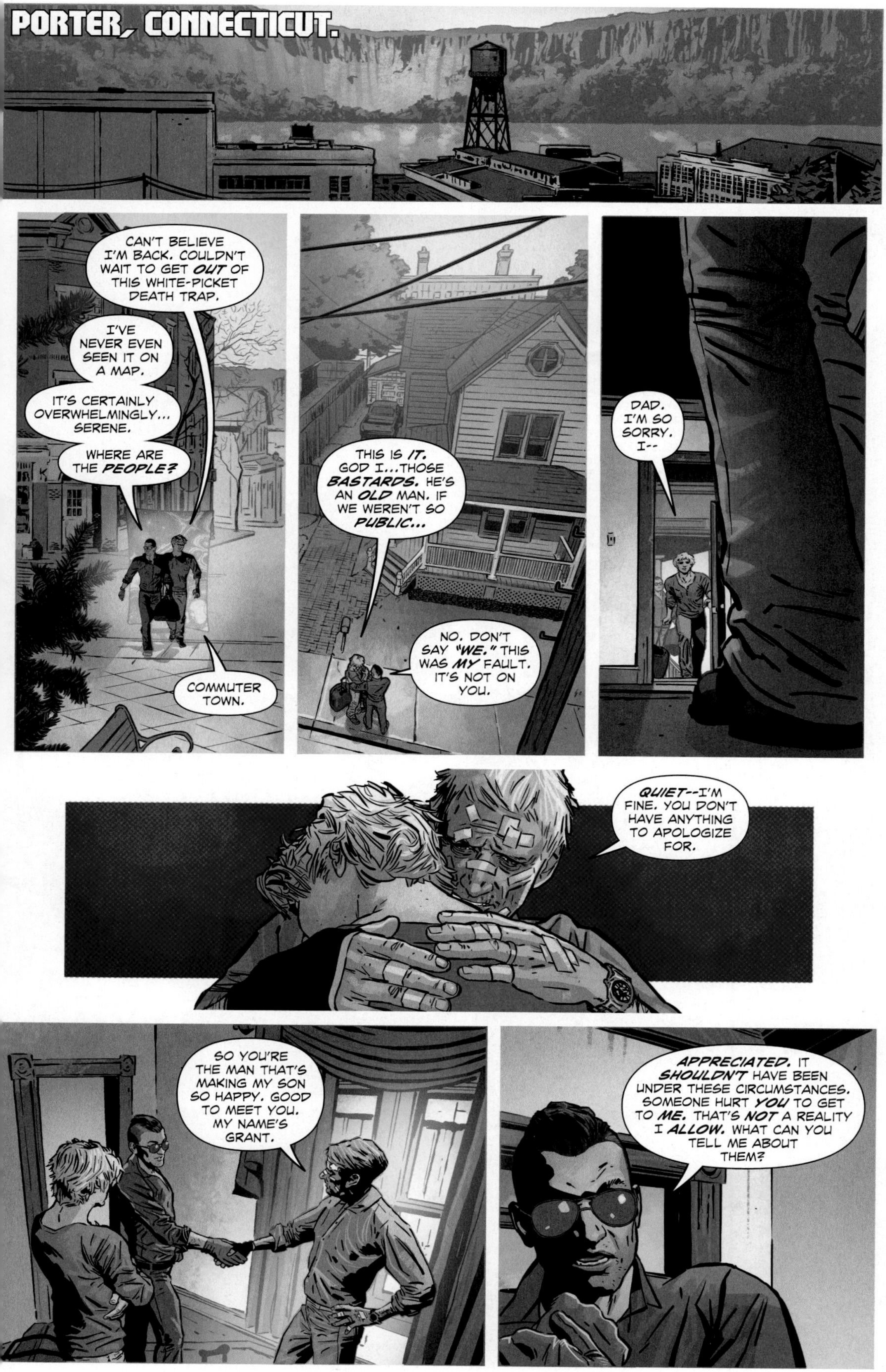
PORTER, CONNECTICUT.
CAN'T BELIEVE I'M BACK. COULDN'T WAIT TO GET OUT OF THIS WHITE-PICKET DEATH TRAP.
I'VE NEVER EVEN SEEN IT ON A MAP.
IT'S CERTAINLY OVERWHELMINGLY... SERENE.
WHERE ARE THE PEOPLE?
COMMUTER TOWN.
THIS IS IT. GOD I...THOSE BASTARDS. HE'S AN OLD MAN. IF WE WEREN'T SO PUBLIC...
NO. DON'T SAY "WE." THIS WAS MY FAULT. IT'S NOT ON YOU.
DAD. I'M SO SORRY. I--
QUIET--I'M FINE. YOU DON'T HAVE ANYTHING TO APOLOGIZE FOR.
SO YOU'RE THE MAN THAT'S MAKING MY SON SO HAPPY. GOOD TO MEET YOU. MY NAME'S GRANT.
APPRECIATED. IT SHOULDN'T HAVE BEEN UNDER THESE CIRCUMSTANCES. SOMEONE HURT YOU TO GET TO ME. THAT'S NOT A REALITY I ALLOW. WHAT CAN YOU TELL ME ABOUT THEM?

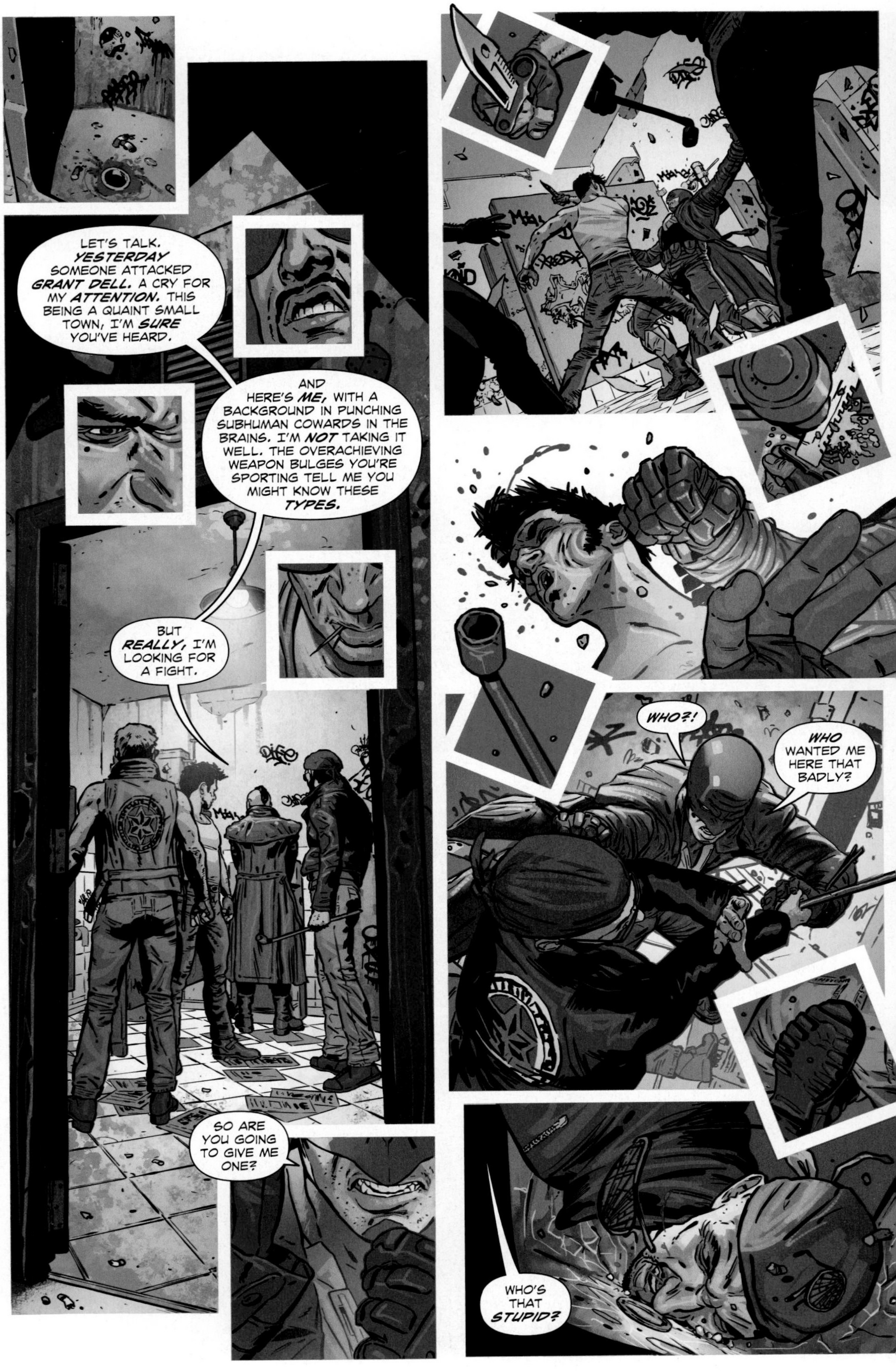
LET'S TALK. YESTERDAY SOMEONE ATTACKED GRANT DELL. A CRY FOR MY ATTENTION. THIS BEING A QUAINT SMALL TOWN, I'M SURE YOU'VE HEARD.
AND HERE'S ME, WITH A BACKGROUND IN PUNCHING SUBHUMAN COWARDS IN THE BRAINS. I'M NOT TAKING IT WELL. THE OVERACHIEVING WEAPON BULGES YOU'RE SPORTING TELL ME YOU MIGHT KNOW THESE TYPES.
BUT REALLY, I'M LOOKING FOR A FIGHT.
SO ARE YOU GOING TO GIVE ME ONE?
WHO?!
WHO WANTED ME HERE THAT BADLY?
WHO'S THAT STUPID?

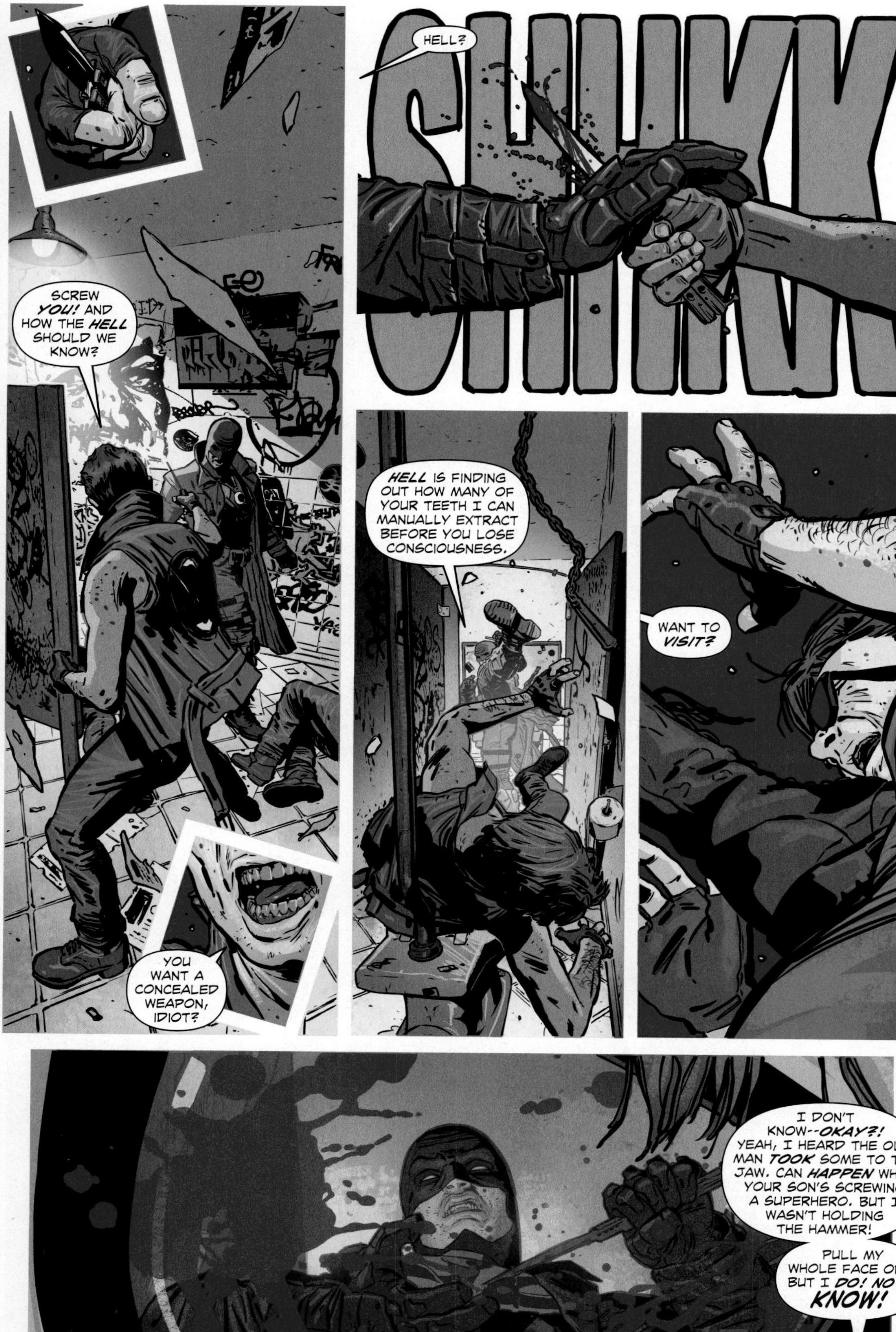

SCREW YOU! AND HOW THE HELL SHOULD WE KNOW?
YOU WANT A CONCEALED WEAPON, IDIOT?
HELL?
SHHKK
HELL IS FINDING OUT HOW MANY OF YOUR TEETH I CAN MANUALLY EXTRACT BEFORE YOU LOSE CONSCIOUSNESS.
WANT TO VISIT?
I DON'T KNOW--OKAY?! YEAH, I HEARD THE OLD MAN TOOK SOME TO THE JAW. CAN HAPPEN WHEN YOUR SON'S SCREWING A SUPERHERO. BUT I WASN'T HOLDING THE HAMMER!
PULL MY WHOLE FACE OFF BUT I DO! NOT! KNOW!

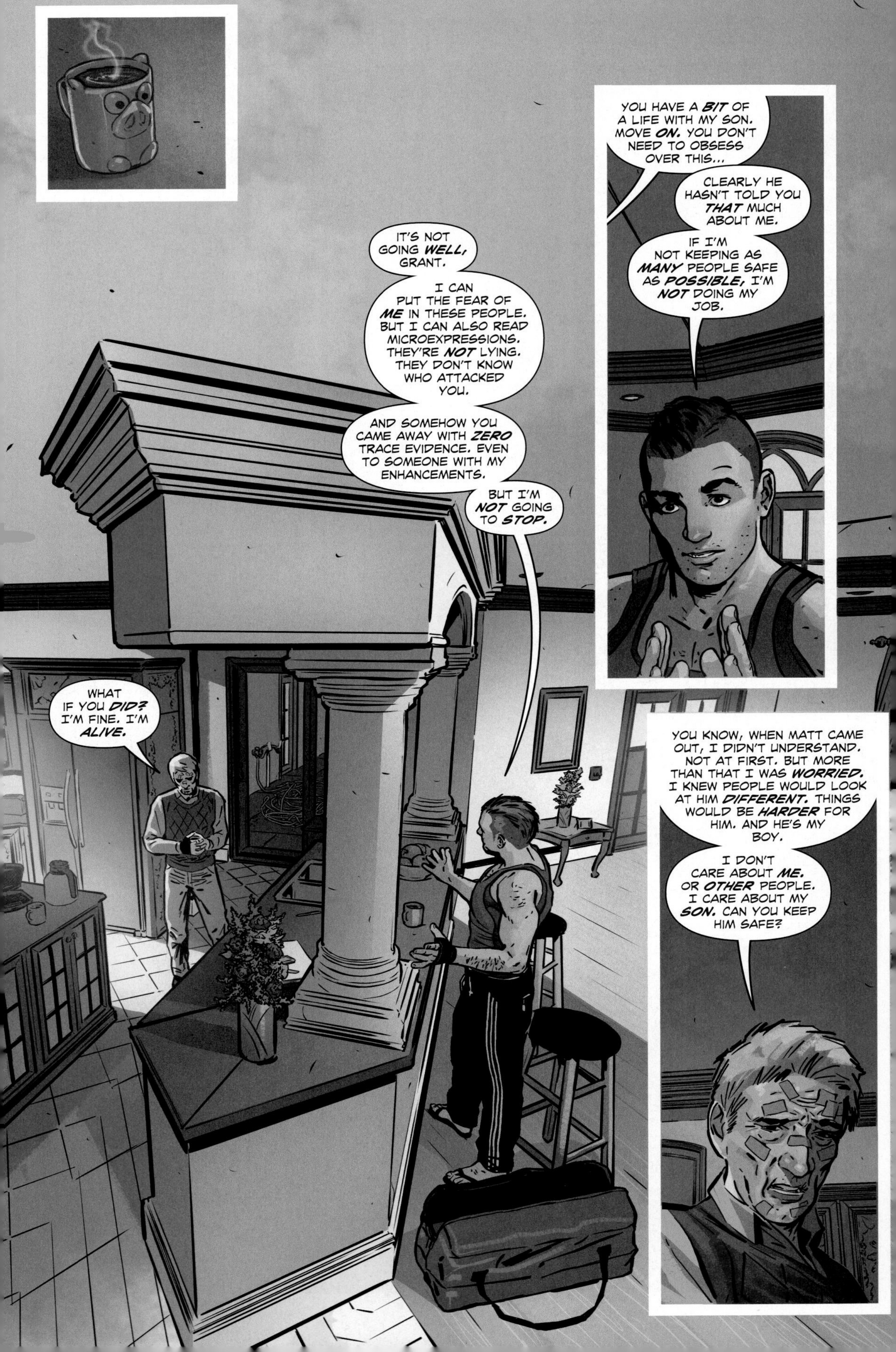
IT'S NOT GOING *WELL,* GRANT.
I CAN PUT THE FEAR OF *ME* IN THESE PEOPLE. BUT I CAN ALSO READ MICROEXPRESSIONS. THEY'RE *NOT* LYING. THEY DON'T KNOW WHO ATTACKED YOU.
AND SOMEHOW YOU CAME AWAY WITH *ZERO* TRACE EVIDENCE. EVEN TO SOMEONE WITH MY ENHANCEMENTS.
BUT I'M *NOT* GOING TO *STOP.*
WHAT IF YOU *DID?* I'M FINE. I'M *ALIVE.*
YOU HAVE A *BIT* OF A LIFE WITH MY SON. MOVE *ON.* YOU DON'T NEED TO OBSESS OVER THIS...
CLEARLY HE HASN'T TOLD YOU *THAT* MUCH ABOUT ME.
IF I'M NOT KEEPING AS *MANY* PEOPLE SAFE AS *POSSIBLE,* I'M *NOT* DOING MY JOB.
YOU KNOW, WHEN MATT CAME OUT, I DIDN'T UNDERSTAND. NOT AT FIRST. BUT MORE THAN THAT I WAS *WORRIED.* I KNEW PEOPLE WOULD LOOK AT HIM *DIFFERENT.* THINGS WOULD BE *HARDER* FOR HIM. AND HE'S MY BOY.
I DON'T CARE ABOUT *ME.* OR *OTHER* PEOPLE. I CARE ABOUT MY *SON.* CAN YOU KEEP HIM SAFE?

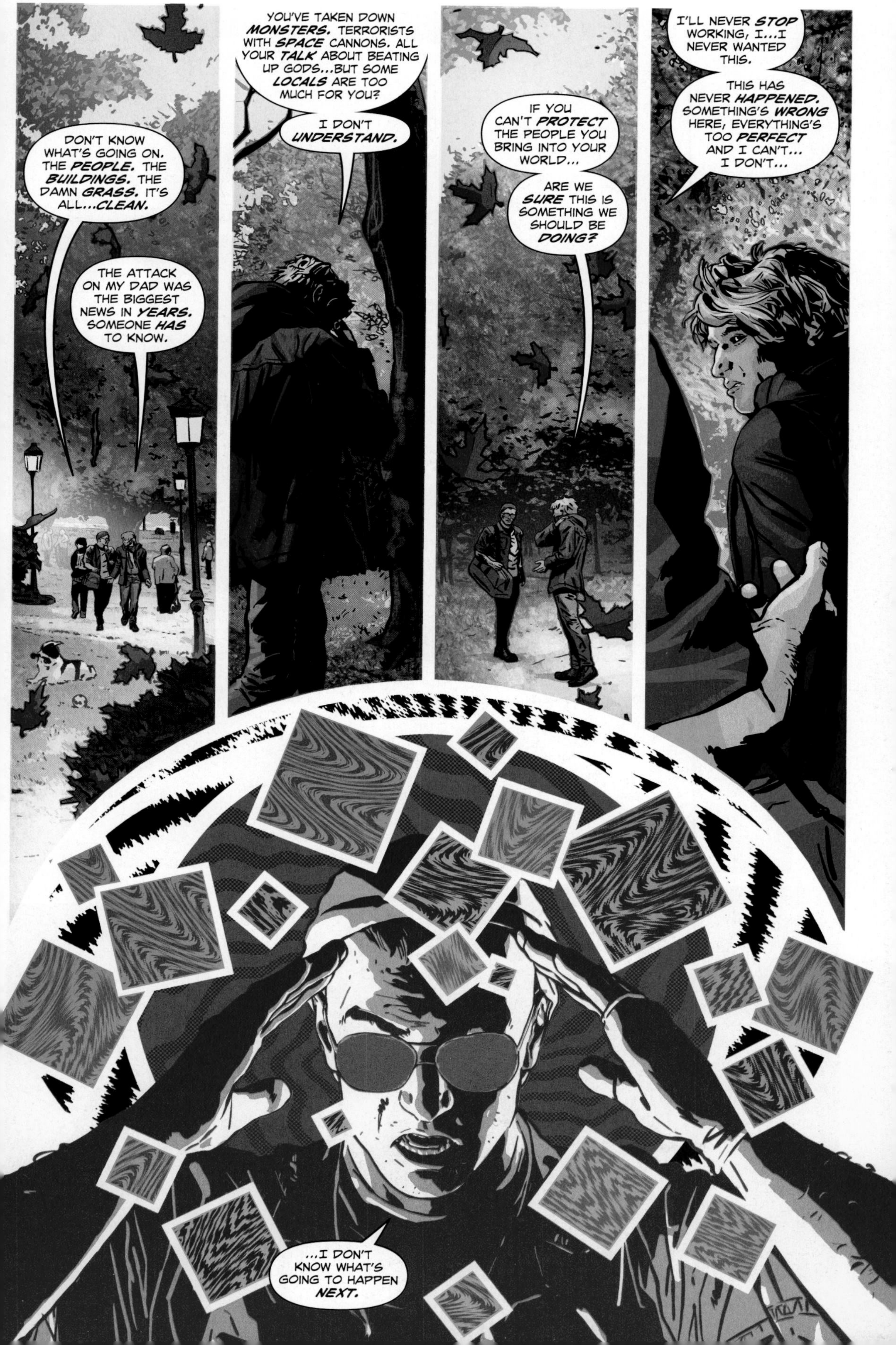
DON'T KNOW WHAT'S GOING ON. THE PEOPLE. THE BUILDINGS. THE DAMN GRASS. IT'S ALL...CLEAN.
THE ATTACK ON MY DAD WAS THE BIGGEST NEWS IN YEARS. SOMEONE HAS TO KNOW.
YOU'VE TAKEN DOWN MONSTERS. TERRORISTS WITH SPACE CANNONS. ALL YOUR TALK ABOUT BEATING UP GODS...BUT SOME LOCALS ARE TOO MUCH FOR YOU?
I DON'T UNDERSTAND.
IF YOU CAN'T PROTECT THE PEOPLE YOU BRING INTO YOUR WORLD...
ARE WE SURE THIS IS SOMETHING WE SHOULD BE DOING?
I'LL NEVER STOP WORKING, I...I NEVER WANTED THIS.
THIS HAS NEVER HAPPENED. SOMETHING'S WRONG HERE, EVERYTHING'S TOO PERFECT AND I CAN'T... I DON'T...
...I DON'T KNOW WHAT'S GOING TO HAPPEN NEXT.

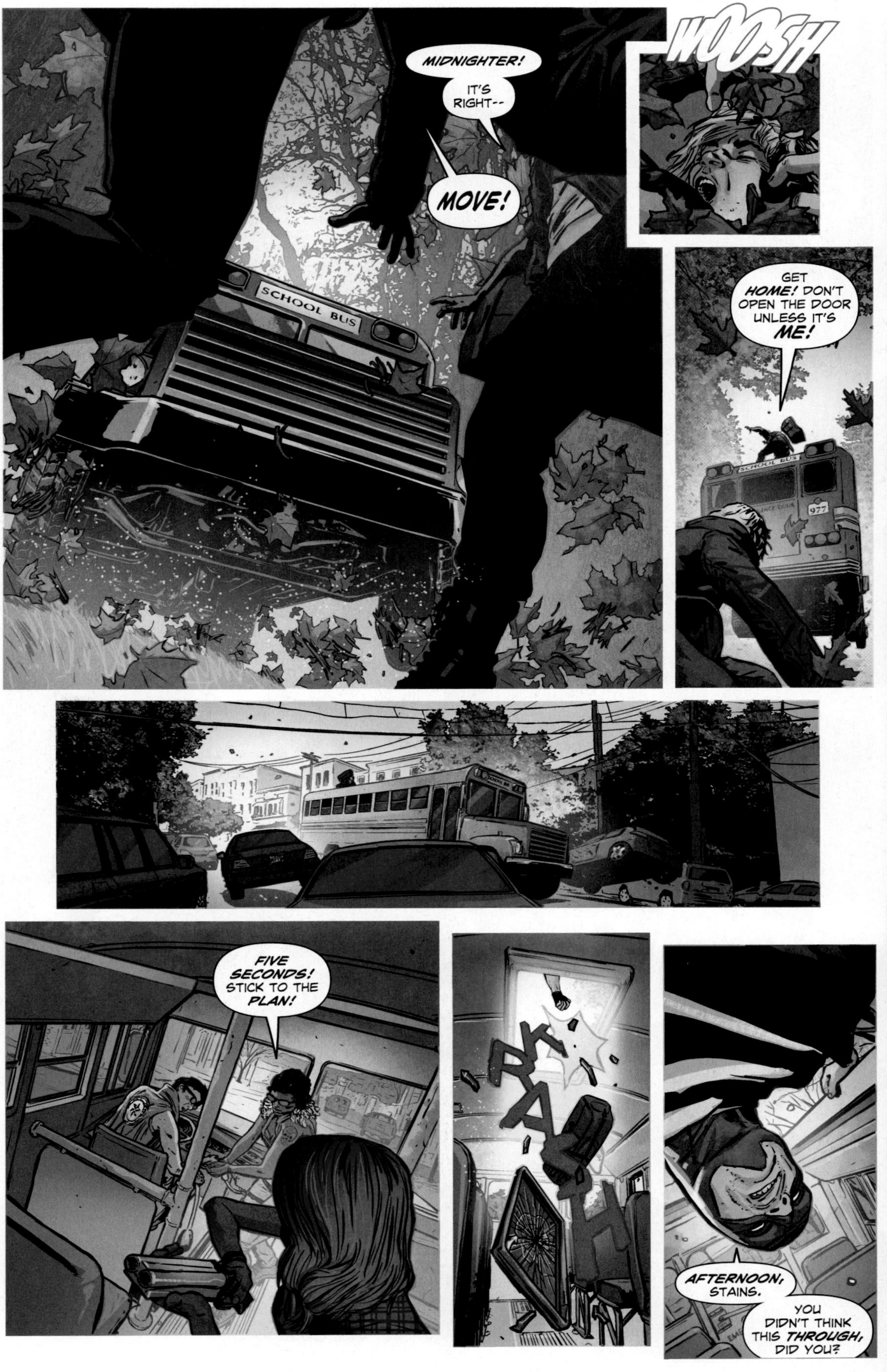
MIDNIGHTER!
IT'S RIGHT--
MOVE!
WOOSH
GET HOME! DON'T OPEN THE DOOR UNLESS IT'S ME!
SCHOOL BUS
FIVE SECONDS! STICK TO THE PLAN!
AFTERNOON, STAINS.
YOU DIDN'T THINK THIS THROUGH, DID YOU?

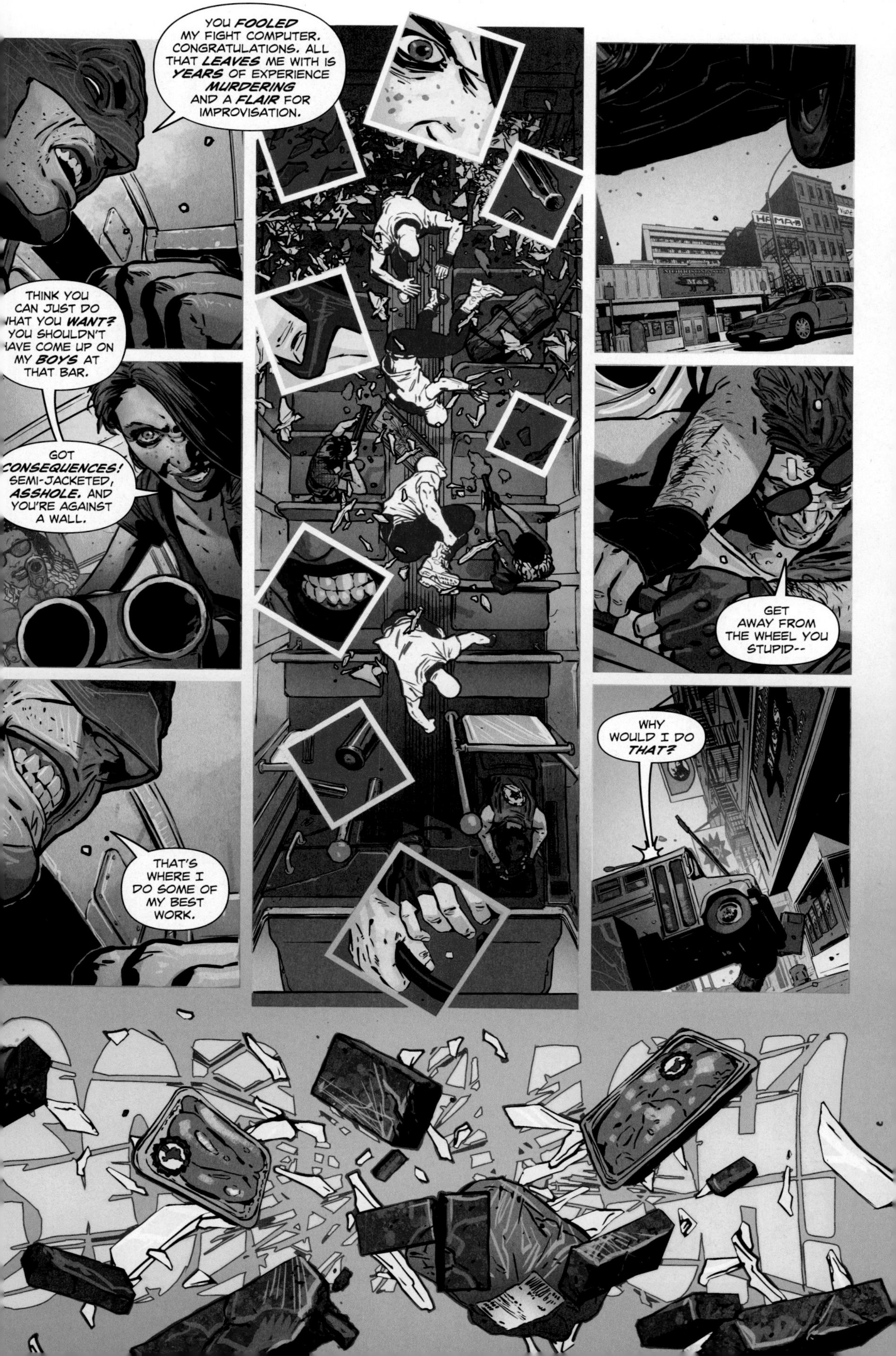
YOU FOOLED MY FIGHT COMPUTER. CONGRATULATIONS. ALL THAT LEAVES ME WITH IS YEARS OF EXPERIENCE MURDERING AND A FLAIR FOR IMPROVISATION.
THINK YOU CAN JUST DO HAT YOU WANT? YOU SHOULDN'T IAVE COME UP ON MY BOYS AT THAT BAR.
GOT CONSEQUENCES! SEMI-JACKETED, ASSHOLE. AND YOU'RE AGAINST A WALL.
THAT'S WHERE I DO SOME OF MY BEST WORK.
GET AWAY FROM THE WHEEL YOU STUPID--
WHY WOULD I DO THAT?

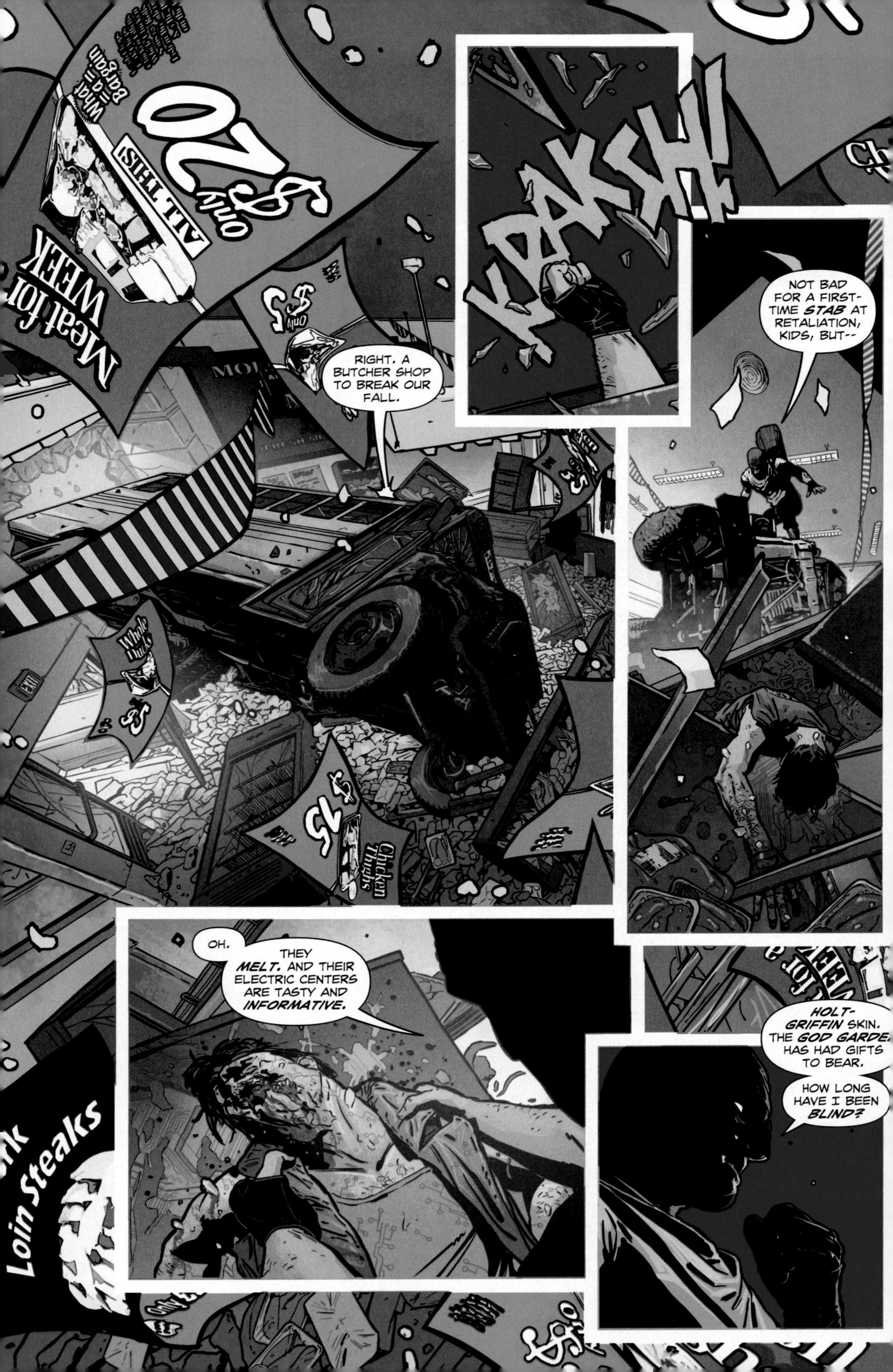
RIGHT. A BUTCHER SHOP TO BREAK OUR FALL.
KRAKSH!
NOT BAD FOR A FIRST-TIME *STAB* AT RETALIATION, KIDS, BUT--
OH.
THEY *MELT.* AND THEIR ELECTRIC CENTERS ARE TASTY AND *INFORMATIVE.*
HOLT-GRIFFIN SKIN. THE *GOD GARDE* HAS HAD GIFTS TO BEAR.
HOW LONG HAVE I BEEN *BLIND?*
Loin Steaks

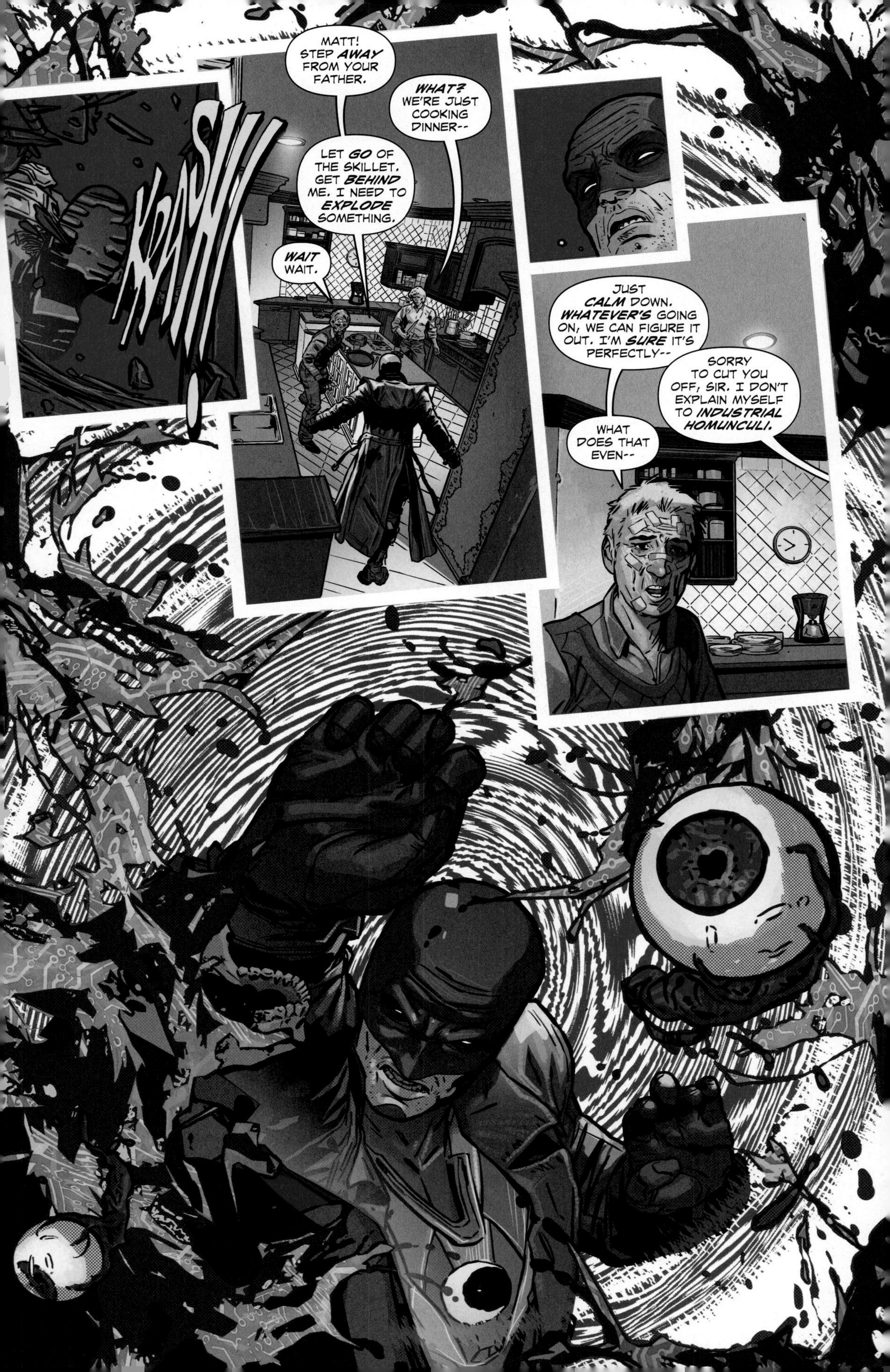
KRASH!
MATT! STEP AWAY FROM YOUR FATHER.
WHAT? WE'RE JUST COOKING DINNER--
LET GO OF THE SKILLET. GET BEHIND ME. I NEED TO EXPLODE SOMETHING.
WAIT WAIT.
JUST CALM DOWN. WHATEVER'S GOING ON, WE CAN FIGURE IT OUT. I'M SURE IT'S PERFECTLY--
SORRY TO CUT YOU OFF, SIR. I DON'T EXPLAIN MYSELF TO INDUSTRIAL HOMUNCULI.
WHAT DOES THAT EVEN--

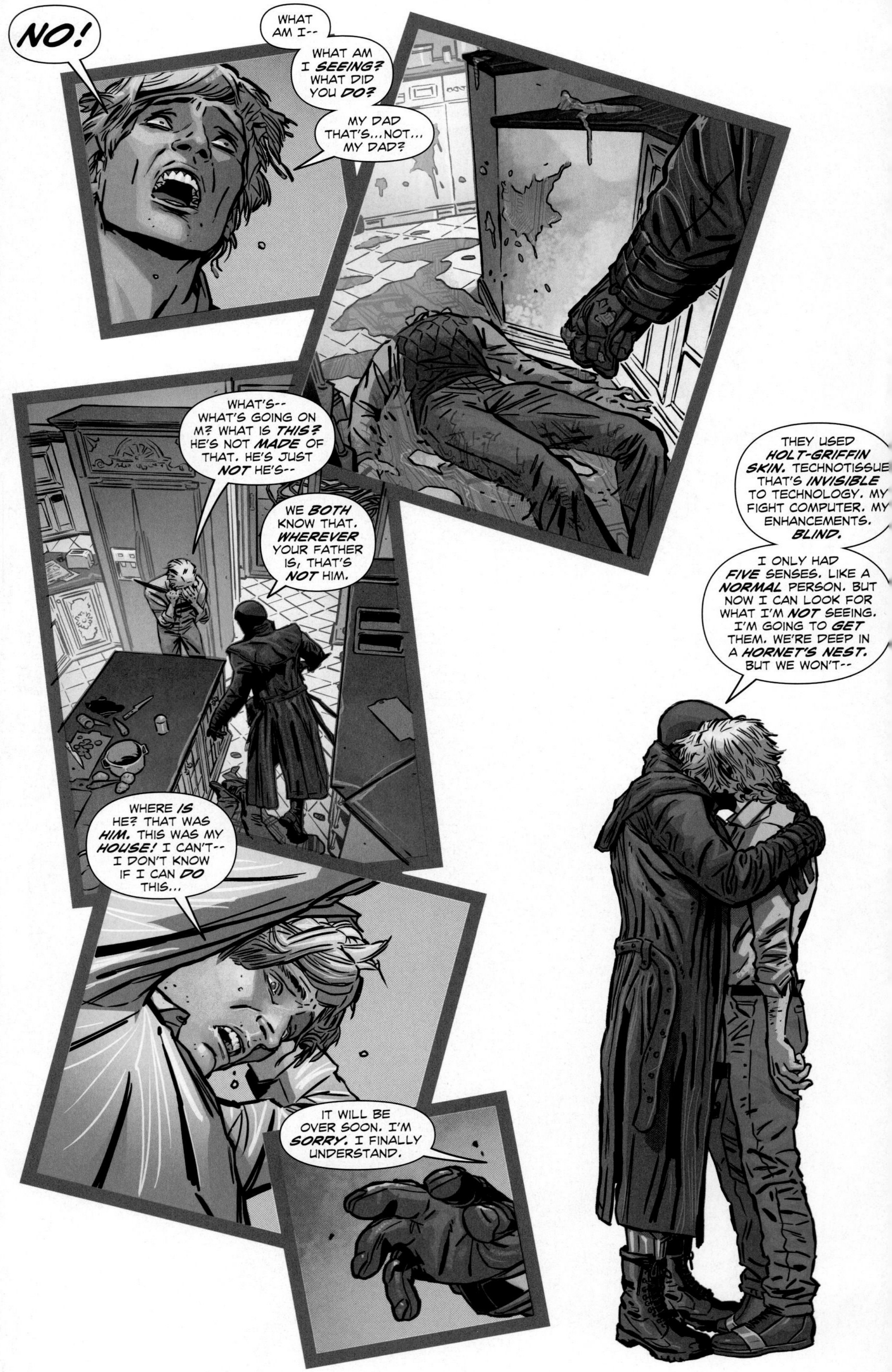
NO!
WHAT AM I--
WHAT AM I SEEING? WHAT DID YOU DO?
MY DAD THAT'S...NOT... MY DAD?
WHAT'S-- WHAT'S GOING ON M? WHAT IS THIS? HE'S NOT MADE OF THAT. HE'S JUST NOT HE'S--
WE BOTH KNOW THAT. WHEREVER YOUR FATHER IS, THAT'S NOT HIM.
WHERE IS HE? THAT WAS HIM. THIS WAS MY HOUSE! I CAN'T-- I DON'T KNOW IF I CAN DO THIS...
IT WILL BE OVER SOON. I'M SORRY. I FINALLY UNDERSTAND.
THEY USED HOLT-GRIFFIN SKIN. TECHNOTISSUE THAT'S INVISIBLE TO TECHNOLOGY. MY FIGHT COMPUTER. MY ENHANCEMENTS. BLIND.
I ONLY HAD FIVE SENSES. LIKE A NORMAL PERSON. BUT NOW I CAN LOOK FOR WHAT I'M NOT SEEING. I'M GOING TO GET THEM. WE'RE DEEP IN A HORNET'S NEST. BUT WE WON'T--

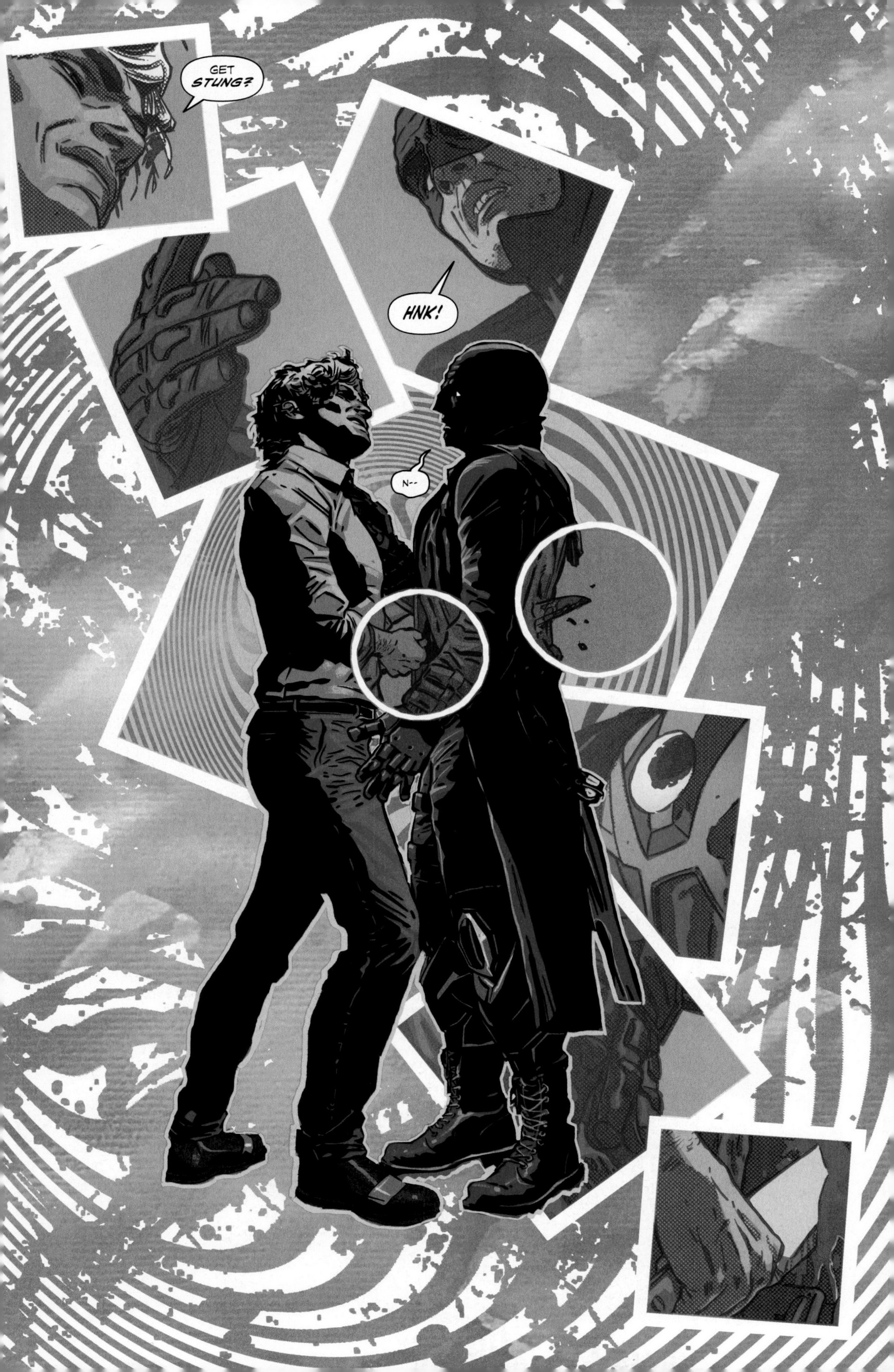
GET STUNG?
HNK!
N--

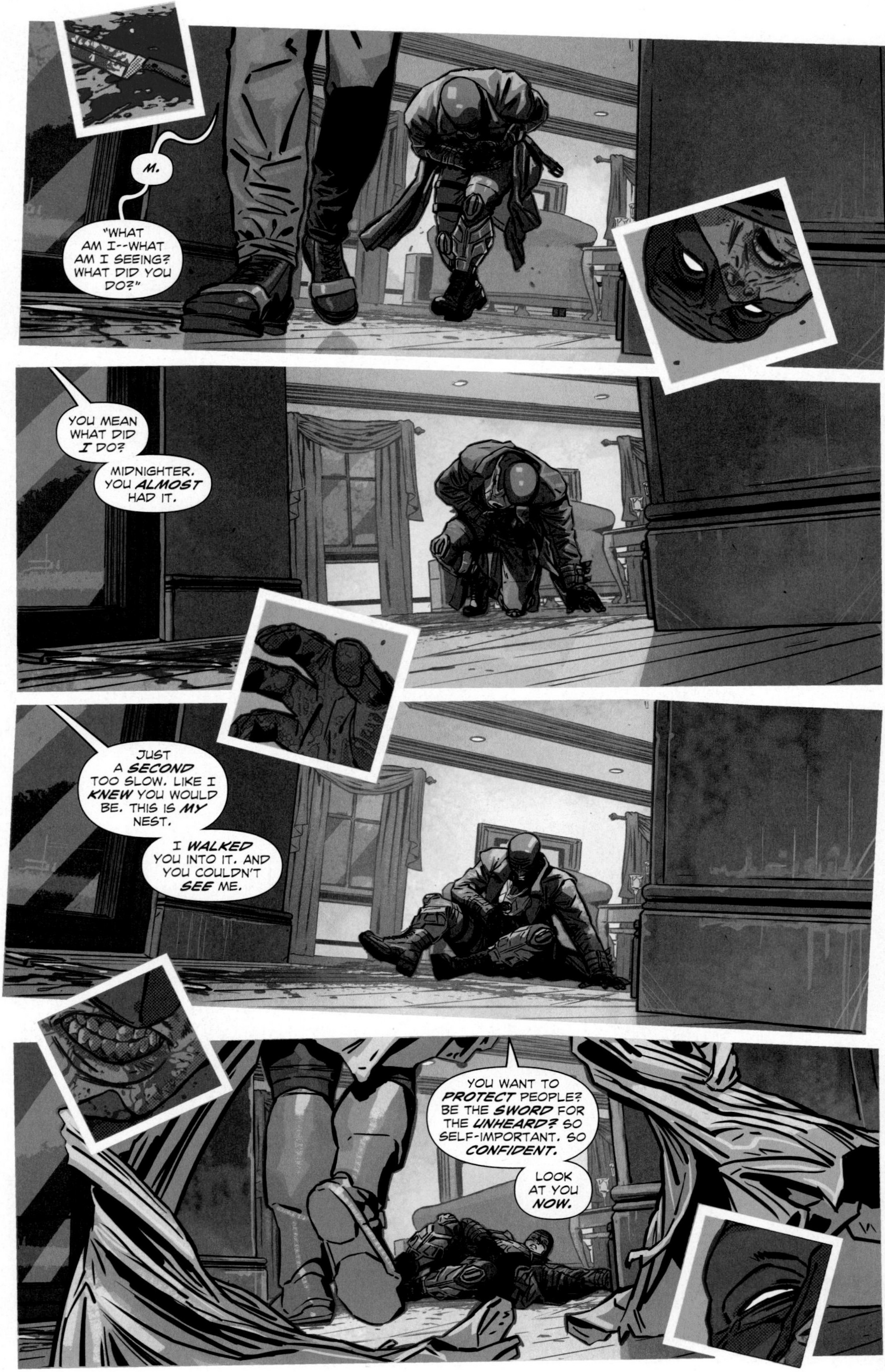
M.
"WHAT AM I--WHAT AM I SEEING? WHAT DID YOU DO?"
YOU MEAN WHAT DID I DO?
MIDNIGHTER. YOU ALMOST HAD IT.
JUST A SECOND TOO SLOW. LIKE I KNEW YOU WOULD BE. THIS IS MY NEST.
I WALKED YOU INTO IT. AND YOU COULDN'T SEE ME.
YOU WANT TO PROTECT PEOPLE? BE THE SWORD FOR THE UNHEARD? SO SELF-IMPORTANT. SO CONFIDENT.
LOOK AT YOU NOW.

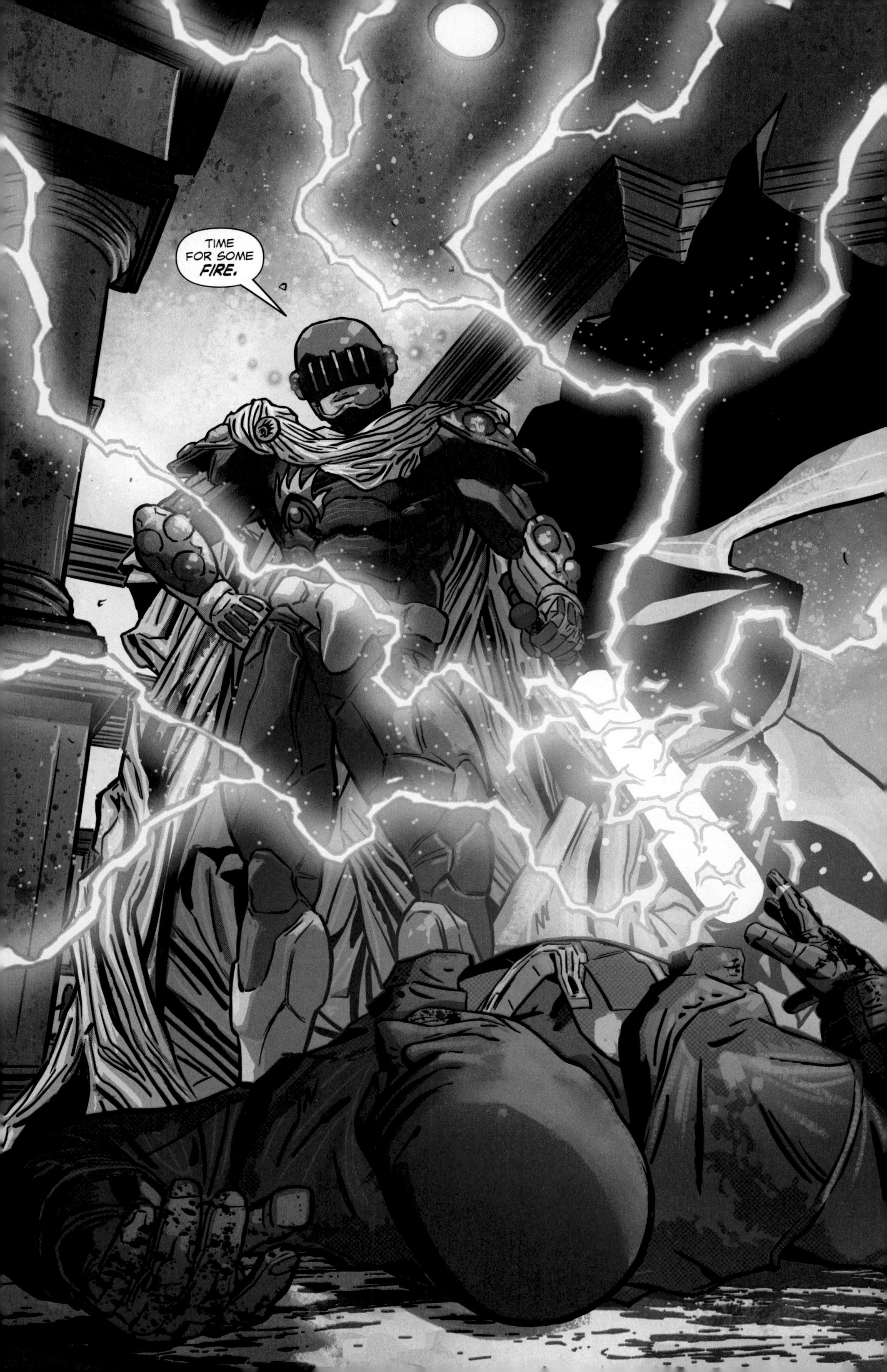
TIME FOR SOME FIRE.

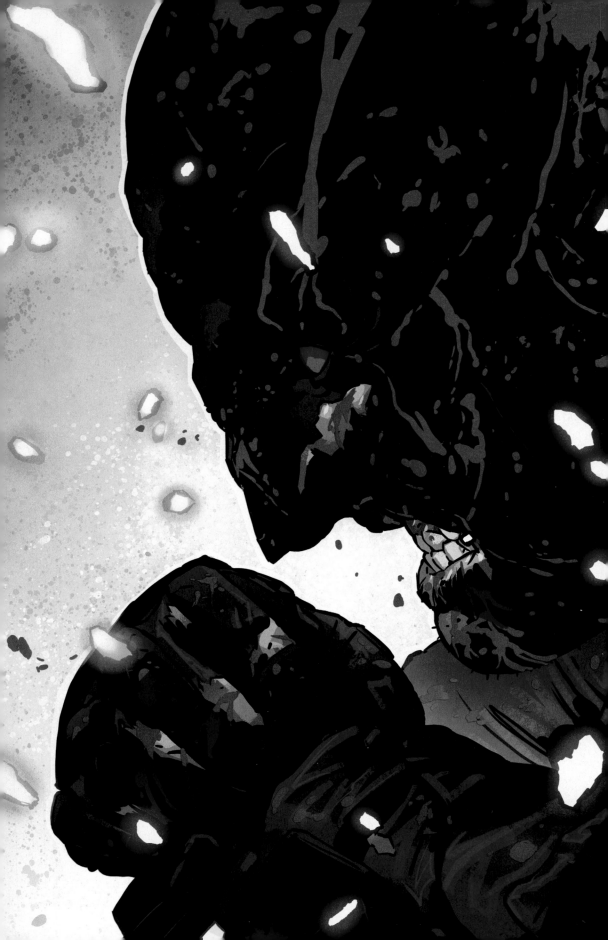

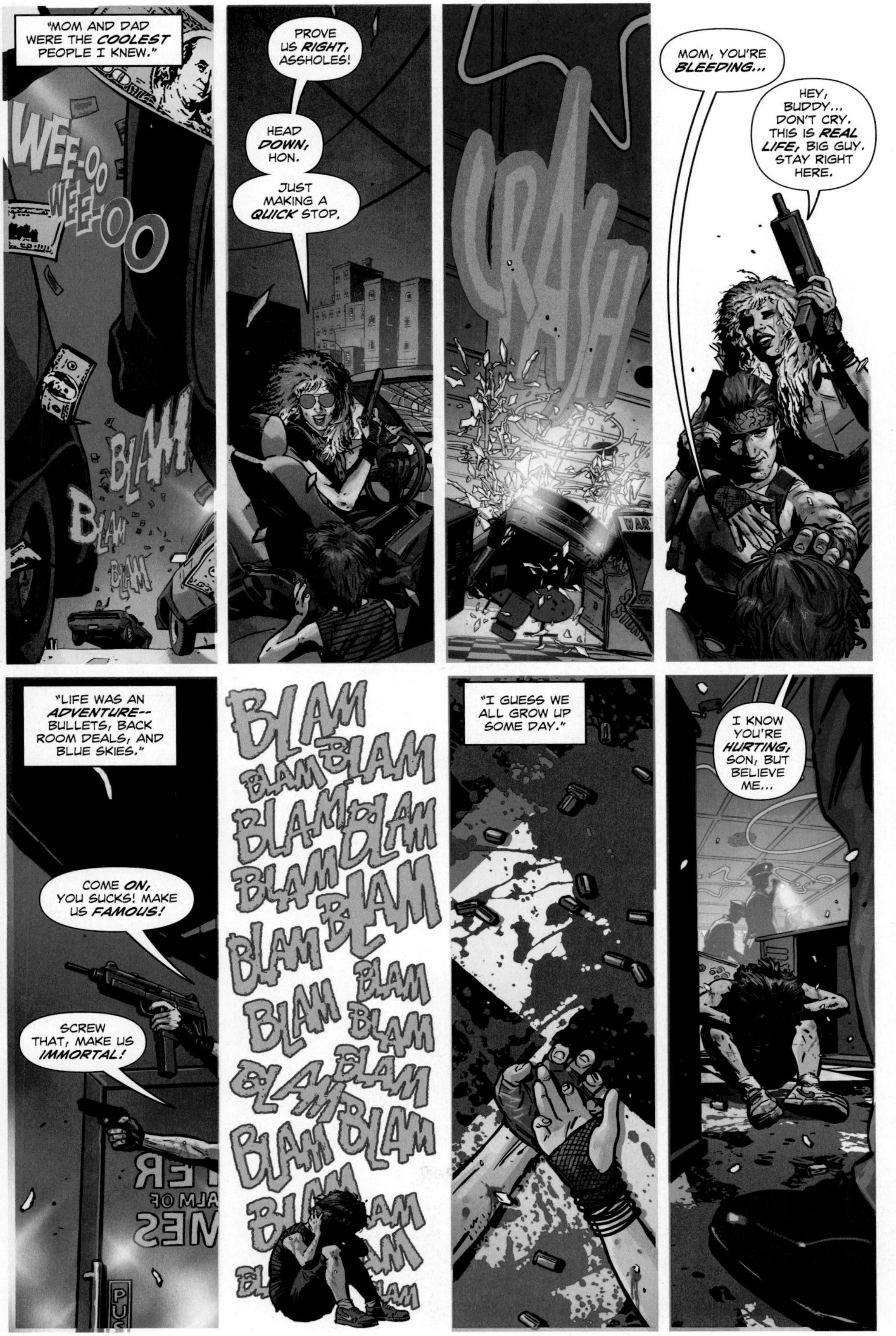
"MOM AND DAD WERE THE COOLEST PEOPLE I KNEW."
WEE-OO
WEE-OO
WEE-OO
BLAM
BLAM
BLAM
BLAM
PROVE US RIGHT, ASSHOLES!
HEAD DOWN, HON.
JUST MAKING A QUICK STOP.
CRASH
MOM, YOU'RE BLEEDING...
HEY, BUDDY... DON'T CRY. THIS IS REAL LIFE, BIG GUY. STAY RIGHT HERE.
"LIFE WAS AN ADVENTURE-- BULLETS, BACK ROOM DEALS, AND BLUE SKIES."
COME ON, YOU SUCKS! MAKE US FAMOUS!
SCREW THAT, MAKE US IMMORTAL!
BLAM
BLAM BLAM
BLAM BLAM BLAM
BLAM BLAM
BLAM BLAM
BLAM BLAM
BLAM BLAM
BLAM BLAM
BLAM BLAM BLAM
BLAM BLAM
BLAM BLAM
"I GUESS WE ALL GROW UP SOME DAY."
I KNOW YOU'RE HURTING, SON, BUT BELIEVE ME...

...WE'RE HERE TO HELP YOU.

HSSSSS!

"MY PARENTS LOVED ME. JUSTICE KILLED THEM. THERE'S NO JUSTICE IN THAT. I HAD TO DESTROY JUSTICE AT THE ROOTS.

"I INHERITED A LOT FROM MY PARENTS.

"THEIR MONEY. THEIR NETWORK. THE UNDERWORLD CARES FOR ITS OWN. AT LEAST WHEN YOUR PARENTS ARE AS FAMOUS AS MINE.

"I HAD TO BE THE BEST, SO NO ONE COULD STOP ME.

"I WALKED AMONG INFLUENCERS. THE TASTE-MAKERS. I STUDIED VIOLENCE IN A DOZEN LANGUAGES.

"IN SHAMBALLA, I EMBRACED UNEARTHLY KNOWLEDGE. I STOLE THE COSMIC KEY, MY DOORWAY TO ANOTHER WORLD.

CLICK

"I WAS READY TO ADDRESS THE PROBLEM OF JUSTICE."

ARE YOU HURTING, "SON"?

PROMETHEUS

STEVE ORLANDO WRITER ACO WITH HUGO PETRUS [PG. 18-19] PENCILLER
ACO WITH HUGO PETRUS INKS ROMULO FAJARDO, JR. COLORS TOM NAPOLITANO LETTERS
ACO & ROMULO FAJARDO, JR. COVER
DAVE WIELGOSZ ASST. EDITOR CHRIS CONROY EDITOR MARK DOYLE GROUP EDITOR

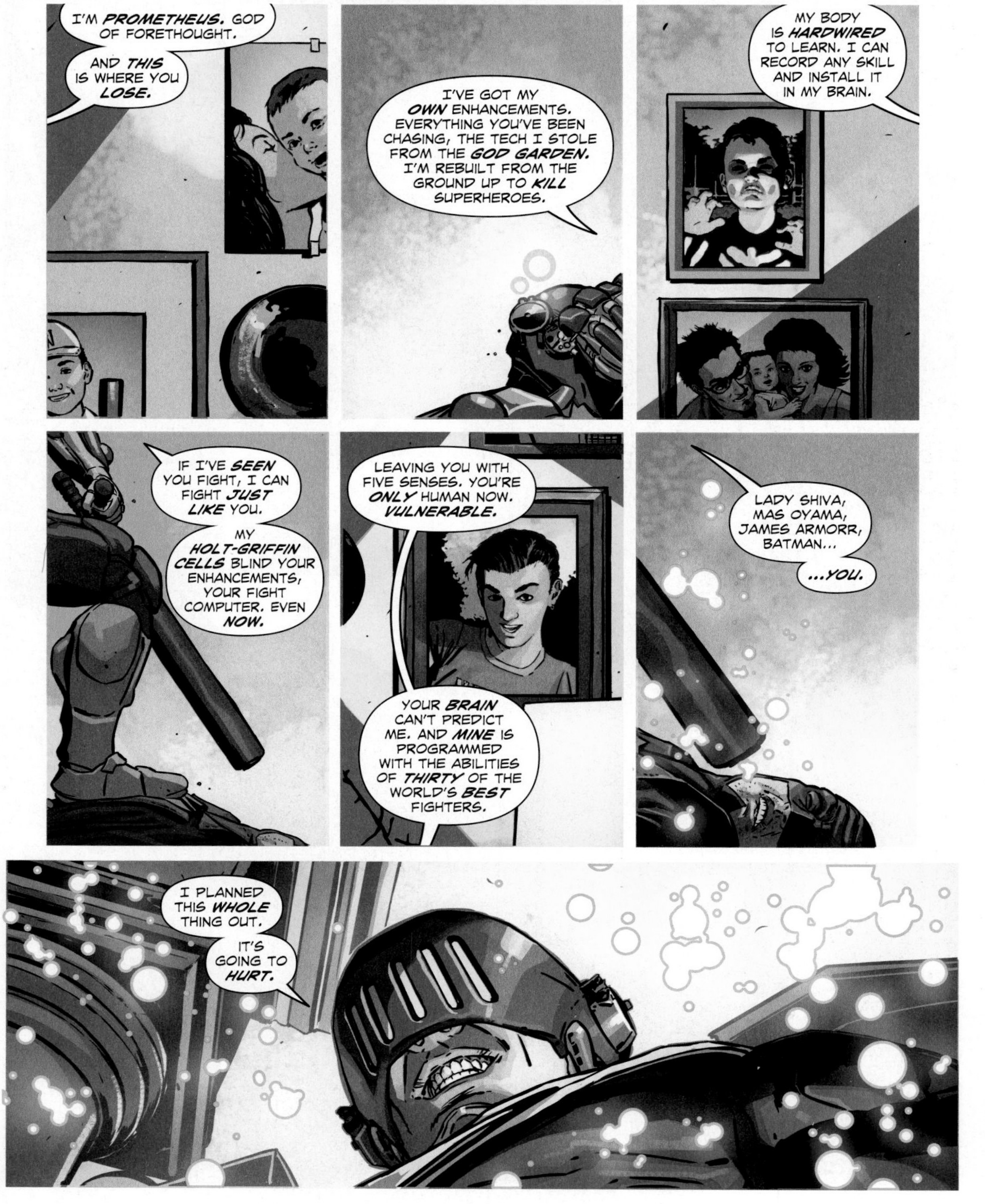

I'M PROMETHEUS. GOD OF FORETHOUGHT.
AND THIS IS WHERE YOU LOSE.
I'VE GOT MY OWN ENHANCEMENTS. EVERYTHING YOU'VE BEEN CHASING, THE TECH I STOLE FROM THE GOD GARDEN. I'M REBUILT FROM THE GROUND UP TO KILL SUPERHEROES.
MY BODY IS HARDWIRED TO LEARN. I CAN RECORD ANY SKILL AND INSTALL IT IN MY BRAIN.
IF I'VE SEEN YOU FIGHT, I CAN FIGHT JUST LIKE YOU.
MY HOLT-GRIFFIN CELLS BLIND YOUR ENHANCEMENTS, YOUR FIGHT COMPUTER. EVEN NOW.
LEAVING YOU WITH FIVE SENSES. YOU'RE ONLY HUMAN NOW. VULNERABLE.
YOUR BRAIN CAN'T PREDICT ME. AND MINE IS PROGRAMMED WITH THE ABILITIES OF THIRTY OF THE WORLD'S BEST FIGHTERS.
LADY SHIVA, MAS OYAMA, JAMES ARMORR, BATMAN...
...YOU.
I PLANNED THIS WHOLE THING OUT.
IT'S GOING TO HURT.

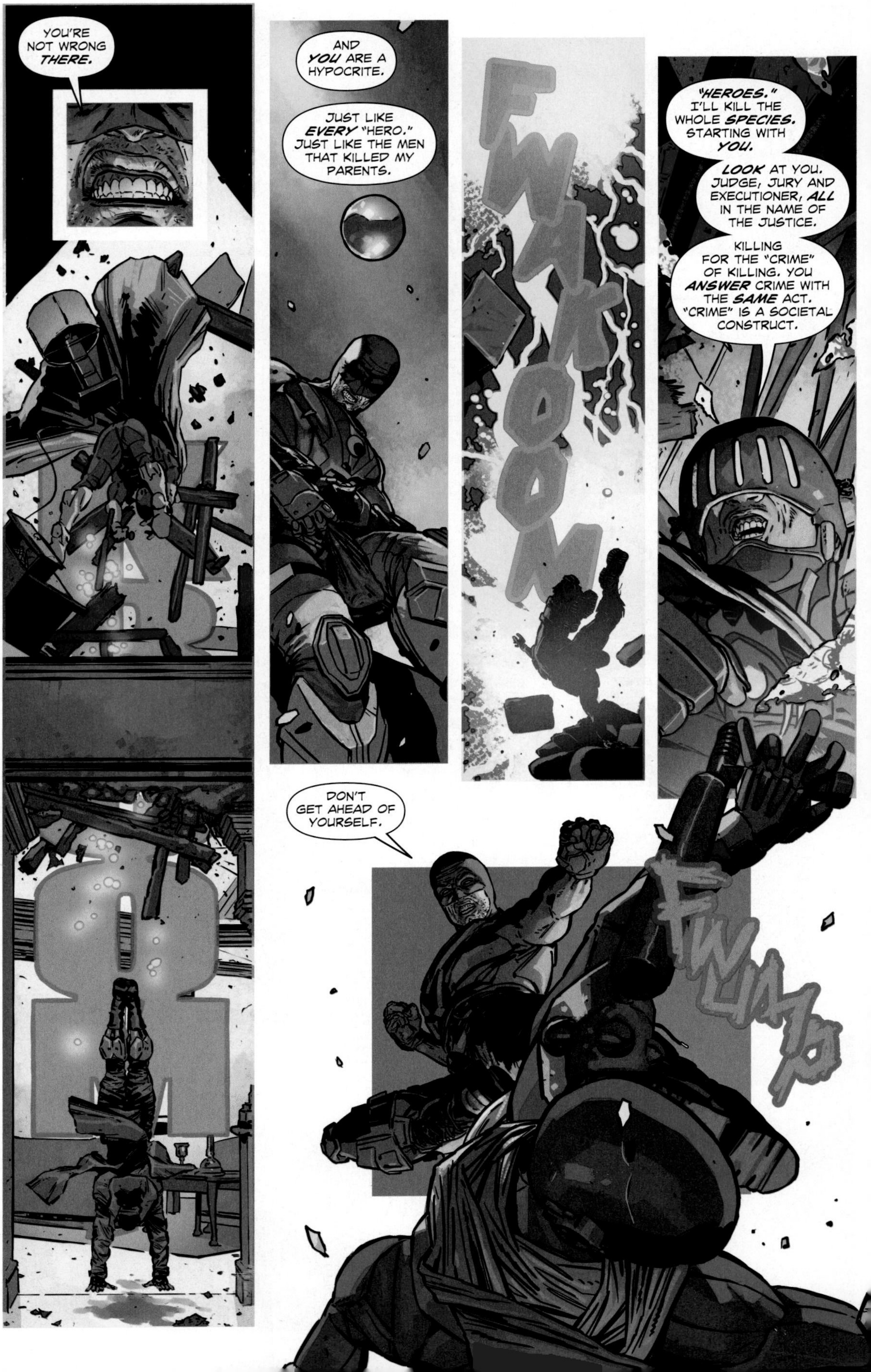

YOU'RE NOT WRONG THERE.
AND YOU ARE A HYPOCRITE.
JUST LIKE EVERY "HERO." JUST LIKE THE MEN THAT KILLED MY PARENTS.
FWAKOOOM
"HEROES." I'LL KILL THE WHOLE SPECIES. STARTING WITH YOU.
LOOK AT YOU. JUDGE, JURY AND EXECUTIONER, ALL IN THE NAME OF THE JUSTICE.
KILLING FOR THE "CRIME" OF KILLING. YOU ANSWER CRIME WITH THE SAME ACT. "CRIME" IS A SOCIETAL CONSTRUCT.
DON'T GET AHEAD OF YOURSELF.
FWUMP

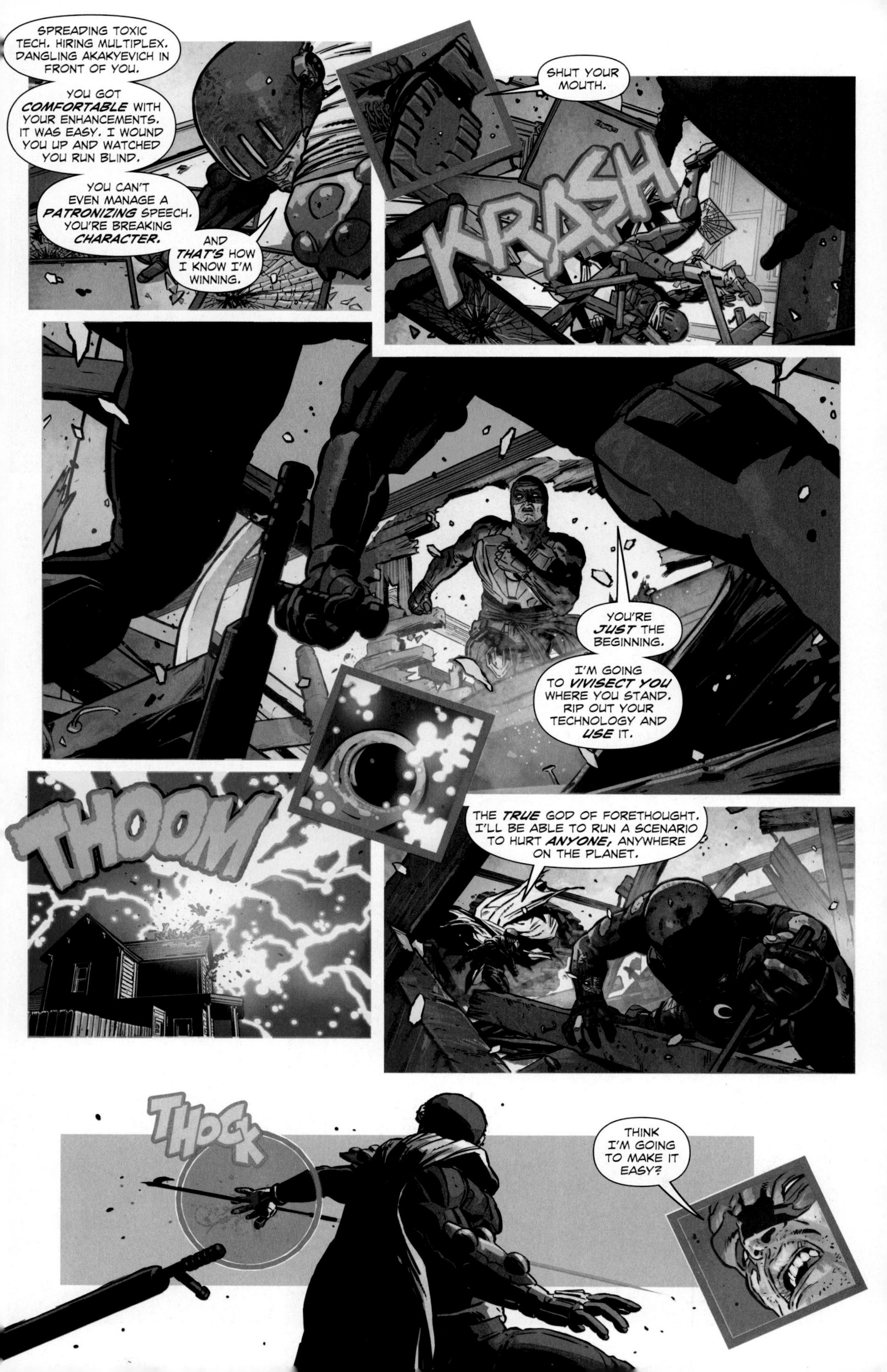
SPREADING TOXIC TECH. HIRING MULTIPLEX. DANGLING AKAKYEVICH IN FRONT OF YOU.
YOU GOT COMFORTABLE WITH YOUR ENHANCEMENTS. IT WAS EASY. I WOUND YOU UP AND WATCHED YOU RUN BLIND.
YOU CAN'T EVEN MANAGE A PATRONIZING SPEECH. YOU'RE BREAKING CHARACTER.
AND THAT'S HOW I KNOW I'M WINNING.
SHUT YOUR MOUTH.
KRASH
YOU'RE JUST THE BEGINNING.
I'M GOING TO VIVISECT YOU WHERE YOU STAND. RIP OUT YOUR TECHNOLOGY AND USE IT.
THOOM
THE TRUE GOD OF FORETHOUGHT. I'LL BE ABLE TO RUN A SCENARIO TO HURT ANYONE, ANYWHERE ON THE PLANET.
THOCK
THINK I'M GOING TO MAKE IT EASY?

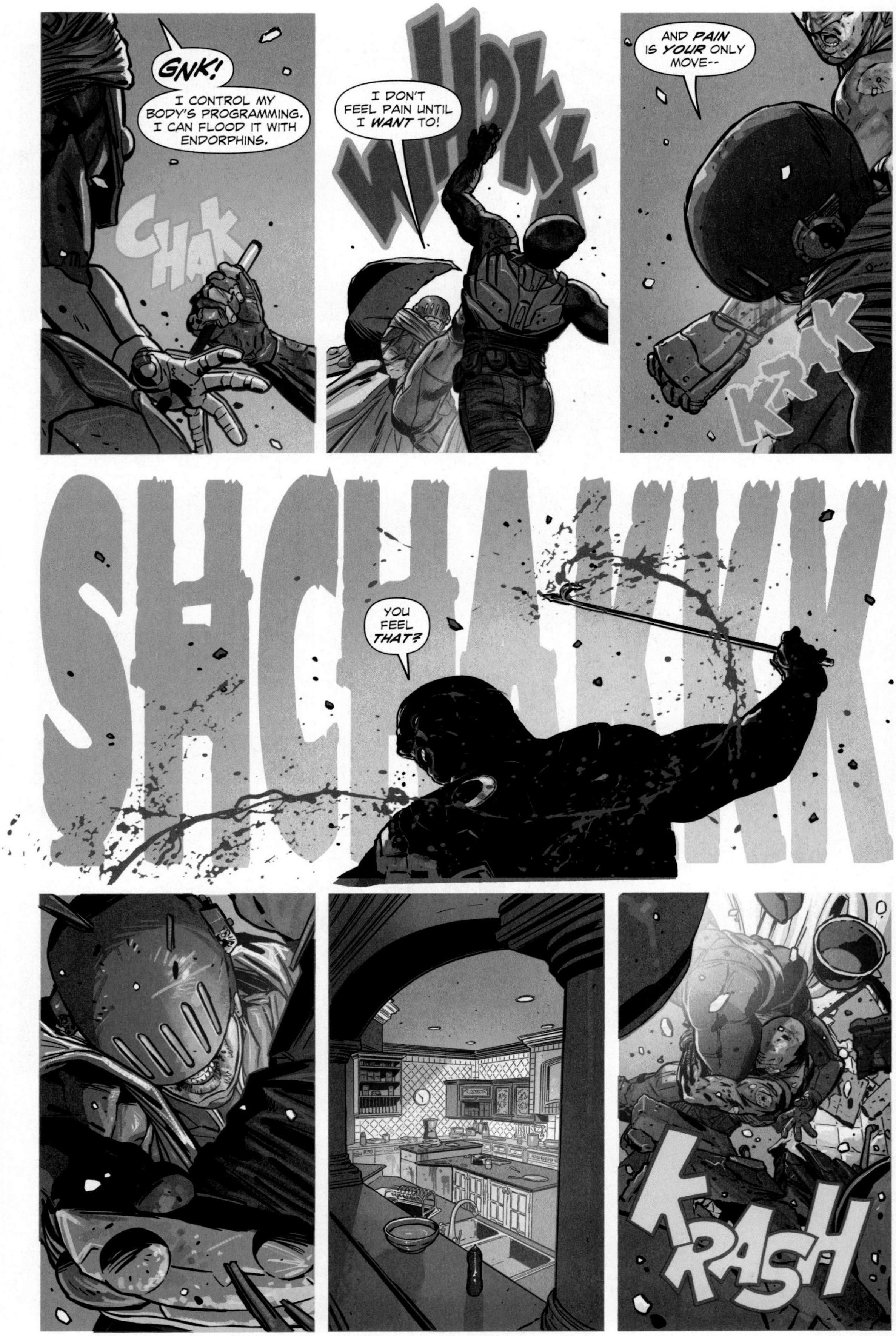
GNK!
I CONTROL MY BODY'S PROGRAMMING. I CAN FLOOD IT WITH ENDORPHINS.
CHAK
I DON'T FEEL PAIN UNTIL I WANT TO!
WHOK
AND PAIN IS YOUR ONLY MOVE--
KRAK
SHCHAKK
YOU FEEL THAT?
KRASH

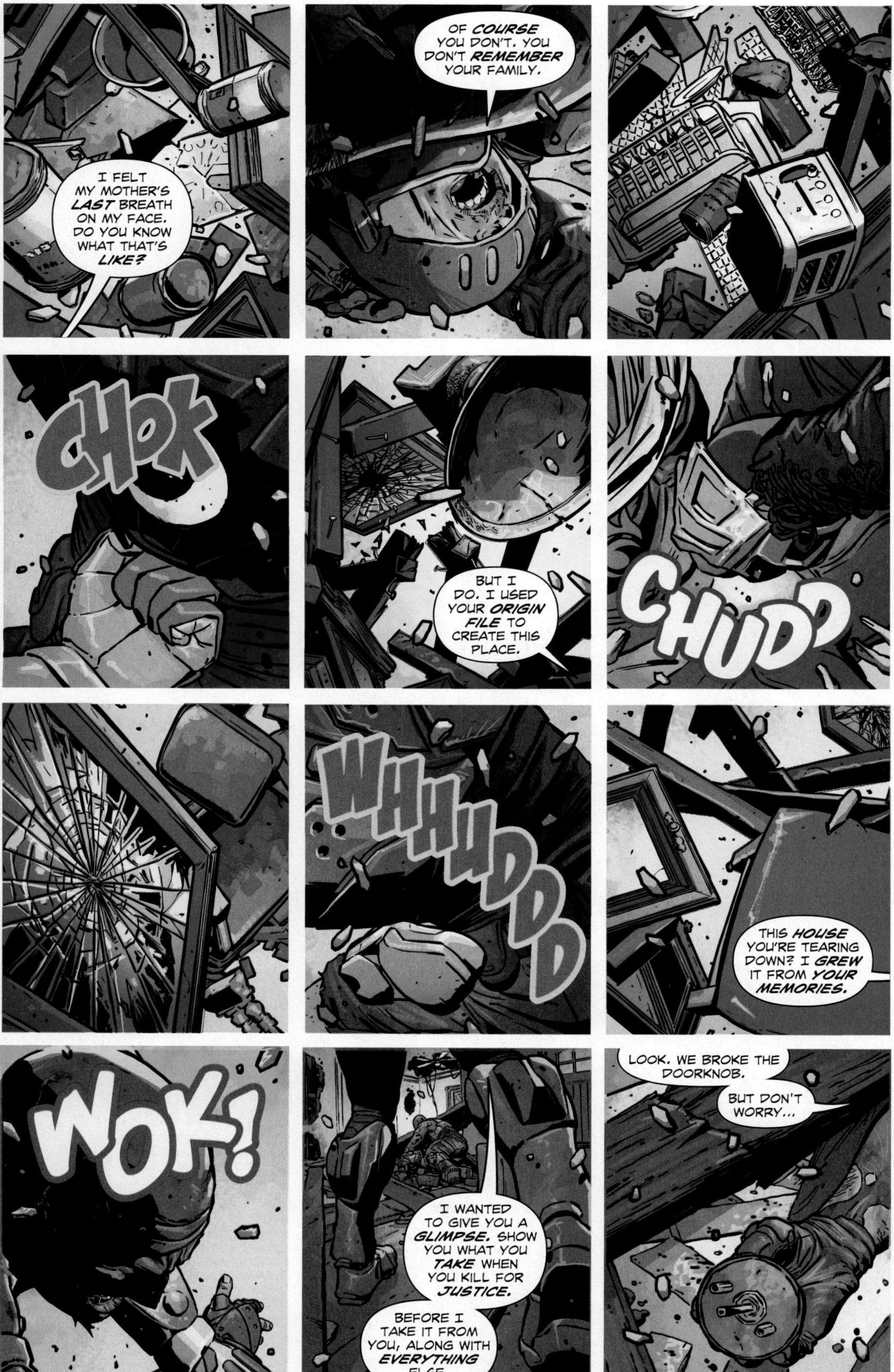
I FELT MY MOTHER'S LAST BREATH ON MY FACE. DO YOU KNOW WHAT THAT'S LIKE?
OF COURSE YOU DON'T. YOU DON'T REMEMBER YOUR FAMILY.
CHOK
BUT I DO. I USED YOUR ORIGIN FILE TO CREATE THIS PLACE.
CHUDD
WHHUDDD
THIS HOUSE YOU'RE TEARING DOWN? I GREW IT FROM YOUR MEMORIES.
WOK!
I WANTED TO GIVE YOU A GLIMPSE. SHOW YOU WHAT YOU TAKE WHEN YOU KILL FOR JUSTICE.
BEFORE I TAKE IT FROM YOU, ALONG WITH EVERYTHING ELSE.
LOOK. WE BROKE THE DOORKNOB.
BUT DON'T WORRY...

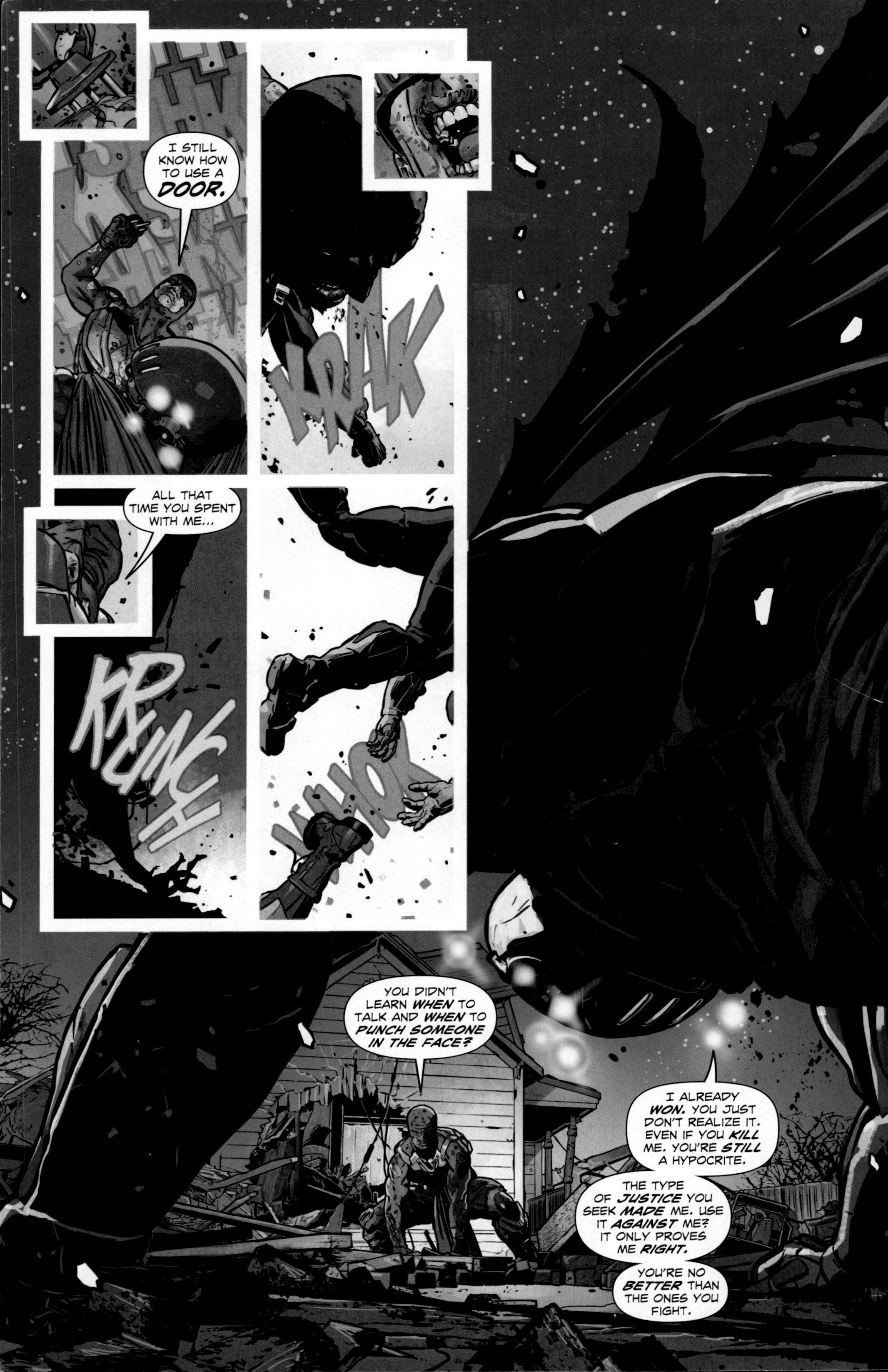
I STILL KNOW HOW TO USE A DOOR.
KRAK
ALL THAT TIME YOU SPENT WITH ME...
KRUNCH
YOU DIDN'T LEARN WHEN TO TALK AND WHEN TO PUNCH SOMEONE IN THE FACE?
I ALREADY WON. YOU JUST DON'T REALIZE IT. EVEN IF YOU KILL ME. YOU'RE STILL A HYPOCRITE.
THE TYPE OF JUSTICE YOU SEEK MADE ME. USE IT AGAINST ME? IT ONLY PROVES ME RIGHT.
YOU'RE NO BETTER THAN THE ONES YOU FIGHT.

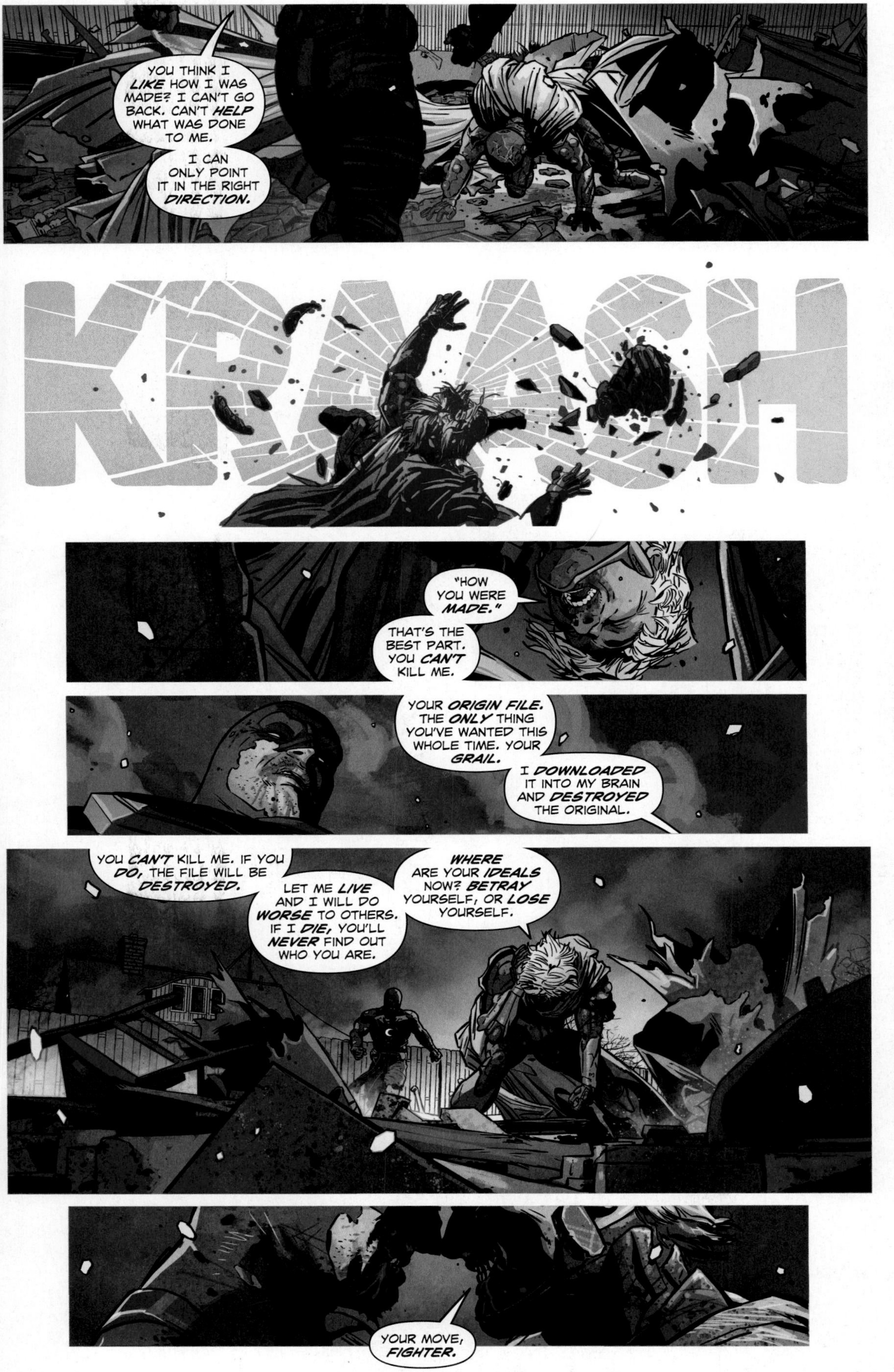

YOU THINK I LIKE HOW I WAS MADE? I CAN'T GO BACK. CAN'T HELP WHAT WAS DONE TO ME.
I CAN ONLY POINT IT IN THE RIGHT DIRECTION.
KRAASH
"HOW YOU WERE MADE."
THAT'S THE BEST PART. YOU CAN'T KILL ME.
YOUR ORIGIN FILE. THE ONLY THING YOU'VE WANTED THIS WHOLE TIME. YOUR GRAIL.
I DOWNLOADED IT INTO MY BRAIN AND DESTROYED THE ORIGINAL.
YOU CAN'T KILL ME. IF YOU DO, THE FILE WILL BE DESTROYED.
LET ME LIVE AND I WILL DO WORSE TO OTHERS. IF I DIE, YOU'LL NEVER FIND OUT WHO YOU ARE.
WHERE ARE YOUR IDEALS NOW? BETRAY YOURSELF, OR LOSE YOURSELF.
YOUR MOVE, FIGHTER.

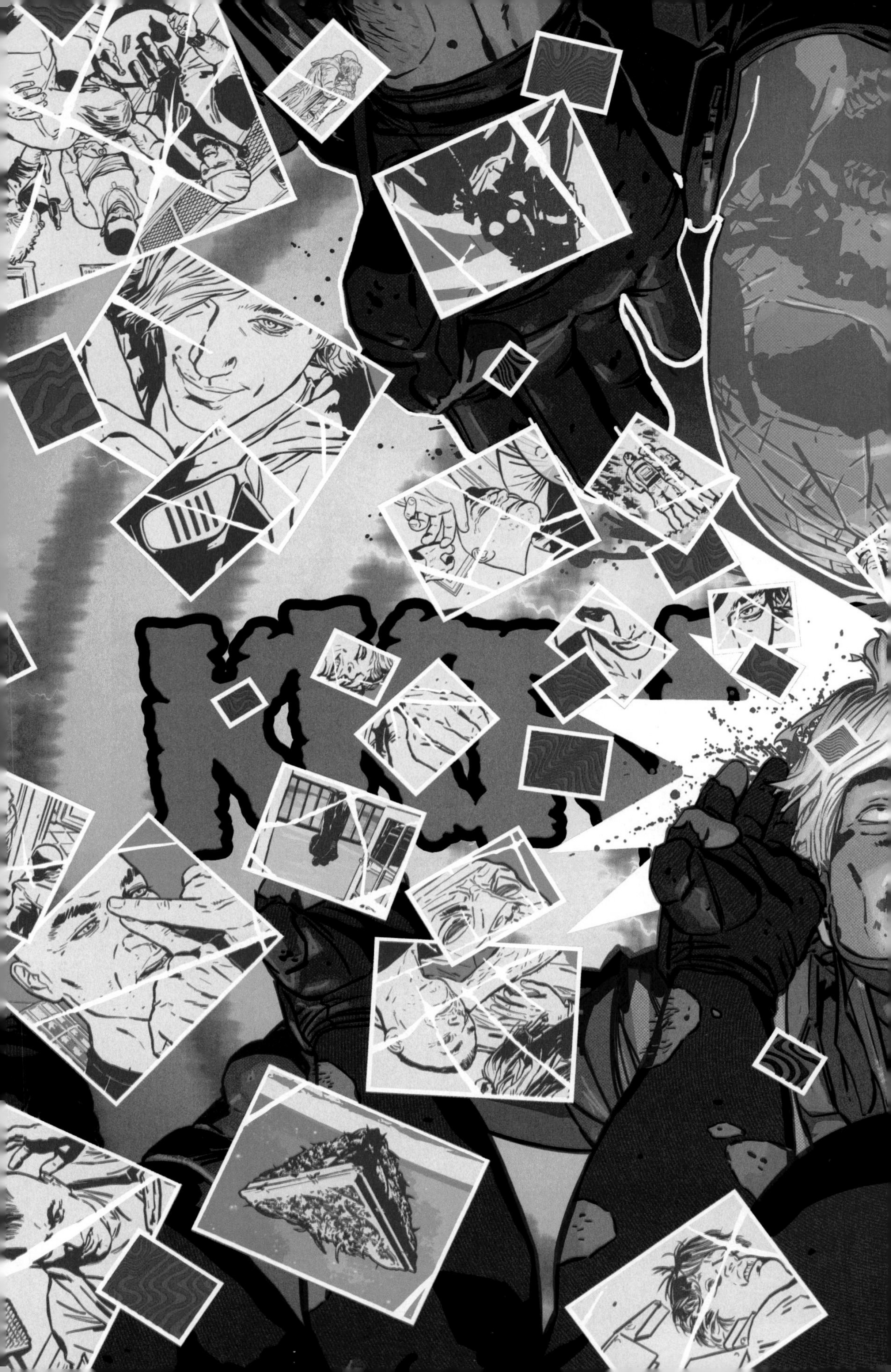

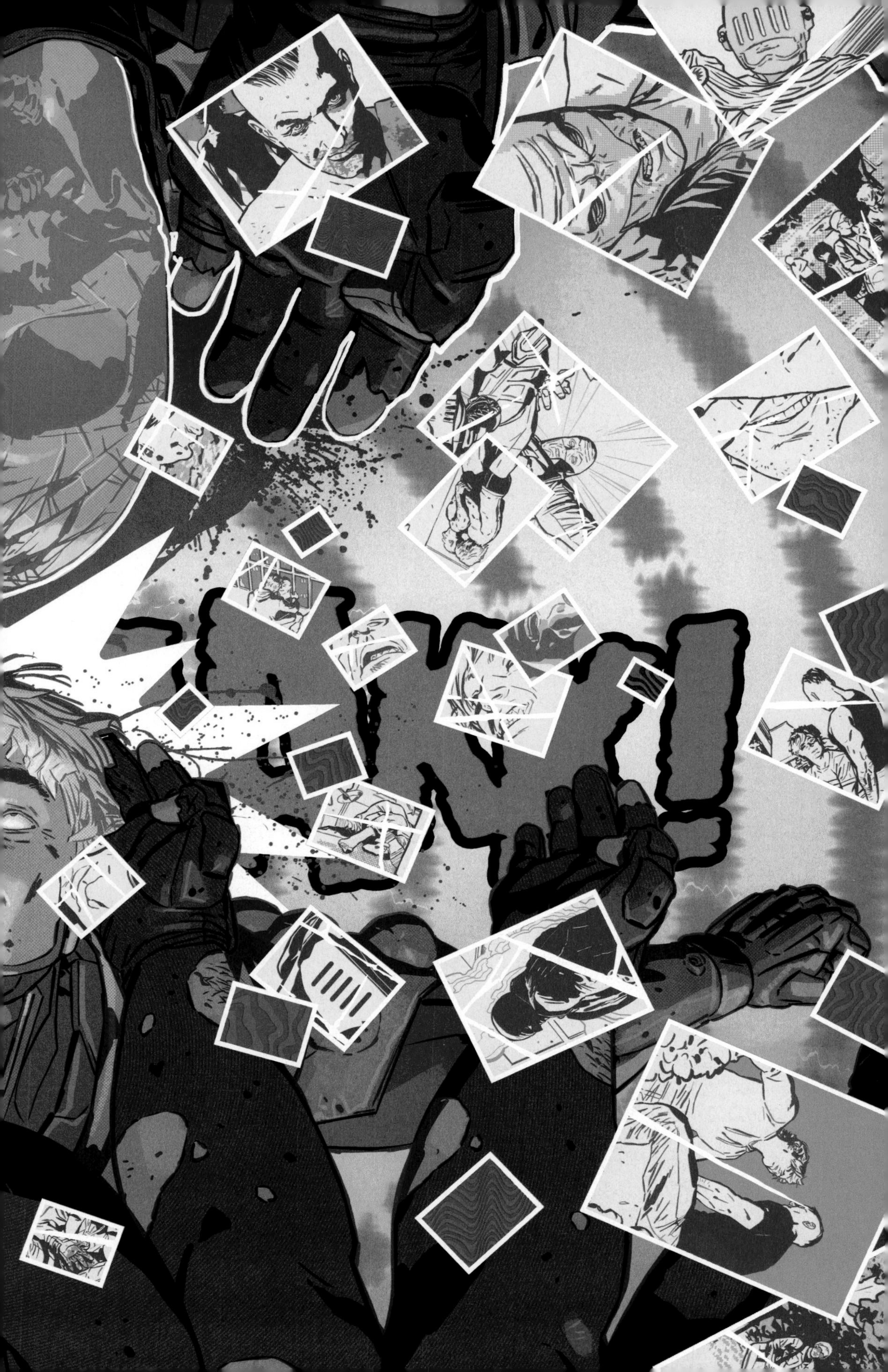

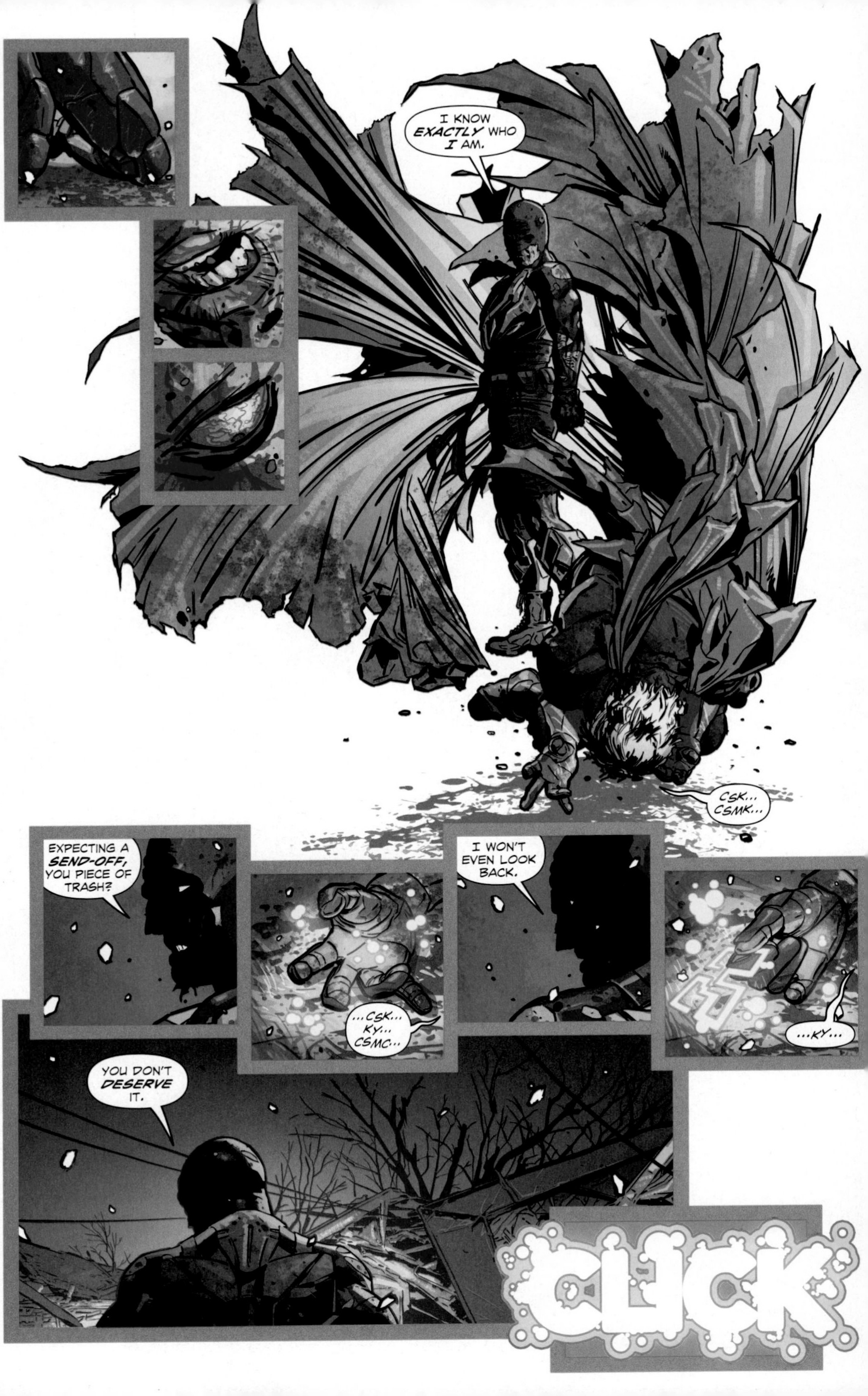
I KNOW EXACTLY WHO I AM.
CSK... CSMK...
EXPECTING A SEND-OFF, YOU PIECE OF TRASH?
...CSK... KY... CSMC...
I WON'T EVEN LOOK BACK.
...KY...
YOU DON'T DESERVE IT.
CLICK

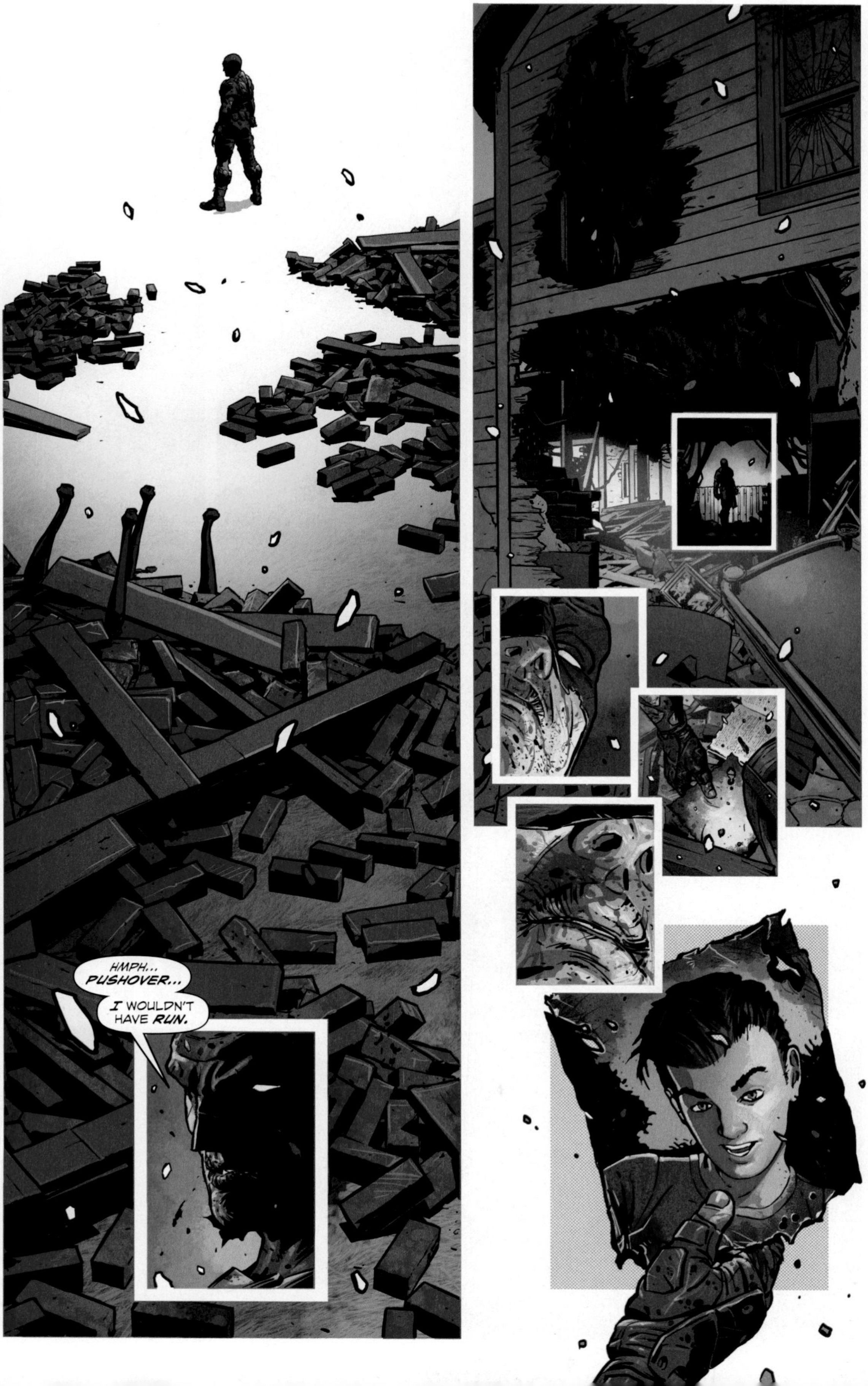
HMPH... PUSHOVER...
I WOULDN'T HAVE RUN.

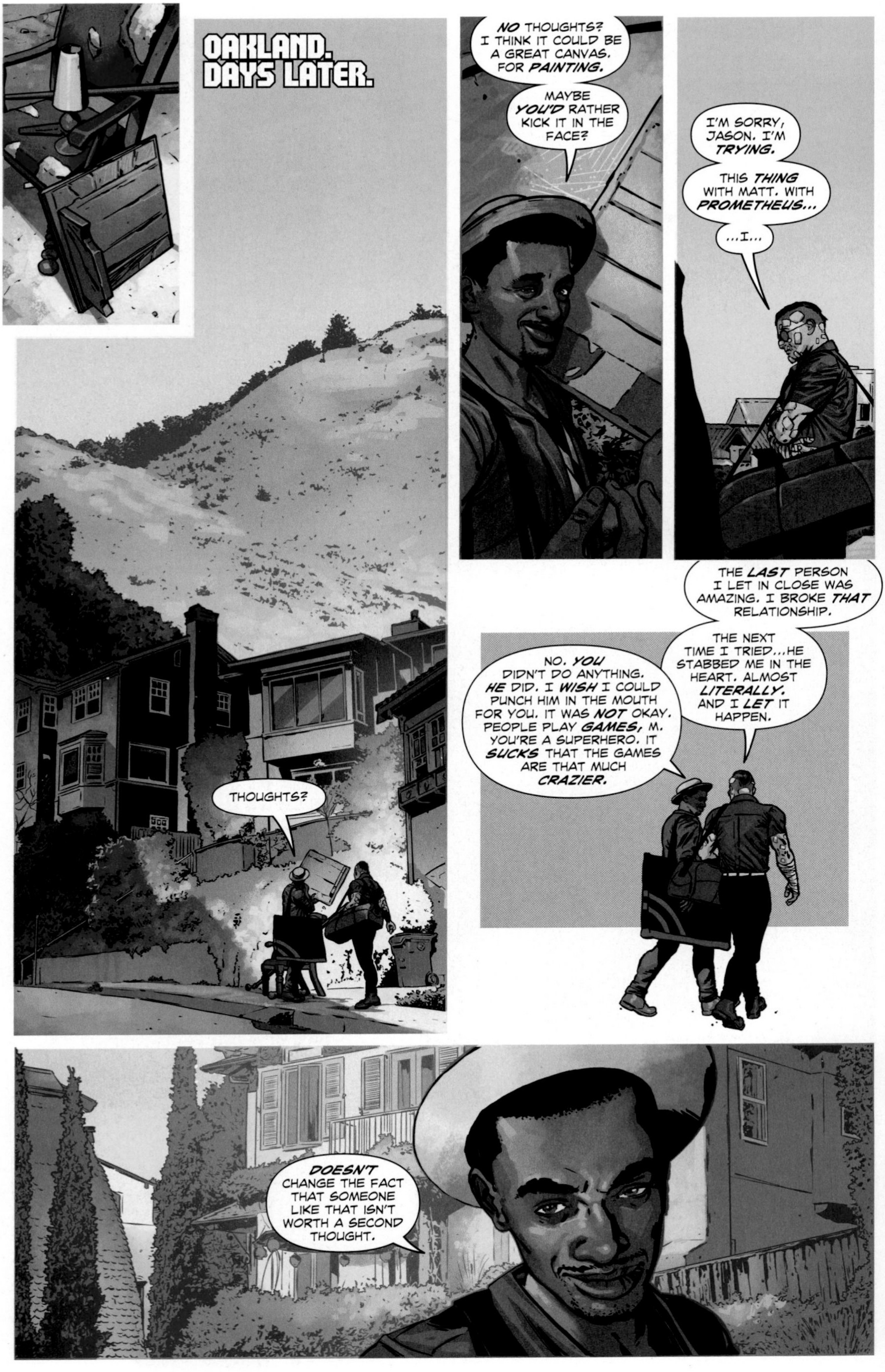
OAKLAND. DAYS LATER.
THOUGHTS?
NO THOUGHTS? I THINK IT COULD BE A GREAT CANVAS. FOR PAINTING.
MAYBE YOU'D RATHER KICK IT IN THE FACE?
I'M SORRY, JASON. I'M TRYING.
THIS THING WITH MATT. WITH PROMETHEUS...
...I...
THE LAST PERSON I LET IN CLOSE WAS AMAZING. I BROKE THAT RELATIONSHIP.
THE NEXT TIME I TRIED...HE STABBED ME IN THE HEART. ALMOST LITERALLY. AND I LET IT HAPPEN.
NO. YOU DIDN'T DO ANYTHING. HE DID. I WISH I COULD PUNCH HIM IN THE MOUTH FOR YOU. IT WAS NOT OKAY. PEOPLE PLAY GAMES, M. YOU'RE A SUPERHERO. IT SUCKS THAT THE GAMES ARE THAT MUCH CRAZIER.
DOESN'T CHANGE THE FACT THAT SOMEONE LIKE THAT ISN'T WORTH A SECOND THOUGHT.

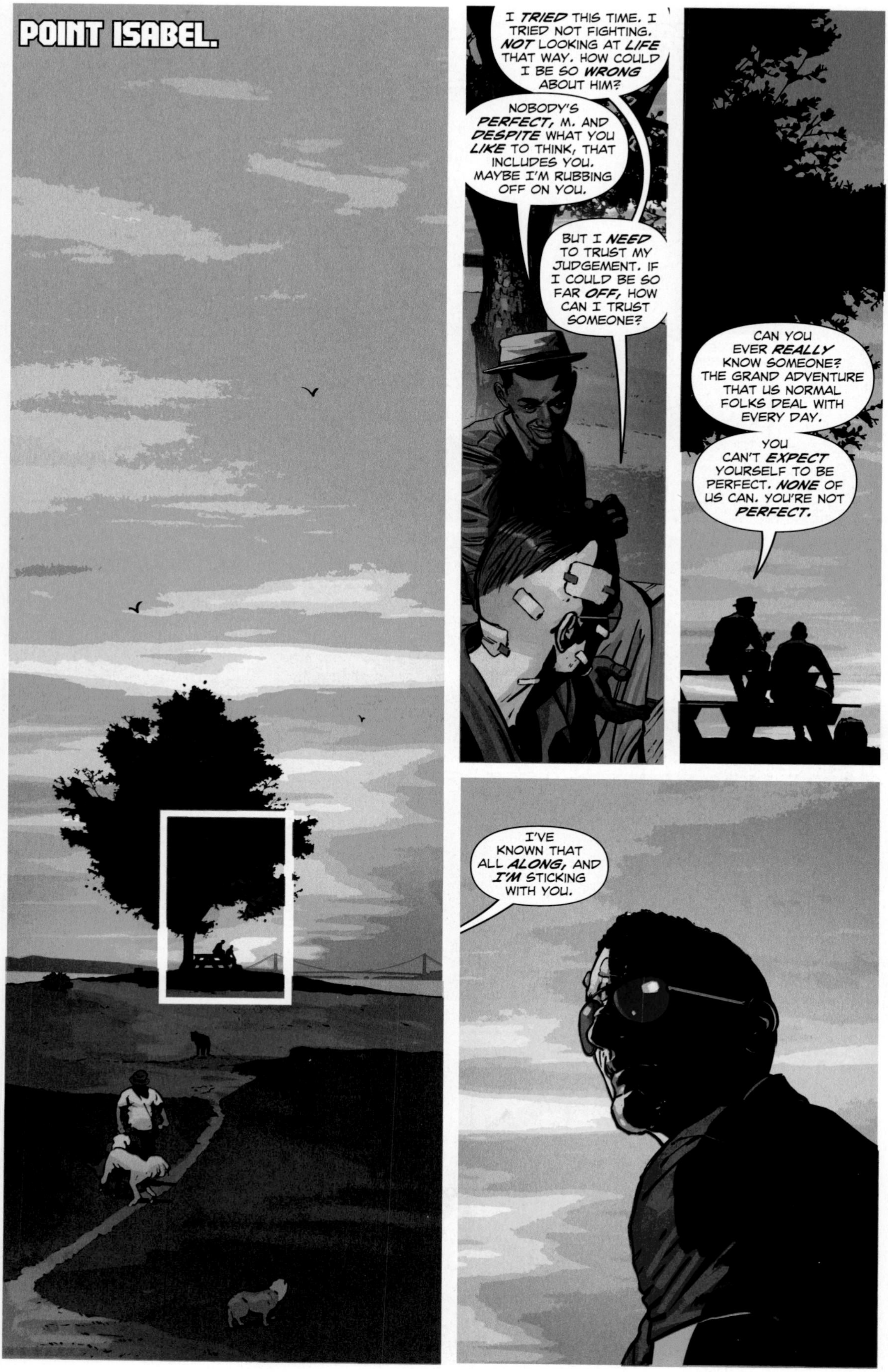
POINT ISABEL.
I TRIED THIS TIME. I TRIED NOT FIGHTING. NOT LOOKING AT LIFE THAT WAY. HOW COULD I BE SO WRONG ABOUT HIM?
NOBODY'S PERFECT, M. AND DESPITE WHAT YOU LIKE TO THINK, THAT INCLUDES YOU. MAYBE I'M RUBBING OFF ON YOU.
BUT I NEED TO TRUST MY JUDGEMENT. IF I COULD BE SO FAR OFF, HOW CAN I TRUST SOMEONE?
CAN YOU EVER REALLY KNOW SOMEONE? THE GRAND ADVENTURE THAT US NORMAL FOLKS DEAL WITH EVERY DAY.
YOU CAN'T EXPECT YOURSELF TO BE PERFECT. NONE OF US CAN. YOU'RE NOT PERFECT.
I'VE KNOWN THAT ALL ALONG, AND I'M STICKING WITH YOU.

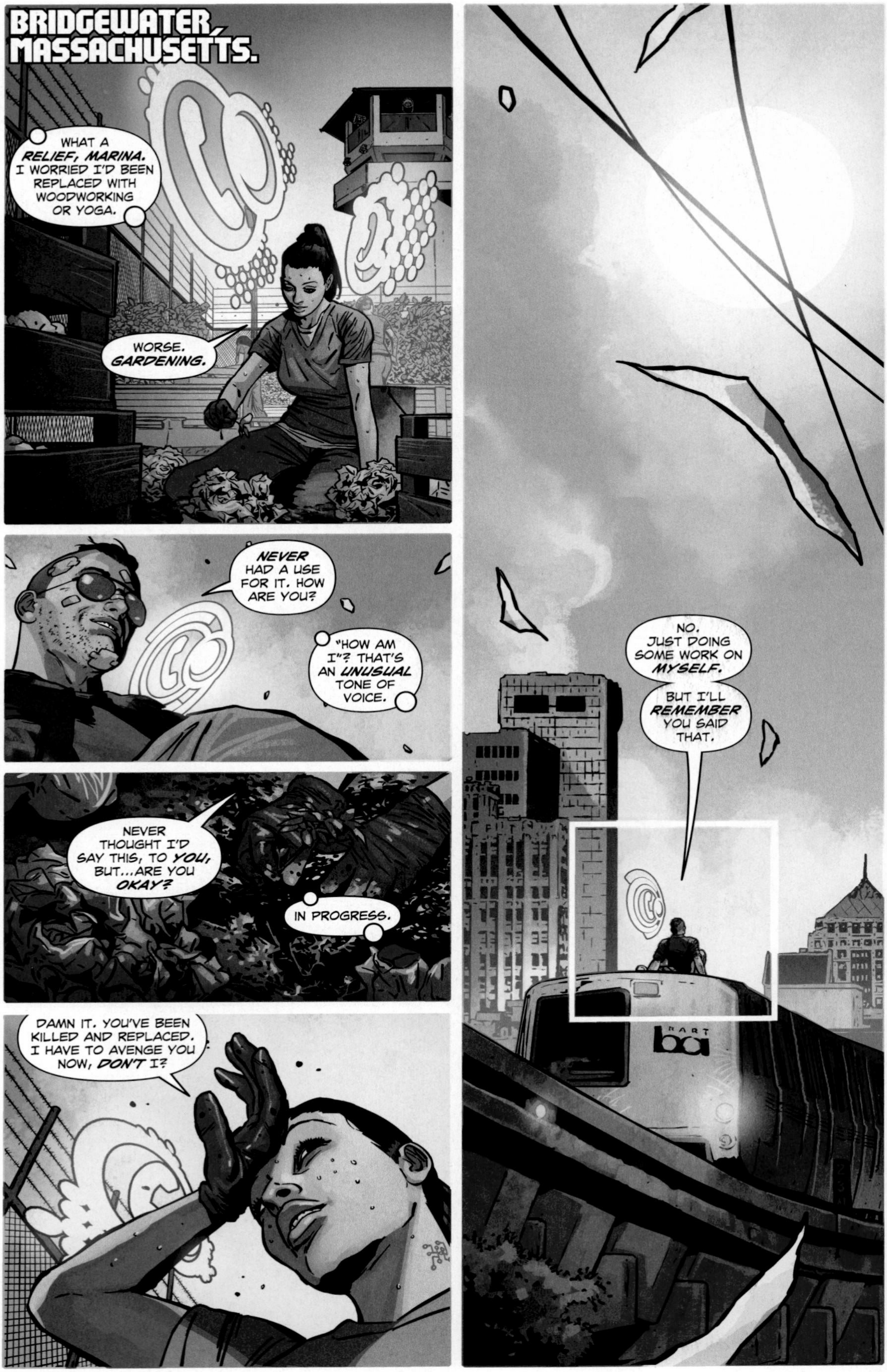

BRIDGEWATER, MASSACHUSETTS.
WHAT A RELIEF, MARINA. I WORRIED I'D BEEN REPLACED WITH WOODWORKING OR YOGA.
WORSE. GARDENING.
NEVER HAD A USE FOR IT. HOW ARE YOU?
"HOW AM I"? THAT'S AN UNUSUAL TONE OF VOICE.
NEVER THOUGHT I'D SAY THIS, TO YOU, BUT...ARE YOU OKAY?
IN PROGRESS.
DAMN IT. YOU'VE BEEN KILLED AND REPLACED. I HAVE TO AVENGE YOU NOW, DON'T I?
NO. JUST DOING SOME WORK ON MYSELF.
BUT I'LL REMEMBER YOU SAID THAT.

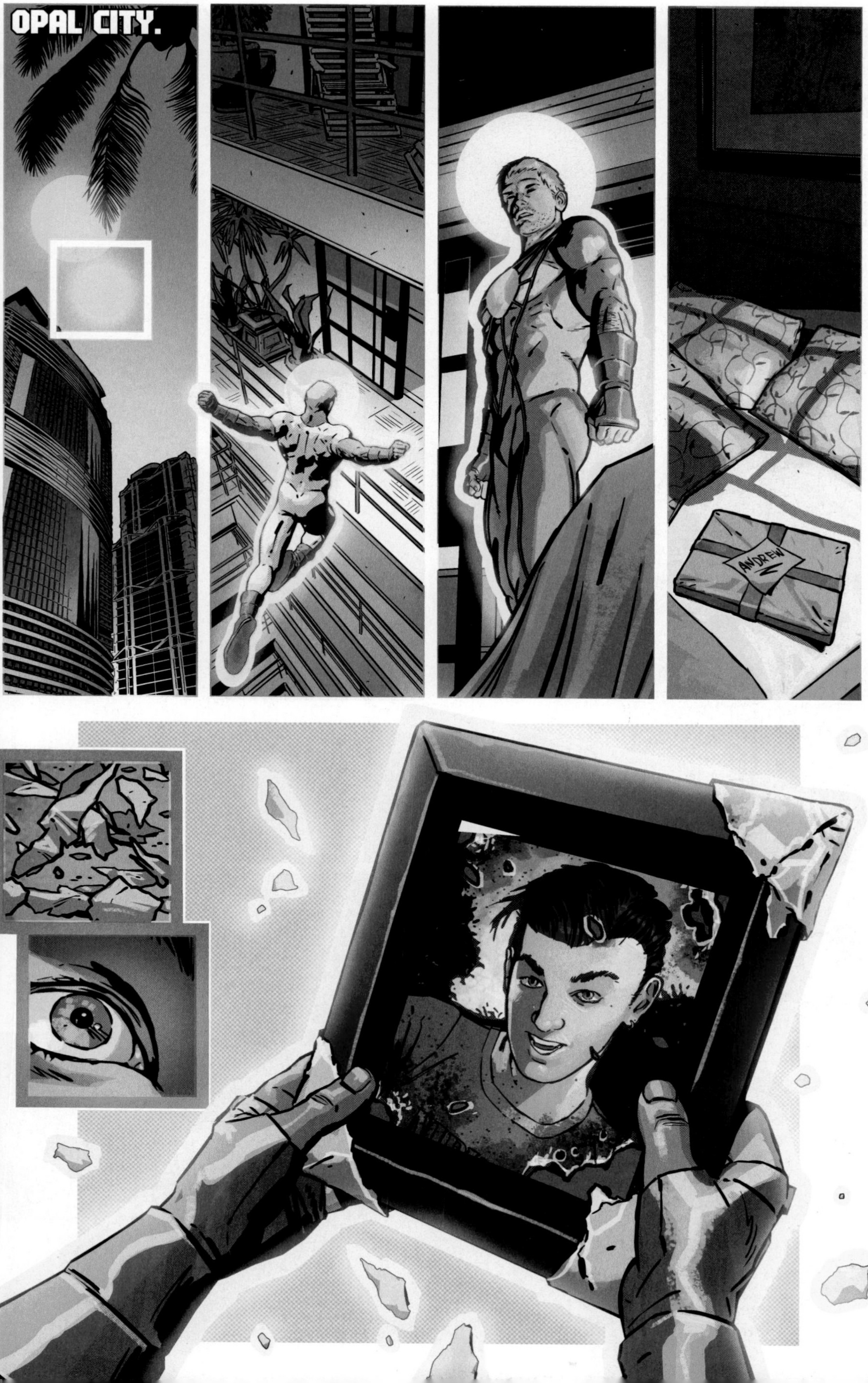
OPAL CITY.
ANDREW

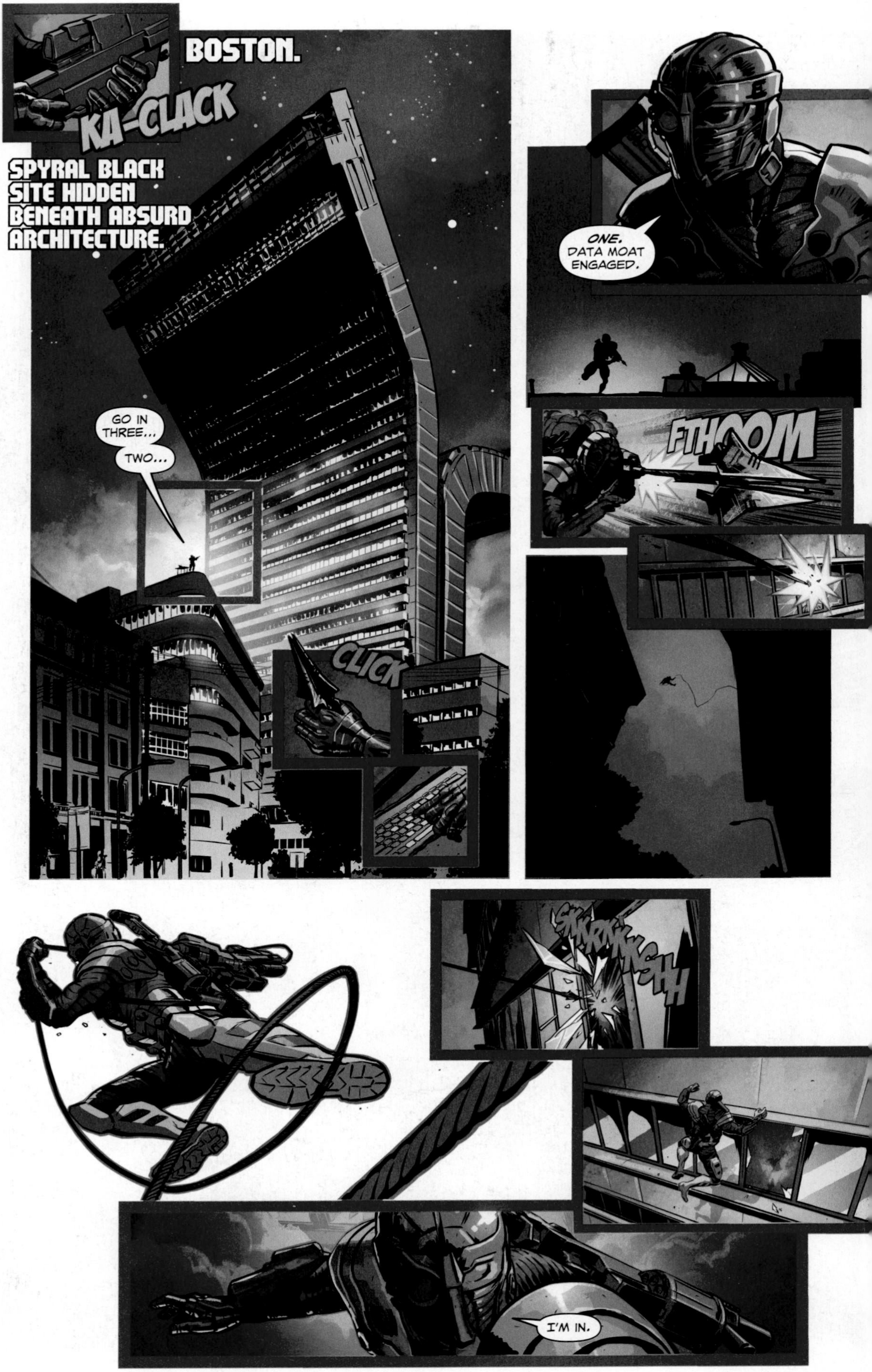
BOSTON.
KA-CLACK
SPYRAL BLACK SITE HIDDEN BENEATH ABSURD ARCHITECTURE.
GO IN THREE...
TWO...
CLICK
ONE. DATA MOAT ENGAGED.
FTHOOM
SKKRNKKSHH
I'M IN.

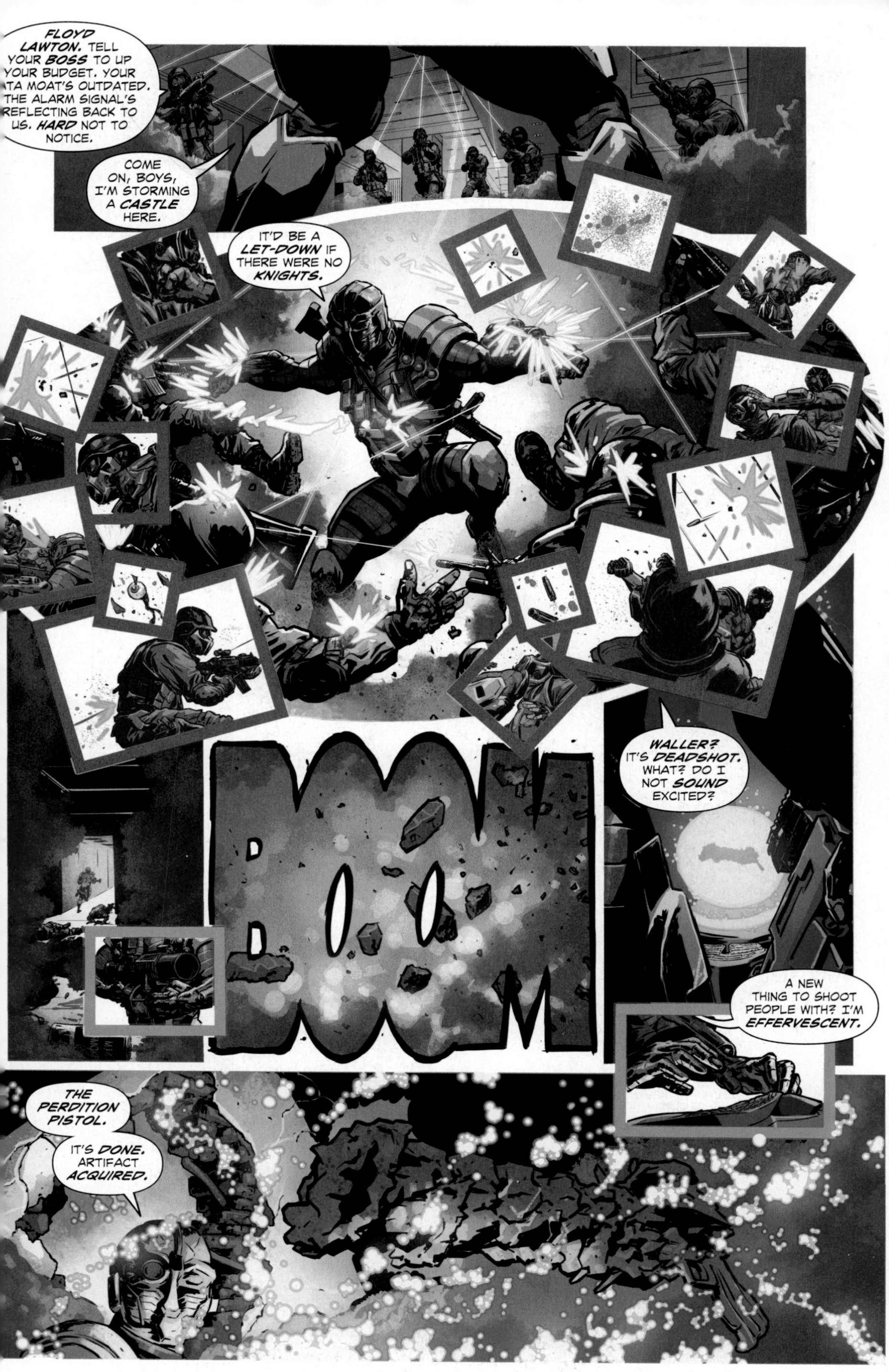
FLOYD LAWTON. TELL YOUR BOSS TO UP YOUR BUDGET. YOUR ATA MOAT'S OUTDATED. THE ALARM SIGNAL'S REFLECTING BACK TO US. HARD NOT TO NOTICE.
COME ON, BOYS, I'M STORMING A CASTLE HERE.
IT'D BE A LET-DOWN IF THERE WERE NO KNIGHTS.
BOOM
WALLER? IT'S DEADSHOT. WHAT? DO I NOT SOUND EXCITED?
A NEW THING TO SHOOT PEOPLE WITH? I'M EFFERVESCENT.
THE PERDITION PISTOL.
IT'S DONE. ARTIFACT ACQUIRED.

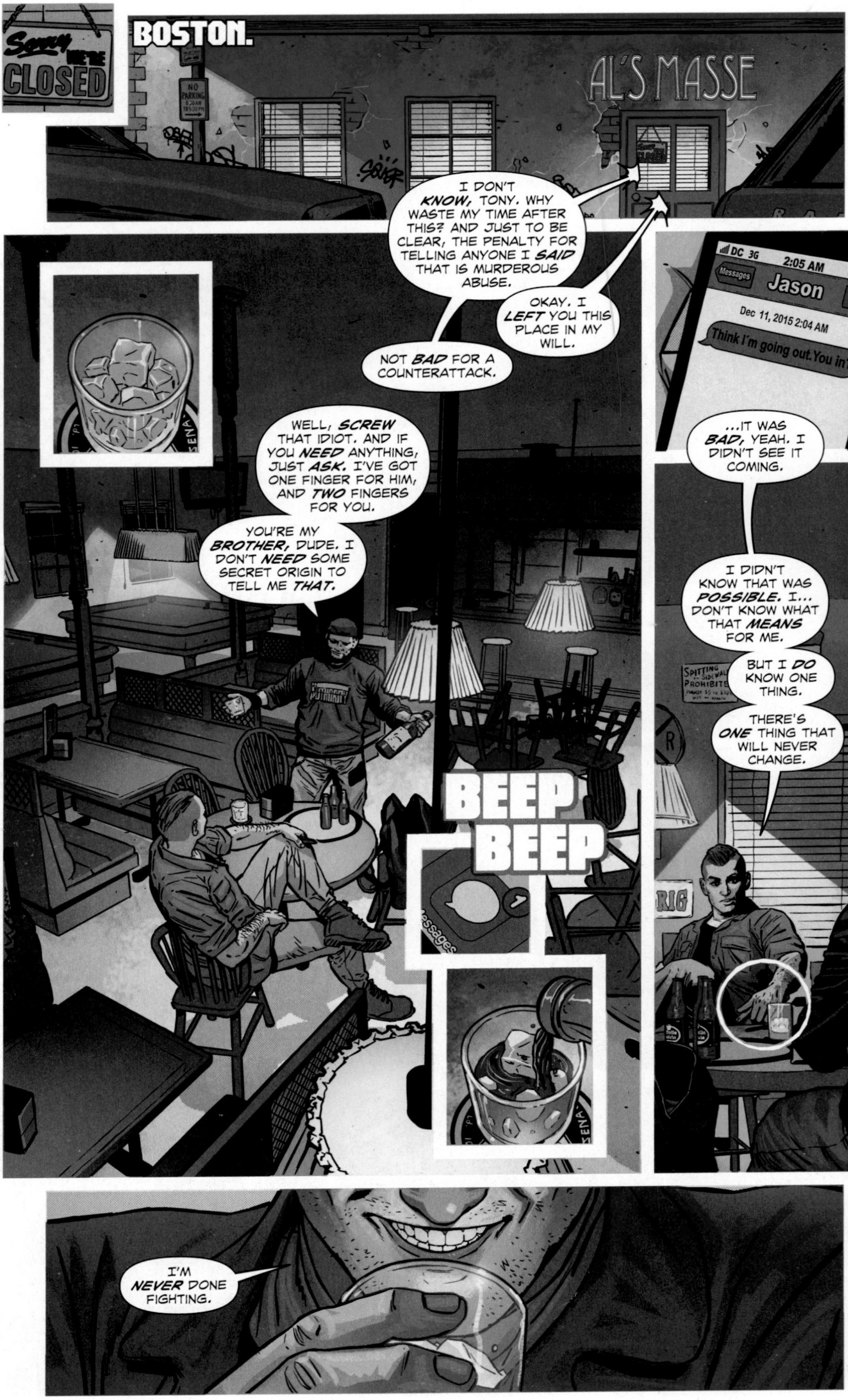
Sorry WE'RE CLOSED
BOSTON.
NO PARKING
AL'S MASSE
I DON'T KNOW, TONY. WHY WASTE MY TIME AFTER THIS? AND JUST TO BE CLEAR, THE PENALTY FOR TELLING ANYONE I SAID THAT IS MURDEROUS ABUSE.
OKAY. I LEFT YOU THIS PLACE IN MY WILL.
NOT BAD FOR A COUNTERATTACK.
DC 3G 2:05 AM 45%
Messages Jason Edit
Dec 11, 2015 2:04 AM
Think I'm going out.You in?
WELL, SCREW THAT IDIOT. AND IF YOU NEED ANYTHING, JUST ASK. I'VE GOT ONE FINGER FOR HIM, AND TWO FINGERS FOR YOU.
YOU'RE MY BROTHER, DUDE. I DON'T NEED SOME SECRET ORIGIN TO TELL ME THAT.
...IT WAS BAD, YEAH. I DIDN'T SEE IT COMING.
I DIDN'T KNOW THAT WAS POSSIBLE. I... DON'T KNOW WHAT THAT MEANS FOR ME.
BUT I DO KNOW ONE THING.
THERE'S ONE THING THAT WILL NEVER CHANGE.
SPITTING ON SIDEWALK PROHIBITED
BEEP BEEP
Messages
I'M NEVER DONE FIGHTING.